THE
SELF
SUFFICIENT-ISH
BIBLE

THE SELF SUFFICIENT-ISH BIBLE

AN ECO-LIVING GUIDE FOR THE 21st CENTURY

ANDY + DAVE HAMILTON

HODDER & STOUGHTON

·ACIDITY·AIKALINITY·
·RAISED BEDS·FEEDING THE S
MAKING CHOICES·BUYIN
FOOD·DRINK·CLOTHES·S
HEMP·ETHICAL BANKING
CHOOSING AN ALLOTMENT
GETTING TO WORK·PONDS·
WILDLIFE·ALLOTMENT ART

HINGS·ELECTRICALS·
TION·HEATING·NATU
WILD

TREE FRUIT·ROOTSTO
LEGAL ISSUES·SOFT FR
PLANTING AND PRUN

FOOD

LIFESTYLE

6245

INTRODUCTION

How often have you dreamed of leading a simpler, less stressful life as your car stop-starts its way through rush-hour traffic on a rainy Monday morning, while you sit at your computer in a fluorescent-lit office or as you push your way through supermarket queues at the weekend? You can picture it now – you're living in a farmhouse by the coast, with the sun streaming in through the windows; you open the back door, breathing in the crisp country air, and stop to collect fresh eggs from the free-range chickens that roam your land. You bake your own bread and grow all the fruit and vegetables you need; your solar panels glimmer on the roof and apart from the bird's chorus the only sound is your trusty wind turbine turning gently in the breeze. You're entirely self-sufficient and removed from the stresses of modern life.

What often stops this blessed existence from becoming a reality is that most people have to work for a living – household bills and mortgages need to be paid every month and, try as you

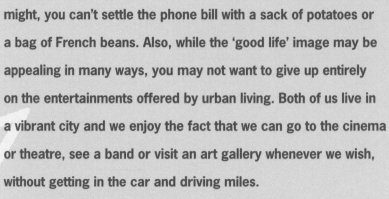

might, you can't settle the phone bill with a sack of potatoes or a bag of French beans. Also, while the 'good life' image may be appealing in many ways, you may not want to give up entirely on the entertainments offered by urban living. Both of us live in a vibrant city and we enjoy the fact that we can go to the cinema or theatre, see a band or visit an art gallery whenever we wish, without getting in the car and driving miles.

Between the pure rural idyll and modern, hi-tech consumerist lifestyle there is a middle path. We all have a choice and it's perfectly possible to lead a more environmentally friendly, more ethical and more self-sufficient life without leaving the modern world behind entirely. By growing your own fruit, vegetables and herbs, for instance, you can bring some of the countryside to your town or city, eat more healthily, save money and do your bit to help the environment – you won't be using harmful pesticides and with no packaging or transportation involved you won't be contributing to global warming. You can also help do your bit for the planet by cutting down on your energy consumption in all areas of life – even small changes will make a difference.

For us it all began in our childhood, when we used to grow and harvest crops under the guidance of our parents and grandparents. Later, we each got an allotment and decided to experiment with self-sufficiency to see whether we could obtain all of our fresh food from the allotment and from foraging expeditions. Within a few months we were able to put home-grown vegetables and fruit on the table every day of the year, supplemented by wild mushrooms, berries and leaves collected from surrounding areas. Inspired by this, we started making our own nettle beer, ale, cider and wine. We couldn't be entirely self-sufficient without keeping livestock for dairy products, eggs and meat or growing wheat for bread – and we weren't ready to give

up our urban life to take on a smallholding, not yet anyway – but being partly self-sufficient (or self-sufficientish) was certainly a step in the right direction as far as we were concerned.

We wanted to share our enthusiasm for growing our own food and brewing our own ale with anyone who'd listen and in 2004 our website www.selfsufficientish.com was born. Although the original idea was to set up a blog, we decided to create a web forum instead, in order to exchange information with a 'community' of people with similar values around the world. As you'll see from the diversity of subjects covered in our forum, the term 'self-sufficientish' has now gone way beyond food and brewing and covers ethical shopping, herbalism, renewable energy and basically everything else that is ethical and ecologically sound.

Changing to a greener lifestyle needn't be a huge upheaval or mean hours and hours of hard labour. Throughout this book there are simple projects and recipes that anyone, regardless of their circumstances, can tackle and achieve. Whether you live in a rented bedsit in a city or in a large country house, our aim is to inspire you to take up the challenge of living in a way that's healthy both for the individual and for the planet. We hope very much that you'll find the self-sufficientish way of life as stimulating, enjoyable and rewarding as we do.

ANDY + DAVE HAMILTON

1.
HOME

THE ECO-FRIENDLY HOME

When it comes to the home, what is kind on the environment is frequently healthy for the individuals living within it. However, a vast number of modern houses are built and furnished using a variety of synthetic, unsustainable materials, which can be harmful for the planet as well as human health. Paints and wood stains can be high in volatile organic compounds (VOCs), increasing the number of indoor air pollutants, and many ordinary household items, such as foam cushions, fibreglass insulation and carpets, are a source of formaldehyde – a chemical that can cause irritation to the eyes and respiratory system and is linked to asthma and possibly some cancers. Ideally, a house will be constructed from natural, sustainable materials, such as managed or reclaimed timber.

Environmentally speaking, natural materials such as wood or reclaimed stone are considerably better than brick, which requires large amounts of energy in its manufacture; for this reason, reclaimed bricks are always preferable to new ones. Timber has the added advantage of keeping carbon locked up for the lifetime of the house. Excellent insulation should always be a priority, to reduce energy consumption in the longer term – there's a wide range of insulation on the market, including a product made from recycled newspaper. An eco-friendly home should also have a sustainable and efficient heating and hot-water system and built-in water-saving devices, which enable you to harvest rainwater and/or to recycle bath and basin water. Organic finishes should be used whenever possible, as they are pollutant-free and allow the underlying material to 'breathe'. Although environmentally friendly options often seem more expensive in the short term, you'll soon get a return on your investment because of their efficiency.

ECO HOME

Designed with sustainability and a healthy living environment in mind, this house is made from 90 per cent wood – one of the most environmentally sound as well as durable materials. It is built using a timber-frame system, which is light, simple to erect yourself and has good insulation properties. Excellent insulation was a priority in order to reduce energy consumption, so once the frame was erected the walls were clad inside and out with 'breathable' sheathing boards, which were pumped with recycled newspaper insulation, and the outside walls were covered with a mixture of timber cladding and lime render. Heating is provided by a wood-burning stove, with back-up from a ground-source heat pump (a form of solar energy). The internal finishes such as the flooring, staircase, roof beams, doors and work surfaces were made from European timber grown in managed forests.

LARGE OVERHANG

An overhang shelters the house in winter and keeps it cool in summer.

WINDOW FRAMES

The window frames are made from thick heartwood from sustainably managed pine forests plus recycled aluminium and are finished with water-based paints.

GROUND-SOURCE HEAT PUMP

An underground pump extracts heat from the ground, which has been warmed by the sun to a near-constant temperature of 11–13°C (52–55°F). Pipes beneath the surface transport heat in the form of warm water to the house interior.

SKYLIGHTS

Windows set into the roof provide natural lighting and ventilation; built-in blinds, which are operated by remote control, prevent temperatures from rising in summer.

LIME RENDER ON WALLS

Lime is less energy-intensive to manufacture and more 'breathable' than cement.

WALLS INJECTED WITH RECYCLED NEWSPAPER

Pulped newspapers have been pumped through holes in the walls and roof, providing highly effective, non-toxic insulation (see page 29).

WINDOWS

Made from low-E glass (see page 31), which insulates the house against cold in winter and heat in summer.

TIMBER CLADDING

Green oak boards form a rain screen; generous expansion gaps allow water to drain well.

FURNISHINGS & ELECTRICALS

Whether you rent or own a house, the furnishings and finishes can be made from the most unsustainable and toxic substances around. Paint and varnishes can give off harmful fumes, forests can be illegally chopped down to make our furniture, and electrical items often aren't made to last because of our incessant desire to own the latest models and dispense with the old. Before you buy anything, consider whether it's made from a renewable source, how long it will last and if there's a more natural, preferable alternative.

Furniture

The most sustainable way of buying furniture is to get it second hand – antique shops, reclamation yards, furniture auctions and www.freecycle.org are great places to start your search. If you're buying new, try to buy a product that's been made from recycled or reclaimed materials and check out the credentials of the manufacturer.

Wooden furniture When purchasing wooden furniture, consumers all too often consider comfort, price and aesthetics and frequently neglect to ask about the source of the timber and its sustainability. The UN's Food and Agriculture Organization estimates that the current rate of deforestation in the tropics is at around 154,000 square kilometres (59,500 square miles) per year. The majority of this deforestation is caused by the timber industry. In 2002 the UK was the biggest importer of illegal timber from Indonesia, where furniture export has led to the destruction of 70 per cent of the country's forests. Bearing in mind tropical rainforest houses over 50 per cent of the Earth's species, it really is inexcusable to be a party to this destruction just for the sake of some cheap furniture.

But how do you know what is ecologically acceptable? First, if you're buying furniture made from new wood, always look for the Forestry Stewardship Council (FSC) logo. This is a mark that is recognized worldwide and indicates timber that has been grown from a sustainable source. Most European wood is from sustainable sources. However, timber from West Africa, Central America and South-east Asia is more questionable, as these are the areas where illegal logging is most concentrated. A full-out boycott is not advisable, as plenty of wood is legally logged from these areas and the money will go to help some of the world's poorest people.

If you can't find FSC-certified timber, it's worth checking the Friends of the Earth website. They've compiled a 'Good Wood Guide', listing a huge variety of woods and giving their origin, uses, global threat status and whether they're available as reclaimed wood. This is useful for buying not only furniture but also flooring or wood for any DIY or construction project. (See www.foe.co.uk.)

Ideally, you should buy local wood, so you don't have to factor transport into its environmental impact. Also, buy better-quality wood that lasts longer rather than inexpensive wood that will soon fall apart. The most ecologically sound furniture is made from reclaimed wood.

Furniture made from other materials
The Victorians used to make furniture such as chairs, tables, bookcases and beds out of papier mâché and the famous Lloyd Loom furniture, so popular in the 1930s, was made from woven paper threads. Today, there are still some furniture manufacturers using paper.

Bamboo furniture is inexpensive and highly sustainable as bamboo is a grass, so it grows back when harvested. The downside is that it has to be shipped from the other side of the world and is sometimes grown using a plethora of pesticides – vast areas of forest can be cleared in order to produce bamboo, so it's vital to ensure that it comes from a sustainable source.

If choosing furniture that's outside the manufacturing loop it doesn't mean you have to buy second hand. There are many types of 'new' furniture available made from reclaimed materials. Companies such as Green-Works (www.green-works.co.uk) design and build furniture made from reclaimed office furniture. Another site to check out is Nigel's Eco Store (www.nigelsecostore.com). There are tables made from washing machines, rocking chairs made

Old wine boxes stacked on top of each other are given a new lease of life as bookcases.

Natural flooring (anti-clockwise from top right): wool, seagrass, coir, jute and two samples made from paper.

from cinema seats and the design-your-own 'rock'n'roll' bookshelf, made from paper rolls stuck together with Velcro. Alternatively, you can create your own reclaimed furniture – Dave made bookcases from wine boxes stacked on top of each other.

Natural flooring

About 1.7 million tonnes of carpets made from synthetic materials end up in landfill in the UK every year, taking anything up to 250,000 years to degrade because of lack of water and sunlight needed for the degrading process. There are other more natural options to consider when replacing your old carpet, among them coir, jute, seagrass, wool, reclaimed wood, natural stone, cork and even bamboo and paper.

Wool Wool has superb ecological credentials as it's sourced in Britain and is completely sustainable as the sheep's coat grows back every year. It's also very soft and therefore ideal for the bedroom. The downside of woollen carpets is the price, so you may want to mix and match, perhaps by having a woollen rug by the side of your bed and using another cheaper flooring for the rest of the room.

Seagrass Seagrass is grown in paddy fields, dried and spun into carpets. It's very difficult to dye, so it generally comes in two colours – green or brown – depending on the time of harvest. Seagrass is not recommended for use in damp areas such as the kitchen or the bathroom.

Coir You've no doubt wiped your feet on a coir doormat, but you may not be aware that you can fit it throughout the home as a relatively inexpensive carpet substitute and that it comes in a range of colours.

Coir is made from the husks of coconut, which means it's one of the most environmentally friendly floor coverings available, as it's 100 per cent renewable and degradable. However, because coconuts aren't grown in this country, the environmental cost of import needs to be taken into consideration. Coir matting is durable but difficult to wash – a regular weekly vacuum clean will suffice and there's also a natural stain protection spray available made by Intec. As coir can absorb water, avoid areas of heavy spillage such as the kitchen or bathroom and don't consider using it where there are signs of damp.

In areas such as the bedroom, where you might want a softer carpet, you could use a woollen rug next to your bed on top of the coir or consider a softer natural flooring such as jute, wool or even a combination of the two.

Jute Jute comes from the inner bark of plants of the Malvaceae family. The bark is harvested by hand before being softened in water and then dried in the sun. The sun-dried fibres are spun into a yarn that can be made into flooring or a variety of other items including paper and shopping bags. Jute can be a lot softer than other natural floorings but its softness comes at a price, as it isn't as durable as other natural floorings such as coir or seagrass. For this reason, it's better to use jute flooring in the bedroom rather than on stairs and in hallways, where it would wear out too quickly.

Paper No – it isn't a misprint, you really can get paper flooring. The paper is made from virgin wood pulp, which is spun into yarn and is then woven into a carpet. Recycled paper is never used as it would offer a less durable product. Most companies use FSC wood sources to make paper flooring, but it's worth checking. Paper flooring is ideal to use in kitchens and bathrooms.

Reclaimed wooden flooring It's possible to have a great-looking wooden floor without it costing the earth. In fact some companies, such as Ashcroft Flooring (www.woodflooringuk.com), offer reclaimed wood that's less expensive than new timber. The best-quality flooring comes from older trees, as it's denser than younger wood and has fewer knots and structural defects. Using reclaimed wood means that you get all the benefits of old timber without destroying ancient woodland to get it and in some cases the wood would have gone to landfill anyway, so it's a totally win-win situation. (See also page 16.)

Stone Natural stone tiles can work very well in your kitchen or bathroom. It's worth looking into where the stone comes from and doing a bit of research into the background of the suppliers and manufacturers. Ask how far the stone's travelled, how sensitively it's been quarried (over-quarrying can irrevocably destroy the habitat) and how it's been shaped (some companies have been known to use child labour for this). To avoid any ethical or ecological minefields, it's worth looking around for reclaimed stone.

Cork Cork is harvested from the thick but light outer bark of the cork oak. It's completely sustainable, because the tree regrows its bark within about 3 years. Cork is biodegradable, it can be recycled and provides very good insulation, making it one of the most eco-friendly flooring substances around.

Bamboo Flooring made from bamboo can look very attractive and you'd be hard-pushed to tell it apart from wood. At first glance, bamboo appears to be a very eco-friendly alternative to any other flooring: as a grass, it's renewable and is much faster-growing than most wood and wood-based products and it's also highly durable and water-resistant. However, there are drawbacks (see page 16). In addition, the long, thin strips that make up the planks for flooring are sometimes joined using a glue containing formaldehyde, which can cause nausea and watery eyes and can trigger asthma; some consider it could also be carcinogenic. Before purchasing a bamboo floor, ask the supplier what types of glue are used and where it's grown, to be sure that you're not inadvertently buying something with less-than-ethical credentials.

Chemical-free paints

Conventional paints and emulsions contain volatile organic compounds (VOCs), which emit toxic gases that can have an adverse effect on our health. These gases are more than 5 times higher indoors, particularly in unventilated areas, where the gases are more highly concentrated than outdoors. VOCs can contribute to 'sick building syndrome', with symptoms such as headaches, memory impairment and respiratory problems (see page 326).

VOC-free paint made from natural oils, herbs and minerals.

There are several alternatives to conventional oil-based chemical paints, including water-based products that use mineral or organic vegetable compounds, such as chalk, talc, cellulose and beeswax. The other commercially available alternative is lower-VOC paint: as the name suggests, this has reduced VOCs.

Organic bedding

The most common material for duvet covers, sheets and pillowcases is cotton. Cotton grows around the seeds of the cotton plant and so is of course natural. However, environmentally speaking it's one of the 'bad boys' – the cotton industry relies heavily on chemical fertilizers and insecticides, it's one of the least fairly traded commodities, many children work for very little in the cotton fields and on top of that it's one of the four main crops to be genetically modified. Around the world, cotton accounts for just 3 per cent of farmland but between 15 and 55 per cent of pesticides are used in its production. The good news is that an increasing number of farmers are producing organic cotton. According to the Organic Consumers Association, the Andhra Pradesh region of India, which was once the pesticide capital of the world, is now returning to more traditional organic farming methods. The disadvantage of all cotton is that it's shipped half way across the globe before it reaches us. (For more information on cotton, see pages 350–1).

There are several natural alternatives to cotton bedding, including organic hemp (see pages 350–1) and wool. Hemp, which can be grown in Britain under licence, is used to make sheets, duvet covers and pillowcases. It has a short growth cycle, at just 4 months, and is up to 4 times more durable than cotton, so it will last longer. Just 0.4 hectare (1 acre) of land will produce about 450kg (1000lb) of hemp fibre, almost 3 times the amount of cotton it can grow. The downside of hemp is the price: it can be more than triple the cost of cotton. Canvas used to be made from hemp and the Arabic word for canvas is 'cannabis'.

Wool is perfect material for bedding, as it has excellent thermal properties that give an even distribution of warmth and aid deeper and calmer sleep. It's used inside duvets, blankets, mattress covers and even for pillow fillings as an alternative to feathers or artificial fibres. There's plenty of wool grown in the UK; for even better green credentials, you could get locally produced wool. Wool is generally cheaper than hemp but more expensive than cotton, although it will usually last longer. Even at twice the price it could be a viable alternative.

Old metal bed frames are available at auctions, reclamation yards and on the internet.

SIMPLE PATCHWORK DUVET COVER

The traditional American patchwork quilt involved piecing together numerous pieces of leftover fabric, making do with what was available. The charm of these quilts lay in their seemingly *ad hoc* nature (although the designs were often meticulously planned) and the fact that each patch had a 'history' of its own. You can make your own patchwork quilt from worn-out clothes and fabric scraps quite easily, although it does take time. Ask friends and family for old clothes and ask charity shops if they have a 'rag bag': they often receive donations that they can't sell as they're not in good enough condition and may be happy to pass these on for a small donation. Asking on www.freecycle.org would be another option. Andy made a patchwork quilt by stitching together patches from pairs of old jeans.

What you need
Piece of cardboard for template
Ruler
Scissors
Wax crayon
Fabric scraps
Paper and pencil
Pins
Needle and thread
10 poppers, buttons or a zip

1.

Draw a square shape on a piece of cardboard using a ruler and cut around it to make a template. The size of the template will depend on the narrowest width of fabric you have: 15–20cm (6–8in) each way would be a good size, but as long as all the squares are the same size it doesn't really matter.

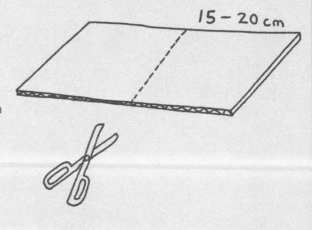

15 – 20 cm

2.

Work out how many patches you'll need to complete your duvet cover. Bear in mind you'll need to allow for seams, about 5mm (¼in) around each square, so the final size of the squares will be about 1cm (½in) smaller than the cut-out shapes. Also, you'll need to make the cover quite a bit larger than the duvet. Using a wax crayon and your template as a guide, mark out the patches on the fabric scraps.

3.

Cut out the squares using a sharp pair of scissors. Arrange the squares across the floor in the pattern you require – for example, alternate-coloured squares or stripes. To make the pattern more interesting, you could cut diagonally across some of the shapes, turning the squares into triangles.

4.

Give each different piece of fabric a number and mark it on the back of each shape with the wax crayon. Draw a plan of your quilt on a piece of paper so that it's easy to follow when you come to assembling the patches.

5.

Take one square and attach it to a second square. Put together the right sides of the pieces to be joined, align the edges, pin and then stitch along one side, 5mm (¼in) in from the edge of the fabric, using running stitch. Weave the needle in and out of the fabric several times before pulling the needle and thread through. To secure the end of the seam, form a few small backstitches on top of each other.

6.

Join all the other pieces together in a similar way until you've completed the top of your quilt, then do the same for the underside.

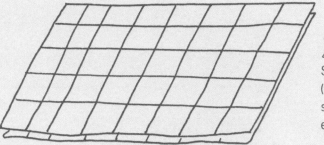

7.

Sew the two sides of the duvet cover together (right sides facing each other), leaving one of the short sides open for the duvet. Add poppers (the easiest option), a zip or buttons and buttonholes.

Patchwork is a traditional way of using up scraps of old, worn clothes.

Energy-efficient lighting

Fluorescent light bulbs cut greenhouse emissions and running costs by 75–80 per cent compared with traditional lighting. They're available as linear tubes or as compact fluorescent lamps. Try to avoid halogen lights, as they use a lot of energy – don't be deceived into thinking that low-voltage halogen lamps mean low-energy lamps; each one generates 1kg (2lb) of greenhouse gas every 15 hours (about the same as a traditional 60-watt bulb, although halogen does provide more light). (For more information on energy-efficient lighting, see pages 326–7.)

Whatever lighting you opt for, remember more watts means more energy used, which means higher bills and greater carbon emissions. Use low-wattage bulbs whenever you can, especially for downlights and spotlights, and dimmer switches are also a good idea if the bulbs will take them. Also, select light fittings with reflectors that direct light where you want it and do not absorb too much light. Clean lamps and fittings regularly, as dirt build-up reduces light output.

In caravans and on narrow boats the lighting system is generally run off a 12-volt battery. This system can also be adapted for the home, either as a back-up for when there are blackouts or as your main lighting system (see www.selfsufficientish.com/12v.htm for more details). If you plan to have outdoor lighting, consider solar-powered garden lights.

Home-entertainment systems

The digital age might be heralded as the second or the third industrial revolution, but environmentally speaking it may not be the great leap forward we all hoped it might be. It's true that DVDs and CDs use fewer resources to make and transport than videos, records and cassettes, but as a result they're cheaper to produce and we're buying many more of them. In addition, formats are updated so quickly and with each innovation an older format disappears, making the equipment redundant and fodder for landfill.

Televisions Televisions use varying amounts of electricity. Plasma screens consume the most at around 300 watts per hour. Also, the more energy-hungry plasma screens don't last as long as lower-energy televisions because they're more likely to experience phosphor-fade and burnout. LCD (liquid-crystal display) televisions use less energy than plasma screens and sometimes less than the old-style CRT (cathode-ray tube) televisions, although this isn't always the case. The manufacturer Sharp seems to be leading the way with low-energy LCD technology – its

entire range of televisions has been awarded the EU Ecolabel (see page 43), which is bestowed upon goods that meet strict criteria devised to minimize harm to the environment and comply with the energy star criteria.

Digital music We all love listening to music but in this technological age are the younger generation leading the way when it comes to buying such entertainment? Many of us who remember buying LPs before they were called vinyl or recollect taping favourite songs from the chart show might still feel that for some reason we need to own the CD, cover and all, to enjoy the music we listen to. But is this really necessary?

In 2006, 164 million CDs were sold in the UK – this is a huge number considering that they could have all been downloaded and stored on hard drives, lowering their carbon footprint from 1.6kg to 0.7kg (3½lb to 1½lb). However, if you then go on to burn the music to CD your music's carbon footprint will increase three-fold. If you prefer to have a CD collection, there's a thriving second-hand market: try charity shops, car-boot sales, internet auctions and specialist record shops.

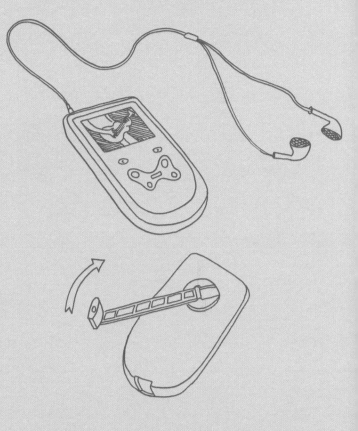

Wind-up eco-Mp3 players are now available, using no energy at all.

As technology has improved, your computer can be your home-entertainment system – our friend John Wells (aka DJ Anorak) uses his laptop to perform to packed clubs. To house your growing download collection, you might want to consider buying an external hard drive of at least 20GB capacity, because filling your computer with music can really slow it down. If you want to listen only to the odd song you can do so online – with websites such as YouTube offering videos of many top artists you can listen to almost anything you wish.

There are eco-Mp3 (media) players out there that are worth looking at (just type 'eco Mp3 player' into Google). These come with wind-up handles, eliminating the need for batteries.

DVDs A TV/DVD player combo is considerably more energy-efficient than having two separate items to power. At the time of writing, just some of the smaller portable sets come in a combined form, but as DVDs get smaller this is likely to change.

Online rental of DVDs is becoming popular and makes excellent sense. This works by compiling a list of films that you wish to see; the disks are then posted to you and when you've finished watching them you return the disks in a freepost envelope provided. Alternatively, you could organize a lending library between your friends, work

mates or within your local community and share your collection of DVDs. Either way, each film can be watched many times over, reducing the need to manufacture and distribute more DVDs.

Radio and internet While writing this book we've often listened to the radio, but rather than turn on another electrical item we tend to listen online. You can listen to all of the BBC stations and most of the independent radio stations online using RealPlayer or Windows Media Player software. Links to these can be found at www.radiofeeds.co.uk.

If you're not online, are perhaps more traditionalist or want to be greener than green, the clockwork/wind-up radio is an ideal way to stay tuned to your favourite shows. It's a false economy to buy cheaper wind-up radios from bargain stores as they have a short working life and will work only with batteries in them. Wind-up radios are available online at www.ethicalsuperstore.com or from leading electrical retailers.

Standby buttons and multi-plugs As far as we're concerned, the standby button is public enemy number one. If everyone in the UK turned off their appliances properly instead of leaving them on standby we'd need two and a half fewer power stations. To put it another way, up

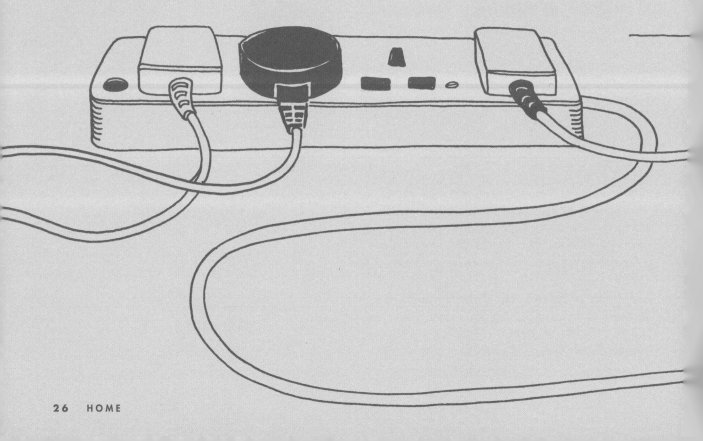

to 10 per cent of your electricity bill could be a result of leaving things on standby – that's roughly 7 years of wasted electricity in everyone's lifetime.

If you know that you simply won't bother to switch off manually, consider getting the 'Bye Bye Standby' device, which turns off all your electrical equipment just with the press of a central button on a remote control, reducing energy consumption, costs and carbon emissions. Alternatively, you could plug your television, digibox, DVD player and video into a four-way multi-plug and switch them all off at once.

DISPOSING OF ELECTRICAL WASTE

In 2005 the EC directive on Waste Electrical and Electronic Equipment (WEEE) came into effect. The aim was to reduce the environmental impact of electronic and electrical waste, increasing recycling and reducing the amount submitted to landfill.

In accordance with point 48 of the directive, when you buy an electrical or electronic item, by law the retailer has to accept your old, broken equipment on a like-for-like basis – they're obliged to recycle all the parts that they possibly can and dispose of the rest safely. Like-for-like doesn't mean you have to buy exactly the same product in order for them to recycle it – for example, if you purchase a DVD player to replace an old VCR or an Mp3 player to replace your broken cassette recorder they have to accept it. However, there are limitations, and the law states, 'A customer should not expect the distributor to accept a television when they buy a kettle, or a washing machine when buying an electric drill.'

If you're not buying new, it's the consumer's responsibility to take old electrical or electronic goods to the local council's recycling depot.

Remote controls and batteries Many households have a number of remote controls – one each for the television, video, DVD player, digibox and stereo. They don't use much power, so batteries that no longer work for other electrical items, such as digital cameras, can be used in remote controls instead of being thrown away. When the batteries are totally used up ensure you recycle them. Some local authorities will collect batteries – check on www.recyclenow.com to see if yours does. Alternatively, some supermarkets and electrical retailers have battery recycling bins, so keep an eye out for these. Better still, use rechargeable batteries.

If you have cordless phones, charge only one phone at a time instead of having all the slave phone cradles plugged in. Alternatively, consider having just the old-style cord phones that do not need extra electricity.

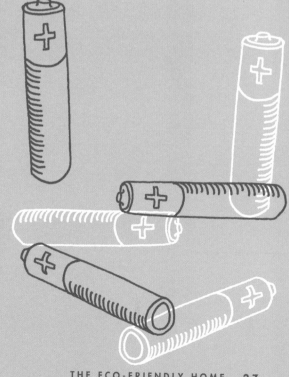

INSULATION & HEATING

In terms of energy conservation the single most important thing you can do is to insulate the home. Heating a home without insulation is like trying to fill a bucket of water with a hole in the bottom. Inadequate loft and wall insulation, alongside poorly or single-glazed windows, all contribute to heat being lost from the house. A 24cm (10in) layer of insulation can save 1.5 tonnes of carbon emissions every year, or the equivalent of an average trans-Atlantic flight. If you had to spend money on just one thing to cut your carbon footprint, it would have to be insulation.

Wall and loft insulation

Around 15 per cent of your home's heat can be lost through the loft and a further 15 per cent through the walls, so insulation will make a huge difference to heat-retention in the home and your heating bills.

The UK government and other governments overseas sporadically offer grants to help with the installation costs of both wall and loft insulation. Those on benefits and the elderly often take priority, but others are occasionally entitled to grants to cover some of the costs.

There are several different types of insulation and they're installed in different ways. In the loft, insulation is usually laid between the rafters in long strips. It's recommended that this type reaches a depth of 270mm (11in), so existing, thinner insulation may need to be added to in order to achieve this depth.

Sheep's wool is a natural, effective form of insulation.

In many houses built after 1930 there's a gap, or a cavity, between the inner and outer walls. This means that heat can leach out of the house to heat the outside wall rather than being reflected back inwards. One method of filling the gap is to drill holes in the outside wall and have an insulating material 'blown' into the gap. This usually needs to be carried out by a specialist.

Solid-wall insulation is a method of insulating a wall that doesn't have a cavity. It can be done on an inside or outside wall. Outside insulation consists of adding a decorative weatherproof layer to the outside of the house, while inside insulation can be either in the form of backed plasterboard or a false wall put in with the insulating material pinned behind it. It's expensive to install and you'll lose a certain amount of room inside your house.

The materials you use for wall and loft insulation depend on your personal preference, budget and space or on the shape of the area to be insulated. Here are the main options available:

Recycled newspaper

In terms of sustainability, cellulose insulation (trade name Warmcel) is probably the best insulation material of all. It's made purely from recycled newspaper, treated against rot, fire and rodent attack, and is completely non-toxic and non-irritant. It can be disposed of without creating toxic waste and takes little energy to manufacture (a lot less than traditional mineral-fibre insulation). Cellulose insulation can be fitted in both walls and lofts. You may need a specialist to install it, as it's usually 'blown' into a wall or loft cavity. In terms of insulation properties, it's comparable with inorganic, more traditional alternatives such as rock wool.

Sheep's-wool felt and flax felt

Sheep's-wool felt and flax felt are also good, sustainable forms of insulation, even though they tend to be slightly more expensive than other products. They come in large blocks, similar to traditional mineral-fibre insulation, but are completely non-toxic, so no masks or goggles need to be worn during their installation and you don't need a specialist to fit them. They're suitable for lofts and solid-wall insulation (they're pinned between two boards in a wall). Both flax felt and sheep's-wool felt are comparable to mineral fibre in terms of insulating properties.

Mineral fibre

Traditional mineral-fibre insulation, which includes rock wool and fibreglass, is made from non-renewable but abundant sources. This type of insulation is relatively inexpensive but it takes a lot of energy to produce and can cause irritation when laid, so installation needs to be carried out while wearing goggles and a mask (you can install it yourself or employ a specialist). There has been some concern recently about the toxicity of fibreglass.

Fossil-fuel-based insulation

Finally, there are types of fossil-fuel-based insulation. These include polyurethane foam and polyisocyanurate foam, which can come either in board form for installing in lofts and solid walls or as a liquid foam which you get a specialist to 'blow' into wall cavities. You can also obtain expanded polystyrene boards for both solid-wall and loft insulation.

These forms of insulation offer the benefit of higher insulation performances. However, the drawbacks are they're made from fossil fuels, which aren't a renewable source, and there are some concerns about their toxicity; they may also use CFCs in their production. The pros and cons of using these high-performance but non-sustainable types of insulation have to be weighed up. They are from non-renewable sources but you will use less fossil fuel during their lifetime because they're so efficient.

Energy-efficient windows

Many old, single-glazed houses are very cold in winter. Those with the original Victorian sash windows can be among the worst offenders. According to the Energy Saving Trust, as much as 20 per cent of heat generated to heat the house can be lost through its windows.

In Scandinavian countries and other parts of Europe, shutters are installed to keep out light as well as to keep in some of the heat during long, dark winters. A physical barrier such as this will help prevent a certain amount of heat loss. Similarly, heavy-backed or interlined curtains are an effective way of reducing the amount of heat lost through windows. It's important to make sure your curtain rails can take this extra weight, as Dave once discovered after two embarrassing phone calls to his landlord and a cut in his damage deposit.

Double or triple glazing

The usual physical barrier to prevent heat loss through windows is double- or in some cases even triple-glazed windows. Double and triple glazing works by trapping an inert gas or creating a vacuum between two or three panes of glass, preventing heat escaping through conduction. Rather than the heat being lost as it is through a thin, single-glazed window, it's reflected back into the room. Although double glazing can be expensive, it will certainly reduce your energy bills considerably and will increase the value of your home.

INSTALLING CLINGFILM DOUBLE GLAZING

Rented accommodation is frequently poorly insulated. However, you can help reduce draughts by insulating your windows in glazing film, which is available from a DIY store, or you can use a large sheet of ordinary clingfilm. It's simple and inexpensive to install yourself and will reduce your heating bills.

1.
Put double-sided sticky tape around the inside frame of the window you wish to 'glaze'.

2.
Stretch the large sheet of polythene or clingfilm over the window frame and stick it to the tape – you may need two people for this job.

3.
Using a hairdryer, go over any wrinkles in the polythene. To prevent melting holes in the film, don't hold the hairdryer too close and move it around rather than fix it in one place for too long.

Low-E glass Low-emissivity (or low-E) glass insulates the house against both the cold in winter and the heat in summer and works by reflecting heat back to its source. The windowpane is coated with a thin, virtually invisible layer of metal oxide. In winter, the sun's rays (short-wave radiation) and light pass through the glass, warming up the room, and radiant heat from the inside reflects on the glass and bounces back into the room, reducing heat loss considerably. In summer, low-E glass reflects unwanted heat (long-wave radiation) back to the outside of the house, helping to keep the inside cooler. The initial expense of these windows can be quite high but it can significantly reduce your heating and air-conditioning costs and will soon pay for itself. (See also page 15.)

SUMMER

Sun's rays reflect off the glass

Sun's rays pass through the glass

Glass reflects radiant heat back into the house

WINTER

Placing aluminium foil behind the radiator reflects heat back into the room.

Conservatories, porches and lobbies

Transition areas such as conservatories, porches and entrance lobbies all act as buffer zones between the inside and outside, protecting the main part of the house from extremes of temperature, especially in winter, and acting as a natural form of temperature control. To make the most of a conservatory's or porch's shielding properties there must be a dividing wall with a door to separate it from the main part of the house, otherwise the cold air will just move freely from the outside of the thin conservatory walls to the inside of the home.

On sunny days, porches and conservatories can become considerably hotter than the outside temperature. This is because the glass gathers the sun's heat and traps it in the fabric of the building (this natural heating process is known as 'solar gain'). While this increase in temperature makes a conservatory an ideal growing space for tropical and subtropical plants, it can become quite uncomfortable in summer for human occupants, so ventilation is often needed if you don't want to feel you're sitting in a sauna. Rather than installing expensive, energy-hungry air-conditioning units you could install blinds to stop the temperature from rising indoors during the hotter months.

In winter, the increased temperature in a well-insulated conservatory can be more than welcome. However, many older conservatories aren't well insulated and they really make a worthwhile extra room for only 8 months of the year. Although it's hard to insulate a conservatory after installation, there are a few things you can do to improve the situation. One is to insulate the floor, because a great deal of heat is lost this way. You do this by installing a 'false floor', creating a cavity between it and the existing floor and filling it with insulating material. It can be a costly business, as both inner and outer doors may need to be raised. You could also install low-emissivity (low-E) glass (see pages 15 and 31), which will hold on to some of the heat coming into the conservatory.

Cellars

Dave knows first hand what it's like to live above a cellar in the winter if it's not properly insulated – it's freezing! The trend for bare floorboards hasn't helped, as a carpet does help to insulate the floor from the cold air below. If you have wooden floorboards, you can lift them and place a layer of insulation underneath. Sealing up the cracks in wooden floorboards with silicon will also go some way to reducing heat loss through the floor.

The walls and ceiling of a cellar can be insulated in much the same way you would your loft and with the same materials (see pages 28–9); ceiling insulation can be kept in place with plasterboard or wood. One important thing to point out is that insulation can restrict the movement of air, which means damp can become a problem, so it's vital to make sure there's adequate ventilation – install an extractor fan or an under-floor vent.

Once properly insulated, a cellar will not only stop heat loss from the house above but it will also maintain the cool temperature within the cellar walls – an added benefit if you're storing wine or home brew. Wine will age quickly at high temperatures, but cellars shouldn't really fluctuate above 25°C (77°F) and should have low humidity. During the secondary stage of fermentation beer will do better in a cellar than anywhere else in the house – if you don't have a cellar, a cupboard under the stairs is the next best place.

Heating the house

There are many simple ways of reducing your heating costs and, at the same time, your home's carbon emissions. Turning the heating off when you're not in and setting a timer are the most obvious ways of doing this. Also, radiators can be turned off in rooms not in use or the thermostat can be set to a lower temperature. Turning the heating down by just 1 degree can reduce a heating bill by as much as 10 per cent a year, so try doing this week by week and see if you get used to a slightly cooler room temperature. A good tip is to reflect radiator heat back into the room by putting aluminium foil behind all your radiators.

If you're using only one room at a time, an individual or stand-alone heater might be advisable. There's no point heating an entire house if you're spending all your time in the study.

There are more advanced ways of improving the heating in your home, and businesses and homeowners alike could consider installing a heat-recovery ventilation system. These vary in size: the smaller ones are ideal for single rooms and larger ones for the whole house. They work by using the warm, stale air leaving the house to heat the incoming fresh, cooler air entering the house. Smaller systems can be placed on an external wall, usually in the kitchen, and two fans will send out the cold air and bring in the warm respectively. Larger whole-house systems can be stored in the loft or made to fit in a cupboard above a domestic cooker extractor. These will mechanically pump warm or cold air around the house. Both systems can also be used in reverse in the summer months or warmer climes to act as an air-conditioning unit.

Keeping warm without heating
As do many couples, Andy and his girlfriend engage in arguments now and then about whether to have the heating on or off, and whether to set the thermostat a few degrees higher or lower. This is not unusual – in general, women have less muscle mass and are smaller than men, and men have more insulating fat on their torso, which helps keep the internal organs warm. Rather than put the heating on, there are several other ways of keeping warm:

- Keep doors shut throughout the house to cut down on draughts passing from one area of the house to another.

- Shut the curtains – up to 20 per cent of a room's heat can be lost through the windows.

- Add another layer of clothing.

- Wrap up in a warm duvet and snuggle up on the sofa.

- Use a hot water bottle.

- Exercise regularly – this is great for the circulation and makes a huge difference.

- Ensure there are no gaps and cracks in old wooden interior doors by painting them.

- Make a draught excluder (you can make a large version of the RSI hand rest, see page 331) and place it at the foot of a draughty door or across a windowsill. It makes a real difference, particularly in older houses.

- Have hot meals rather than cold food.

Heating water
Thankfully, the days of heating a caldron of water over a fire in order to have a bath or a wash are well and truly over. In the majority of homes, water is heated in a boiler, although there are other methods that we'll go into later.

Boilers come in all shapes and sizes and run on a myriad of different fuels – gas, oil or wood/biomass. If your boiler is over 10 years old there's a good chance that it's very inefficient. Some old boilers work at less than 65 per cent of their energy efficiency, in contrast to modern condensing boilers that work at a level of up to 85 to 95 per cent. If you decide to replace your boiler, try to get one in the A or B energy-efficiency bands. Although it will be more expensive than a less-efficient boiler, in the long run it will more than pay for itself. The cost of replacing a boiler can be prohibitive, so many people decide to insulate their boilers as a temporary measure. A useful website to check out the efficiency of your boiler is www.boilers.org.uk.

Limescale build-up can reduce the efficiency of a boiler sometimes to the extent that a band A boiler will be reduced to a band C in terms of efficiency. There are several chemical products on the market to reduce the amount of limescale in a system or a filter can be fitted to prevent the problem in the first place.

Condensing boilers
Although they run on fossil-fuel gas, condensing boilers are seen as one of the greenest ways of heating water. Their efficiency means that the extra cost of replacing a conventional type of boiler with one of these can be recovered well within 3–4 years.

With a conventional boiler a lot of the heat can be lost into the atmosphere via a waste flue. A condensing boiler contains a heat exchanger (sometimes two), which not only reclaims a lot of this heat but also condenses much of the waste water vapour back into water, trapping its latent heat as it does so (hence the name 'condensing boiler').

Combination boilers
A combination boiler will fire up only as and when it needs to. This reduces the standing losses associated with other boilers that can have whole tanks of hot water completely unused. Combination boilers

work by splitting the hot water and heating demands within the boiler so one or the other (or both together) can be used at one time. They're not always suitable for large houses, as the demand for hot water can come from more than one place – for example, by someone washing up while another has a shower. However, they're perfect for smaller houses or flats with a low demand for hot water. Condensing combi-boilers are now available, which further improves their efficiency, and are a great choice for those living in small houses or flats.

Biomass boilers These use energy from a renewable source and are usually cheaper to run than gas-powered boilers. Wood and wood-chip pellets are the main fuels and some more advanced biomass burners provide not only heat but also a certain amount of electricity. (For more information on biomass and wood-burning in the home, see pages 319–20.)

Solar water heaters If you've ever left a can of drink in the sun and then taken a swig from it later in the day, you'll understand the principle behind solar water heaters. In warm climates and in summer in Britain, solar water heaters can provide the majority of a house's hot water.

Even in winter the sun can sometimes be hot enough to 'help out' a conventional boiler. A solar water heater can save 250kg (550lb) of carbon being released into the atmosphere every year, or the equivalent of driving 1610 kilometres (1000 miles) in a small petrol-powered car.

As with photo-voltaic (PV) solar panels, solar water heaters are best mounted on a south-facing roof, but we've seen them ground mounted and on east- and west-facing roofs. Solar water heaters can be bought and installed for very little these days and you can see a return on your investment quite quickly.

A simple and inexpensive way to make a solar water heater is to use an old salvaged radiator and paint it black. It should be placed on the roof in an insulated glass-fronted box with silver paper on the back to reflect the heat more efficiently onto the surface of the radiator. Water is then run through the radiator and is fed back into your hot water tank via an insulated pipe. For further information on making your own solar water heater visit the website www.diydata.com/projects/solarpanel/solar_collector.php.

You could perhaps also rent a solar water heater (contact your local energy-efficiency advice centre, as you may be eligible for a grant). (For more information on solar power, see pages 314–15.)

A roof-mounted solar water heater absorbs heat from the sun.

OUTDOOR AREAS

Building a house creates a man-made space where nature once thrived and has a knock-on effect for wildlife, plant life and the water cycle in that particular area. It is, of course, impossible to return things to how they were before the house stood there. However, there are measures we can put in place to make a home sit more harmoniously with its surroundings. Green roofs and gardens can be havens for wildlife and this has meant that natural diversity can be greater in some urban areas than in rural settings. In addition, both front gardens and green roofs can help balance the water table and by holding on to water reduce the chances of flooding after prolonged rain or storms.

Rainwater-harvesting systems

With droughts and hosepipe bans becoming ever more commonplace, increasing numbers of people are starting to harvest rainwater for all sorts of activities from washing the car or watering the vegetable garden to flushing the toilet. It's very easy to store the rainwater in butts or large containers. Over the last 10 years the technology for saving water has become considerably more advanced: by using high-specification filter systems, such as UV or micron filtration, some households can now boast an entire water system using only filtered rainwater harvested from the roof (see page 36).

Collecting rainwater in a butt

USING HARVESTED RAINWATER

Here are just a few of the ways you can use rainwater stored in a water butt or pumped from a whole-house water-collection system:

- Watering plants and the lawn

- Car washing

- Washing mud off vegetables (as contaminants can be washed into the water from roofing material, rinse food first in rainwater, then give it a final rinse with fresh tap water)

- Topping up a pond during dry weather

- Filling up bird baths

- Washing hands after being in the garden

- Cleaning muddy boots and tools

- Flushing the toilet

Water butts (or rain barrels) By far the easiest way to harvest rainwater is to install a water butt. Most rainwater flows down the roof into the guttering to the down pipe and straight into a drain, where it joins all your sewage waste. A water butt simply stops the last part of the rainwater's journey and collects it for you to use at a later date. Water butts are available in most garden centres and many local councils in the UK offer schemes for reduced-priced butts. They're very easy to install and in some cases they can even be fitted for you.

Many commercially sold water butts are produced completely or partially from recycled material, so not only are you saving water but a little less goes to landfill too. Alternatively, you could recycle previously used containers such as large barrels, oil drums, big dustbins or any container that's able to hold liquid without leaking; Dave uses an old packing crate as a water butt. Juice concentrate is shipped around the world in large barrels and these are now available on the internet for rainwater collection, already fitted with a tap (see www.smithsofthedean.co.uk). Always put a lid on your water butt or barrel to keep the water free of contaminants.

Whole-house rainwater-collection systems

A more sophisticated version of the water butt is a whole-house rainwater-collection system, in which rainwater is collected, filtered and then pumped back into some or all of the house's water supply. The water can then be used for flushing the toilet, washing clothes, for gardening and, in some cases, as drinking water.

Rainwater is harvested from the roof during wet weather and sent from the guttering down the down pipe. The water is then filtered in a settlement tank to remove small particles, leaves and other debris and is collected in a large container (this is usually buried underground to prevent stray birds, insects and other small animals from falling into the water). When the water is needed – for flushing, for example – it's pumped from the large container up to the house, again passing through a filter. For drinking water, you need to have a UV-sterilization unit, where the water is filtered twice at 5 and 25 microns, to make sure that it is totally safe to drink.

At the time of writing, many homes across the UK were cut off from the mains water supply for about 10 days after a water treatment plant flooded. Despite record levels of rainwater falling, many had to rely on bottled water and large containers provided by the local authorities. The households with their own rainwater-collection system were not as badly affected, as they obtained water from large storage tanks rather than relying on it being pumped in. *Nature* magazine published a paper in July 2007 suggesting that the floods were linked to global warming and that problems of this kind are set to increase.

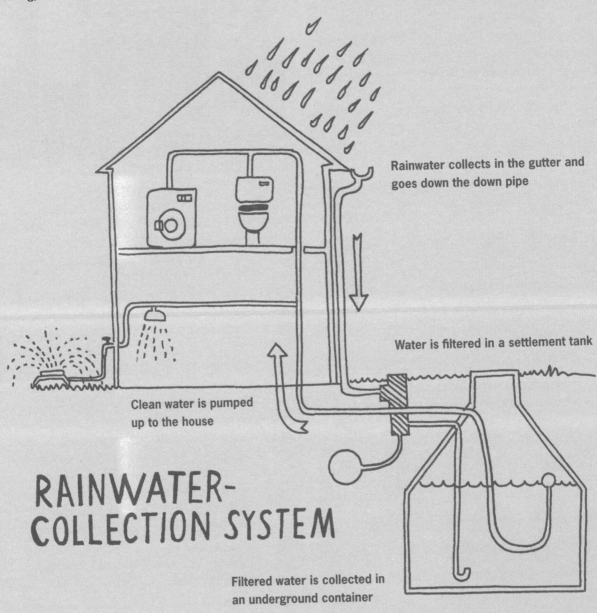

Rainwater collects in the gutter and goes down the down pipe

Water is filtered in a settlement tank

Clean water is pumped up to the house

RAINWATER- COLLECTION SYSTEM

Filtered water is collected in an underground container

A reed-bed system is a natural way to clean and process sewage, grey water and storm water.

Natural sewage and drainage systems

Reed-bed drainage and sewerage systems are an amazing example of modern technology utilizing a natural phenomenon. Reeds take in oxygen through their leaves and release it through their roots. Aerobic micro-organisms (those that need oxygen) that live at the plants' roots use the oxygen to break down soluble waste and ultimately purify the water using biological action. In this way, reed-beds can clean storm water, 'grey' water (see page 59) and sewage water and send it back into the water system without using potentially hazardous environmental pollutants. Power is not required with the natural reed-bed method, and the only maintenance needed is regular emptying of the tanks (these are used to remove gross waste before allowing it to enter the reed-bed).

Another benefit of reed-bed systems is that while the micro-organisms are digesting the solids in the waste water they give off a considerable amount of heat, which can then be utilized with underground piping to heat water for the house in much the same way as solar water heaters do with solar energy (see page 34).

Other wetland plants, most notably willow, are often used in combination with reeds in natural sewage and drainage systems. The willow and reeds can be burnt as a biomass fuel (see pages 319–21) and replanted again and again, making the house's sewage system a completely renewable source of energy.

Many of our native wetlands were drained for use as farmland long ago, but artificial wetlands and reed-beds that are now being created will have a positive impact on the surrounding environment.

Green roofs

If you're building a new house, repairing an existing roof or putting up an outbuilding it's well worth considering the option of a green roof. The word 'green' in this case doesn't just mean this type of roof is environmentally friendly; it also refers to the fact that there's vegetation living and growing on the surface.

A green roof is very important for wildlife, as it can in part restore the habitat that was destroyed when the house was built. The soil can provide a home for beetles, worms, millipedes, ants and a host of other subterranean species and microbial life forms. Flowering plants attract bees and butterflies and all of these insects in turn will feed the local bird population. The lack of human interaction also means that rare plant life can grow in these removed havens. On a Swiss green roof dating from 1914, rare orchids have been found growing undisturbed yards above the ground.

It's not only wildlife that benefits from a green roof – it provides an extra layer of insulation in winter and deflects rather than absorbs ultra-violet (UV) rays in summer. Roads and buildings absorb heat from the sun, whereas vegetation reflects it. This heating-up of man-made areas is known as the 'urban heat-island effect'. In the USA, the EPA (Environmental Protection Agency) claims that cities can be as much as 2–6°C (4–11°F) warmer than rural air temperatures, and a green roof in urban situations will help to counteract this.

A green roof is also beneficial in storm conditions. With conventional roofs, water flows straight into storm drains. However, the vegetation on a green roof acts like a giant sponge, slowly releasing water (up to 85 per cent) from its surface and putting far less strain on the system.

There is also evidence that a green roof has a longer lifespan than a normal roof, because as a living thing it will naturally replenish itself rather than need to be retiled or resurfaced every 10 years or so.

Installing a green roof If you're considering installing a green roof, especially on an existing structure, you have to ensure that the building has sufficient load-bearing capability, because green roofs are considerably heavier than many other types.

First the waterproof layer is installed. Traditionally this is made from impenetrable rubber, PVC or a glass-reinforced polythene membrane on top of a wooden framework. In recent years, waterproof concrete has come on the market, negating the need for this layer and thereby reducing the installation costs. Next comes a protective layer, usually concrete or paving slabs. Some roofs then have an additional layer of insulation. Finally the top layer is added: this consists of the growing medium (substrate layer) for the plants.

There are two types of green roof, intensive and extensive. Intensive green roofs are more like roof gardens. They're strong enough to walk on with a deep soil of 15cm (6in) or more and can grow anything from grasses to small shrubs and even trees. Extensive green roofs are not designed for walking on and have shallow soil. They're best for drought-resistant, succulent plants such as sedums or similar plants that are able to go without water for long periods of time or hold on to it when it's there. They're mainly for wildlife and holding water rather than 'gardening' as such. Intensive roofs, of course, need more maintenance than the extensive type, and the heavier the plants, the stronger the roof will have to be.

Front gardens

As car ownership continues to rise, the need to have somewhere to keep the car also increases. With the added incentive of reduced insurance payments and no need for costly permits, it's perhaps not surprising that hundreds of thousands of front gardens are now being tarmacked over to provide off-road parking. It's estimated that two-thirds of London's gardens have been covered in this way, losing an area of about 31 square kilometres (12 square miles).

The problems caused by the loss of a front garden have an immediate impact on the surrounding area. As with a green roof, during times of heavy rainfall garden vegetation absorbs rainwater and then slowly releases unwanted water over a period of days rather than immediately dumping it in the water system the moment it falls. If there's no vegetation in the vicinity, water just builds up on driveways and on tarmacked gardens with nowhere to go. As freak rainstorms are thought to be on the increase, it's clear that we have to do whatever we can to lessen the impact of these potentially devastating downpours. If you consider a drive essential, use gravel or similar porous material, which will reduce the likelihood of flooding.

Concreted, bricked or tarmacked land also spells a loss of habitat for birds, insects, plant life and small mammals. Over the last 10 years the demise of the front garden has led to house sparrow populations dropping by nearly 70 per cent. It's not only animals that suffer the loss of the front garden – it also means an increase in carbon-dioxide levels, as the plants are no longer there to absorb it from the atmosphere. In addition, bushes and trees act as a barrier to wind, noise, dirt and dust and the loss of these can have a negative impact on human health.

A green roof provides a habitat for wildlife and absorbs rainwater.

THE KITCHEN

The finger is often pointed squarely at industry whenever climate change is mentioned, possibly as it's an easy way to disassociate ourselves from any responsibility, but the truth is that 27.5 per cent of Britain's energy is used in the home (transport uses 34.5 per cent and industry just 19 per cent). It's vital that we cut back on this usage and the kitchen is the place to start, as this is by far the most energy-hungry room in the house.

There are many ways to cut down on energy consumption without going back to wood-burning stoves and washing clothes by hand – with the rising costs of fuel, it makes environmental and economic sense to do so. It's possible to run a kitchen without using any electricity or gas and still have cooked food, refrigerated items, clean dishes and clothes. You can cook your food using solar energy, which will also heat your water. A fridge can be made from two flowerpots and some sand and you can even wash your

clothes and get fit at the same time by using bicycle power with the originally named 'Cyclean' (see www.cyclean.biz). If you're slightly less adventurous and don't want to make your own white goods, you can still benefit from this chapter. At present, you may well be throwing money away and emitting far more carbon than you need to by not running your kitchen appliances efficiently – we'll be exploring ways in which you can increase efficiency and, as a result, shave a considerable amount off your fuel bills.

ENERGY IN THE KITCHEN

People consume vast amounts of energy and water in their kitchen, but there are many things you can do to reduce this consumption, saving money and reducing your CO_2 emissions in the process. When buying any kitchen appliance, check the energy label carefully (see opposite). Although you may pay slightly more for an energy-efficient appliance in the first instance, you get more for your money in the long run, as you won't use so much electricity or gas. You can also save money and power by using appliances efficiently: for example, by running washing machines, washer-dryers and dishwashers only when you have a full load, using economy and low-temperature settings and spin-drying clothes before you tumble-dry. Also, whenever possible consider using appliances and food preparation methods that require no electricity.

COVER PANS
Put lids on pots to keep heat in and save energy.

FRIDGE
Buy an energy-efficient fridge; locate it far from the oven and use it properly to save energy (see page 48).

KETTLE
Kettles are among the highest consumers of power in the home; don't over-fill and keep them free of limescale (see page 52).

COOKER
Hobs and ovens use a lot of power use them efficiently (see page 44) and consider fuel-less options (see pages 45–7)

WASHING MACHINE
'Grey' water from the washing machine can be treated and used in the garden (see page 59).

By law, the European Community Energy Label (below) must be displayed on all of the following products: fridges and freezers, washing machines, tumble dryers, dishwashers, electric ovens, lamps and air conditioners.

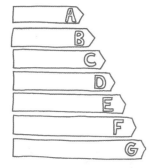

Products are rated from A–G, with A being the most energy efficient and G being the least. The most efficient fridges and freezers are marked A+ and A++.

Some products are awarded the European Ecolabel, which indicates that a product meets strict environmental criteria, putting it among the best in its class.

MICROWAVE

A microwave can use a lot less energy than a conventional oven, particularly if you're cooking or heating up small quantities.

ECO-FRIENDLY WASHING-UP LIQUID

Use eco-friendly washing-up liquid and natural cleaning products that are less harmful to the environment than strong detergents (see page 55).

DISHWASHER

Dishwashers generally use less water than washing up by hand (see page 52).

COOKING

A conventional hob or oven can use a lot of power in the kitchen, but there are plenty of easy steps you can take to reduce the amount of energy you consume when cooking, simply by changing your habits. In addition, there are several fuel-less alternatives to conventional cookers including the solar oven and the hay-box cooker. Neither of these methods uses electricity or gas, so they'll save you energy and help to reduce carbon emissions, whether they're used instead of or in conjunction with conventional appliances.

Hobs and ovens

Here are a few tips to help you save energy when cooking:

● Keep a careful eye on timings to avoid consuming surplus energy – Using a timer and reading up on cooking times before starting a recipe will help.

● Don't always preheat the oven – Many recipes will state that you should warm the oven before putting in your food, but this isn't always necessary, unless you need hot fat or are baking bread, cakes or pastry. You may have to alter the cooking time by adding a couple of minutes at the end to compensate, but as the oven stays hot for some time after cooking you might want to experiment by turning it off towards the end of the cooking time and adding a few minutes to the time stated in a recipe.

● Make use of the excess heat from the oven – After your oven is switched off, there's still enough heat left to start the drying process for herbs or mushrooms. This is especially useful in the autumn months, when you'll be thinking about preserving food (see page 247).

● Adjust cooking times and temperatures – Fan-assisted ovens are hotter and faster than conventional ovens. If cooking with a fan-assisted oven, as a rule of thumb set the oven temperature about 20°C (36°F) lower than stated in the recipe.

● Check the oven seal – Ensure that the seal on your oven is tight or heat will escape. If it isn't on properly it's worth getting a professional to fix it.

● Use an electric rather than a gas oven – A gas oven uses 65 per cent more power than an electric oven, because much of the heat escapes from a gas oven as a result of the flue that exhausts the combustion gases from the oven area. Also, if you get an electric oven and switch to a green-energy supplier at least a percentage of the electricity used will be carbon-free (see page 312).

● Use a microwave oven when you can – The wattage on many microwaves varies, as it does with the elements in most conventional ovens. The largest ring on an electric hob uses 1.5 kilowatts as standard. This is twice the number that many microwaves use. Even if something takes more time to cook in a 750-watt microwave it's still using less power than an electric hob.

● Put a lid on your pans – One of the simplest ways to reduce your energy usage is to put a lid on your pots when cooking. It's simple physics but often forgotten: less heat escapes, so more is retained when you put a lid on a pan of boiling water. If you haven't got lids for all your saucepans, just put a plate over the top instead.

● Flat-bottomed pans are best – Ensure the whole base of your pans touches the electric or gas ring. A pan with a warped bottom uses 290 watts to boil 1.5 litres (2½ pints) of water, while a flat-bottomed pan uses only 190 watts.

● Use a smaller pan whenever possible – A larger pan means a larger surface area to heat and therefore more energy is required.

● Choose the right ring for the pan – If you put a small pan on a big ring, heat will escape either side and won't be put to any use. Ideally, the pan should fit the ring almost exactly. Opt for a small pan on a small ring whenever possible.

● Use a pressure cooker – This is especially useful if you're cooking a lot of food. Food will cook in a third of the time and you'll be using fewer saucepans. To boil 1.5 litres (2½ pints) of water, a pressure cooker uses just 60 watts

Steaming uses less water than boiling and retains nutrients.

rather than the 190 watts used by an ordinary pan. It's worth investing in a really good model that will last.

● Simmer, don't boil – You'll use less energy and many dishes, such as soup, will actually benefit from simmering rather than boiling.

● Steam your food – This has two benefits: it uses less water than simply boiling your food and it also keeps the nutrients in the food itself. We steam all our vegetables in a metal colander placed on top of a saucepan full of boiling water, putting the saucepan lid on top of the food to keep the heat in.

● Clean your hob – Dirt or grease on your hob can reduce the heat flow to your pans, resulting in a slightly longer cooking time.

Solar-powered cooking

Solar cookery, in which the heat of the sun is used to cook food, is by no means a recent invention. In 1767 a Swiss scientist named Horace de Saussure experimented with glass 'hot boxes'. He managed to achieve a temperature of 88°C (190°F). With a bit of fine-tuning this idea was developed over the next few years and in 1774 the famous French chemist Antoine Lavoisier built a solar furnace that could reach temperatures of 1750°C (3182°F)!

There's little recorded on the evolution of the solar oven until a century later, when Auguste Mouchout designed and built solar ovens for French troops in South Africa. He boasted that they could cook 1kg (2lb) of potatoes in an hour. We have to jump another century, to 1957, to find a commercial solar hot plate, invented by American solar scientist Dr George Löf. He named his invention the 'umbroiler'. It was essentially an umbrella lined with silver foil to reflect light from the sun so that food could cook. It used to be available commercially in the 1950s and 1960s but it never really caught on and was phased out.

There are currently two American companies that sell solar ovens. Both of them are run by not-for-profit organizations offering low-cost cooking for developing nations that have a lot of sunshine but are short of fuel. They are the Solar Oven Society (www.solarovens.org) and Solar Cookers International (www.solarcookers.org). Made from recycled plastic drink bottles, aluminium and state-of-the-art insulation, their ovens are claimed to cook just about anything – they can roast meats, bake fish, chicken and bread, steam vegetables and even cook rice, beans, lentils and pasta using only solar energy. Solar ovens are a real benefit in developing nations, because they free women and children from the burden of gathering and carrying firewood (this is a dangerous activity in places where there are landmines), and they're helping to reduce deforestation as there's no need to cut down trees for cooking fuel.

Although solar ovens haven't yet taken off in the West, there are those who swear by solar cookery, particularly in warmer countries. Our friend Nev Sweeney frequently uses his homemade solar oven in the hot Australian sun and it really works. It's basically an insulated plywood box, painted black inside to absorb the heat, and is fitted with reflectors to channel more sunlight into the oven for higher temperatures. For further information on Nev's oven, visit our website www.selfsufficientish.com/nevssolaroven.htm. There's also a very good book by Beth and Dan Halacy called *Cooking with the Sun: How to Build and Use Solar Cookers*, which we recommend if you want to find out more about this way of cooking (see Useful addresses & further reading, page 385). Perhaps as the price of gas and oil increases, using solar technology for cooking and heating will become a necessity for all of us. (For more information on solar energy, see pages 34 and 314–15.)

Hay-box cooker

The hay-box oven is a tried-and-tested method of cooking and was used extensively during the Second World War, when fuel and cooking oil were scarce. It's useful for making liquid-based foods, such as soups or stews, which cook in their own heat, and works by trapping heat in the air spaces in the hay.

Quite simply, a hay-box oven consists of a box (this can be made of wood, metal or cardboard or can even be a cool box) filled with hay (you could also use shredded newspaper or old rags). Ideally the box should have a tight-fitting lid so no heat escapes, but if you use a cardboard box, covering the food with a pillowcase stuffed with hay will help retain heat (see opposite). The hay insulates the contents and the food will carry on cooking.

Food actually tastes better when cooked by this method, particularly meat casseroles, which you cook in advance and then leave for the flavours to develop and for the meat to become tender. A big difference between hay-box cooking and conventional cooking is that there is no evaporation. This means that less water is used and higher amounts of nutrients are retained. By using a hay-box oven regularly in conjunction with your standard cooker you'll make a considerable difference to your fuel consumption, which is a great bonus as fuel prices continue to soar. It's also an ideal way of transporting food and keeping it warm – Andy uses a hay-box oven when he's out all day on his allotment and wants something hot to keep him going.

HAY-BOX COOKING TIPS

● Don't be tempted to peek at the food, as it will reduce the heat inside the hay-box cooker and the dish will subsequently take longer to cook.

● Avoid spilling liquid on the hay as this will reduce heat.

● Foods cook better if the pot is full.

● Use pots without long handles, as they'll be easier to fit inside the box.

● Keep the hay box out of cold areas when possible, as the colder it is outside the box, the more quickly it will cool down inside.

● You can reuse the hay but if you don't use it within the week put it on the compost or fork it into your vegetable patch between plants as a mulch.

● Check for rodents before use if the box has been left outdoors.

MAKING A HAY-BOX COOKER

A simple hay-box cooker can be made from just a cardboard box and some hay, which you can get from a pet shop, or other insulating material. The food will stay warm for up to 8 hours.

1.

Prepare your soup or stew in a pot with a tight-fitting lid. The pot should be as full as possible. Bring the food to boiling point before putting it in the box.

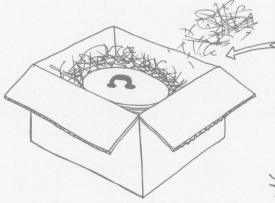

2.

Line the base of the box with hay to about half way up and put in your covered pan of food. Stuff hay or other insulating material around the sides of the pot.

3.

Fill a pillowcase with hay and place it over the pot.

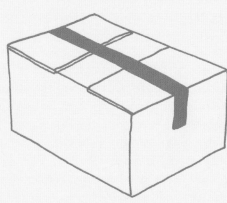

4.

Seal the box and leave undisturbed for 4–5 hours.

KEEPING FOOD COOL

In the days before fridges, food was kept fresh in snow, ice, cellars, caves and cold water, vegetables were buried underground or dried (see pages 247–9) or turned into pickles and chutneys (see pages 252–4) and meat was preserved by salting and smoking. It wasn't until after the Second World War that that mass-production of electric fridges began. They were hailed as one of the great modern inventions until the 1980s, when people came to realize the negative effects that fridges were having on the environment.

Fridges

Fridges are certainly among the most useful of all modern kitchen appliances and greatly reduce the chance of getting food poisoning. However, we despair when we go to our friends' houses, peer into the fridge and find just one mouldy fish cake and half a tomato – it seems such a waste to run a fridge to keep practically nothing cool. In the last 3 years, energy prices have gone up by almost 50 per cent and there's every possibility that they'll continue to rise. There are plenty of ways you can maximize your fridge's efficiency and greatly reduce your energy bills in the process.

The first step to energy-saving is to buy an energy-efficient fridge – fridges, like many electrical goods, are graded for energy efficiency, with A being the most efficient and G the least. This is shown on the front of the fridge when you buy it. If you're buying second hand, ask the person or dealer to supply you with the energy rating. The cost of an energy-efficient fridge can be recouped in just over 6 years, because you'll be using 30 per cent less energy. If you're upgrading a working fridge, offer your old one on www.freecycle.org. If you're replacing one that's broken, take your old fridge to the retailer, as by law (according to the WEEE directive, see page 27) they have to dispose of it safely for you.

Energy-saving tips for fridges

● Keep your fridge at an optimum temperature of 3–4°C (38–39°F) for maximum efficiency.

● Check the door seals by putting a banknote in the door and shutting it. If you can pull the note out easily, you might need to replace the seal on the door.

● Cover all liquids and moist food with lids or used bread bags. Added moisture will make your fridge work harder and waste energy.

● Locate your fridge as far from the oven as you can and out of direct sunlight.

● Don't box in your fridge. The heat from the compressor and the heating coil both need to be able to escape freely or they'll heat up the fridge. Dust can collect at the back of the fridge and this will have the same effect.

● A small hole drilled in the floor beneath your fridge can help cool the element and save more energy.

● Rather than running the cold-water tap to obtain colder water it's worth filling a bottle with water and placing it in the fridge. This way you're saving electricity as well as water, because the more items there are generating colder temperatures in your fridge (such as bottled water), the less your fridge will need to generate cold.

Cool larder

In pre-refrigerator days it was common to have a larder or pantry in many houses. Today they're rare in modern homes but they have many benefits. Foods such as cheese, eggs, bread and butter are better kept in a larder than a fridge, as they have more flavour and are ready to use immediately. Most fruit is also better kept out of the fridge and root vegetables are happy in a cool place. Another useful aspect of a cool larder is that when fridges aren't large enough to accommodate all the food, particularly in a big household, it can take the overspill, eliminating the need for a second fridge.

If you plan to create a larder, build a cupboard on a north-facing wall, add a ventilation brick and include some shelving. Situate the larder away from any source of heat: it needs to be as cool as possible, as well as fly-proof and rodent-proof. Some larders have small windows that are unglazed but are covered in a fine mesh, allowing ventilation without flies entering, and some have stone shelves or surfaces to keep food as cool as possible.

Covering moist foods with lids or old bread bags means your fridge doesn't have to work so hard.

Pot-in-pot cooler

In the semi-desert of northern Nigeria there is no electricity and this of course means no refrigeration. Mr Mohammed Bah Abba, a teacher born in 1964 into a family of pot-makers in the region, wanted to help reduce disease among the rural poor caused by decaying foods. He came up with the simple but ingenious idea of using traditional African terracotta pots to keep perishable food cool, based on a principle of physics already known in ancient Egypt. Two terracotta pots of different diameters are placed one inside the other, wet sand is placed between the two pots and the sand is kept constantly moist so the pots remain damp and cool. Perishables are then placed inside the smaller pot and covered with a damp cloth. Mohammed Bah Abba set up production of the pot-in-pot and personally paid for 7000 pots to be made. This gesture did not go unnoticed, as he was given the Rolex Award for Enterprise in 2000 and a sum of $75,000 for his 'desert refrigerator', which has revolutionized the lives of numerous impoverished Nigerians.

You can make a pot-in-pot cooling system at home relatively cheaply out of earthenware flowerpots that you or your friends and family may not need any more. Alternatively, ask at your local www.freecycle.org group. The cooler works best in the shade indoors or outdoors. Although heavy, it can be used for many practical applications, such as at a festival or barbecue for keeping your beers cool. It uses less water than filling a bin full of ice or water.

MAKING A
POT-IN-POT COOLER

1.
Take one large, unglazed terracotta pot and one slightly smaller pot. You'll need to plug drainage holes at the base with some putty sealed with gaffer or duck tape to ensure that no moisture leaks out.

2.
Put a layer of coarse builder's sand about 2.5cm (1in) deep into the larger pot, then put the smaller pot onto the sand. Fill the rest of the gap between the two pots with more sand. Leave a slight gap at the top of the pots.

3.
Pour cold water over the sand, a bit at a time, allowing it to be absorbed before pouring more in. The water needs time to soak into the terracotta. Keep filling with water until you can't fill any more.

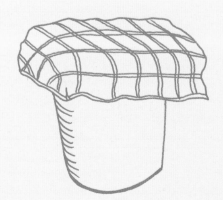

4.
Place a wet tea towel or bit of hessian over the top of the pots. Keep it damp by rewetting as necessary. The 'fridge' should stay cool for about 2 days.

The pot-in-pot cooler is a highly efficient but low-tech, portable refrigerator.

KITCHEN APPLIANCES

For every task that you undertake in the kitchen there seems to be an electrical item that can do the job for you. Sometimes this can be a total waste, as in the case of the electric tin opener (unless you're physically unable to open a tin), but very occasionally it can be more economical than using the conventional method.

Kettles

Here in Britain the humble cup of tea is the life-blood of many households; since its introduction to these shores 400 years ago, it has become entrenched within our culture. Climate change means tea is even grown in the UK, down in Cornwall. However, this enthusiasm for the beverage (and to a lesser extent coffee) is not without its drawbacks. You could power all the streetlights in the UK on the amount of energy wasted by kettles every year (1,270,000,000 kilowatt hours) and it's an area in which we should try very hard to cut down our energy usage.

To save energy, don't over-fill the kettle – fill it with just enough water for your needs. If there isn't a measuring level on the side, simply pour in as many mugs of water as you require and no more (provided the element is covered). If you have a clear kettle, indicate in marker pen on the side the various levels of water required for one cup, two cups and so on. Always empty your kettle after use and keep it clean. If you don't, limescale builds up, especially in hard-water areas such as parts of southern Britain and the Midlands. A build-up of limescale means that the kettle will take longer to boil and it will eventually stop working. To remove limescale, boil white vinegar mixed with an equal amount of water inside the kettle rather than buying expensive removers. After ridding your kettle of limescale you must ensure that it's well rinsed.

An electric kettle can be 3 times more efficient than heating a pan of water on the hob and slightly more efficient than using a gas ring and traditional kettle. However, if you have an Aga, Rayburn or wood-burning stove that is in use you might as well boil a traditional kettle on that as the heat is already there.

One of the best green gadgets that we've come across recently is the Tefal Quick Cup kettle, a piece of kit that could have been invented entirely for Andy's girlfriend, who can become impatient when she's gasping for a cuppa and the kettle takes so long to boil. The water is passed through a spiral heating system that heats the water within 3 seconds. It heats only the water you need and Tefal claim that this saves one-third of the energy of a standard kettle. It also filters fresh cold water within seconds.

Bread-making machines

The bread-maker is one of the few electrical gadgets that is more economical than its more traditional counterpart. Essentially, it's a mini bread oven the perfect size for a loaf. There's no area of the oven that is being heated up unnecessarily and even if you take into account the kneading action it requires less energy than an oven.

Blenders and grinders

Although useful for many things, an electric blender is really a bit of a luxury. There are hand-cranked blenders on the market, which are certainly harder to use than simply flicking a switch, but obviously they're more energy-saving. Another interesting option is a blender that can keep you fit – you can put an attachment on your bike and pedal to blend. Before you reach for your blender automatically, remember some jobs are easier to do by hand, particularly when dealing with small quantities, such as baby food. If puréeing fruit it's often better to use a sieve and push fruit through the mesh. For spices and nuts you could use a traditional pestle and mortar rather than an electric grinder.

Dishwashers

According to a study by DEFRA (Department for Environment, Food and Rural Affairs), washing dishes in a dishwasher uses up to 4 times less water than when washing up by hand. The study looked at washing 140 items. The results showed that 63 litres (14 gallons) of water were used to wash them by hand and less than 20 litres (4½ gallons) using a dishwasher. Some manufacturers claim that dishwashers are also more energy-efficient, if you take into account the heating of the tap water, but the study concluded that there was in fact not a strong case for or against using a dishwasher to save energy.

Microwave ovens

Some people seem almost scared of the microwave, but when used properly it can save you a lot of energy and reduce your electricity bill considerably. Consider the 10-minute zap in the microwave compared to at least an hour in a conventional oven that it takes to cook a jacket potato.

We drink 160 million cups of tea a day in Britain, or 62 billion cups a year. Kettles are one of the main consumers of energy in the home.

Lemons, vinegar and soap pods are all natural
and effective cleaning products.

NATURAL CLEANING

Many of today's cleaning products may well get rid of the dirt in your home but a large number of them contain some very strong, harmful chemical agents, which are bad not only for the environment but also people's health. Below are a few examples of natural products that will do the job just as well. Some ovens become particularly dirty – if you feel you need the help of a cleaning product, we'd recommend the Ecover range. When it comes to washing clothes, there are some natural products available, but if your clothes aren't very soiled you may be able to wash them without using any detergent or soap at all. Some dirt (and smells) are totally water-soluble, so a quick spin in the washing machine may be all you need.

Bicarbonate of soda This works as a deodorizer when you mix it with water. You can use it to dissolve grease – for example, on the hob and grill pan. Sprinkle it onto the surface and scrub with a sponge. If used dry, it will lift stains from carpets, too.

Lemon juice This is effective at cutting grease on electric hobs and surfaces. Squeeze the lemon juice onto a surface, then wipe clean with a damp cloth. If you have limescale marks on your taps, cut a lemon in half and leave it on the taps overnight; rinse off in the morning.

Vinegar You can use any type of vinegar to clean your kitchen. Use it neat or put it into a spray bottle as a dilute mixture (about 1 part vinegar to 3 parts water). It's particularly useful for cleaning draining boards. White vinegar is better for use on white surfaces as malt vinegar can sometimes leave a residue.

Eco-balls These are used instead of detergents in your washing machine and work by agitating dirt off your clothes; they're not ideal for heavily soiled clothing but they do work for the average wash. In addition, anyone who suffers from allergies such as dermatitis from washing detergents will really benefit from eco-balls. An added bonus is the fact that they will reduce your energy bill, as there's no need for the rinse cycle that's used to wash away the detergents.

Soap pods Another good alternative to washing powder, these are nuts from the Indian soap nut tree (see opposite and right), a deciduous tree that grows in hot climates. It produces a berry-like fruit, the skin of which contains saponin, a substance with similar properties to soap. As soap pods are natural the whole berry can be composted. They are available from specialist health shops and online. One bag lasts for about 25 washes.

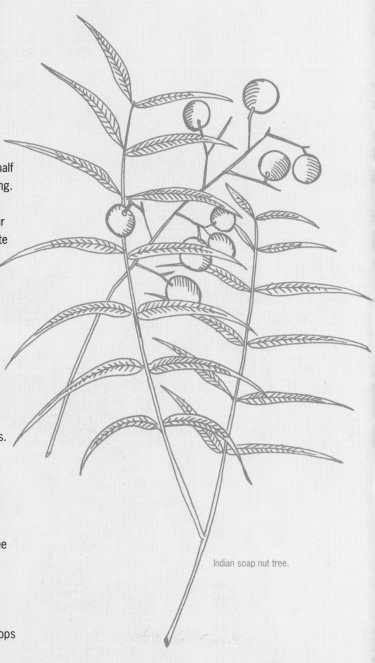

Indian soap nut tree.

WASTE & RECYCLING

Through our kitchens, we generate a huge amount of domestic waste, of which up to 60 per cent can be composted. In the not-so-distant future we could be looking at an increase in our council tax bills to pay for excess waste, as the cost of landfill will be passed on to the taxpayers. If we start to compost and recycle now, it won't be a shock to the system when this time comes.

Compostible food waste

The more you grow your own produce, the easier it is to reduce waste, as your food won't involve so much packaging and will consist more of peelings and scrapings. During the Second World War, pig clubs sprang up around Britain to supplement the meat rations. Several people would group together and buy, feed and look after a pig in exchange for bacon and pork when the animal was slaughtered. People would save their kitchen scraps and give them to the clubs to feed the pigs. Today, the majority of people don't know a pig to take the scraps off their hands, so the ideal way of using vegetable scraps is to compost them (see pages 81–2).

If you live in a flat and don't have access to a garden or an allotment and your council doesn't collect your organic waste, ask friends, family and neighbours if anyone is willing to take your vegetable waste for their compost heap or bin. If so, get a bucket with a lid and pop scraps into it as you go. Try to get them to collect the bin once or twice a week, depending on how much waste you create. Flies may become a problem, especially during the summer months. Andy's small flat became infested with fruit flies. They seemed to be everywhere – small clouds used to form in the centre of the kitchen whenever he opened a cupboard. So he bought a carnivorous plant called a pitcher plant in an attempt to combat this and it worked extremely well – within a week the flies had gone. To keep flies at bay, always keep your bucket sealed and clean it after use.

Wormeries If you don't have room for an outdoor compost heap but want to compost your own kitchen waste, a wormery might be for you. This is a self-contained system that uses worms to digest organic kitchen scraps. Wormeries are inexpensive and will fit in any available space in your kitchen. Since the units are sealed, you needn't worry about the worms escaping. A wormery will create two beneficial products to help the gardener:

Most councils now recycle aluminium cans.

compost and liquid feed (also called 'worm tea'). Both are very nutritious and will give your plants a boost. Worm casts have 5 times more nitrogen, 7 times more phosphorus and 11 times more potassium than soil.

Worms will eat almost all of your kitchen scraps, except for citrus fruit, meat and fish, and onions and leeks should be kept to a minimum. You can also throw in garden waste, although it's better to start a separate compost bin for this, as they don't like large quantities of the same thing. Try not to over-feed the worms or you could kill them; wait until they've dealt with your last offering before adding more scraps. If flies are a problem, cover the contents of the bin with a whole damp newspaper, as this will stop the flies laying any more eggs and they should soon die out. Worms are sensitive to heat and moisture, so make sure the bin doesn't get too hot or too cold and that it doesn't dry out or get too wet, or it could kill your worms. The optimum temperature inside the wormery is between 15°C and 25°C (59°F and 77°F).

For outdoors, we recommend the Can-o-worms wormery available at www.wigglywigglers.com. If you have no choice but to keep your wormery indoors we would strongly advise buying an all-in-one container, available on www.bullybeef.co.uk.

Bokashi composters The Bokashi system, developed in Japan, is another excellent way of composting food scraps. It's the perfect method for smaller households and flat dwellers, and everyone we know who uses the system swears by it. Like the wormery, the Bokashi composter is small and neat – about the same size as a small pedal bin – and can be kept under the kitchen sink or indeed anywhere you can find room for it.

One of the main advantages of the Bokashi system is that as well as breaking down vegetable matter it composts foods that you can't use in a wormery, such as meat, fish and citrus fruit. There's no need to turn the waste and there's no smell.

After adding your kitchen waste to the bin you sprinkle a little Bokashi bran over the surface. The bacteria and

MAKING A WORMERY

You can make your own wormery out of a 40-litre (9-gallon) plastic or wooden bin. Place it in an outhouse, porch or garage or close to the back door. A wooden bin provides the ideal habitat for worms but a plastic bin is easier if you're making your own.

1.

Drill 5mm (¼in) holes around the side of the bin, 4cm (1½in) apart and about 7.5–15cm (3–6in) up from the base. Also drill 2mm (⅛in) holes in the lid and in the side, about 30cm (12in) down from the top. This is so air can circulate.

2.

Place the bin on a tray to prevent 'worm tea' from seeping through the drainage holes.

3.

Add a layer of coarse sand to the bin, about 10cm (4in) deep. On top, place a polythene bag with holes in it – these are needed for drainage.

4.

Add a layer of bedding material – you can use moistened newspaper, cardboard (corrugated works best), seaweed (cleaned of salt), used compost or leafmould. You should aim for about 7.5cm (3in) of bedding.

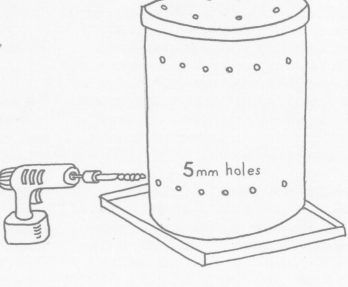

2 mm holes

5 mm holes

5.

Put in as many worms as you can. Make sure they're the right kind – tiger worms are best. You can order these on the internet.

6.

Throw about 1kg (2lb) of chopped vegetable waste into the bin, cover the contents with a whole soaked newspaper and put on the lid. As a rule of thumb, if you see worms feed them and if you can't, hold back. Little and often is the key to a healthy wormery.

PAPER ⇒
WASTE ⇒
WORMS ⇒
BEDDING ⇒
POLYTHENE ⇒

SAND

yeasts in the bran break down your waste and eliminate nasty odours. Every 2 or 3 days you need to strain off the excess fluid this creates, which can make a very nutrient-rich plant food, diluted at 1:100. Alternatively, you can just pour the liquid down the sink: the bin manufacturers claim that it cleans your pipes and stops any sink odours. Once the bin is full, you leave it for just 2 weeks for the composting process to take place. After this time, the waste can either be added to your compost heap or wormery, or dug straight into the garden or allotment, where it will release nutrients into the soil. The waste will be pickled by this time, so it won't attract vermin.

The one possible downside of this system is the cost, because you need to invest in two Bokashi bins (one for using in the kitchen and the other waiting to go on the compost heap) and bags of bran. However, if you work out the costs of plant food, drain cleaner and compost, this could come close to the same figure. Bokashi bins are not currently widespread but they're available online at www.greengardener.co.uk/bokashi.

Other waste

Your local council should inform you of all the recycling services that it offers. It's also a good point of call for every recyclable item and will be able to tell you if there are any local businesses that will collect unwanted items. Some councils will also supply you with bags or recycling boxes and inexpensive compost bins.

Bin bags and storage boxes

The 'normal' bin bags that you buy in most shops are thought to take 400 years to degrade in a landfill, although this could be longer. In addition, they're made from plastic, meaning that petrochemicals are used in their manufacture. We don't actually use bin bags at all, as we have waste bins with a removable inner bucket, which we then empty into a wheelie bin. We put any rubbish that rots either in the home compost or in the council's organic collection bags, so there isn't food for rats and maggots in the wheelie bin. Although you shouldn't put meat waste in your home compost bin it is acceptable in some councils' compost collections because the waste is taken to a huge compost heap that generates enough heat to break down such items in a shorter time than in home-compost systems, where rats can be a problem. It's worth noting that some councils insist on bin bags in wheelie bins.

There are other options for those who want to use a bin bag but don't want to harm the environment. Goodness Direct (www.goodnessdirect.co.uk) offers what it calls the most environmentally responsible refuse sacks, d2w. There are swing-bin liners, pedal-bin liners, wheelie-bin liners and various other types of bags that degrade to CO_2, water and a small amount of biomass. They take about a year to degrade.

If you don't have a kerbside recycling scheme, or if you generate a lot of waste, you might have the problem of storage. Your local discount shop could come to the rescue – for very little you can buy stackable boxes to store your recycling items. The boxes should fit into any spare space that you might have in the house, such as a porch or an alcove.

Recycling cans, bottles and Tetra Pak cartons

Many councils now collect cans and if they don't there are plenty of can-recycling banks around. If you crush used cans you can fit far more into your recycling bin; if you get through a lot of cans, you might consider obtaining a can crusher.

Keep hold of your glass bottles and jars, as these can come in handy for storing foods, particularly when preserving and home brewing. If you don't intend to use them yourself, pass them on to someone who could use them through your local www.freecycle.org group.

Tetra Pak is the company that makes most drink cartons that we use. Although these can be recycled in theory, the majority of councils don't collect them. However, you can post your cartons to the Alliance for Beverage Carton Manufacturers.

'Waste' water

'Grey' water is the 'waste' water that's left when you do the dishes, have a shower or run the washing machine. The other waste water, from the toilet, is called black water.

Grey water from the kitchen sink can contain detergents, food residue and fat, and waste water from the washing machine or dishwasher can contain nitrogen and phosphorus, which will eventually get into the ground water and cause algal growth. For this reason, you should never use grey water unless it's been treated (although in some countries, where water is scarce, this does occur). The treatment process involves passing grey water through a filter to remove any solids, then through a sand and gravel filter or a reed-bed (see page 37). Once it's been treated you can use it on non-edible plants, but you should never use it on your vegetable plot because it could still contain pathogens. Japan is a good example of a country using grey water intelligently – there, water is often diverted from the bath to the washing machine.

THE BATHROOM

The main purpose of the bathroom is washing, but it's also a place to freshen up for the day or unwind and relax in the evening. Most bathroom activities involve using water – and plenty of it. Today we take hot and cold running water and flushing toilets for granted, but the fact that this precious resource is so readily available can result in a tremendous amount of water being wasted.

There are many simple ways in which you can modify your habits to save water – take showers rather than baths, keep showers short, install low-flow plumbing fixtures and turn taps off when you're not using them. If your water bills are high, you might consider switching to a water meter – you may find it's less expensive than paying a fixed rate and it'll make you more aware of water consumption.

The bathroom is also a place for grooming, beautifying and pampering, but with so many of our soaps, shampoos and cosmetic products containing petrochemicals and synthetic perfumes we could be doing our bodies more harm than good by using them. It strikes us as rather contradictory that many people buy or grow organic food because they're concerned about what goes into their body but won't think twice when it comes to putting a cocktail of chemicals on their skin and hair. In this chapter, we look at natural alternatives that are better for you as well as for the environment.

USING WATER

In a typical household in Britain, bathing and showering account for about 20 per cent of annual water use, but in recent years manufacturers of plumbing equipment have come up with numerous water- and energy-saving appliances. You can now get low-flow showers, new toilet cisterns use a lot less water than their archaic forebears and dual-flush toilets give you the option of high-volume and low-volume flushes.

Toilets

Unless you're a gardener, toilets use more water than any other installation in the home, amounting to about 40 per cent of the total consumption. Typically, they will use 9–12 litres (2–3 gallons) of water every flush, so a family of four flushing 5 times each a day could use up to 7200 litres (1600 gallons) of water a month. Huge amounts of energy are used to supply us with water, purify it and take it away after we've used it, so reducing the number of times you flush the toilet on a daily basis will make a big difference. If in doubt, just remember this little rhyme: 'If it's yellow let it mellow, if it's brown flush it down' – it's pretty self-explanatory.

To reduce water usage, you could make a 'cistern brick' by putting one or two plastic bottles filled with sand, earth, grit or water in the toilet cistern (we find the shorter, wider bottles work best); you could save over 2 litres (3½ pints) per flush this way. If you find yourself frequently having to flush twice, remove the bottle as you'll be using more water. This 'brick' is not to be used in modern dual-flush toilets, which already save water.

Another option is to use rainwater in your toilet. Collect water in buckets or in a butt and pour a bucketful down the toilet after use. Alternatively, you could install a more sophisticated whole-house rainwater-collection system, which saves rainwater in a tank and pumps it into the house for flushing (see pages 35–6).

Dual-flush toilets There are many dual-flush toilets on the market, all of which enable you to choose between two different flush volumes, depending on whether you need to dispense of solid or liquid waste. They operate by having two buttons on the top of the cistern – one will release around 3 litres (5 pints) of water and the other about 6 litres (10 pints).

Compost heaps and straw-bales There are several basic toilets you can use for liquid waste, both of which are beneficial for the garden. The most basic is the compost bin: simply wee into it every couple of days (really, this is one for the men – it would take quite a feat for a woman to perform this task). The reason for using this method, apart from saving water, is that urine is nitrogen-based and can help speed up the composting process. However, if you do it too frequently the compost will become excessively watery.

Adam Hart-Davis, the historian, broadcaster, author, photographer and toilet enthusiast has modified this idea in his straw-bale lavatory. It's a lot easier to use than the compost-heap method and women can participate too. He stuffs tightly packed straw (about a third of a bale) into a plastic stacking box, with the cut end facing upwards. After a few months, he removes the straw and puts it on the compost heap or digs it straight into the ground. Adam put one of his straw bales into a trench and planted runner and climbing French beans on top.

Compost toilets If you have enough space, a proper compost toilet is the greenest option possible for dealing with your solid waste (you need to urinate elsewhere). It avoids the need for water, sewers and treatment works and puts soil to good use.

In the bathroom, compost toilets can look very much like conventional ones at first glance, but without the chain and cistern. It's below the toilet where the real difference lies, because there's a chamber underneath to collect waste. Human waste contains a whole host of trace elements and nutrients that are beneficial to plants, including nitrogen, magnesium, sulphur, phosphorus and potassium. After about 2 years, once aerobic bacteria has broken down your waste, the compost can be used on garden trees and bushes, but not vegetables or herbs as there's risk of infection from the pathogens. In some communes, compost toilets have been set up over wheelie bins, with sawdust added to each deposit. The bins can be wheeled off once full and stored for later use as compost.

You do need quite a lot of space to accommodate the underground chamber, so bear this in mind before you consider installing one in your home. You'll need a ventilation shaft reaching from the chamber to the outside

A compost toilet has a collection chamber beneath the floor.

of the house, and the entrance of the shaft should be covered in wire mesh so air can enter to break down the waste but flies are unable to pass through. To get the compost out, you'll need to build access panels into the design. There has to be a considerable amount of heat for the composting process to work: an average family's waste will generate enough heat, but in a house or flat containing one or two people, or a holiday home, there might not be enough generated, so you have to weigh up whether running a heater all the time to make very little compost is really worth it, and the answer is probably not.

You need to add carbon-based 'soak materials' to the compost to help the process of breaking down the waste. Keep a bucket of sawdust, shredded paper or leaves nearby and throw some down the toilet after use.

Showering and bathing

Showers are generally considerably more eco-friendly than baths, using about one-third of the water and energy of an ordinary bath. However, power showers have increased flow rates, which means that they can use at least as much water as a bath, if not more.

A friend of ours takes an egg timer into the shower. He limits his showering time to 5 minutes, which is more than enough time to get clean, saving precious hot water and money in the process. Some people like to shower every day, sometimes twice a day: this is unnecessarily wasteful and it's not good for your skin or hair either. Try showering only when you need to – perhaps cut down to 3 times a week. A thorough wash of the essential areas from the basin with soap and water will ensure that you keep clean.

Of course, not everyone has a shower just to get clean: many do so to wake themselves up in the morning, or perhaps they take a bath to unwind after a day's work. Try cycling to work to make you more alert in the morning and have a footbath instead of a bath or shower to help you relax in the evening. If getting to sleep is a regular problem, try other methods to relax you that don't involve using water (see pages 284–5).

Low-flow showerheads A low-flow showerhead is a device that you attach to your shower to reduce the amount of water that comes out, meaning that less water is heated. It's easy to install – simply unscrew your traditional showerhead and replace it with the new low-flow version. Some people complain about the more basic models, as they obviously reduce the flow, but we find them perfectly adequate. They benefit from a monthly dip in a 1 part white vinegar to 2 parts hot water solution,

especially in hard-water areas. There are also slightly more expensive low-flow showerheads on the market, which add oxygen to the water and increase velocity. They have the advantage of being made from a non-stick metal too, so you'll rarely have to de-clog the head. These showerheads can be bought from www.naturalcollection.com. The cost will soon be recuperated when you consider that a low-flow shower will use about half the amount of hot water of a normal shower.

Solar showers Many campers and outdoor types will already be aware of the solar showers on the market. These are essentially a bag that you fill up with water, hang in the sun for 3 hours for the water to heat up then shower under. Solar showers are inexpensive and are available from shops specializing in camping and sailing equipment.

Consider using one for everyday use on hot days – put down a couple of patio slabs under a tree, with a fence panel secured next to it for modesty, and you could have your own outdoor summer shower. If your backyard is overlooked, this may not be such a good idea – we wouldn't want to recommend anything that would lead to readers being charged with indecent exposure!

WATER-SAVING TIPS

- Don't leave the tap on when brushing your teeth.
- Shower instead of having a bath.
- Power showers use as much water as a bath; consider alternatives before having one fitted.
- Fix any dripping taps.
- Insulate your hot-water pipes – the hotter the water stays, the less time you have to run a tap to get hot water.
- Fill a basin to wash instead of a running tap.
- Share a bath or shower.
- Take less time in the shower.
- Use an electric razor instead of 'wet' shaving.
- Report mains' leaks to your water supplier.
- Don't flush the toilet unless you need to.
- Put a 'brick' in your toilet cistern (see page 62).

BATHROOM PRODUCTS

Next time you're in the bathroom, pick up a bottle of shampoo or beauty product and read the ingredients on the label: it's a long list and only those with a degree in chemistry will be able to make sense of it all. We frequently wonder whether we really need all of these chemicals just to wash our hair or keep our bodies clean when we've managed for thousands of years without. And why buy chemical products when organic alternatives are readily available or you can make your own?

Soap

Standard soap often contains petrochemicals and can leave your skin feeling quite dry. Many people can be very sensitive to these chemicals. You can buy organic soaps, made from vegetable oils, or why not combat these problems in a fun way by growing your own?

An eco-friendly alternative to soap is the root of the soapwort plant. Simply boil up the whole plant in about 500ml (17fl oz) water, cool, then strain into a spray bottle. Use it as you would liquid soap. Soapwort can be grown from seed in most soils. Be aware, however, that once established it may become invasive.

Deodorants & antiperspirants

Fresh sweat contains sex pheromones, which are chemicals that aid attraction. This means that natural smells are more likely to help you attract a mate than unnatural scents in perfumed products, which often contain animal pheromones. So if you find yourself attracted to someone wearing a certain body spray, perfume or aftershave, just think – you might be attracted to a wart hog.

However, the human scent is not always pleasant, especially if it's not fresh. You can reduce the amount of unpleasantness your armpits emit in a number of ways without using deodorants or antiperspirants. Give your armpits a good wash every morning with soap and water and watch what you eat. Sweat glands excrete toxins from your body, so if your diet's bad you'll probably smell bad. Avoid excessive amounts of caffeine, refined sugars and processed foods, eat plenty of fresh fruit and vegetables and reduce your fat intake.

Most deodorants contain aluminium, which is considered to have damaging, long-term effects on the brain and it's thought to be one of the possible factors in developing Alzheimer's disease. There's also some conjecture about the link between aluminium-based underarm deodorants and breast cancer, although deodorant manufacturers have dismissed such claims. You can find deodorants made without aluminium in large healthfood shops – brands to look out for include Jason Natural Products and Weleda.

Another option is to use a deodorant stone, made from potassium mineral salts. To use, you simply wet the stone and run it under your arm; it works by creating a hostile environment for the bacteria. Deodorant stones are available from large healthfood shops or online.

Basil and lovage deodorant

The cost of buying a natural organic deodorant is often at a premium, and it's much cheaper to make your own. The recipe below, which should keep for about 10 days, is for a deodorant rather than an antiperspirant, so it allows the body to sweat naturally but will mask any unpleasant smells. Lovage is usually available from your local herbalist or healthfood shop or you could grow it yourself.

2 tbsp fresh or 1 tbsp dried basil leaves
2 tbsp fresh or 1 tbsp dried lovage leaves
600ml (1 pint) water

1. Put the basil and lovage leaves into a saucepan with the measured water. Bring to the boil, then simmer, with the lid on, for 5 minutes.
2. Meanwhile, place a glass jar into a second pan with enough water to cover the jar and boil for 2 minutes to sterilize, then remove it from the pan and allow to cool.
3. Take the pan with the leaves off the heat and leave with the lid on until it has completely cooled.
4. Strain the liquid into the jar and compost the leaves.
5. To apply, dip a flannel into the liquid and dab under your arms or put it into a mister and spray under your arms.

Hair washing

Ordinary shampoos contain vast numbers of chemicals that surely can't be good for us. We suggest buying organic shampoos made by companies such as Jason Natural Products (www.jason-natural.com), Aubrey Organics (www.aubrey-organics.com) and Korres (www.korres.com), which all make chemical-free, vegan shampoos that are available from most healthfood shops as well as online. Alternatively, baby shampoo is usually free of chemicals.

Natural hair care These quick tips will keep your hair looking and feeling healthy, without using any unnecessary chemicals.

- Massage a beaten egg into your hair and wash out with cold water.

- If you have dark hair, rub cider vinegar into your hair and rinse out.

- For light hair, massage in lemon juice and rinse.

- Use olive oil instead of hot-oil products (warm it up, massage it in, shampoo and rinse it out).

- Wet your hair before swimming, so it soaks up less chlorinated water (or wear a swimming cap).

The no-shampoo method The most eco-friendly way of treating your hair is never to use shampoo. If you leave your hair for about 6 weeks the natural oils will start working to keep it naturally clean. This takes dedication, and you have to go through a stage of having pretty greasy and sometimes smelly hair. The reason for this is that your sebaceous glands over-produce sebum, which is a lubricant, to compensate for the drying effects of shampoo, which strips your hair of its natural oils. Once you leave your hair alone it will adapt and the sebaceous glands will settle down. You can wet your hair as and when you need to, but just use water. The no-shampoo method isn't advisable in areas with hard water (such as many areas in southern Britain, including London, and the Midlands), because wetting hair with hard water can interfere with its natural oils.

Some people using the no-shampoo method massage bicarbonate of soda into their scalp, leave it there for a couple of minutes and then rinse out with water. After doing this, mix 1 part cider vinegar to 7 parts water in a mug and apply it to your hair followed by the final rinse.

Facial skincare

Although we're a couple of blokes there are the odd occasions when we indulge in a little bit of male grooming – as ever, we wouldn't pay through the nose for bottled treatments and instead opt for what we can find in the kitchen and make ourselves.

Marie Antoinette's face mask

Marie Antoinette, the wife of King Louis XVI of France, was a legendary beauty. Many believe that this facial treatment was the secret of her clear, glowing skin – so much so that it's still popular in France. This mask is suitable for normal or oily skins, but the witch hazel and lemon can be harsh on dry skin.

1 egg
Juice of 1 lemon
4 tbsp non-fat milk powder
1 tbsp witch hazel

1. Put all the ingredients into a blender or food processor and mix well. Alternatively, blend them together by using a fork or a wire whisk.
2. Apply the mixture to your face and neck and allow it to dry for around 15 minutes.
3. Rinse your face thoroughly with warm water and pat dry with a clean towel.

Butter face mask

Butter is a good source of vitamin A, which works as a restorative for damaged skin. This face mask is suitable for all skin types. Keep the mask in the fridge and use within 5 days.

1 tbsp unsalted butter, softened
1 tbsp lemon juice (for oily skin)
   or 2 mashed strawberries (for normal skin)
   or 1 egg yolk (for dry skin)

1. Beat the butter in a bowl, then beat in the ingredient that matches your skin type.
2. Apply the mask immediately and leave on for 10–15 minutes.
3. Remove the mask with a warm, wet cloth. Rinse your face with water, then pat dry.

This butter face mask is ideal for dry skins.

Wooden toothbrushes with natural bristles can be composted after use.

Toothbrushes

Around 240 million plastic, non-biodegradable toothbrushes enter a landfill every year in the UK, which is around 4320 tonnes of waste, so it's well worth seeking out alternatives even though they're not easy to come by. Wooden-handled toothbrushes with natural bristles, which can be put in your council compost bin, are available online and in leading healthfood shops. For children you can get natural wooden toothbrushes made from local beech wood and natural hygienically treated pig hair at www.smilechild.co.uk.

The only other alternative that's dubbed as an 'eco-toothbrush' is a bit of a cop-out in our opinion. It's a toothbrush with a changeable head and will help cut down by about one-third the number of toothbrushes going to landfill. However, it's still made of plastic. Changeable-head toothbrushes are produced by various manufacturers and are available from some healthfood shops.

In some parts of the developing world, people chew bitter-tasting twigs from the meswak tree rather than use a toothbrush. The sap that is released is thought to freshen breath and keep your teeth strong; when the twigs are chewed for longer periods, the 'splinters' act like floss. You can buy meswak twigs from some Islamic shops in the UK and they can be composted after use.

Toothpaste

Most brands of toothpaste contain sodium lauryl sulphate, a foaming agent that can lead to mouth ulcers, as it dries out the inside of your mouth, causing the tissue to become weaker. Toothpaste can also contain triclosan, a chemical used for its anti-bacterial properties, which it's thought could become carcinogenic when it comes into contact with water. In 2005 Marks and Spencer stopped selling their products containing triclosan as a precaution.

There are plenty of organic and natural toothpastes available from good healthfood shops or online. Companies that make natural toothpastes include Jason Natural Products, Green People, Kingfisher and Lavera.

Toilet paper

During our schooldays in the early 1980s there was an insult that used to do the rounds: 'I bet you use recycled toilet paper.' Thankfully, times have changed and recycled paper is no longer considered to be infra dig. In fact, if anything it's the reverse.

Several brands of toilet rolls made from recycled paper are now widely available and they're often cheaper than 'new' paper. Our toilet paper of choice is Nouvelle, as it's made from 100 per cent recycled paper, uses entirely recyclable packaging, contains no optical brightening agents and it's also much softer than many other recycled products; in addition, the company supports the Woodland Trust in several ways. If your shops don't stock Nouvelle, look for the FSC symbol on packaging. This means that at least the paper comes from managed woodland.

Sanitary products

Many sanitary products on the market are bleached and contain a by-product called dioxin. Dioxins can soon accumulate in your body and may contribute towards thyroid disorders, diabetes and possibly even cancer, and may damage the immune system. Look out for Natracare tampons, panty liners and pads as they're unbleached and also made from 100 per cent organic cotton.

An alternative to disposable tampons is the Mooncup, a reusable menstrual silicon cup, about 5cm (2in) long. It is inserted like a tampon but collects rather than absorbs fluid. It needs to be emptied at the end of each day and should be washed by boiling it in a pan of water for 5 minutes. Using a Mooncup can help stop the 11,000 tampons or sanitary pads that a woman is likely to use during her lifetime from being thrown in a landfill. It can be a big step to try one out, as it's a different approach to feminine hygiene from the norm, but many women swear by them once they've tried them. Mooncups can be bought from larger Boots stores, independent healthfood shops or online.

Also available are washable menstrual pads that can be reused again and again and will soon pay for themselves. Women who use them report that they're very comfortable. After initially rinsing them under a cold tap and leaving them to soak in water for a couple of hours, put them in the washing machine.

Toilet cleaners

If you look on the side of a toilet cleaner bottle it's alarming to read a whole list of cautions. This stuff is being poured down our toilets and eventually enters our waterways, affecting both wildlife and humans. Try using natural cleaning products, which are chemical-free and considerably better for the environment.

Bicarbonate of soda This helps to control odour and also prevents clogging. Try buying bicarbonate of soda in bulk to keep the costs down, as you'll need to put about 100g (3½oz) a week down your loo to make a difference. You can buy non-cooking bicarbonate of soda in bulk from suppliers of swimming-pool equipment (they call it sodium bicarbonate).

Borax and lemon juice This is a good solution for getting rid of very stubborn stains. Mix together 125g (4oz) borax and 60ml (2fl oz) lemon juice until you have a paste, then apply the paste to the stain. Leave it for about an hour, then scrub clean with an old toothbrush. Borax is difficult to find and it comes in different strengths. We don't recommend buying it straight from a chemical supplier, as it could be far too strong for your needs. You can buy natural household borax on www.naturalcollection.com. If using borax, avoid contact with the eyes, ensure the room is well ventilated and as an added precaution wear rubber gloves. Keep it out of the reach of children and do not ingest.

Bicarbonate of soda and lemon juice If the above precautions are enough to put you off using borax, you can also consider using this mix in the same way, although it's slightly less effective. We use 60g (2oz) of bicarbonate of soda and the juice of half a lemon per application. Any leftover mixture can be used on taps to give them a great shine.

Vinegar Pour neat white vinegar into the toilet instead of bleach and leave overnight. This helps to get rid of limescale, a particular problem in hard-water areas such as some regions of southern England and the Midlands. To clean the toilet bowl, use a solution of 3 parts water to 1 part vinegar.

Cola If you've ever put a copper coin into a glass of cola overnight, you'll have observed its corrosive qualities – the coin comes up like new. For the same effect, pour cola into the toilet, leave overnight and flush in the morning.

Air fresheners

In many houses you'll see a bottle of air freshener to mask unpleasant odours. While this may seem harmless enough, some products, according to the *Ecologist* magazine, can actually alter your sense of smell, making it less acute. Also, a study of 14,000 pregnant women and mothers in 1999 reported that women who used air fresheners more than once a week were more likely to suffer depression and their babies were 30 per cent more likely to fall ill with ear infections and diarrhoea.

A lavender plant or rose petals in a bowl will help give your bathroom a more natural smell. You could also place a bowl of lemon juice in the bathroom, on the radiator during the winter or by a window in the summer; as the lemon juice evaporates it helps to neutralize the air. For a more powerful freshener, boil a few slices of lemon in a pan of water and leave the pan in the bathroom. Alternatively, hang up some herbs to dry in your bathroom – basil, thyme, rosemary and mint are all very fragrant and will also work as a natural insect repellent.

MAKING YOUR OWN POT POURRI

Shop-bought pot pourri often contains over-pungent, synthetic-smelling perfumes that can have an adverse effect on people who are sensitive to chemicals. Making your own means that you know exactly what's in it and it's less expensive too.

1.

Use a potato peeler to peel the skin of half an orange. The peel gives the pot pourri a sharp, tangy fragrance.

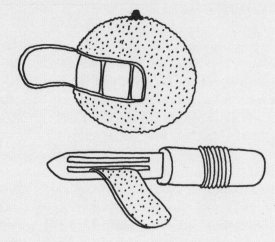

2.

Lay the orange peel, together with a cup of scented rose petals and a tablespoon of lavender flowers, in a single layer on a tea towel, baking sheet or tray. Leave them to dry naturally for 3 days in the sun, on a windowsill or in an airing cupboard.

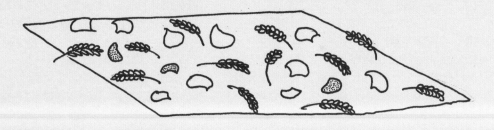

3.

Combine the dried ingredients in a jar with half a cinnamon stick, breaking up the stick a little. Seal the jar and shake it every day to mix the contents.

4.

After 2 weeks put the pot pourri into a shallow bowl and enjoy the spicy, floral fragrance.

Homemade pot pourri made from dried roses, lavender, orange peel and cinnamon.

2.
OUTDOORS

THE SOIL

Whatever the size of your vegetable garden, your success will depend on one vital element – the soil. It's very easy to neglect and just sow your seeds and hope for the best. Some plants – nasturtiums for instance – will thrive in poor soil, but the majority will struggle and the results can be very disappointing. Seeds can rot in a waterlogged clay soil before they've had a chance to germinate, and in free-draining sandy soils plants can fail to germinate or grow through lack of water. Taking a little bit of time to find out your soil type and making appropriate changes before you start sowing or planting your crops will yield far better results than attempting to grow plants in a neglected soil – later, as you admire the little Eden you've created, you'll realize the extra work has all been worthwhile.

The ideal garden soil is generally considered to be a rich loam, which is made up of a balance of ingredients with a healthy amount of organic material; it is free-draining, holds on to nutrients and has an adequate amount of aeration. This nutrient-rich loam is what all gardeners crave and can spend a lifetime trying to achieve. However, more often than not the soil you inherit in your garden or allotment will be predominately clay, silt or sand. There are other soil types, for example chalk, green sand or (if you're lucky) peat, and more specialist gardening books will go into these in further detail; however, we'll deal only with the three main types here.

A good starting point for finding out what soil you're likely to have in your garden or allotment is to ask your neighbours. Allotment-holders are well known for talking about their plots at length and will be happy to tell you the hardship they've suffered digging the clay or the joy of working their light, fertile ground. Likewise, your next-door neighbour with her prize dahlias will be pleased to give you advice on the soil. For those in new-build properties, asking the neighbour may not be an option, but it's a fact that most new builds have very poor garden soil, because the topsoil is often removed during building work and rubble may well be buried in the ground, so you'll need to incorporate as much organic matter as possible before planting. Even the Eden Project had to overcome this hurdle, and tonnes and tonnes of compost were imported to the site (a reclaimed china-clay pit) near St Austell, Cornwall, before it could begin to grow the wonderful array of plants that now flourish in the gardens.

In these times of unpredictable weather, when we're experiencing long dry spells followed by either inconsequential or, at the other extreme, prolonged downpours, it makes sense to work organic matter into all types of soil, in order to retain and make the most of rainwater when it's there.

Improving soil texture

The easiest and quickest way of identifying your soil type is probably the finger test. This involves taking a handful of moist soil and gently squeezing it to about the size of a golf ball. Next, rub two fingers across the surface of your soil ball. If it's gritty you have sandy soil, if it feels silky and powdery, almost like talcum powder, you have silty soil and if it feels smooth and slippery it has a high clay content.

Clay A clay soil has the disadvantages of being sticky and hard to work with when it's wet and setting like concrete in hot, dry weather. It does, however, hold on to nutrients far more effectively than any other soil. Dave's grown by far the biggest parsnips he's ever seen in a clay soil. Once established, most plants do very well in clay, but it's getting them started that can be the problem. The process of turning clay into a fine tilth (loose, easy-to-work, fertile soil) can be long and arduous, but will prove worthwhile.

The main trouble with clay is that it's often too wet to work with; sometimes you seem to get more on your feet than on your spade. Working with over-wet, sticky soil can also damage the soil structure, causing it to become compacted, which results in slow drainage and poor aeration. If you're planning to dig over a clay soil it's vital to get the timing right: ideally you'd do it in late autumn, at the end of the growing season, before it gets too wet; alternatively, late spring is a good time, just as the soil is beginning to dry out.

When preparing clay soil for planting, for best results dig it well in advance and leave it clear over winter; in cooler climates, frost can be very useful for breaking down hard lumps of compacted clay and eliminating weeds. Use a hand claw, garden fork or sturdy rake to break apart big clods of earth, working to 15–30cm (6–12in) deep, and incorporate compost or other organic material, such as manure, into the soil. It's also important to remove any

weeds and roots by hand at this stage. Once you've dug over the plot, leave the frost to get in and do the rest of the work for you. The best method of eliminating persistent perennial weeds, such as couch grass and bindweed, is the black plastic mulch method (see page 80).

With established plants in a clay soil, just keep adding a mulch of suitable organic matter, for example wood chippings, compost, comfrey or rhubarb leaves, and you'll find the soil quality will gradually improve over time.

Dos and don'ts with clay
DO incorporate organic material.
DO dig in coarse sand or grit (but not fine sand).
DON'T work when it's too wet.
DON'T tread on the ground more than you have to, as this will compact the soil; instead, put boards down to walk across the beds.

Sand A sandy soil is at the opposite end of the spectrum from clay: it's very manageable, even when wet, but it holds on to very few nutrients. A small number of plants grow happily in sandy ground, provided it's not too infertile: potatoes, carrots and parsnips all do well, because they can push their roots and tubers through the light soil. However, for any other vegetables it's best to add manure, leafmould, garden compost, straw or other organic matter to improve the soil texture – you may find you're working in large quantities of soil improvers year after year if the sand content is very high. Unlike clay, sandy soil can be improved at any time of year and it's very easy to work. Since sandy soils don't hold on to moisture very well, it's worth mulching around plants with organic matter, especially after rainfall, to retain what moisture you can.

Silt A silty soil consists predominantly of ground-down rocks and can therefore be quite rich in minerals. Silt isn't as free-draining as sand, and isn't as heavy as clay, so it can be a relatively productive soil type, holding on to nutrients and water quite effectively. The particles are much smaller than sand, so silt doesn't feel gritty to the touch, but it can have a soapy texture when wet. These smaller particles mean a silty soil can become compacted more easily than a sandy soil. It's worth adding some manure and garden compost to a silty soil to encourage crumb formation, but be careful not to overdo it. Work in a little before planting your crops and be sure not to tread on the beds more than necessary to prevent compaction. You could also add small amounts of clay to a silty soil to improve soil structure if necessary.

Acidity and alkalinity

If vegetables are failing in your plot, it might be worth getting a pH test kit to see if the soil is too acidic or too alkaline. These are available at most garden centres or on the internet and are relatively inexpensive. However, a kit isn't always necessary, as nature can give us some clues. For a general indication of a soil's pH, it's well worth taking a look at the types of weeds growing. For example, if you have wild mustard it's likely that you have an alkaline soil, and if you have creeping buttercup there's a good chance you have a more acidic soil.

Weeds in acidic soil	Weeds in alkaline soil
Bracken	Black henbane
Creeping buttercup	Honeysuckle
Daisy	Nodding thistle
Hawkweed	Sow thistle
Heather	Stinkweed
Horsetail	Wild mustard

Alkaline soil An alkaline soil has a pH of 7.4 or above and is perfect for plants in the brassica (cabbage) family. Many other crops, such as lettuce, spinach and onions, can all tolerate a slightly alkaline soil, while other vegetable crops may not do so well. If you have a very alkaline soil, add generous helpings of leafmould to redress the balance (see 'Avoid peat!' box, page 78) or consider putting in raised beds filled with organic matter (see page 80).

Acidic soil An acidic soil has a pH of below 7. Blueberries do particularly well in an acidic soil, and rhubarb, potatoes and endive will tolerate it. However, many other plants may struggle to survive in this medium. A good helping of organic matter, such as garden compost, will go some way to balancing the pH, and consider adding lime to the soil if it's particularly acidic (below pH5). Never add leafmould, especially from oak leaves, because it can be extremely acidic and will only exacerbate the problem.

Horsetail (shown here with dock) is a good indicator of an acid soil and can also indicate an underlying problem of bad drainage.

Blueberries thrive in a very acidic soil, ideally with a pH of around 4–5.5. They also prefer a cool, moist climate.

AVOID PEAT!

In acidic conditions, such as a marshy area, moss, trees, fungi, insects and other organic matter sometimes do not fully decay. When this happens, the substance that remains is called peat, and it's highly prized by gardeners who require more acidity in their soil.

Peat bogs store a lot of carbon – the equivalent of about 20 years' worth of industrial carbon emissions is stored in British peat bogs alone – but continuous erosion of the bogs means that carbon dioxide is being released into the atmosphere. Climate change is making the situation worse: as the planet warms up, these areas are quickly drying out, releasing even more carbon; it is an ecological disaster waiting to happen. In addition, peat bogs are home to an array of wildlife, particularly wetland birds, and their precious habitat is being eroded too.

The first step we can take in trying to avert these disasters is to stop buying peat or peat products for our gardens. Check every packet of compost that you buy, and if it doesn't say 'peat-free' on the packet the chances are it contains peat. Also, if you're about to buy pot plants, find out if they've been grown in peat and refuse to buy them if they are; it is simple supply-and-demand economics, and it won't be harvested if no-one buys it. There are several alternatives to using peat – peat-free composts are available from garden centres (often made from a mixture of coconut fibre or leafmould). Even better, make your own leafmould by filling a black plastic bag with leaves from deciduous trees in autumn, seal up the bag and leave it until spring. It can then be used as a nutritious mulch or added to the soil as an improver.

You can also help by joining groups that campaign against using peat, such as Friends of the Earth and the Royal Society for the Protection of Birds or the Wildlife Trusts (see pages 384–5).

FROM WEED BED TO SEED BED

When you inherit a garden, allotment or vegetable plot, in most cases you won't be fortunate enough to have a weed-free, worked bed ready to pop your seeds into. More often than not you're confronted with a thick mass of weeds or a patch of lawn. There are many methods used to work a plot of land into a viable place to grow fruit and vegetables. Most gardeners have their own tried-and-tested methods – some are labour-intensive and require a lot of elbow grease, but there are often quicker options as well.

Single and double digging

There are no two ways about it – digging over an entire plot to ensure all weeds are removed before planting is extremely hard work but highly effective. During the Second World War the 'Dig for Victory' campaign published leaflets advocating people put their gardens over to vegetables; the initial stage of this process usually involved double digging the soil to prepare the land for cultivation. In those days, the population seemed to be made of sterner stuff: they walked more, there were fewer office-based, sedentary jobs and the diet was a lot more wholesome, making for a fitter population, so digging over a plot of land in a single day may not have been a great effort for them. If you have time, and are physically capable, digging is undoubtedly the most effective method of getting rid of weeds; even if you don't have time to do this thoroughly for the whole plot, try to dig over as much as possible and place a barrier, such as planks of wood salvaged from skips, sunk at least 10cm (4in) into the soil around the dug area, to prevent couch grass and other weeds from creeping back in. Digging has the added benefit of improving drainage.

Single digging involves the methodical digging of the soil to the depth of a spade; double digging means that the soil is worked to a depth of two spades. Ideally, prepare the ground in autumn, winter or early spring, depending on your soil type (see page 76).

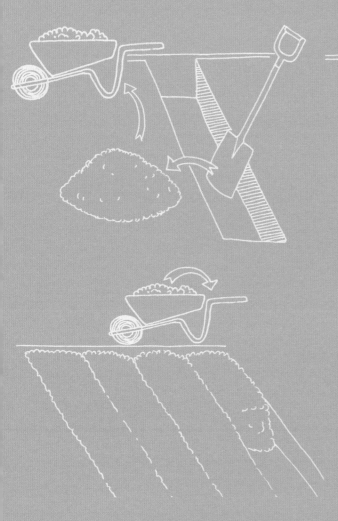

No-dig methods

Mulches are a very effective way of eliminating persistent perennial weeds from a plot. A mulch is any barrier put on the soil to prevent weeds from germinating, growing or setting seed. It can be comprised of organic material, such as compost, wood chippings or leafmould, or it can be a simple layer of cardboard, a piece of old tarpaulin, black plastic sheeting or a specialist porous weed-suppressant material available from a garden centre.

The really lazy, no-dig method This involves considerably less effort than digging. The cardboard, which will eventually break down, will exclude light and keep weeds from growing back; it will also help to retain moisture in the soil.

1. Pull out any large perennial weed roots you see, such as bramble and dandelion.

2. Take several large cardboard boxes, remove all the staples or tape, flatten them out and lay them over the bed (alternatively, you could use thick layers of newspaper).

3. Dig in planks of wood to surround the bed, using small pegs to secure them in place. Try not to leave any gaps between the cardboard and the wood as weeds can creep in.

4. Fill the bed with as much peat-free, organic matter as you can – ideally, a mix of compost and rotted manure. You can sow your seeds directly into the bed, but you may need to dig holes through the cardboard if you're growing root crops. The cardboard will eventually rot down into the soil.

The single-dig method

1. Using sticks and string to make lines, mark out the area to be cultivated.

2. If digging over a lawn, cut out the top layer of grass using a spade and pile up the turf away from the plot. The turf will eventually rot down in a year or so and can be used as compost to improve the soil.

3. Dig a ditch to a spade's depth and about one spade's-length wide across the width of the bed, pulling out any weed roots you come across. Place the soil you've dug in a pile at the other end of the plot.

4. Dig a trench next to the first and put the soil from it into the first ditch, mixing it with organic matter such as garden compost or manure as you go along. If you have clay soil, this is also a good time to incorporate some sand or grit. Continue to do this until the whole bed is worked over. Put the soil taken from the first trench into the last trench.

5. Dig in planks of wood to surround the bed using small pegs to secure them in place.

Planting through black plastic prevents weed growth.

Planting through plastic and weed-suppressant material
Crops can be grown through a plastic mulch or specialist porous weed-suppressant material, such as Mypex, eliminating the need to weed or dig an entire bed. We've seen potatoes and Brussels sprouts that have been cultivated using this method, with good yields in both. In the past, people would have used old hessian-backed carpet. We would prefer to recommend this, as it's a free resource and is reusing something that would normally go to landfill. However, carpet has now been banned on many allotments, because unless it's made of 100 per cent wool, chemicals are released into the soil as it rots down.

1. Cut large perennial weeds, such as brambles and grass, to the ground.

2. Lay the plastic or weed-suppressant material on the area to be covered and cut out a sheet a little larger than the plot to allow for the edges. Place the sheet on the soil and weigh down the edges with stones or bricks.

3. With a sharp knife or spade, cut X-shaped holes into the plastic, where you wish to grow your crops. Weed the area immediately beneath the 'X' mark, removing as many of the roots as you possibly can.

4. Mix compost or manure into the soil and plant your seedling into the centre of the 'X'.

Black plastic mulch
Covering the soil in black plastic is an ideal way of eliminating weeds permanently from a plot. The roots of bindweed, horsetail and couch grass can weave their way into the soil and no matter how much you try to dig them out, the tiniest bit of root left in the ground is enough for them to return again and again.

A layer of black plastic will block out light, thus preventing further weeds from germinating and eventually killing the weeds already present. It can take a while to kill off all perennial weeds, so it's best to leave the plastic in place in spring and summer, during the growing season. In addition, the heat of the sun will help to burn the weeds dry. It's also useful to have a plastic mulch in place over winter, to prevent weed seeds from being blown in and to raise the soil temperature, so crops can be sown earlier.

RAISED BEDS

The raised-bed technique is one that is growing in popularity. A physical barrier, usually of disused wood, is put around the individual beds and each bed is dug over and/or filled with organic material. It can be a very effective way of turning a lawn into a vegetable patch and marking the plot off from other parts of the garden. The raised bed also improves drainage, especially on a clay soil, and helps to enrich poor soils. Raised beds should never be walked on as this can compact the soil – instead, lay a plank across the ground and use this as a walkway and as a useful guideline and kneeling board for planting.

COMPOSTING + FEEDING

No matter what soil type you have, it will benefit from a generous helping of organic material in the form of compost. Compost is a truly amazing thing. You mix together your cleared old plants, kitchen waste, cardboard and all manner of organic waste and just leave it to rot, turning occasionally. Months later, you're treated to a natural, rich growing medium for absolutely no cost at all and very little effort. A layer of compost makes a useful top-dressing in the spring, ready to feed your plants, or it can be worked into the soil to improve its structure. Homemade compost can also be used in the very early stages of your crop's life as a potting compost or for young seedlings. Liquid feeds are highly beneficial to plants too, providing additional nutrients for healthy growth and increased productivity.

Composting

There is a common myth that compost is hard to make – well, it's not. Anything that has been living in recent years will compost. That's not to say you should compost anything and everything, as there are a few 'rules' you should adhere to, listed below. It's worth having two compost bins if you have the space, one to rot down following the first year and one that you keep topping up with fresh scraps and garden waste.

 Try not to include too much of any one thing in the compost and remember that all kitchen scraps will struggle to be broken down.

 Put your compost bin on soil rather than concrete, to encourage the migration of beneficial insects and microbes to the bin.

 To get them started, most compost bins will need an activator such as urine, nettles (without the roots), comfrey leaves or chicken manure. Alternatively, just add a couple of shovelfuls from an existing compost heap.

 The more you turn a compost heap, the quicker it will break down – about once a week or fortnight should do it. So, if you want compost in 6–10 weeks, in the words of the Byrds, 'Turn, turn, turn.'

 Rats and other vermin can be attracted to cooked food in a compost heap, so it's best to put this in your organic waste collection bin, if your local council permits it.

 The acid in oranges and other citrus-fruit skins in large quantities will deter worms and other organisms, so keep citrus-fruit peel to a minimum.

 Woody material will break down *very* slowly – shredding woody stems and branches before you put them on the compost heap can speed up the process.

 Weed leaves are generally fine for the compost heap, but as a general rule avoid roots or seeds, as they will make new weeds. You can, however, add annual weeds that haven't gone to seed, such as hairy bittercress or chickweed. Also, if you dry out weed roots in hot sun or in a black plastic bag for a few months they can also sometimes be added.

Do add:

Kitchen waste, floor sweepings and Hoover-bag contents (unless they contain glass, plastic, screws or other non-organic material)
Tea bags and coffee grounds
Hair from plug holes and hairbrushes
Grass clippings
Crushed eggshells
Annual weeds that haven't seeded (preferably dry them out first)
Used paper tissues
Cotton wool
Wood ashes (but not too often)
Leaves (including those of weeds)
Shredded pine needles in small quantities (too many will make the heap acidic)

Don't add:

Cooked meat, fat and bones
Weed roots or seeds
Dog and cat poo
Glossy magazines
Thick branches, brambles and other woody material
Coal ashes (the chemicals in spent coal can harm the composition of your compost)
Diseased plants

Four wooden pallets are all you need for the bin's sides.

Attach the pallets to upright battens for support.

Getting a compost bin The easiest way to get a compost bin is, of course, to buy one. A huge range is available online, from the high street and even at a reduced price from some local councils. (To find your local authority website, visit www.selfsufficientish.com/councils.htm.) As composting is primarily a method of reducing landfill waste, it seems illogical to us to buy a bin made from new rather than recycled material. The best option is of course to construct one yourself out of old wood. Making your own compost bin from wood is very easy, and as a bonus it will work better than a bought plastic one, as it allows the contents to 'breathe'.

Compost bins are simple to make from just four pallets or scraps of wood nailed together, with upright battens secured at the corners to provide additional support; if you had two old doors you could saw them down the middle and make a bin using the same method. Make the front easily detachable so you can remove the compost later.

Composting in a small place Many local councils will now take scraps away as part of their doorstep recycling collections. This makes it possible for anyone to recycle kitchen waste, even those living in flats or houses without gardens. However, if you live outside these areas or still want a little compost for pot plants there is an alternative. Wormeries are an excellent way of recycling kitchen waste for anyone living in a small space (see pages 57–8). Contrary to popular belief, they don't smell and they can deal with the majority of kitchen waste. They're available on the internet or from your local garden centre.

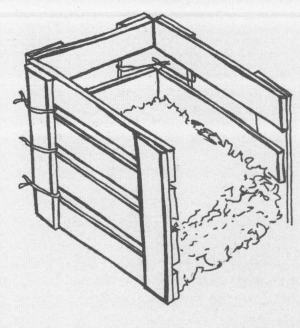

Liquid feeds

Most plants benefit from a little extra help when growing. You can buy expensive organic plant feeds from garden centres, and in the past we've used these on tomatoes grown in bags at home. However, it didn't take us long to realize that they're not necessary, as most feeds can be made from nothing more than weeds naturally cleared when working a plot. Weeds often have roots that go deep into the soil or creep in all directions. They seek out nutrients that are locked in the soil, such as nitrogen, phosphorus and potash, which will aid their growth. Once rotted down in water, these nutrients are released and can be fed to your growing crops.

Comfrey makes a good liquid feed.

Comfrey A liquid feed of comfrey is our favourite way of giving plants the extra boost they need to help them to fruit or flower or just to aid their growth; it's particularly effective for tomatoes, courgettes and squash. Dave once had a patch of comfrey at the top of his allotment and would regularly cut the leaves and leave them to rot in a bucket in the summer sun. When picking comfrey leaves you might want to wear gloves, because the foliage can be quite coarse and may irritate your skin.

The recipe needn't be too scientific: simply fill a bucket or any large container with as many comfrey leaves as you can, cover them with water and leave until the mixture starts to smell really bad (5 days to a week in summer, up to a month in winter). Some gardeners put a tap on the bottom of the bin in order to extract the liquid, but we find the tap can get clogged up, so we plunge plastic bottles into the bottom and fill them up instead.

The resulting liquid is very high in potash and nitrogen and will need to be diluted before applying it to your plants. Water it down at a ratio of anywhere between 5:1 and 20:1. Different plants respond to different amounts of feed, so the desired strength is based on trial and error and observing what the crops respond to. Try a weaker 10:1 solution to begin with, and up the strength if it doesn't seem to make much difference. We usually feed our plants once a week using a weak solution when the plants are small, gradually building up to a stronger one.

The main downside to comfrey is the smell of the rotting leaves and the fact that, once established, the plant will grow and grow, so much so it can become a bit of a pest. If the smell of rotting comfrey gets unbearable, the unrotted leaves can be used as a mulch for growing potatoes, soft fruit or anything that would benefit from a physical barrier against weeds and extra nutrients for the soil. (For details on growing comfrey, see page 157.)

Couch grass Couch grass is the bane of most gardeners wherever it grows, and the vast amount that can be pulled out of the soil, especially on a new plot, can seem to be never-ending. The long, spindly roots need to be completely eliminated, as they can grow back from the tiniest piece of root. However, the roots do have some interesting uses. They can be boiled down and used as a tonic for those with sinus problems, or fresh roots can be used as a plant feed. Simply place a good-sized bunch of the roots (as many as you can fit) into a porous bag such as a hessian sack, tie the end and submerge the bag in a bucket of water. Leave this for a few days, then use the water as a plant feed, diluted to a ratio of 4:1.

Nettle Nettle is another very useful plant that is often considered a weed. However, it can be used as a food in the same way as spinach (see page 222), it can be made into rope and fabric for clothing and it's a good plant feed. In the same way as comfrey's, the leaves are beneficial and need to be steeped in a bucket of water. Simply cut up some plants with a pair of shears, put as many as you can into a bucket and then let them rot down for a week or two. The resulting feed can then be diluted to the same ratio as comfrey feed (see left) and used to water your crops.

Other liquid feeds Lawn clippings can also be rotted down and used as a plant feed, in the same way as leaves, and the liquid run-off from a compost bin or wormery is beneficial too. Dilute the liquid to a ratio of around 5:1 before feeding your plants. Some gardeners steep manure in a bag in water in much the same way as couch grass roots, to act as a feed (see above).

THE ALLOTMENT

There are many benefits of having an allotment – you can eat organically and inexpensively and it's also good for your wellbeing – putting good, healthy food on the table is incredibly rewarding and the physical work involved makes for a healthier lifestyle. Single plots of land set aside for agricultural use have arguably been around in the UK since AD 100 and were used by the Celts. Allotments in their present form, however, were not introduced until 1845, basically to keep the population out of the pub and to stop peasants from revolting. The government set aside 2200 acres (890 hectares) of land for allotments, and in 1887 the Allotment Act was passed, which meant authorities had to provide allotments if there was a demand. In the Second World War the government introduced the 'Dig for Victory' campaign and demand increased, but once the war was over it dwindled, until recent years. As people become increasingly concerned about food scares, excessive use of pesticides and their effects on the environment, they're taking up their forks and returning to allotments *en masse*.

In some areas there are now waiting lists of 6–10 years for good allotment spots. This is compounded in some London boroughs by the practice of selling a house with an allotment as an asset, even though in most cases this goes against the allotment's tenancy agreement. In order to find an allotment, first telephone your council and ask to be put through to the person in charge of allotments. In Bristol you're sent a map of all the allotments in the area and armed with this you can visit them and choose the one that suits you. In some regions it will be your local parish council that you'll need to contact. In areas where all the plots are taken you can get together with five other people and lobby your council to provide more plots. Alternatively, you could go on the waiting list or ask friends and neighbours with gardens if they're prepared to give up a patch of their garden in return for some lovely organic veg.

CHOOSING AN ALLOTMENT

Although it may seem obvious, when choosing an allotment take on only what you have time for. There's no point in getting a full-sized plot on your own if you work full time and expect to be there solely at weekends. A full plot is enough space to grow vegetables for a family of four, so if there are just two of you to feed it will be wasted space. We've seen single people take on a plot and try to stay on top of it; it can be a Sisyphean task, especially for a novice. Unless your need is great, take on half a plot and run it well instead.

The allotment site is also a very important consideration. Andy made a poor choice with his first plot, so we've come up with five points that we'd recommend taking into consideration if you're thinking about getting an allotment:

1. Check the soil – is it full of weeds? Make a close inspection of your prospective plot and look out for perennial weeds such as couch grass and bindweed. If you're using organic methods it's a lot of work to remove these and only a short root of either plant left in the soil can mean the plant will grow back. If the plot is riddled with weeds it's best avoided, unless you like the challenge of lots of digging or are prepared to wait for the black plastic method to work (see page 80).

2. What's the journey like? Consider how you'd get to your allotment. Is it sufficiently close to walk? You might have the best intentions that a 5-mile walk after work will do you some good but, realistically, how often are you truly going to want to do that? Imagine yourself taking this route frequently armed with seedlings, tools or bags of compost.

3. Is it secure? Unfortunately, theft and vandalism are concerns on many allotments. Ask other allotment-holders in the vicinity if there's a history of incidents on your proposed plot or in surrounding areas.

4. Is the plot close to any potential problems? Potential problems include a rubbish tip (rats), a park (if it's frequently vandalized, your plot may be too), or a river (flooding). Infestations such as clubroot or blight can also cause problems. Check the neighbouring plots. If they're covered in weeds the seeds will soon set on yours.

5. Is there a water supply? Although most plots have their own water supply, this is sometimes at an extra cost to the rental of a plot. The water supply will be either a trough that refills or a tap. In areas where hosepipe bans are common the trough is a better option, because you can dunk your watering can straight in and fill it quickly. Some plots come without a water supply. Although this is obviously less convenient it need not pose too much of a problem if you collect rainwater in a series of water butts.

ALLOTMENT TIPS

- **Work backwards** – If you work with your back to the work that needs to be done facing the work that has been done it will seem less of a daunting task.

- **Don't be afraid to ask** – If someone has prized carrots or a glut of beans, don't be afraid to ask them for tips. Allotment folk are generally very approachable people and will offer a helping hand. In summer we end up talking more than working on our plot – they can be very sociable places!

- **Research the history of your plot** – If your plot was used the year before, ask the allotment rep or neighbouring allotment-holders what was grown on it. You might be digging up an established rhubarb plant or shrub. Also, you might find that potatoes were grown in the spot where you plan to have tomatoes and this can considerably increase your chances of getting blight (an airborne disease that can destroy solanaceous plants such as tomatoes and potatoes, see page 131).

GETTING TO WORK

The first task that most people have to tackle when they take on an allotment is clearing the plot of weeds and improving the soil. If you feel energetic, you could dig over the soil really well, using the single- or double-digging technique (see pages 78–9). Alternatively, you could use the no-dig approach, which requires less work than traditional methods and is ideal if you have a patch of land that's almost unworkable. This method involves covering over the area with a weed-retardant material, such as cardboard, black plastic or Mypex, which excludes light from the weeds and stops them from growing (see pages 79–80).

Growing in rows or deep beds

When you go past allotments on a train you may have noticed that they generally consist of neat rows of vegetables. This is the approach that most of the older generation adopt and it's not without its merits: you can walk easily between the rows and water your crops. However, it isn't the best use of space for maximum yields, and walking between the rows can compact the soil, resulting in slow drainage and poor aeration.

A few carefully managed beds can give you high yields and are also much easier to manage. Weeding one bed at a time gives you a sense of achievement, so is good for morale. Many first-time allotment-holders carve out just a few beds to start with and keep them weed-free, popping in only at weekends or after work for a few hours. Once you've worked out how much time this can take and know what you've embarked on it's easier in subsequent years to make more beds and utilize the whole plot efficiently.

Tools of the trade

A compost bin is vital on an allotment (see pages 81–2), as is somewhere dry and secure to store your tools. The first-time gardener might be unaware that tools can easily become damaged and unusable if they're not taken care of in the proper manner. Andy learnt this lesson the hard way when he managed to snap the handle off two garden forks in two consecutive seasons because of improper care. Tools should last a lifetime if well looked after, and there are some simple measures to follow to ensure that you don't make the same mistakes as Andy.

- Scrape off any soil and dirt from your tools after use.

- If you have wooden-handled tools, rub linseed oil into the handles every few months to help preserve the wood.

- Keep your tools inside when not in use.

- If you have no choice but to leave your tools open to the elements, put them into a bucket of sand to prevent rust and cover the bucket to make sure the sand doesn't get wet. You could also tie plastic bags around your tools, especially where the handle meets the metal part, to keep them dry and to protect them from frost.

- If thieves are a concern, store tools out of view.

- Dry out your tools before storing. On wet days, use an old towel or rag to help speed up the process.

- Use a sharpening tool or sharpening stone on your secateurs and shears.

- If storing your tools inside, keep them on nails or hooks so that they don't touch the ground.

- Oil the metal parts of your tools once a year.

Protecting seedlings from cold

Many gardeners are caught out in early spring with a late hard frost (frost that penetrates the ground) and their seedlings may die before they've had a chance to grow. With a little forethought, you can prevent this.

- Harden off your seedlings gradually in a cold frame (see pages 88–9). Place them inside the cold frame in their pots and leave the lid open on milder nights for several weeks before planting them outdoors.

- Water your plants with ice-cold water first thing in the morning (freezing water slowly releases heat).

- Put straw around your plants.

- For bigger plants and trees invest in some thermal fleece and wrap it around them.

- Cut the bottom off 3-litre bottles and place them on top of seedlings and young plants (see overleaf).

- During prolonged cold snaps, take tender plants in containers indoors.

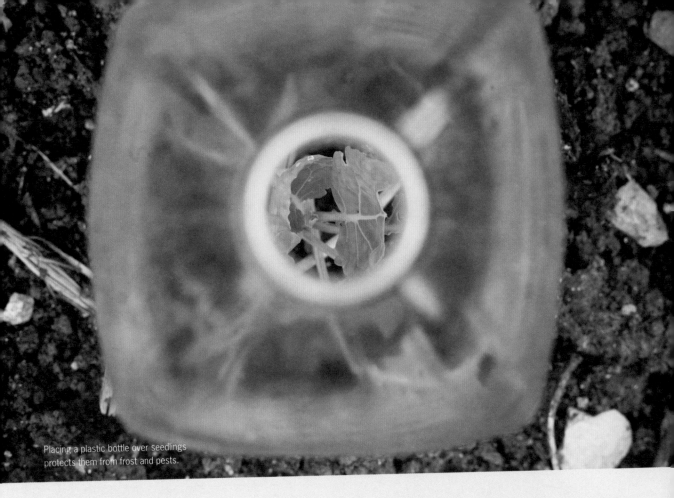

Placing a plastic bottle over seedlings protects them from frost and pests.

Cloches and cold frames

A cloche or a cold frame is an easy way to protect young plants from a late frost in spring, to harden off plants or to extend the growing season at the end of the year to ensure fruit ripens. They're also perfect for protecting early seedlings from extremes of temperature as well as from damage by insects such as slugs and weevils. You can make a simple cloche yourself by placing a plastic bottle with the base cut off over young plants; a more complex version is a cold frame that resembles a miniature greenhouse, with a wooden frame and a glazed lid.

MAKING A COLD FRAME

A cold frame is useful if you grow frost-tender fruit and vegetables that need hardening off before you can plant them out in spring. Stand the plants in the cold frame a few weeks before you expect the last frost, open the lid every morning and shut it in the evening, then plant out.

This cold frame should be placed against a wall. A sturdy stick can be used to prop open the windows during the day to help the plants harden off.

What you need

Hammer

Saw

2 wooden-framed windows, the same size and thickness (A)

1 length of timber, around 10–15cm (4–6in) wide and the same thickness as the window frames (B)

2 lengths of timber, around 20cm (8in) wide (C)

2 lengths of sustainable, outdoor-grade plywood (D)

Nails

4 hinges

Enough screws to fit the hinges

1. Find two wooden-framed windows of the same size (A). Ideally, your window frames should be no smaller than 30 x 30cm (12 x 12in) and no bigger than 1.5 x 1m (5 x 3ft). Place the windows on the floor next to each other and put the 10–15cm- (4–6in-) wide piece of timber (B) between them.

2. Place two other lengths of timber (C), approximately 20cm (8in) wide, along the length of the two windows plus the timber divider, and saw them to the right size.

3. The two sides of the cold frame are now made from plywood (D). Saw a piece of plywood in half diagonally, so that the windows will be able to rest on the slope. Straighten off the pointed ends of the plywood 'triangles' so that they form flat sides.

4. Nail the lengths of timber (C) to the plywood at the top and bottom of the frame. Nail the smaller length of timber (B) between where the two windows will be. Finally, attach the windows to the hinges.

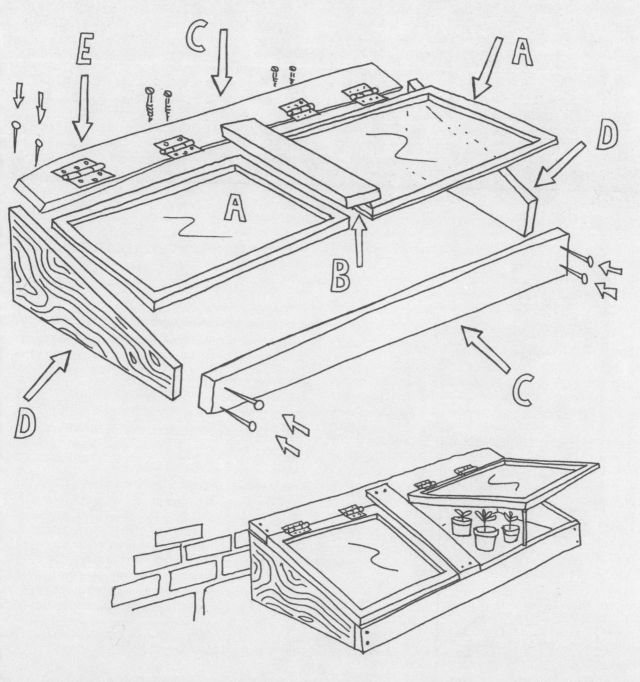

Cover brassicas in netting to keep birds away.

CDs make perfect bird scarers, as does Dave.

Protecting plants against birds

You'll find that birds, especially pigeons, can be a real pest on the allotment, pecking at young seedlings, damaging the leaves and sometimes digging the plants clean out. We lost a whole crop of sweetcorn this year because of birds eating it. Plants in the cabbage family (brassicas) are particularly susceptible to pigeon attack. It helps to cover the plants in netting (you can get this from a garden centre), securing the netting in place with sticks or bamboo poles; score an X-shaped hole in the top of old yogurt pots and push these down the sticks or poles for added security. Plastic netting can be a problem on the allotment, and Andy is still digging up some on his plot left by the previous owner. However, there is a biodegradable alternative made from corn starch – it starts to degrade within a few months, and so can be left on the plants until it rots into the soil.

Better still, keep the pigeons away entirely. A simple bird scarer can be made by stringing some CDs along a length of string. What better use is there for the free CDs or DVDs from Sunday papers that never get played? All but the bravest of pigeons will stay away, as they mistake the discs for the huge eyes of a predator staring at them.

WILDLIFE-FRIENDLY ALLOTMENT

Bearing in mind greenfield sites, gardens and other habitats are slowly being eroded across our country, we feel it's the duty of allotment-holders to encourage wildlife to their plots. If you help wildlife, you'll also be helping yourself, as birds will eat insect pests and caterpillars, and hedgehogs and slow-worms will munch on the dreaded slug population. It helps to leave just one small area of the allotment totally untouched. Also, a pile of logs will lure insects, bushes will attract birds and you could provide drinking water for hedgehogs. In addition, you could make a pond to provide a home for amphibians.

Ponds

Frogs, toads and newts should become your friends when you have an allotment. They're hungry little critters and will eat slugs and snails for you (not that you'd want to eat them!). This is one good reason for creating a pond on your allotment. In addition, you'll be making a home for a whole host of other wildlife. You may have to clear it first with your allotment rep, but they should be happy to have an increase in amphibious life on the plot.

One of the things we enjoy most about our allotments is the pond, although some of the more traditional plot-holders think that it's a waste of useful space. There's nothing more magical than sitting by the water and seeing your first frogs peering up at you, or watching damselflies darting around the surface. Although the initial outlay may seem costly, the joy of watching wildlife makes it one of the best investments we've ever made; also, if you attract frogs and toads to your plot the saving on slug-destroyed crops alone should help it to pay for itself.

Safety first – you need only 5cm (2in) of water to drown in, so if small children visit your allotment you'll have to think about protecting them against this; consider also the other plot-holders with children. Erecting a small fence is one solution. To be safer yet, try covering the pond's surface with wire mesh that's big enough for frogs but not children to pass through. Ensure that it's very secure – as a child, Andy fell into a pond with mesh on it at a party. He'd managed to pull up the mesh and the next thing he remembers is wearing someone else's pyjamas with a horde of worried parents around him.

The simplest possible way to make a pond is to sink a watertight container in your plot. We've used a plastic baby bath in the past that we bought from a charity shop for £2.50, but an old washing-up bowl or any container that holds water will make an adequate pond. Because the water can evaporate in a small container in hot weather, collect some rainwater in an old dustbin and keep topping up the pond. Alternatively, you could make a larger pond using a special pond liner (see overleaf).

Aquatic plants encourage wildlife such as grasshoppers.

MAKING A POND USING A LINER

You can make a simple pond using a butyl liner, available from a garden centre or on the internet. Pond weed is obtainable from garden centres specializing in aquatic plants and fine sand from a garden centre or a builders' merchant.

What you need
Butyl liner
Fine sand
Spade
Pond water
Pond weed
Wire mesh or small fence (optional)

1. Dig a hole that is at least 60cm (24in) deep. One end of the pond will be deeper than the other in order to provide aquatic life with an area that will not freeze in the winter or get too hot in summer.

2. Remove all sharp stones so that they don't break the liner and dig out the area required for the pond, ensuring that the pond gently slopes at an angle of about 15–30 degrees. A gentle gradient is important for different types of wildlife – birds can wade on the slope, frogs and toads can hop out with ease and small mammals can drink from it.

3. Line the hole with a layer of fine sand, about 2cm (¾in) deep, then place the butyl liner over the sand. Don't worry if it seems too baggy, as it will take shape when filled with water. Dig a small trench, 5cm (2in) deep, around the pond so that you can bury the edges of the liner later.

4. Throw in a handful of subsoil from the surrounding area (soil from below the top layer), as it will benefit the pond, then fill up your pond with rainwater or, if that's not possible, tap water. Fill it right up to the top, so it looks like it might overflow, and leave the water to settle for about 48 hours.

5. To get the ecosystem started, it's a good idea to add some pond water from an established pond if you can and some pond weed. Don't take pond water from any source – make sure you get permission from the pond owner beforehand. Pond water from as close to your pond as possible is the best source, as similar conditions mean a similar ecosystem that's adapted to that area's conditions.

6. Bury the edges of the liner in the trench and put a little turf around one or both sides. This will undoubtedly appear to die off at first, but grass is sturdy and after a little while you should have tall grass around your pond, which frogs love to hide in. You could also put some rocks or a ramp of bricks on one side for hedgehogs (see opposite).

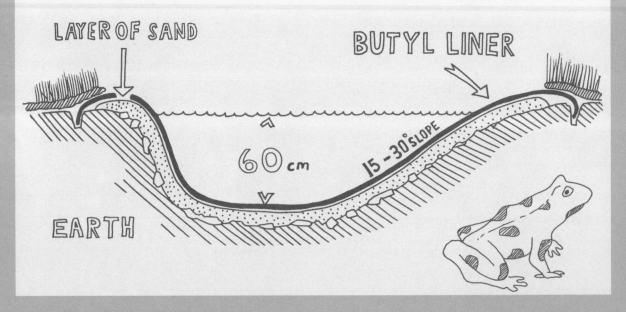

LAYER OF SAND

BUTYL LINER

60 cm

15–30° SLOPE

EARTH

POND TIPS

🐸 Ensure that the pond is surrounded by long grass for frogs to hide in and leave a patch of grass to one side of the pond for amphibians to rest on.

🐸 If using a sunken container, make sure that amphibians can climb out of the pond. This is achieved by placing a stick running from the bottom of the pond to the side.

🐸 Place your pond away from overhanging trees. Sun encourages a greater abundance of wildlife.

🐸 Local hedgehogs might visit and they also eat slugs, so make life easier for them and build a little ramp of bricks next to your pond. Ensure that it's not too high, as they could fall in if they have to stretch. They're mostly nocturnal, so you might see only the odd footprint.

🐸 If your pond turns green with algae, place a fine mesh bag containing cut lavender or barley straw in it. This will attract micro-organisms that will destroy the algae.

🐸 Put a bit of frogspawn in the pond, but not fish, as they will eat the frogspawn. (Don't take frogspawn from the wild, but from a neighbour's pond with permission.)

🐸 Situate your pond in a place where you can enjoy it, such as near a bench. It's great to sit and watch the pondskaters, frogs, damselflies and other wildlife that will visit your pond.

Pond life thrives in an open, sunny site.

Encouraging birds and insects

Our feathered friends make excellent pest controllers and should be encouraged on organic allotments. A good example is the blue tit, which will collect up to 15,000 caterpillars to raise a brood, leaving fewer to devour your plants. To attract birds to your plot, you could make a basic bird table from scraps of wood (see opposite). Put food and a small bowl of water on the table and keep an eye out as the birds arrive. To keep birds healthy you'll need to clean and disinfect the table regularly and don't allow old food to accumulate.

You can also make a simple 'insect hotel' to attract beneficial insects, such as ladybirds and lacewings, to the allotment. In winter they need protection against cold weather, so if you provide a home for them at this time they'll be ready to help you with your fight against pests when spring and summer arrive. There are several types of 'accommodation' you can make in no time from recycled food and drink containers.

The margarine-tub hotel is perhaps the simplest: fill a margarine tub with straw, make several holes in the lid using a knitting needle and place the tub on its side under a bush; this will be a warm refuge for insects over winter. Alternatively, for the drinking-straw hotel, bunch some straws together, tie them up with string, leaving part of the string dangling, and attach them to a tree or bush. If you use various-sized drinking straws you'll attract different insects, so you could have lacewings living side by side with ladybirds. A really simple option is the hotel made from a plastic pop bottle (see below).

HOW TO MAKE AN INSECT HOTEL

1. Cut the bottom off a 2-litre plastic pop bottle.

2. Cut a sheet of corrugated cardboard (about 1m/3ft) long and roll it up so that it fits inside the lower part of the bottle.

3. Tie the bottle to a tree or bush using string and watch for your first guests.

MAKING A SIMPLE BIRD TABLE

What you need
Hammer
Saw
Wooden board, about 50 x 30cm (20 x 12in)
Strips of wood, 2cm (¾in) thick
Nails and/or wood glue
Wooden pole or stake, 1.8m (6ft) long
2 metal brackets

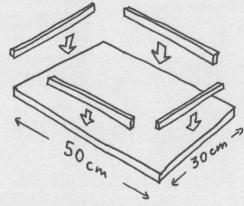

1. Saw the strips of wood to fit your board; they should be about 2cm (¾in) smaller than each edge. Nail or glue the strips of wood along the sides of the wooden board, leaving a 1cm (½in) gap on either side. The gaps allow rainwater to drain off so it doesn't accumulate on top of the table.

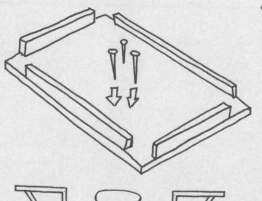

2. Nail the board to the pole or stake. Ensure that the pole is smooth and not full of knots or anything that can act as a cat or squirrel ladder. If you can't get a smooth pole, attach a piece of drainpipe around your pole to stop unwanted wildlife from scaling the table.

3. If the top of the table is loose, add brackets (the metal ones used to put up bookshelves are ideal). Half hammer a few nails into the wooden board near its edge so that feeders can be attached to the sides.

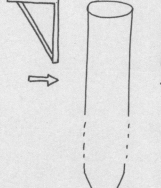

4. Choose a place for your table. It needs to be close to bushes to provide cover for birds but not so close that the local cats will be able to get to it easily. Push the pole or stake into the ground, about 30cm (12in) deep. Add food and water and wait for the birds.

Taking a break under Dave's homemade arbour.

HEALTH + WELLBEING

Gardening on an allotment is an excellent way of getting regular exercise. You don't have to be a very keen gardener either: studies show that 30 minutes a day of moderate activity, such as gardening, can help to decrease the risk of many ailments including heart disease, strokes and Type 2 diabetes, not to mention burning off some calories. An allotment is also a wonderful place to relax and socialize and it gives you a great sense of satisfaction and achievement, contributing to a general feeling of wellbeing.

During dry summers you can get a great upper-body work-out on your allotment just by carrying two 10-litre (2 gallon) watering cans back and forth. In autumn and winter, digging provides vigorous exercise, and even when weeding and pruning or just pushing a full wheelbarrow around you're exercising without really realizing it.

In a study by Bristol University and University College, London, it was found that working with soil can help lift depression, thanks to an enzyme in the soil called *Mycobacterium vaccae*. We've also found that being outside, completing goals (such as weeding one bed) and exercising make you feel more positive about life generally.

Social life on the allotment

Allotments can be a great way to meet new people. You'll often find that plot-holders have a set routine, going up in the morning or evening during the week or just at weekends. It might be that you'll never see some allotment-holders, despite the fact that their plots are obviously worked. If you've just moved to an area and are short of human contact, consider going to your plot at different times of the day. While writing this book we've found that it can be a lonely experience at times and the chats on the allotment have been very welcome.

Some allotments hold competitions, seed swaps or meetings and sometimes even have a clubhouse. One of the overgrown plots near Andy's allotment is going to be turned into a communal orchard over the winter, with all the allotment-holders chipping in and helping to create it. If there's a redundant plot on your allotment, you could ask to do the same. In the orchard, they're going to grow a few hazel trees so that all the allotment-holders can harvest their own bean sticks, coppicing the twigs when they've grown to a sufficient size, rather than importing bamboo poles from China. Gardeners in Britain have used wood from the hazel tree for centuries, but because of the convenience and accessibility of bamboo poles, hazel has sadly become neglected. If you can't grow your own hazel there are places you can buy hazel poles (see page 176).

Making a bean den

One of Andy's fellow allotment-holders, Barbara, has small children and wanted to create a sociable area where they could sit in the summer. It's a simple but effective idea and costs next to nothing to make.

1. Dig a small round trench about 2m (6½ft) in diameter and 50cm (20in) deep using a spade.

2. Get 10 bean sticks (preferably made from hazel branches), about 3m (10ft) long, and push them in around the hole, sticking them 20cm (8in) deep into the soil and angling them so they meet at the top in a wigwam formation.

3. Tie the sticks together at the top with string and plant a bean plant or two at the base of each stick.

Relaxation

When you've been working hard on the allotment it's a great feeling to take a break, have a cup of tea and a chat and sit and admire the work you've done. For this reason, it's a really good idea to construct some kind of built-in seating. An arbour is ideal, as it doubles as a place to sit and you can also grow plants up the structure. It's often associated with rose gardeners, but it's just as appropriate for the fruit or vegetable gardener, and has the benefit of allowing vegetables to grow vertically – a great advantage where space is at a premium (see page 176). Dave built his own out of salvaged wood (see opposite), and it's a wonderful place to relax after an energetic day's work on the allotment. He sowed a mix of sweet peas and nasturtiums on one side, and French beans, squash and more nasturtiums on the other; the beans made their way right up to the arbour roof by summer. It wasn't until all the plants flowered that the arbour really came into its own and it soon became a haven for pollinating insects. Nasturtiums attract beneficial insects that feed off aphids and can act as decoy plants so caterpillars leave your main crops behind.

Old rusty gardening tools and metal rescued from scrap heaps can make striking sculptures for the garden or allotment.

ART ON THE ALLOTMENT

An allotment can be much more than just a place to grow food. It's a home from home, and moreover a personal area of land where you can be creative and express yourself. Allotment art can take many forms, from willow sculptures and woodcarvings to simply laying out beds in an interesting formation or being inventive with old pieces of gardening equipment. It's well worth wandering around allotment sites just looking at how other people have expressed themselves in their small, rectangular plots – the ingenuity and sheer creativeness can be tremendously inspiring.

If you're not artistically inclined you may know someone who is, in which case you might get them involved in creating a work of art for your allotment – it can be immensely enjoyable, needn't be over-complicated and the artist will have a ready-made, captive and semi-public audience for his or her work.

Using natural materials

Many people make fabulous sculptures out of willow, as it's such a good material to work with. When fresh it's very flexible and it's also extremely tough and resilient, which is why it's been used for making baskets for centuries. It grows very quickly, is easy to propagate from cuttings and is completely renewable. If you grow a small amount of willow on your allotment it will act as a windbreak and will provide you with material for making fences, hanging baskets, plant supports and sculptures year after year.

Wood is also a good material for allotment-art projects. You can carve most solid wood, as long as it's not wet or rotten. Pine, oak, lime and sycamore are among the best, and you can use the composted wood chippings for paths and to dig into the soil. Small tree stumps are good to experiment on when you first start carving. It's best to follow the grain of the wood and to incorporate knots and any branches into the overall sculpture.

When you're out and about, you could also collect natural objects, such as beautiful stones, shells or a large piece of driftwood, and display them in their raw state.

Recycling scrap

As allotment-holders we're well aware of the amount of 'stuff' that can accumulate on a plot – plant pots, scraps of wood and broken tools just seem to be everywhere. The obvious thing to do is to burn all the wood and put the rest into a skip. However, with a little imagination these items can be put to good use. Some people choose practical uses for scrap on the allotment – Dave has a scrap wooden seat underneath a scrap wooden arbour with climbing plants growing across the top and a bird table made from an old bin lid screwed to a wooden post. However, others may choose more sculptural uses for scrap – you can make scarecrows out of broken canes and plant pots, and broken tools arranged in certain ways can make intriguing sculptures. The most ambitious use of scrap we've ever seen is the WEEE (Waste Electrical and Electronic Equipment) man sculpture, which now stands in the Eden Project in Cornwall. It's a 7m- (22ft-) high figure of a man made entirely from scrap consumer goods.

A hand-carved wooden totem pole on Dave's allotment.

THE VEGETABLE PATCH

With a well-organized vegetable patch it's possible to put fresh food on the table every day of the year. Even the novice gardener on a small plot can be more or less self-sufficient in vegetables during the summer months, and growing your own will always be cheaper than buying fresh organic vegetables. Cost-saving may have been our starting point, especially as students, but now it's not just cost that drives us both to plant year in, year out. There are few simpler pleasures than digging up a glut of potatoes or cutting courgette after courgette from just a handful of plants, and once you've started to grow your own you'll realize how much better they taste than shop-bought vegetables – there's nothing quite like a fresh carrot pulled from the ground or peas straight from the pod.

It took us a long time to get around to growing our own vegetables, despite being brought up by parents and grandparents who did. As teenagers, we were much more interested in pubs and gigs than helping out our granddad with his onions. It wasn't until Dave, by then in his mid-twenties, put an old sprouted potato in a small patch of ground that either of us caught the growing bug. He had no idea what he was doing, didn't follow any procedures such as chitting, earthing up or even watering, and was amazed to discover he'd somehow produced a new and quite substantial crop from this one vegetable. Plants have been doing well without our help for thousands of years for one key reason – they want to grow. However, if you grew all your vegetables this way you couldn't expect a successful harvest every time. Dave was fortunate in having very fertile soil and there was frequent rainfall that year, so there was no risk of the ground drying out. If he'd earthed the potatoes up, paid more attention to spacing and dug in some manure or organic matter, his first harvest would probably have been even better.

> "On average, each human sends household waste weighing as much as a cow to landfill each year."

We strongly believe that one of the most important things you can do from an environmental perspective is to grow your own food. Household waste accounted for 89 per cent of municipal waste in the UK, according to figures published by the Department for Environment, Food and Rural Affairs (DEFRA) for 2005/2006. This made a staggering 505kg (80 stone) per person per year, or roughly the same weight as an average cow. Next time you look at a field of cows grazing, count one for each year you've been on this earth and it may give you more of an impetus to reduce the amount you put into landfill each year. Growing your own food means all the waste can be composted. There are no plastic bags to dispose of, no plastic containers for your green beans and no cellophane wrapping for your broccoli; all come as nature intended and as we have traditionally enjoyed food since humans first settled into farming communities thousands of years ago. In addition, the backyard or allotment plot means zero or very little transport is required, which is another good reason for growing your own.

Neither of us has ever used any chemicals when growing our own food. In this chapter we'll explore some of the ways you can grow vegetables without reaching for chemical sprays every time your plants get a little nibbled or diseased. If you're going to use as many chemicals as an intensive farmer it seems to us you'll negate one of the prime reasons for growing your own.

CROP ROTATION

If you're growing a number of different crops you need to start some kind of crop-rotation scheme. Crop rotation is important for a number of reasons. First, if you rotate your crops you avoid a build-up of diseases in the soil. For example, if your brassicas have been struck by clubroot or your potatoes have been damaged by blight, it's better to plant them in fresh ground the following season rather than leave them in the same contaminated ground. Different diseases strike different types of vegetables, so what damages peas and beans, for example, won't affect a member of the carrot family. Another reason is that each different type of vegetable crop needs specific nutrients; this means that the same crop grown on the same soil year after year will simply not get the nutrition it needs, because it will have drained the soil of the required nutrients in previous years. If you move the crops around, you give the soil a chance to recover.

How to rotate crops

Crop rotation revolves around five main groups of vegetables: the potato family (potatoes, peppers, tomatoes and aubergines); the carrot family (carrots, parsnips, celeriac, celery, fennel and parsley); the onion family (garlic, leeks, onions and shallots); the legumes (peas and beans); and the brassicas or cabbage family (broccoli, cauliflowers, cabbages, kale, Brussels sprouts, radishes, swedes and turnips). The remaining vegetables (lettuces, marrows and courgettes, pumpkins and squash, sweetcorn and beetroot) form a miscellaneous group and they have a more flexible role in crop-rotation schemes in the vegetable garden (see right).

4-year rotation scheme

On the facing page is a 4-year plan for rotating the main family groups of vegetables. Our parents use this plan by splitting two large beds into two, making sure the potatoes are as far away from outdoor-growing tomatoes as possible, to minimize the risk of blight spreading. The 'miscellaneous' group, which includes lettuces, marrows, courgettes, pumpkins, squash, sweetcorn and beetroot, can be planted anywhere within this plan, but remember to add plenty of manure before planting summer and winter squash. This plan ensures that no vegetable is planted on the same land year after year and also makes full use of the land available.

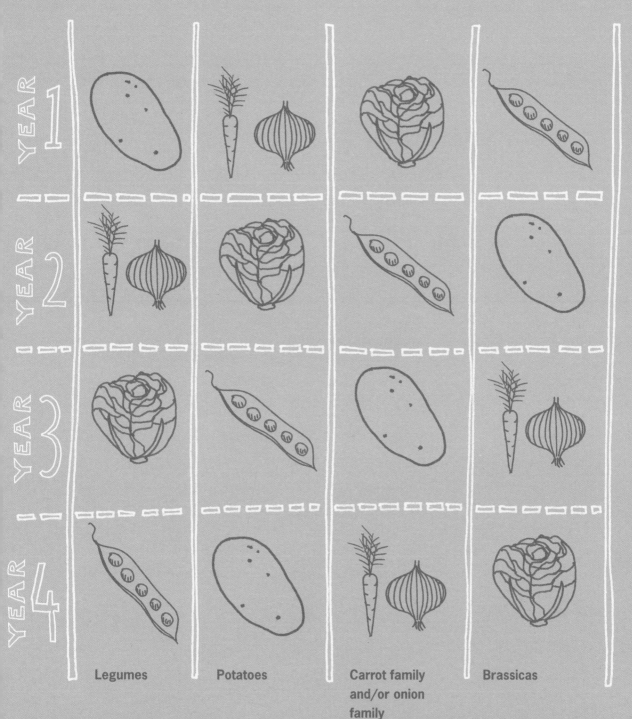

BED 1　BED 2　BED 3　BED 4

YEAR 1

YEAR 2

YEAR 3

YEAR 4

Legumes　　Potatoes　　Carrot family and/or onion family　　Brassicas

A fine example of companion planting: the corn supports the climbing beans and the beans leave deposits of nitrogen in the soil.

GREEN MANURE

A green manure is a fast-growing plant sown in the vegetable plot to improve the fertility or structure of the soil and/or as ground cover to prevent weeds from taking seed when you're not using the ground. You can plant a green manure in fallow times, after harvesting a crop, or before planting a new crop. To sow green manure, scatter the seeds on the soil and rake them in. When the plants are lush and leafy, dig them in, before they flower. Allow 2 weeks before sowing or planting your vegetables.

Examples of effective green manures include red clover and winter tares, both of which fix nitrogen into the soil, and alfalfa, which is used to break up heavy soils. If using a crop-rotation scheme (see pages 102–3), it's worth remembering that mustard is in the cabbage family and clover is in the bean or legume family.

RED CLOVER

COMPANION PLANTING

Plants have always lived side by side, and sometimes they've benefited from this partnership and sometimes they haven't. Companion planting involves growing a combination of plants that will benefit one or more of the plants in the area. For example, planting a row of onions next to members of the carrot family (which includes parsnips and celery) is beneficial to both the carrots and the onions – the conflicting smells confuse and deter both the carrot fly and the onion fly, so it's an ideal partnership.

One of the most successful planting combinations we've come across is the squash, bean and maize matrix. This is a traditional method of companion planting that has been used for centuries across the New World, in what is now the southern United States, Central America and the northern countries of South America. Most notably the Mayans in Mexico have been using this method for around the last 700 years. The plants together are often called the 'three sisters'. The basic principle behind planting squash, beans and corn together is quite simple: the corn provides a support for the beans, the squash helps to suppress weeds by providing ground cover (a bit like a living mulch)

and the beans fix nitrogen into the soil. Once the corn matures, the squash should be close to reaching maturity and the corn can be harvested, allowing the squash to take over the plot. This method of planting is an excellent way to grow a number of different crops in a small space. It works best in tropical countries but it can also be applied in Britain or any other temperate climate.

Some herbs are also very useful planted among vegetables: tarragon, in particular, is said to improve the flavour of most vegetables and its scent should deter a number of pests. Overleaf is a table showing what will help and what will hinder the growth of young vegetables.

VEGETABLE	COMPANION VEGETABLES	COMPANION HERBS	NON-BENEFICIAL/ HARMFUL PLANTS
ASPARAGUS		Basil, tarragon	
BEANS	Squash, sweetcorn, cucumbers, potatoes (for dwarf bean varieties), celery, garlic	Rosemary, sage, tarragon	Onions, leeks, garlic, chives
BROCCOLI		Chamomile, peppermint, dill, sage, rosemary, chives, tarragon	Strawberries, tomatoes, climbing beans
CABBAGES	Celery, onions	Mint, nasturtiums, dill, rosemary, oregano, chives, chamomile, sage, thyme	Strawberries, tomatoes, climbing beans
CARROTS	Lettuces, radishes, onions, tomatoes, garlic	Chives, rosemary, sage, tarragon	Dill
CELERY	Beans, cabbages, tomatoes	Tarragon	Dill
CUCUMBERS	Sweetcorn, beans, garlic	Nasturtiums, oregano, chamomile, tarragon	Sage
FENNEL		Tarragon	Coriander
GARLIC	Carrots, onions, tomatoes	Tarragon	Beans
LETTUCES	Garlic	Dill, tarragon	
ONIONS, LEEKS, SPRING ONIONS	Tomatoes, carrots	Chamomile, tarragon	Beans
PEAS	Beans, carrots, celery, chicory, sweetcorn, cucumbers, peppers, potatoes, radishes, spinach, turnips, garlic	Parsley, rosemary, tarragon	Onions, chives
PEPPERS		Basil, oregano, tarragon	
POTATOES	Dwarf beans, brassicas	Coriander, oregano	Tomatoes, rosemary
PUMPKINS AND SQUASH	Sweetcorn, beans, cucumbers	Nasturtiums, oregano, tarragon	Sage
RADISHES	Peas, cucumbers	Nasturtiums, tarragon	
TOMATOES	Onions	Basil, mint, nasturtiums, parsley, petunias, French marigolds, chives, oregano	Potatoes, sweetcorn, kohlrabi, dill

French marigolds help to repel whitefly on tomatoes. Tomatoes also grow better and bear more fruit when marigolds are planted around them.

Salad leaves can be sown in trays in spring for transplanting into the ground in summer.

A YEAR IN THE VEGETABLE GARDEN

The gardening year starts just a few months ahead of the regular year, in October and November. It's a time when many will want to spend longer indoors as the weather becomes colder and dark evenings draw in. However, it can be one of the most important times of the year in the vegetable garden, because this is when most of the preparation needs to take place for the following season. It's the perfect time to dig beds over, add manure and generally tidy up your plot. If you've been well organized, winter needn't be a fallow period, as parsnips, sprouts, kale, leeks and other vegetables can still be put on the table throughout this season.

The first few hot days of the year often prompt us into sowing seeds too early, but be warned – even in these times of global warming, a sharp frost can still damage tender young seedlings. For this reason, plant under cover, in a greenhouse or indoors, and then harden off the plants gradually, perhaps in a cold frame, before planting them outdoors in the garden (see pages 88–9).

Spring is a strange time in the vegetable garden. It's one of the busiest periods of the year in terms of sowing, planting and preparing the soil, yet there's very little around to eat. Even with careful planning, sometimes all there is to harvest in early spring is the last of the winter kale and perhaps a leek or two. However, by late spring things improve quickly and we're treated to the delights of the first spears of asparagus and florets of sprouting broccoli.

Summer can be a time of abundance in the self-sufficientish garden, and with the warm weather comes the first real glut of fresh vegetables. Flowers are in full bloom, courgettes are coming thick and fast and we usually have more beans than we know what to do with. At this time it's all too easy to let things slip, and leaving a plot for just a couple of weeks during August can mean the weeds will soon take over and it can be a real effort to get the plot

working well again – we found this to our cost in the summer of 2004, when we organized a festival for our 30th birthdays. But it's not all work, and the effort you put in during winter and spring will really start to pay off during these few months.

As the long evenings come to a close and the temperature drops, autumn brings with it a bounty of fresh squash, pumpkins, leeks, sweetcorn and the last of the tomatoes. It's the time when the vegetable garden would naturally store all its goodness for the following year and is therefore when many vegetables are at their very best. Autumn is also a time when all the year's growth can be put into the compost, ready to feed the following year's crops.

On the following pages we've given details about how to grow the vegetables we enjoy the most. We've provided sowing and planting times, but bear in mind these vary according to where you live; also, they change from year to year depending on the weather. With plants that need planting out after the danger of frost has passed, this usually means April to June, but it can be as late as July in colder areas. For ideas on what to make with your home-grown vegetables, see Seasonal Cooking (pages 186–203) and Preserving (pages 244–57).

Asparagus

Asparagus is not for the impatient. However, once it's established it can provide a crop year after year for up to 20 years. It's best to buy asparagus crowns from a nursery rather than grow it from seed. Plant the crowns in March or April into a weed-free bed with plenty of rotted manure added, allowing 45cm (18in) each way between crowns. Leave the ferns to grow uncut for the first year; don't be tempted to harvest any of the spears, as this will weaken the plant. In the second year after planting, harvest from April to June and cut down the ferns only once they've turned yellow, in autumn. Asparagus needs to be kept weed-free, because long-rooted weeds can damage a crop. It's a coastal plant and salt can be added to the soil to aid growth. Water well in the growing season.

• See Chicken and asparagus stir fry, page 193; Quinoa and asparagus salad, page 190.

Aubergines

We've always found aubergines incredibly hard to grow. They need a long period of time to ripen fully, and as they're not frost-tolerant the ripening process has traditionally had to take place under glass. However, in these days of global warming they can be grown outdoors in the south of England, although there is a risk of losing them if a hard frost hits or if temperatures fluctuate towards the end of summer. They are therefore best sown on a windowsill or in a heated greenhouse in March, and if planting out leave until May and do so only under a cloche, in a cold frame or in an unheated greenhouse. Allow around 50–60cm (20–24in) between plants in both directions and keep well watered. They're ready to harvest in August and September.

Beetroot

Beetroot is easy to grow and doesn't suffer from many problems. It does prefer a light soil but we've grown it in heavy clay before without any major difficulties. Sow seed *in situ* from April to June (or you can sow seed under a cloche in February or March). Insert two seeds at about a thumb's depth (5cm/2in), leaving a couple of thumbs' width (10cm/4in) between each sowing. Thin out the weaker plant and use the leaves in a salad. Harvest from June to October. If harvested young, when they're about the size of a golf ball, they have a delicious sweet flavour and can be grated raw into a salad or roasted with other seasonal vegetables. One or two leaves can be harvested from each plant and used as an extra salad leaf. Stored beetroot will last for several months (see page 248).

'Burpees Golden' is a yellow to orange-coloured beetroot with leaves that taste similar to those of beet spinach. 'Cylindra' is a fairly common beetroot that grows longer and thinner than the conventional globe-shaped 'Boltardy' varieties and is ideal for slicing and therefore pickling.

• See Autumn salad, page 196.

Broad beans

If you're lucky (and organized) the beans you sowed in autumn should start to flower by spring. For a continuous supply over early summer, sow a row every couple of weeks from March until the end of May. We plant them about a thumb's depth and cover the seeds with compost if the ground is too tough and crumbly to cover them. Ideally, they should be spaced around 20cm (8in) apart. Pinch off the top 7.5cm (3in) once the first bean has developed and/or if they're covered in blackfly. Once you've picked all the beans you can,

dig the whole plant into the ground as a green manure (see page 105).

• See Grilled lamb with broad beans and rice and Quinoa and asparagus salad, page 190.

Broccoli

There's a much wider array of broccoli types than you might first consider. Dave's favourite for looks and taste is purple sprouting broccoli, but there's also a white sprouting variety, the psychedelic, lime-green Romanesco and of course the familiar calabrese broccoli. Broccoli is a brassica, so it will benefit from a bit of lime in the soil or some crushed eggshells. It's not for the impatient: the sprouting variety can be in the ground for nearly a year before it's ready.

For calabrese, start seed off in pots indoors or in a greenhouse in April or May and plant out after 5–7 weeks, in June or July. Alternatively, sow seed *in situ* in May, June or July, with 15cm (6in) between rows, to be thinned when the plants are 7.5cm (3in) high. Harvest between June and October. For purple sprouting broccoli, sow outdoors in April or May and harvest between January and April. Thin out or sow the seedlings around a boot-and-a-half's-length for sprouting varieties and just a boot's length for the green varieties.

• See Steamed sprouting broccoli with lemon dressing, page 188; Chinese winter salad, page 203.

Brussels sprouts

Brussels sprouts land firmly in the category of a vegetable that not everyone likes. Many people have unpleasant memories of overcooked, soggy sprouts. We'd suggest, however, if you haven't tried them since being forced to eat them as a child, that you try them again. They're particularly delicious in stir fries.

Harvesting beetroot in summer.

Brussels sprouts are very useful, because they're ready from September to March, just as many other vegetables are coming to an end.

Sprouts need an alkaline soil to thrive, so if necessary either lime the soil or add eggshells to alter the soil pH. They're best started off on a windowsill in March or April and then planted out in May or June. Leave a couple of boots' length between each plant, as they need plenty of room to grow in. When they've reached the size of a walnut, cut off the sprouts with a sharp knife, starting from the bottom and moving up. The leafy tops are also a tasty spring green and can be removed sparingly as and when you need them.
• See Brussels sprouts with satay sauce, page 200.

Cabbages

Like all brassicas, cabbages contain anti-carcinogenic properties and are a good source of iron, calcium and other essential vitamins and minerals. The two main problems with growing cabbages are slugs and birds. Birds will largely leave them alone in the summer months, but come winter – when there isn't much food around – they'll tear a cabbage plant to shreds. The cabbage white butterfly (see page 126) and cabbage root fly can also be a problem. If planting cabbages in an acidic soil, add lime or eggshells.

There are so many different types of cabbage that planting times can vary across the year depending on when you want to eat the cabbages and how much space you have. Winter cabbages are useful when there's little else around. Varieties such as 'Tundra', the good old 'Savoy' and red cabbage can be sown in pots indoors in spring and put out in May or June ready for a winter harvest.

Alternatively, a spring cabbage such as 'Primo' is a good choice. Spring cabbages are useful to keep a plot productive when other crops have finished. However, they can take up a lot of room, and if space is short we'd suggest having sprouting broccoli growing over winter, although this can always be interspersed with some spring cabbages for a bit of variety. Spring cabbages are best sown outside in August or early September, about a boot's length to a boot and a half apart. They should be ready to harvest by March to June the following year.

Neither of us has ever attempted to grow summer cabbages, because there seems to be plenty of choice of green leaves around in the summer months. However, our Granddad used to grow the 'Greyhound' variety, which he would harvest throughout the summer. Sow summer cabbages in pots indoors in February or March or directly into the ground in April or May. Transplant seedlings to their final growing positions or thin out plants grown outdoors in April, May or June.
• See Crunchy cabbage stir fry, page 189; Christmas red cabbage, page 200; Stuffed cabbage, page 201; Chinese winter salad, page 203.

Carrots

The orange carrot is relatively recent in botanical terms, having been introduced by Dutch plant breeders in the 15th or 16th century. In their wild form in Afghanistan, where they've grown for hundreds if not thousands of years, carrots are purple.

A fresh organic carrot is one of the best flavours you'll get from a home-grown plant, and given the right conditions they're quite easy to cultivate. They prefer a light, stone-free soil. We've grown them in a back garden littered with stones and the

results are a 'hand' shape where the carrot has tried to grow around the stone. As with parsnips, on heavier soil make a hole with a crowbar or tool handle and fill with compost or lighter soil, then sow the seed into this hole. The most damaging pest is the carrot fly.

Sow carrots outdoors between February and June, depending on whether they're late or early varieties (early carrots are ready to harvest in July, later ones in December or beyond). You'll need a cloche for early sowings. They can be sown by scattering seed and thinning out to 7.5–15cm (3–6in) apart, or sow seed in rows, thinning out the weaker plants as the crop matures.

'Harlequin' is a great 'show-off' carrot, as it grows in various colours, including purple and white as well as the usual orange. We think the white ones taste particularly sweet. 'Purple Haze' is a winner if you want coloured carrots. As their name suggests, they come in purple.
• See Spring salad, page 188; Crunchy cabbage stir fry, page 189.

Cauliflowers

Cauliflower is a fairly difficult vegetable to grow; it needs a very rich soil and regular watering or the heads will never reach their full size. Late frosts can also harm the developing heads, so they often need to be covered in horticultural fleece.

You can start off summer varieties indoors or in a heated greenhouse as early as January through to March, to be transplanted out in April or May. Autumn varieties can be sown straight outside in April or May and winter varieties should be sown in May. Plant out the seedlings or thin them out (if sowing direct) to about 60cm (24in) for summer varieties and 75cm (30in) for autumn and winter ones.

Brussels sprouts are ready to harvest when they're about the size of a walnut.

Courgettes need harvesting when small
if they're not to turn into marrows.

Celeriac

In our modern society, where convenience is such a priority, vegetables that are hard to prepare and need a little more attention than most in the kitchen are quickly vanishing from the shelves – celeriac is one of these, which is a shame as it's an extremely delicious and very versatile vegetable. It can be put into soups, included in mashed potato for extra flavour, stir fried, made into chips and roasted along with other vegetables for a Sunday dinner.

Celeriac does have quite a long growing period and needs constant watering and mulching during its lifetime. However, even the inexperienced gardener can get some results from growing this plant. When we first started growing celeriac it didn't get particularly large, but the flavour was incredible so we persisted, and we'd strongly recommend anyone to have a go at growing it.

Sow seed indoors in pots on a windowsill or in a heated greenhouse in March or April, planting out a boot's length apart in late May or early June. It can be harvested from September right through to March, so is useful to fill the 'hungry gap' early in the year.
• See Creamy roasted vegetable soup, page 203.

Celery

Celery isn't the easiest vegetable for the beginner to grow. It requires a lot of care and attention – you can't just plant it and expect a good crop with little aftercare, as you can with some other vegetables. There are two main types of celery: trench celery, which is grown in a trench in order to blanch the stems (this makes it less stringy and improves the flavour), and self-blanching celery, which is not grown in a trench. The self-blanching variety is less tender and has less flavour, but if you're growing it for soups and stews rather than for eating raw in salads, self-blanching is fine and is much easier to grow.

For trench celery, prepare the soil early in the year by digging a trench about a spade's depth and lining the bottom 5–10cm (2–4in) with manure or compost. For self-blanching celery, work in a generous layer of manure a few months before planting. Start both types off on a windowsill in late March or early April and plant out when you have four to six true leaves, in May or June. Harden off fully for a week or two before planting out when the risk of frost has passed. Don't plant near parsnips, as the same pests can attack them, and plant near onions to avoid carrot fly. Unlike some other plants, celery will bolt (go to seed) if the weather gets too cold in its early stages, so don't be tempted to plant them out too early.

Trench celery will need blanching and earthing up at regular intervals. This is a fiddly job, but thankfully quite a simple one. When the crop is around 30cm (12in) high, cut off any small side stems and tie some corrugated cardboard loosely around the stems, leaving the leaves poking out from the top, then fill the trench up with compost or well-rotted manure. It may be necessary to blanch the plant again in this way as it matures.

Self-blanching celery should be harvested before the first frosts, in late summer or early autumn, while trench celery can be harvested in late autumn and early winter. It is often useful to leave celery in the ground to eat over the winter months, when there is little of anything else around in the vegetable garden, rather than eat it all straight away.
• See Quinoa and asparagus salad, page 190; Summer salad, page 195; Winter warming soup, page 201.

Courgettes
and marrows

To settle an argument heard every year on allotments across the country, courgettes and marrows are from the same plant – marrows are just courgettes that have been left to grow and courgettes are immature marrows. You can buy seeds that will make for a better courgette than marrow, and vice versa, but the thing to remember is if you want courgettes don't let them put all their energy into producing a marrow; pick them small and often and you'll get a bigger crop.

There are two main varieties of marrow and courgette, the bush and the trailing. Trailing varieties can be grown vertically (see page 177) or across the ground and will help reduce the number of weeds; bush varieties are easier to harvest and plan into a planting scheme, as their size is usually more uniform.

Dig a hole about as deep and as wide as a spade and fill it with well-rotted manure, compost or other organic matter. Leave a crater shape for the plant to sit in, as they're thirsty plants and this helps retain a lot of the water. You can sow seed in pots on a windowsill or in a heated greenhouse in April and harden off before planting out once the risk of frost has passed, or sow straight into the soil in May or June. Space them the length of three boots apart or slightly more for trailing varieties (it's beneficial to plant them around sweetcorn). Water generously and frequently. 'Golden Dawn' is a yellow bush courgette that crops very heavily over a long period and 'Rugosa Friulana' is a knobbled, yellowish bush variety. Courgettes are ready to harvest from July to October.
• See Stuffed courgettes, page 195; Autumn salad, page 196; Stuffed marrow, page 198; Marrow and ginger jam, page 256.

Cucumbers

We resisted growing cucumbers for years, thinking they were more effort than they were worth, but then we were given a packet of seeds for the outdoor ridge cucumbers and since then we haven't looked back. We grew some in pots and some up a back fence that caught a bit of sun and they all flourished, giving us tasty fresh cucumbers from summer to early autumn. After a while we decided to harvest them small and keep them as gherkins, pickling them in a mixture of vinegar and spices to add flavour and zest to winter meals.

Cucumbers do best in a rich but not-too-heavy soil. They can be started off in pots indoors in a heated greenhouse from March to May and put out once the risk of frost has passed. Some gardeners prefer to sow seed *in situ* after the last frost. The *in situ* method can be useful, because sometimes cucumbers don't transplant very well. The downside is that you won't get cucumbers as early this way, so it may be worth trying both methods if you have plenty of seeds to spare. Sow the seed into a mix of compost and manure at about a boot's length deep and leave about the same distance between pot-raised plants. Harvest July to October.

We've found that cucumbers tend to be more productive when they're allowed to climb rather than trail across the ground. Send them out over a trellis, perhaps combined with sweet peas or runner beans. Because the fruit is 99 per cent water it's important to not let the plant dry out, so water regularly.

• See Summer salad, page 195.

Florence fennel

There are two types of fennel: one which is a herb grown mainly for its seed and leaves and which you sometimes find in the wild (see page 158), and the other which is a cultivated, bulb variety known as Florence fennel and is eaten as a vegetable, cooked or raw in salads.

There are early and late varieties of Florence fennel. These can be sown indoors from April to June, to be transplanted in June to early August, or they can be sown directly in the ground between April and July. This lengthens the harvesting time, and planting a mix of varieties can mean a longer harvest.

When the bulb is about the size of an egg, you'll need to earth up the bulb, as you would with potatoes (see page 122). Cut off seedheads as they appear. Harvest the bulbs from July to October. The leaves and stalks can be harvested as soon as they're ready, from June onwards; over-harvesting will restrict bulb size.

• See Trout baked with fennel and herbs, page 194.

French beans

There are two varieties of French beans, namely the climbing French bean, which does well growing up a support, and the dwarf French bean, which forms a small, bush-like plant (hence its alternative name of bush bean). French beans are a must for the first-time grower, as they're very easy to cultivate and extremely rewarding. The dwarf bean makes an ideal companion plant for many vegetables, especially squash and courgettes, because it fixes nitrogen in the soil, helping to feed the other plant. In our experience, dwarf beans seem to do well in a clay soil, even if it hasn't been improved, so they're extremely useful for areas that you haven't got around to preparing fully.

Climbing French beans seem to grow as tall as you let them – most books will say they grow to around 2m (6½ft), but they can grow taller. However, the more you allow the leaf to grow, the smaller the crop will be. For a good crop, plant climbing beans up a bamboo wigwam, an arbour or a trellis, or even up sweetcorn (see pages 104–5) or a sunflower.

Sow seed of dwarf and climbing beans indoors in April or May and transplant seedlings in May or June, or sow outdoors from May to July. Plant them at a thumb's depth and spaced well over a hand span apart.

Harvest French beans regularly for a constant supply from around June until October. They should be picked when fully sized but while they're still young and tender. To save the seed, leave a few pods on the plant to mature and dry out and then put the dry beans into an envelope, ready for the next year. Select pods from the most productive plant as they will be acclimatized to your region and are likely to produce a big crop.

• See Summer salad, page 195.

Jerusalem artichokes

Jerusalem artichokes are very useful for breaking up the ground and don't need an over-fertile soil. They will grow like a weed if not fully harvested and can come up year after year. For this reason, many gardeners choose to leave some in the ground and have a permanent bed for them. They're ready to harvest between October and February, so fill a gap when other foods are scarce. Plant them straight into the ground in April, more or less as you would potatoes – about 15cm (6in) deep and 45cm (18in) apart, leaving twice that between rows. If the ground is very heavy, add compost or manure to the soil in autumn before planting.

• See Jerusalem artichoke crisps, page 203.

Kale is extremely nutritious and is an excellent antioxidant. It's rich in lutein, which is useful in reducing cataracts.

Kale

This is one of those vegetables, like Brussels sprouts, that is very good for you but bad experiences in childhood seem to put so many off eating it. We suggest you try kale again. It should never be overcooked and must be eaten only when young, as mature leaves are very bitter. Blanched kale can be made into a winter salad; it can be steamed with some butter and lemon juice or added to soup for extra texture and flavour.

Kale does take up a lot of space and is slow to grow, but it will put food on your table when there's very little else in the ground. You can start off seedlings on a windowsill in April or May, to plant out between late June and early August, or sow outdoors in May or June. They need about a boot's length and a half between them once mature, so either let them take and thin out the weaker plants, or plant the seedlings at this spacing. They can follow on from early potatoes, peas or broad beans, so are useful in crop rotation and keeping a plot productive over winter. The taste is best after the first frosts and they can be harvested any time from November until April, sometimes May.

• See Kale and leek with tagliatelle, page 188.

Leeks

Leeks are a very useful winter vegetable. They can be sown indoors from January to March, to be planted out from April to June at about 15cm (6in) apart, or directly into the soil in April or May to be thinned out in June and July to the same spacing. They grow in most well-drained soils, and although they benefit from a little rotted manure added well before the growing season it isn't essential.

Harvest them between September and April, lifting earlier if you need the space, or if you can wait let them grow large. They're very useful for breaking apart heavy soil, but unless you wish to save the seed be sure to lift them before they bolt, because they will self-seed quite easily. It's worth letting one or two turn to seed if you have the room, as the flowers of the leek are quite stunning.

• See Kale and leek with tagliatelle, page 188; Winter warming soup, page 201.

Lettuces
and salad greens

As they're prone to many pests and diseases, over 85 per cent of lettuces bought in our shops are sprayed 4 times or more in their short life span. Residues of these pesticides, including dimethoate (listed by the EU as a suspected 'hormone disrupter') are often still on the plant by the time it gets to you – this is reason enough to grow your own, not to mention the fact that the flavour's so much better.

There's a bewildering array of salad leaves available, but most need the same kind of conditions to grow – preferably evenly spaced, in a light, loamy, not too acidic soil with plenty of organic matter and water; the bed should also be free of slugs (see pages 128–9). The latter can be an uphill struggle. Through trial and error, we've found that for some reason slugs are more likely to avoid red salad greens.

Timing is crucial with lettuces: planting a whole row at once can mean a sudden glut, so they're all more likely to go to seed or 'bolt' at the same time. To avoid this, plant at 2-week intervals, in rows about a boot's length apart. We usually make a groove of about half a thumb's depth and shake in the seeds in a thin row, thinning them out to about a boot's length between plants once

they germinate to a decent size. Always thin leaving the strongest plants at any one station. We generally eat the salad leaves we thin out there and then.

It's possible to have lettuces all year round. The names often give you an idea of the time they'll be ready to eat: for example, 'Imperial Winter', 'All Year Round' or 'May Queen'. One of our favourite lettuces is the red-leaved 'Lollo Rosso'. 'Buttercrunch' is very popular among gardeners, and although not remarkable in taste it is very easy to grow and has the advantage of being bolt-resistant.

For more unusual salad leaves we would strongly recommend sowing both American land cress and rocket. American land cress has a fiery, peppery taste and will grow through the winter; it's also very easy to grow. Rocket is quite easy too and if you can't find a wild source of it, it's well worth planting a couple of rows.

• See Spring salad, page 188; Summer salad, page 195; Autumn salad, page 196.

Onions
and spring onions

There are two main ways of growing onions – from seed or from sets, which look like baby onions. We've tried both methods and have found the results from sets are more satisfactory. Onion sets can be planted in autumn for the following spring, or in spring to harvest in late summer or early autumn. Push the sets into well-prepared soil in rows, about 15cm (6in) apart.

Spring onions are started from seed rather than sets from March to July and you can harvest them about 3 months later. Sow thinly at a depth of 1cm (½in), in rows 15cm (6in) apart, in rich soil and in a sunny spot.

• See Pickled onions, page 252.

Leeks are a useful crop in the cold winter months.

Harvesting first earlies on the allotment in July.

Parsnips

Despite being one of our only truly native vegetables, parsnips are very hard to get going. Once they're established they can grow to monster-sized proportions without you having to do a great deal. However, it's difficult to get the seed to germinate. The trick seems to be to save the seed from a plant growing in your area rather than buying commercial seed. This isn't always possible, though. There are countless methods of germinating seeds, so try any or all of them and see what works for you.

● In January or February, place the cardboard tube from inside a toilet roll upright on a tray and fill the roll with potting compost. Sow a couple of seeds in the compost and place the tray by a windowsill. Once the seedling is a few inches high, make a hole in the ground using a dibber, broom handle or trowel. Parsnips hate having their roots disturbed, so the cardboard roll is planted along with the seedling and will rot away as the plant grows.

● Make a hole in the ground and backfill with sand or fine compost. Sow the parsnip seed direct in March, April or May.

● Broadcast the seeds *in situ* from March to May, cover them with a fine layer of compost and thin them out once they've germinated.

There should be about a boot's length between plants, so thin them out to this spacing, leaving the strongest plants, and keep well watered in dry weather. 'Student' grows very long and has a great taste.
• See Winter warming soup, page 201; Creamy roasted vegetable soup, page 203.

Peas

A fresh pea from the pod is a treat to look forward to every year; frequently we find that our peas don't make it to the kitchen but are instead eaten on the spot in the allotment. Prepare the bed ready for peas in late winter or early spring. Peas prefer a rich soil, so add plenty of well-rotted manure or compost to the bed before sowing.

We've found peas do better if they're started off in a pea collar (see page 180). We normally sow first early varieties in March or April, then second earlies in late April. Maincrop peas can be sown straight into the ground every couple of weeks from May until June, then a second batch of early varieties at the end of June. A mix of varieties means you can harvest peas from June until October.

Peas will need some support as they grow. You could buy pea sticks, available from garden centres, or if you are an economic/more self-sufficient gardener simply dig some twigs with many side branches into the soil and allow the peas to climb up them. Peas can also be trained to grow up trellises and arbours and can be decorative with other climbers.

Potatoes

In many ways, potatoes are one of the easiest vegetables you can grow. They're very useful for breaking up heavy clay soils and will grow in most conditions. There's a bewildering array of potato varieties available, and one of the great benefits of growing them yourself is that you don't have to stick to the traditional bland choice of spuds in the supermarkets. There are three main types of potatoes: first earlies, which are planted in March and April and ready in June and July; second earlies, which are planted in April and harvested in July and August; and maincrop, which are planted in April or May and ready in September or October. We've had a lot of success with the old classics such as 'King Edward' and good all-rounders such as 'Maris Piper' (both maincrops). However, as potatoes are quite cheap to buy it is well worth experimenting with more unusual types such as the maincrop 'Pink Fir Apple'. A particular favourite of Dave's is the 'Anya' potato. The 'Anya' is a second early variety, so in areas prone to blight the crop can all be harvested before the disease properly hits. It's also a very light-tasting potato, so perfect for salads.

There are also many methods of growing the humble potato. As well as growing them straight into the ground, Dave's had good results growing them in large pots and Andy's grown them in tyres, stacking a new tyre on top of the last as the foliage increases. It's a good idea to use a mixture of growing methods to maximize the space available. Some swear by growing potatoes under black plastic mulch with the leaves poking through holes in the plastic, although we've never tried it. The plastic mulch method saves the effort of earthing up your crop (see overleaf), but it can also be a breeding ground for slugs.

Preparing to plant To prepare the ground, add manure in the winter and turn the ground over roughly with a fork so a couple of frosts can get in and break up the soil, killing off weeds and pests in the process.

Before planting, potatoes are normally chitted, which means placing them in a light, cool but frost-free place (indoors) to produce little shoots. There is a debate if this is necessary or not. As a rule of thumb it's probably worth chitting them if you've bought them in good time, but if it's been a mad rush to buy them and you put them in late, don't worry too much as they'll still grow. To chit potatoes, place them in an open cardboard egg tray or other shallow box and leave on the windowsill until they produce little sprouts. This usually takes about 6 weeks. Remove all the 'eyes' or sprouted bits except the top two strongest before planting.

Planting, earthing up and harvesting
Dig a trench of just over a hand's depth (20cm/8in) and plant in a row about a boot's length apart with the 'eyes' pointing upwards. You could add some comfrey leaves before planting. Ideally, leave 1m (3ft) between rows to allow room to earth up and walk between the rows. Some gardeners plant rows closer than this, and you can get round the earthing-up issue by covering the plants with straw or hay as they grow; you may find the yields are lower this way, but experiment and find out what's best for your plot. The spacing between plants is also determined by the variety of potato.

The main reason for earthing up potatoes is to exclude light, because this will cause them to turn green as they produce a toxin called solanine. The easiest way to earth up potatoes is to pull surrounding soil, using a hoe or ridging hoe, to the green foliage surrounding the plant, forming a small mound around it and covering all but the very top leaves.

Harvest your potatoes when the foliage starts to die down, or, if you want new potatoes, about 8 weeks after planting. If you're careful, you can harvest one or two new potatoes from each plant by digging lightly around the plants' periphery; harvest the rest when they're fully mature.
• See Healthy roast potatoes, page 200; Butternut squash and apple soup, page 196.

Radishes
Radishes are a great crop for kids or the impatient, as they're among the fastest-maturing vegetables. Summer varieties need only 10 weeks to mature and if sown at 2-weekly intervals will guarantee a crop through the growing season. They're ideal for salads but are also useful for adding extra flavour to soups, grated raw on the top of rice dishes or in chutney.

Radishes are often referred to as a 'catch crop'. This simply means they can be sown in between slow-growing crops, such as parsnips or sweetcorn, and cleared before the bigger plants grow and need the space. As a member of the cabbage family they should not be sown on the same land as any other brassica for at least 2 years.

Sow radishes from early spring to late summer. They don't need to be sown very deeply; you could make a groove in the soil with your finger and slowly shake them in with your hand. Thin out to around 2.5cm (1in) between plants. Rows should be about a hand's width (15cm/6in) apart (slightly more for winter varieties).

Runner beans
You'll see runner beans running around wigwams of poles on almost any allotment during summer, offering a splash of fiery red with their flowers. Their popularity is probably down to the fact that they're one of the easiest and most abundant of all crops; sometimes you can even harvest them right up to the first frosts. They also freeze well and make an excellent chutney.

Runner beans require a well-drained, quite rich soil. Add plenty of manure or compost in autumn ready for a late spring planting. Sow seed indoors in March or April to transplant in May or June, or plant directly into the soil in May or June. They'll need some support as they can grow up to 2.5m (8ft) or more, so plant them up a fence, trellis or on a cane wigwam or similar support. Pick the beans before they grow too long and stringy; picking will encourage cropping.

Spinach
There are two main types of spinach grown in the UK: beet spinach (sometimes known as perpetual spinach), which is a relative of the beetroot, and the thinner-leaved 'true' spinach that we're more familiar with.

Beet spinach has advantages over conventional spinach in that it's very easy to grow and has few predators. Swiss chard is a close relative of this plant and can be sown in the same way. Sow from early spring to late summer, in rows about a boot's length and a half apart, thinning the plants to just over a hand span. If it doesn't bolt (go to seed), beet spinach can be harvested right through the year and is very useful for adding a fresh green vegetable at times when there's little else growing. Bolted beet spinach will self-seed prolifically, and the resulting seedlings can be moved to more ordered positions.

True spinach can be a hard crop to grow, as slugs like the tender young leaves of the new seedlings and caterpillars can make short work of an established crop. For this reason, it makes good sense to sow in any available space rather than in rows to reduce the chance of a whole crop disappearing in one go, and spray with soap spray or rhubarb-leaf spray at the first sign of infestation (see page 126).

True spinach can be sown slightly earlier than many crops and will do reasonably well if sown in late March. For a steady supply over summer, it can be planted every 2 weeks until

This pumpkin will be ready to harvest in about a month's time.

late June. Sow thinly, at about a thumb's depth, and thin out to about 10cm (4in) between plants, allowing a boot's length between rows. Use the thinnings in salads, and for a crop of baby leaf spinach sow throughout the growing season, picking the small leaves before the plant fully matures.
• See Quinoa and asparagus salad, page 190; Autumn salad, page 196.

Squash
and pumpkins

Treat squash and pumpkins as you would courgettes and marrows for sowing methods and general care (see page 115), although you harvest squash and pumpkins considerably later than summer squash. The seeds can be used from last year's fruit dried over the winter or, as Andy found one year, seeds from a shop-bought plant can grow into very productive squash plants. Trailing squash and pumpkins will need extra room to grow and some choose to grow them vertically up canes or wigwams, which is a useful method in a restricted space (see pages 178 and 182). However, as they're ready later in the year they often only really spread out after other plants have already been harvested. Cut squash and pumpkins when the fruit is mature, usually in late summer or early to mid-autumn, and let them dry out for a week or so in the sun. If wet weather persists, leave them to dry on an indoor windowsill.
• See Butternut squash and apple soup, page 196; Pumpkin and chestnut risotto, page 199.

Swedes

Swede is another vegetable from the ever-diverse cabbage family and has been bred for its swollen roots. It's best suited to colder climates. Sow very thinly from late May to mid-June, scattering the seed and covering with a layer of soil. Keep thinning the seedlings until they are just over a hand span apart. Keep the crop well watered to stop the root turning thick and woody. Harvest from late September through to March as the roots become large and swollen.
• See Creamy roasted vegetable soup, page 203.

Sweetcorn

Once you've grown it successfully, sweetcorn (or maize) is one of those vegetables you'll want to grow year after year – it tastes delicious and is quite a show piece in the garden. Sow it with squash, pumpkins, courgettes and beans for maximum use of space (see pages 104–5).

Prepare the ground by adding well-rotted manure or compost in winter and turning the soil before raking into a flat surface. Corn needs to be sown in blocks of at least eight plants, as it's a grass and is therefore wind pollinated. Traditionally, sweetcorn is sown under cover in April or May and transplanted in May or June, or sown *in situ* in June, although in some areas of Britain you might be able to sow direct earlier.

If sowing direct, sow two seeds at each station, with about a boot's length and a half between in both directions. Later, remove the weaker of the two plants and allow the stronger to grow on. If planting seedlings, plant one at each station at the same spacing. They can be grown slightly closer together, about 30–35cm (12–14in), especially if planted in very fertile soil. With luck, each

Young sweetcorn on the allotment.

plant should grow one or two cobs. They may need support and they'll need plenty of water in dry weather. Tap the plants when the seedheads form to aid pollination and use a comfrey or nettle feed when the cobs start to form (see page 83).

Don't be tempted to harvest the cobs before they're fully ripe, no matter how big they look. To test for ripeness, pull back one part of the outer casing as if you were peeling a banana until you see the top three or so rows of corn. If the kernels are still white and small, pull the sheath back over it. If they're turning yellow, squeeze one of the kernels and if a creamy liquid oozes out the corn is ready (if it's watery, leave for a while longer). Twist the cob from the stem or cut with a knife just before cooking.

'Strawberry popcorn' is a stunning variety – the cobs look like big strawberries and can be microwaved to make popcorn. It's relatively small, growing to around 1.2m (4ft) tall, so is good for smaller gardens.

Tomatoes

Tomatoes are best grown in a greenhouse or under cover, especially if there's a risk of blight or an early frost in your area. However, they can do well outdoors in a sunny site. Start them off in a greenhouse or on a windowsill in March and April. If planting outside or in a greenhouse, leave about a boot's length and a half between plants, and for plants grown in the open ground leave 75cm (30in) between rows. (For growing tomatoes in containers, see page 182.)

There are two types of tomato – bush and cordon. Bush varieties are perhaps best for an outdoor crop and the first-time grower, as they're very easy to maintain. You don't need to stake them (they will grow only a couple of feet high) or remove the

sideshoots. However, the yields may be smaller and the season shorter than that of their cordon cousins, and the fruit is generally a lot smaller too.

Cordon tomatoes do require a little extra attention. They need staking and tying to a support. You'll also need to remove the sideshoots – that is, any shoots growing at a 45-degree angle from the plant. Cut these when they're about 2.5cm (1in) long and remove any yellowing leaves.

There are numerous varieties of tomatoes. 'Moneymaker', a cordon cultivar, is very popular, easy to grow and usually provides a healthy crop, and the American heritage 'Hillbilly' tomato, a bush variety, is very sweet for a large tomato.

Harvesting and ripening

Harvest tomatoes between July and October, when the fruits are red and fully matured. Tomatoes aren't frost-resistant, so if they haven't ripened by the time of the first frost they can be ripened indoors. To ripen fully, tomatoes need ethylene, which is emitted by ripe fruit – a ripe tomato will usually have a knock-on effect, ripening all the other fruits on the vine. You can mimic this natural process by putting a number of green tomatoes in a draw or box with a ripe banana or ripe tomato. Alternatively, harvest while still green to make chutney.

Tomato problems The main
problem we've found with outdoor tomatoes is the dreaded blight. The first sign is that your crop will look frost damaged, with the leaves and the fruit turning brown and eventually black, sometimes with a downy white growth killing off all the leaves.

 To minimize the risk of blight, keep tomatoes well away from potatoes and other members of the potato

family, such as peppers and aubergines, and avoid sowing them in an area where potatoes have grown within the past 2 years.

 Blight needs at least 2 days of near-constant consecutive rain to flourish, so in these conditions spray with Bordeaux mixture (copper sulphate and lime). A makeshift greenhouse or cloche made from bamboo poles and a sheet of clear plastic seems to help and will also extend the growing season.

 Problems can occur from mineral deficiency, causing yellowing of the leaves, so give a liquid feed from a wormery, comfrey or nettles (see page 83) or an organic tomato feed.

 Don't let tomato plants dry out – intermittent watering can split the developing fruit.

 Dark patches can appear on the fruit – this is known as blossom end rot. It can happen in growbags when the plant dries out or in over-acidic soil. Grow cherry tomato varieties and don't let the plants dry out.

 Whitefly can be a problem – companion plant with basil and/or marigolds to avoid this.
• See Summer salad and Stuffed courgettes, page 195.

Turnips

Turnips are grown in a similar way to swedes but they're a lot smaller and will grow much more quickly, typically taking between 6 and 12 weeks. Sow thinly from March to August and cover with a layer of soil. Thin out to about just over a hand span for maincrop varieties or about 12cm (5in) for early varieties. They can be harvested from May through to January. Turnip tops can also be grown as a spring green (these shouldn't be thinned out).

COMMON PESTS

Aphids

Aphids are by far the most common insect pests you'll come across in the vegetable garden. There are two main types – blackfly, which often appear earlier in the year and affect mainly bean crops (particularly broad beans), and greenfly, which tend to be more abundant on greenhouse plants but can damage almost anything you grow.

The only virtue of aphids that we can see is that they're great food for ladybirds. If the ladybirds don't seem to be doing a good enough job of controlling your aphids, take as many aphids off the plants as you can by hand or with a damp soft cloth; in the case of broad beans, pinch out the top few leaves of the plant. Once you've removed them, make a pesticide by mixing some washing-up liquid and water together in a plant mister and spray the plants to stop the aphids from re-emerging. One application is usually enough, but save the liquid for further applications if necessary. Alternatively, make a rhubarb-leaf spray by rotting two to four rhubarb leaves for a couple of weeks in a bucket of water. The resulting mixture can be sprayed on your infected plants with a mister or pump spray.

ENCOURAGING LADYBIRDS

In its lifetime, a ladybird can munch its way through hundreds if not thousands of pests, such as red spider mite, whitefly, mealy bugs and aphid adults and larvae. It's a good idea to encourage nesting sites in which ladybirds can hibernate during the winter – they particularly like patches of nettles, and gather around the base of clump-forming grasses (especially pampas grass); if you grow grasses, it's well worth leaving some uncut for the ladybirds to stay in over winter. Ladybird nests can be bought commercially and placed around the vegetable patch; alternatively, you could make an insect hotel (see page 94). Hoverflies are also beneficial as they prey on vegetable-plot pests.

Ants

Although ants can be beneficial, by feeding on other garden pests such as caterpillars and larvae, some ant species can cause a certain amount of root damage to young seedlings or established plants. Another unwelcome characteristic for the gardener is that ants 'farm' blackfly for the sticky honeydew they secrete. Although it's an amazing and fascinating fact of nature that one insect can 'farm' another, it doesn't make it any less annoying when you find blackfly thriving on your beans.

Pouring boiling water over an ants' nest, provided it's at a safe distance from your vegetables, is an age-old and effective method of destroying them. However, Dave (unlike Andy) can't bring himself to kill anything over the size of an aphid, so a more Buddhist approach for getting rid of ants is to leave a near-to-empty jar of jam at the base of the plant for the ants to feed on. They much prefer the jam to the aphid honeydew, and without the ants there to farm and protect them, large numbers of aphids will be eaten by ladybirds.

Some gardeners believe that ants don't like the smell of tansy and lavender, so it could be worth experimenting by planting these near your crops to keep ants at bay if they are a persistent problem.

Cabbage white butterfly

One year we didn't get round to starting our cabbage plants off from seed, so we bought in a couple of trays of cabbages at great expense. Within days of planting out they had all been shredded by very hungry caterpillars, and only skeletons of the original plants remained. They never fully recovered and in the end we had to sacrifice our entire crop to the marauders.

The only really effective way we've found to prevent damage caused by caterpillars is either to put a fine-mesh net around the plants, which will also stop birds having a nibble, or if you visit your plot regularly enough to remove the eggs and caterpillars by hand – although this is an effective method, it does take time. Encouraging birds into your garden by having winter feeders for them will also help to keep caterpillar numbers down.

Ladybirds prey on the number
one garden pest – the aphid.

The caterpillars of the cabbage white butterfly and cabbage moth will devour brassicas.

Pea and bean weevil

When we first saw the telltale square notches on the leaves of our peas and sweet peas we had no idea what had caused them. We eventually narrowed it down to the pea and bean weevil, and have since found a very simple method of dealing with it. The weevil seems to affect only the bottom part of the plant as it's growing, so a pea collar made from a juice or milk carton and placed around the emerging plant seems to help deal with this pest (see page 180). In addition, you may want to spray the plants with homemade aphid spray (see page 126).

Vandals

Vandalism is a problem we've both suffered from and unfortunately there's no real answer to it. One year Andy had his entire crop of squash and pumpkins kicked around his plot; it's this kind of thing that makes many people give up growing vegetables altogether. Sadly, there is little you can do except accept a certain amount of loss on your plot if it's in a public place and plant crops that aren't that attractive to vandals. Pumpkins do seem to be a firm favourite, and the slow maturing of these plants can sometimes make it totally disheartening when they're

destroyed in minutes by a mindless act. Potatoes and other root crops are harder to vandalize, as most of the plant is underground. Planting much more than you need is also an option, as there's only a limited amount of interest in trashing a plot. Having plastic windows on sheds limits damage of broken glass, and not keeping expensive tools outside will also prevent a certain amount of theft.

Slugs

Slugs are perhaps the worst of all pests. They can have up to 27,000 sharp rasping teeth and will make short work of tender young seedlings, cabbages, lettuces or indeed just about anything they can sink their teeth into. Whole books have been written on methods of getting rid of these slimy characters, and all ways of eliminating them can be hit-or-miss affairs at best. Rather than give you one definitive way of banishing slugs, we suggest you try a combination of some of the ideas below.

TOP 10 WAYS OF DEFEATING A SLUG

1. Build a pond and encourage frogs, newts and toads, as they will eat slugs.

2. Place a plank of wood or a large stone between the rows of your crops. The slugs prefer a dark, moist area to stay in, so will tuck themselves under the wood, allowing you simply to pick them off in the morning.

3. Introduce nematodes, microscopic worms that feed on slugs. They're worthwhile only for raised beds or small gardens, and don't do well on heavy soil, which restricts their movement.

4. Make a beer trap by sinking a pint of homebrew dregs or cheap beer into the ground near your veggies. Slugs and snails from the surrounding area will be attracted to the smell and will drown in the beer – it's not a method for the squeamish.

5. Place barriers around plants. Slugs like a smooth surface to slither over, so anything sharp will deter their movement – dried brambles, sharp sand and other spiky objects. We've placed jagged plastic collars made from milk cartons around some of our plants in the past, and this seemed to work.

A fine-meshed net will also help, especially with lettuces, and should prevent birds from eating your tender young leaves too, although slugs will find their way through any gap if sufficiently determined. Another barrier method is a copper strip placed around a plant: slugs will refuse to cross this barrier and so will leave your plants alone.

6. Plant red leaves. We've found that slugs tend to avoid red-leaved plants, such as 'Lollo Rosso' and Swiss chard. Planting a barrier of red leaves might be one possible solution.

7. Pour coffee grounds around plants. Slugs and snails can't cope with caffeine, and a generous trail of coffee grounds is enough to make them flee.

8. Mulch around your plants with pine needles, as these are acidic and slugs prefer a more alkaline medium.

9. Put your plants in pots, then secure the pots to a builder's plank suspended by wires. This makes it impossible for the slugs to get to your veggies, but it might make them more susceptible to wind and vandals who may be intrigued by your contraption. Hanging baskets for your salad greens is also a viable option and perhaps easier to install.

10. Many organic gardeners shy away from the use of slug pellets. However, the pellets approved by Garden Organic (formerly the Henry Doubleday Research Association) can be a useful weapon in your armoury against the spineless plant munchers.

Overleaf is a chart showing other pests that you might find are damaging your plants, with suggestions of what you can do about them.

Slugs can have up to 27,000 sharp rasping teeth and will make short work of tender young plants.

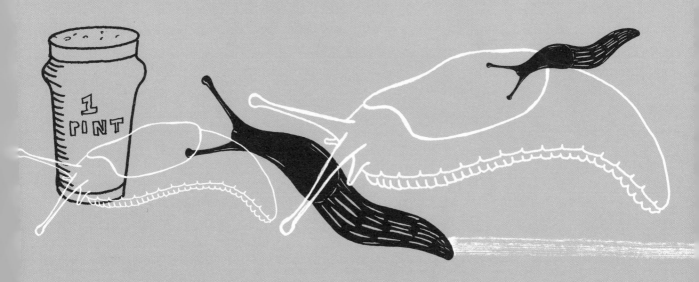

A digging mole dislodges plant seedlings.

PEST NAME	PLANTS AFFECTED	PROBLEM	POSSIBLE SOLUTIONS
CABBAGE ROOT FLY	Anything in the brassica family, including cabbages, kale, broccoli, cauliflowers, Brussels sprouts, radishes, swedes and turnips	Larvae make holes in the root and sometimes up the stem	Salvage what you can of the crop to eat immediately, burn the plant and don't grow brassicas on that piece of land for at least 3 years. The pest can be prevented by placing a homemade plastic disc, 7.5–15cm (3–6in) across, around the base of the plant. Make a cut in the disc to its centre so it can fit around the stem of the plant and place it snugly in the soil. Alternatively, grow pest-resistant varieties.
CARROT FLY	Carrot family, especially carrots, parsnips and celery; sometimes parsley	Tiny maggots bore into the vegetables, leaving rusty brown marks and holes running throughout	Companion plant with vegetables in the onion family (see pages 105–6). Cover with a physical barrier such as horticultural fleece or a plastic cloche. A raised bed has some success as the flies fly close to the ground. Plant to avoid the egg-laying season – late April to end of May and late July to end of August. Plant pest-resistant varieties.
MOLES	Seedlings of any plant	Small mammal digs holes, disturbing the ground and affecting the growth of seedlings and established plants	Two amusing but effective ways of getting rid of moles are placing an annoying musical card in their hole or urinating into it. They hate loud noises and the smell of another animal's urine (including human). Alternatively, use a humane trap or install a physical barrier such as a deep fence or a trench filled with compacted, stony or heavy clay soil.
BLIGHT	Potatoes, tomatoes, peppers, aubergines (see also page 125)	Leaves and fruit turn brown and rot on the vine, especially after wet weather	Plant tomatoes as far from potatoes as possible or plant under cover. Spray with Bordeaux mixture.
WHITEFLY	Tomatoes and brassicas	Tiny, white, moth-like bugs, which fly up in small clouds when the plant is brushed	Plant yellow flowers (poached-egg plants, marigolds, nasturtiums, etc.) near the plants to encourage predators. Use sticky yellow whitefly traps.

PLANTING + HARVESTING CALENDAR

This chart is an at-a-glance guide to the growing and harvesting times of the vegetables described in more detail earlier in this chapter. These are guidelines only – climatic conditions vary greatly from one part of Britain to another (there can be a difference of up to about a month between the south and north of the country). Another consideration to take into account is that weather conditions vary from year to year – at the time of writing, we're experiencing one of the hottest springs on record and the planting season is around three weeks ahead – so you'll need to adapt accordingly.

	DEC	JAN	FEB	MAR	APR	MAY	JUN	JUL	AUG	SEP	OCT	NOV
Asparagus (crowns)												
Plant outside				●	●							
Harvest					●	●	●					
Aubergines												
Sow indoors				●								
Plant outside under cloche							●					
Harvest										●	●	
Beetroot												
Sow outside					●	●	●					
Harvest							●	●	●	●	●	
Broad beans												
Sow outside				●	●	●						●
Harvest							●	●	●	●	●	
Broccoli (calabrese)												
Sow indoors					●	●						
Transplant seedlings							●	●				
Sow outside						●	●	●				
Harvest							●	●	●	●	●	
Sprouting broccoli												
Sow outside					●	●						
Harvest		●	●	●	●							
Brussels sprouts												
Sow indoors				●	●							
Transplant seedlings						●	●					
Harvest	●	●	●	●						●	●	●
Winter cabbages												
Sow indoors				●	●	●						
Transplant seedlings						●	●					
Sow outside					●	●						
Harvest	●	●	●	●						●	●	●

	December	January	February	March	April	May	June	July	August	September	October	November
Spring cabbages												
Sow outside									●	●		
Harvest				●	●	●	●					
Summer cabbages												
Sow indoors			●	●								
Transplant seedlings					●	●	●					
Sow outside					●	●						
Harvest							●	●	●	●	●	
Carrots												
Sow outside under cloche			●	●								
Sow outside					●	●	●					
Harvest	●							●	●	●	●	●
Summer cauliflowers												
Sow indoors		●	●	●								
Transplant seedlings					●	●						
Harvest							●	●	●	●		
Autumn cauliflowers												
Sow outside					●	●						
Harvest										●	●	●
Winter cauliflowers												
Sow outside						●						
Harvest			●	●	●	●						
Celeriac												
Sow indoors				●	●							
Transplant seedlings						●	●					
Harvest	●	●	●	●						●	●	●
Celery												
Sow indoors				●	●							
Transplant seedlings						●	●					
Harvest	●	●	●						●	●	●	●
Courgettes, marrows												
Sow indoors					●							
Transplant seedlings						●	●					
Sow outside						●	●					
Harvest								●	●	●	●	
Cucumbers												
Sow indoors				●	●	●						
Transplant seedlings						●	●					
Sow outside							●					
Harvest								●	●	●	●	

	DECEMBER	JANUARY	FEBRUARY	MARCH	APRIL	MAY	JUNE	JULY	AUGUST	SEPTEMBER	OCTOBER	NOVEMBER
Florence fennel												
Sow indoors					●	●	●					
Transplant seedlings							●	●	●			
Sow outside					●	●	●	●				
Harvest								●	●	●	●	
French beans												
Sow indoors					●	●						
Transplant seedlings						●	●					
Sow outside						●	●	●				
Harvest							●	●	●	●	●	
Jerusalem artichokes												
Plant outside					●							
Harvest	●	●	●								●	●
Kale												
Sow indoors					●	●						
Transplant seedlings							●	●	●			
Sow outside						●	●					
Harvest	●	●	●	●	●							●
Leeks												
Sow indoors		●	●	●								
Transplant seedlings					●	●	●					
Sow outside					●	●						
Harvest	●	●	●	●	●					●	●	●
Lettuces												
Sow indoors				●	●							
Transplant seedlings				●	●	●						
Sow outside/under cloche					●	●	●	●	●	●	●	●
Harvest	●	●	●	●	●	●	●	●	●	●	●	●
Onion/shallot sets												
Plant outside				●	●					●	●	●
Harvest				●	●	●	●	●	●	●	●	
Spring onions												
Sow outside				●	●	●	●	●				
Harvest							●	●	●	●	●	
Parsnips												
Sow outside				●	●	●						
Harvest	●	●	●								●	●
Peas												
Sow indoors				●	●							
Transplant seedlings						●	●					
Sow outside						●	●					
Harvest							●	●	●	●	●	

	DECEMBER	JANUARY	FEBRUARY	MARCH	APRIL	MAY	JUNE	JULY	AUGUST	SEPTEMBER	OCTOBER	NOVEMBER
1st early potatoes												
Plant outside				●	●							
Harvest							●	●				
2nd early potatoes												
Plant outside					●							
Harvest								●	●			
Maincrop potatoes												
Plant outside					●	●						
Harvest										●	●	
Radishes (summer)												
Sow outside				●	●	●	●	●	●			
Harvest						●	●	●	●	●		
Runner beans												
Sow indoors				●	●							
Transplant seedlings						●	●					
Sow outside						●	●					
Harvest								●	●	●	●	
Beet spinach												
Sow outside				●	●	●	●	●	●			
Harvest	●	●	●	●	●	●	●	●	●	●	●	●
True spinach												
Sow outside				●	●	●	●					
Harvest						●	●	●	●	●	●	
Squash, pumpkins												
Sow indoors					●	●						
Transplant seedlings							●	●				
Harvest										●	●	●
Swedes												
Sow outside							●	●				
Harvest	●	●	●	●						●	●	●
Sweetcorn												
Sow indoors					●	●						
Transplant seedlings							●	●				
Sow outside							●					
Harvest										●	●	●
Tomatoes												
Sow indoors				●	●							
Transplant seedlings						●	●					
Harvest									●	●	●	●
Turnips												
Sow outside				●	●	●	●	●	●			
Harvest	●	●				●	●	●	●	●	●	●

THE FRUIT GARDEN

Few things can beat a nice fresh bowl of strawberries and cream on a hot July day, although waking up to a chilled raspberry, strawberry and blackberry smoothie or tucking into a hot apple pie drenched with custard on a cold wet autumn evening have to be close contenders. It might seem strange therefore, given its popularity, that fruit is so often overlooked by gardeners and allotment-holders. Contrary to what people often think, you don't have to own acres of land, an orchard and a fruit cage to grow fruit, and as with vegetables the flavour is so much better when you pick the produce and eat it on the same day.

When growing up in Northampton, we were lucky enough to have Bramley and Cox apples, an elder tree and a patch of rhubarb and raspberries as permanent fixtures in our parents' garden. Our parents still live in the same place, and raspberry fool continues to be a firm family favourite in the summer months. Despite our upbringing, we – like many gardeners – neglected fruit for many years in favour of vegetables. However, more recently we decided to venture beyond and experiment a little, and discovered that it's not at all difficult to produce impressive yields of fruit in

a relatively small space. Strawberries can be grown in a strawberry planter, blueberries in a pot on a patio, raspberries along the edge of a plot and even currant bushes can be grown in the sometimes-neglected corners of an allotment.

In this chapter we show how to grow fruit trees and soft fruit that we've experimented with ourselves, in southern Britain. It's all fairly straightforward and doesn't require a lot of work. The great thing about growing fruit is that once it's planted it will be with you for years to come.

'Winter Gem' apple grown on a dwarf rootstock.

TREE FRUIT

It's possible to grow fruit trees in almost any outside space. Gardeners fortunate enough to have a large plot can plant a small orchard, or train apples or pears to grow over an arch above a path, but for those with only a tiny outdoor space there are numerous smaller fruit trees that do well in the ground in confined spaces or even in containers. You can also grow tree fruit against walls, which saves space, provides some protection against frost, cold and winds and helps the fruit to ripen earlier.

A major advantage of fruit trees is that once planted they need very little care and attention, and year after year they'll produce fruit with little input from the gardener. When Dave moved into a rented terraced house in Oxford, there was a pear and an apple tree growing in a compact bed in the garden. The pear never yielded much fruit – only six or seven pears – but Dave could enjoy the fruit without having to do a great deal because it was an established tree.

Apples

The main benefit of growing your own apples is that you can grow varieties that are difficult to find in the shops. It seems senseless to us that apples are flown across the world during the British apple season when we can grow so many delicious varieties here.

Apples are among the most long-lived elements of the kitchen garden. If a mix of varieties is grown, they can be harvested from August until September, and if wrapped in newspaper and put in a box so they're separated from each other they can be stored right through winter.

Apples are prone to woolly aphids; planting nasturtiums can help with this, or tie an environmentally friendly glue- or grease-band around the lower trunk of the tree (these are available in garden centres and on the internet). Holes in the fruit can be caused by the larvae of the codling moth, and codling moth traps can be hung up in summer to help prevent this pest.

Like most fruit trees, apples benefit from being pruned from time to time to enhance fruiting and to keep the tree healthy. During winter, cut away any diseased wood or crossing branches, allowing air to circulate around the branches.
• See Butternut squash and apple soup, page 196; Autumn salad, page 196; Apple chutney, page 254; Apple jam, page 256; Scrumpy cider, page 269.

Figs

Milder winters and warmer summers have helped fig trees to thrive in Britain in recent years. They're native to the Mediterranean and prefer warmer weather, so have in the past done well only under cover or in the south of the country. Since figs are susceptible to frosts, gardeners in Scotland and the far north should consider growing them under cover or in pots, bringing them in over winter. If possible, plant fig trees against a south-facing wall.

You need to restrict the roots of fig trees in order to get a good crop. The simplest way to achieve this is to plant the tree in a large pot dug into the soil. Alternatively, dig a hole 1m (3ft) square and place boards on either side with a base of rammed rubble to restrict the downward roots. You then plant the tree in the hole and backfill with a mix of compost and soil.

ROOTSTOCKS

A large proportion of fruit trees don't grow on their own roots. Instead, the crown of a tree (the fruiting top part) is grafted onto an existing rootstock (the bottom part of the tree). This is especially true of apples, and they've been grown in this way since the Middle Ages. This not only produces a better crop but also determines the size of the tree, making it easier for gardeners to choose the right-sized tree for their needs.

Harvest pears before they're ripe, as soon as they come off the tree easily.

If planting in a pot you'll need to dig the pot out at the end of each season and cut any roots that have escaped through the drainage hole. Mulch and water well each year, but don't add manure, as this will aid leaf rather than fruit growth. In October pick off any small immature fruits (unless growing in a greenhouse) as they won't fully mature.

Figs can become frost damaged in the winter, so prune away any damaged branches in spring. On older, more established trees, thin out any branches that are crossing over, or diseased and dying. To promote new growth, also cut some of the branches down to where the first bud appears. During summer, around June or July, figs can benefit from a second pruning, cutting away all but five or six leaves on each new shoot. Wasps can be a problem, so to discourage their presence pick up any windfalls and remove any damaged fruit.

Pears

Pears are a little harder to grow than apples, but the crop can be just as sweet and they make an excellent dessert. One of our favourite ways to eat a pear is to poach it in red wine and cinnamon, then finish it off with a generous helping of double cream. It's the perfect antidote for those days when the weather is getting colder and the nights are drawing in towards the end of summer. Depending on the variety, pears are ready between August right up until December.

Pears grow best in sheltered positions, as the early blossoms are susceptible to frosts. To get around this, many gardeners choose to train pears against a south-facing wall. If you're in the north of England or in Scotland you should do this anyway.

Plant as you would any other fruit tree (see overleaf) and each spring add a top-dressing of well-rotted manure. If planting on a lawn, you'll need to remove grass surrounding the pear tree, as it will do much better without any competition. Water regularly, especially in the first few years, and mulch around the base of the tree. However, a mulch can rot the base of the tree in winter, so remove it in November and weed around the base. Pears can struggle in containers, so ideally plant them in a permanent position.

If you have room for only one pear, ensure you have a self-fertilizing variety. Alternatively, if your neighbours have a pear tree, plant yours as near to theirs as possible.

Pears are very similar to apples when it comes to pests and diseases, so it's worth putting up glue- or grease-bands if aphids are a problem and hang up codling moth traps. Always prune in autumn, removing any diseased or crossing branches.

Plums

Plums are a very versatile fruit in the kitchen – as well as being delicious eaten straight off the tree, they can be used in puddings and preserves such as plum jam and chutney. Plums and their dried counterpart, prunes, have a high fibre content and they produce a rather laxative effect, so eat them in small quantities.

Like many other fruit, some plums require a cross-pollinator while others are completely self-fertile. It's important to avoid digging too near the roots of a plum tree, because it can cause suckers to grow. For this reason, it's best to plant plum trees away from your fruit beds. Keep the ground well watered and mulched.

Prune plums in the summer months, between June and August, to prevent infection from silver leaf fungus. Keep the ground beneath the tree clear and well weeded. It's a good idea to plant climbing nasturtiums at the tree's base, because they'll attract beneficial insects. Birds can be a problem with plum trees, so it may be an idea to cover smaller trees with netting. On larger trees, bird scarers such as old CDs hanging in the branches will help keep the birds away (see page 90), but you may just have to accept a certain amount of damage.

FRUIT-TREE LEGALITIES

Special permission is often needed to grow fruit trees on an allotment. Most allotment societies will allow trees with small rootstocks that will never grow to be too imposing, but check with your allotment rep first. If planted in the garden, legally speaking your trees are classed as part of the house, so if you wish to take them with you when you move this needs to be written into the contract when selling the house.

Planting fruit trees

October to March is the best time to plant most trees. This is because once the leaves have dropped off in autumn, the tree effectively 'falls asleep' for the winter – storing valuable nutrients in its roots – and will 'wake up' the following spring. Moving a tree in winter is similar to putting someone who's passed out at a party to bed – they'll put up less of a fight if they're asleep. Leave planting until spring if you have a heavy soil or are in a low-lying area, because the ground may become waterlogged.

Pot-grown trees are the exception and can be planted at any time of year. However, because they've been grown in a container they can have weaker roots than bare-rooted trees and will need lots of watering if they're planted during dry weather. It's worth being a little patient and waiting until autumn or winter, when you can get a bare-rooted tree, and growing a green manure on the chosen site in the meantime (see page 105).

Try to plant when the soil isn't too wet and avoid planting if there's been a ground frost, as this can damage the tree. The type of soil and cultivation requirements vary according to the fruit. For example, a mulch of grass clippings can damage cherries and plums because of its high acidic content, while apples and pears will benefit greatly from the added moisture. However, broadly speaking most fruit trees and soft-fruit bushes do share a number of similar requirements, as follows:

- **A well-drained, not waterlogged site**
- **Plenty of organic matter**
- **Full sun**
- **Regular mulching**
- **Protection from wind and frosts (not usually a problem in most small, urban back gardens)**

How to plant a fruit tree So now you've found the perfect spot for your tree, the next stage is digging the planting hole. Dave's allotment mate Simon is built like a shire horse and is perfect for these kinds of jobs, but with no Simon to hand you'll just have to dig your own hole.

The hole should be sufficiently deep to cover the roots and wide enough so the roots aren't bent or broken when planting. This is especially important for bare-rooted trees, and a wide hole will help the roots spread evenly. With a fork, roughly loosen up the soil at the bottom of the hole to allow the roots to move downwards into the ground. For a pot-grown tree, tease the outer roots from the rootball to help the tree to establish and put a layer of well-rotted manure or compost in the bottom of the hole.

It's best to plant a tree with two people. First, insert the stake. For bare-rooted trees, position the stake vertically and in the direction of the prevailing wind; for pot-grown trees, the stake should be angled at about 45 degrees and on the side away from the wind. Drive it in at about 60cm (24in) below soil level. The next stage is to place the tree and then backfill the hole with compost or well-rotted manure. To ensure the right depth when planting, lay a board or plank across the hole – the plank should be at the original depth the tree was planted at; if planted too deep, the tree can rot. Put the compost in a little at a time and firm with your hands as you go along. Once the hole is filled, gently pull the tree up as much as it will go (only with small trees) and shake it a little, then put it down again. This should ensure the tree is tight in the hole and well planted. Firm again and leave a slight mound of earth around the outside of the tree to retain water. Finally, tie the tree to the stake so that it's taut but won't rub against the tree and damage the bark. Water well.

Aftercare

After planting, keep the tree well watered if the weather is dry and make sure it doesn't dry out. To aid moisture retention, mulch around the base of the tree every spring with compost or well-rotted manure, bark or wood chippings, cardboard or hay. This mulch should also help to keep the weeds down, but watch out for pernicious weeds such as bindweed and brambles creeping in. Weed around fruit trees regularly and consider planting climbing nasturtiums at their base – these attract beneficial insects that prey on aphids and other pests and will grow with little interference to the tree's roots.

Pruning fruit trees It's important to prune fruit trees to enhance fruiting and reduce the chance of infection. It will also maintain the shape or style of the tree. The main thing to look for when pruning is maintaining supporting branches and cutting any that are crossing or sticking straight upwards. Cut away any diseased or dead wood to allow air to get into the healthier branches, but bear in mind that fruit grows on the previous year's branches, so cut these away only if they've become badly infected.

Some fruit trees are trained as a cordon, espalier or fan rather than as a standard or half-standard. These are ways of growing fruit on a series of wires secured to a wall, fence or posts; they're useful for small areas and look attractive, but need regular pruning to keep them in shape.

Cordon-trained apples require summer pruning to control their growth.

SOFT FRUIT

In our opinion, of all the produce you can grow yourself there is the most marked difference in taste between soft fruit grown at home and its shop-bought counterparts. Not only does home-grown fruit beat bought fruit hands down in flavour, but it's also healthier. Once a piece of fruit has been picked its vitamin C content is depleted through exposure to ultra-violet light; eating directly from the plant means fruit retains vitamin C and its levels of other antioxidant vitamins are much higher too.

It's not uncommon to find strawberries on the shelves in the middle of December or raspberries in February. Our obsession with demanding food out of season means that many people are forgetting that the season for most soft fruit really lasts only for the summer months in Britain. Strawberries flown in from North Africa or South America now fill the gap across the winter months normally filled by our own native hard fruits such as pears and apples. Even without relying on foreign imports, some British farmers are supplying soft fruit all year round through the use of heated polytunnels. Transportation of foreign imports and in most cases heat for British

polytunnels rely on fossil fuels. Growing your own soft fruit removes this reliance on non-renewables, and quite frankly it tastes so much better when ripened naturally in the sun and eaten directly from the plant.

Blackberries

For a long time, neither of us saw any point in growing blackberries. They grow so abundantly in the wild, why even attempt to grow them yourself, we thought. Then one year, while living in Oxford, Dave had a variety of thornless blackberries growing in his garden. Day after day he could put them on his breakfast cereal (being able to harvest them in his dressing gown was a definite bonus) and the

yields of big, juicy blackberries off just one or two canes was incredible. The taste of cultivated blackberries can be far superior to that of wild blackberries, and the thornless varieties are much easier to harvest than their wild relatives. On our web forum, some members have talked about falling into blackberry bushes head-first trying to pick them – this is another reason for growing them at home or on an allotment, where you have access to ladders for those hard-to-reach berries, so there's no need for any accidents.

Plant blackberry bushes from October to March, when they're dormant. They can grow very vigorously in any soil type and the main problem will be stopping them from growing like weeds. Choose less vigorous varieties and train them against wires, fences, walls or trellises, pruning any unwanted growth.

Blackberries are relatively trouble-free, but they can suffer from cane spot – purple spots on the withered leaves and canes. Many gardeners recommend spraying with Bordeaux mixture. This has been a permitted spray in organic gardening but it can be damaging to aquatic animals, so it's best avoided if you have a pond nearby. Effective, regular pruning and good garden hygiene should cut down on any problems you may have.

• See Blackberry fool-ish, page 195; Blackberry and elderberry jam, page 255.

Blueberries

Blueberries are a great fruit to grow at home and even those without gardens can grow them in pots on the patio. In recent years they've been given the title of 'superfood', because they're very high in antioxidants and other beneficial compounds. It's doubtful that they're any better for you than our native berries, but this has massively increased their popularity within Britain and the rest of the world. They're not grown on any great scale in the UK and we rely heavily on imports to get them to our breakfast tables. Most of the other berries can be and are produced commercially on a large scale within our shores. For this reason, blueberries are a very important berry plant to cultivate in terms of food miles, and if you were going to grow one berry plant we would suggest it should be the blueberry.

Blueberries are acid-loving plants. If you don't have the benefit of an acidic soil, you can grow them in terracotta pots filled with ericaceous (lime-haters') compost. Dig the containers into the soil to keep the moisture in and to reduce the amount of watering. Ensure each pot is a little bigger than the plant's roots so it has room to grow and won't become pot-bound. Mulch the plants regularly with acidic mulch, such as oak leafmould or pine needles, and don't let them dry out, especially if growing in pots; some gardeners add stones to the top of the pot to aid water retention. Always water blueberries with rainwater rather than tap water.

It's best to plant bare-rooted blueberries in March or April but pot-bought ones can be planted out any time. Leave around 1m (3ft) between plants and plant at least two or three together (like apples, they need a partner plant to pollinate with). Ideally, combine different varieties so you get a longer crop. Blueberries can take a few years to establish, so don't be disappointed if you don't get a good crop in your first year.

Currant bushes
red-, white- and blackcurrants

Once established, currant bushes can yield huge amounts of fruit every year. Unfortunately, it can take a while to get them to this stage and we find maintaining an older bush is easier than planting a new one. However, that's not to say that you shouldn't try, just that it can take a while for fruit to appear, so if you're going to have your plot for only a year or two perhaps currant bushes aren't for you: it may be 3 years before they produce a decent crop. (For growing and propagation details, see box overleaf.)
• See Blackcurrant jam, page 255.

Gooseberries

Gooseberries are one of those fruits that seem to be more associated with the older generation, probably because they're hard to find in supermarkets and greengrocers. They're thankfully quite easy to grow, and as many varieties are ready earlier than other soft fruits they're an important addition to the self-sufficientish garden.

Plant gooseberries when they're dormant, from October to March, ensuring the ground isn't frozen. Bushes should be spaced about 1.2m (4ft) apart so they can fill out when fully grown. They do well in most soil types but prefer a well-drained soil. Prune in autumn, as for all soft-fruit bushes. A further pruning can be done in June to neaten up the plant, as it can become quite bushy, and this will reduce the risk of mildew. Cut to about four to five leaves, leaving the main supporting branches intact. (For growing and propagation details, see overleaf.)

Raspberries

Andy grows his raspberries against the fence on his allotment and they utilize space that would otherwise be neglected. Raspberries are often overlooked in favour of strawberries, which is a shame as they're relatively easy to grow (once you get the hang of them), freeze very well and make good jam. They also tolerate a little shade and can be planted in a town garden that doesn't get much sun.

SOFT-FRUIT BUSHES: GROWING + PROPAGATING

Soft-fruit bushes, such as gooseberries, currants and blueberries, are planted in much the same way as fruit trees (see page 142). Try to plant bushes the day you get them, or plant them within 2 days. If you have to leave them any longer, protect the roots from drying out by packing them loosely with wet newspaper and soak the plants well before planting. To keep birds away it may be worth investing in netting for all your soft fruit. Aphids can cause problems, so use rhubarb-leaf spray (see page 126). Caterpillars are also keen on some soft fruit, but they can be shaken off: place a sheet or piece of cardboard under the bush and shake – the caterpillars will fall onto it. Prune soft-fruit bushes in autumn, when they're dormant.

Taking a cutting from a soft-fruit bush

Taking cuttings from your soft-fruit bushes is a productive and inexpensive way of increasing your stock of fruit plants. Blackcurrants, redcurrants, whitecurrants and gooseberries all readily root from cuttings taken in October.

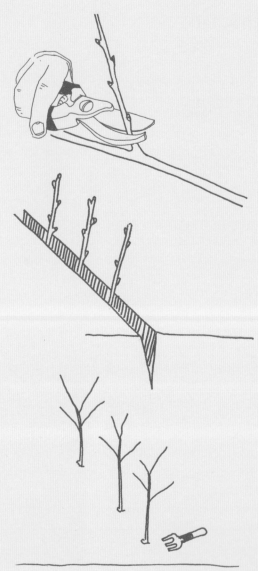

1. Choose a healthy stem from the summer's growth and cut lengths of 30cm (12in), cutting flush with the main stem.

2. Cut off all the leaves and the soft growth at the tip of each cutting. Trim to just below a bud, leaving the top four or five buds. For blackcurrants, leave all the buds intact.

3. Dig a narrow trench about 15cm (6in) deep and line the base with a little sharp sand.

4. Insert the cuttings into the trench to approximately half their length, spacing them about 10–15cm (4–6in) apart. In the case of blackcurrants, bury the stems so that only two buds show above ground. Backfill the trench with compost and firm around the cuttings.

5. Within about 10–12 months the cuttings should have produced roots. Carefully lift the new plants and transplant them to a well-prepared plot where you want them to grow on, or leave them to grow where they are.

How to grow raspberries

Raspberries should be planted in November, December or March in rich, free-draining soil. Insert the canes a little over a boot's length apart, allowing about 1.8m (6ft) between rows. Cut the plant to the first bud, about 30cm (12in) above soil level. This may seem a strange thing to do but it encourages the raspberries' roots to grow, meaning that stronger plants emerge from the rootstock rather than having the plant focusing its energy on cane and leaf production and growth.

The plants will need some support as they grow. Most gardeners recommend putting in training wires before you plant raspberries. Secure wires to stakes either side of the plants, attaching three wires for summer-fruiting canes at 75cm (30in), 1.1m (3½ft) and 1.5m (5ft) high, and two wires for autumn-fruiting canes at 75cm (30in) and 1.2m (4ft). An easy way to remember is the first wire is at the level of the bottom of a trouser pocket, the second just above the belly button and the third at chin height – but then we're only 1.7m (5ft 8in). In years when we've had little money to buy training wire we've found that strong garden twine does the job just as well, but you may need to put in more support posts. The alternative is to grow them up an existing wire fence.

In the first summer after planting, cut the original cane down to ground level in spring, when new growth starts to appear at the base. After fruiting, cut all summer-fruiting canes down to ground level and for autumn-fruiting canes do this in winter. Thin out any stray canes and plant them or shred and compost. For any growth that hasn't yet fruited, tie up the plant ready for next year's fruit.

Like most other crops, raspberries will pick up diseases in time and shouldn't therefore be planted where raspberries have been grown for the last 7 years. They won't do well in waterlogged areas or soil with high alkaline content. If drainage is a problem, put in some raised beds (see page 80). Although raspberries like to be weed-free they don't like their roots to be disturbed, so don't hoe too deeply around the plants.

Raspberries need plenty of well-rotted manure as well as compost to do well, so be sure to dig plenty of both of these into the soil before planting the canes. Once planted, mulch them with manure or leafmould every spring, before the start of the main growing season.

Birds are the chief problem with raspberries; if possible, protect the plants with netting. The best method of keeping the plants disease-free is to prune and weed out any diseased plants regularly and to clear any brambles in the near vicinity. Most plants bought from a garden centre should be certified disease-free, but take care if you inherit any plants.

Aphids can be a problem on raspberry canes, so spray them regularly with rhubarb-leaf spray if your plants are susceptible to attack (see page 126).

Getting new plants from old

Despite all their fussy ways, raspberries are quite hardy and will pop up like weeds all over your plot if not kept in check. This can be a real bonus when you're trying to propagate more canes. Simply remove any suckers (new plants that have grown from the existing plant's roots) in October or November by cutting them away from the parent plant and plant them straight away. Cut the suckers at the base, below ground level, to ensure you have enough roots on the cane for it to grow.

• See Raspberry jam, page 255.

Rhubarb

Rhubarb is a useful perennial in any fruit or vegetable garden. Technically, it's not a fruit at all but a vegetable. However, it has long been treated as a fruit because it's good in puddings and pies. In the Middle East it's treated as a vegetable and although it takes some getting used to, a curry made with spinach, chickpeas and rhubarb is an excellent way to enjoy this crop.

Plant the crowns in autumn or February/March. Make sure the ground is thoroughly free of weeds and work in a good helping of well-rotted manure before planting. Rhubarb can take up a lot of room, so allow around 75–90cm (30–36in) each side of the plant. Don't harvest it in the first year, as it needs to establish leaf growth. Water in well and mulch regularly.

Once established, rhubarb requires little maintenance and it will just keep cropping year after year. You can leave it to crop naturally or, for more tender rhubarb stalks, you can force it.

Forcing simply means to deprive the growing stalks of light. Covering the plant with a large upturned bucket or dustbin, weighed down with stones or bricks, or a special terracotta pot designed for the purpose, is the simplest way of doing this. Late January or early February is the best time to start forcing your rhubarb and it should be ready in March.

Sometimes the plant may seem to wither and disappear in its first year, but don't worry too much too soon. The plant could have rotted in wet ground but it could also be concentrating on root growth – a friend of Dave's found her rhubarb had disappeared completely in its first year only to come back as a healthy plant the following year.

Strawberries

Strawberries are by far the favourite of all the soft fruits in the self-sufficientish garden. Unlike many other soft fruits, strawberries need no sugar added to reduce their tartness and when they're taken fresh from the plant there is little to compete with their taste. They're quite an easy fruit to grow and once they're established there's a good chance you could have more plants than you know what to do with.

Growing strawberries

Strawberries prefer a well-drained, weed-free soil on the slightly acidic side. Adding plenty of leafmould before planting should help things along. They also like a good helping of rotted manure to sit in as they grow, so work some of this in, ideally a month or so before planting.

If you buy potted varieties of strawberries you can plant them at any time of year, although spring and autumn tend to be best. We find if you want a crop in the first year it's best

to do this in March or April in the southern half of Britain or April/May in the north and Scotland. Water them well before planting.

If you order them online, there's a good chance you'll be sent bare-root plants. These must be planted in autumn or spring. If the plants are small and sown in autumn, remove the blossoms in the first year to let the plants establish their root and leaf growth before concentrating on fruit in the following year. Again, water well after planting.

It's important to mulch strawberries; this can be done by planting through black plastic (see page 80) or by putting down a layer of straw. If planting through plastic, try to work the ground up into a mound or ridge before planting to prevent the roots from rotting.

Keep strawberries well watered throughout the growing season. Remove any unwanted runners and diseased leaves. Strawberries will support a few runners, and they can be propagated this way (see page 150), but more than two or three will put too much strain on the parent plant. When the plants are established, top-dress the soil with well-rotted manure in spring and weed regularly.

If you're short of space, consider investing in a strawberry planter. This is a terracotta pot with holes in the sides to allow the strawberries to grow through. It holds on to moisture and also helps to keep the fruit away from slugs. Slugs are such a problem with strawberries that commercial growers plant them in troughs raised off the ground. For the same reason, Andy often grows his strawberries in a hanging basket outside his front door; another advantage is that he can give them to departing guests as they're chatting on the doorstep.

Tall terracotta pots are ideal for forcing rhubarb; the
stems grow longer and are more succulent.

PROPAGATING STRAWBERRY PLANTS

Strawberries propagate from seed but also, in the same way as a spider plant, by sending out runners that will grow into adult plants by the following year. With a little encouragement, these small runner plants can be rooted into pots. Do this with healthy plants, after they've fruited and as the runners start to form, and clear any diseased plants at the end of each season.

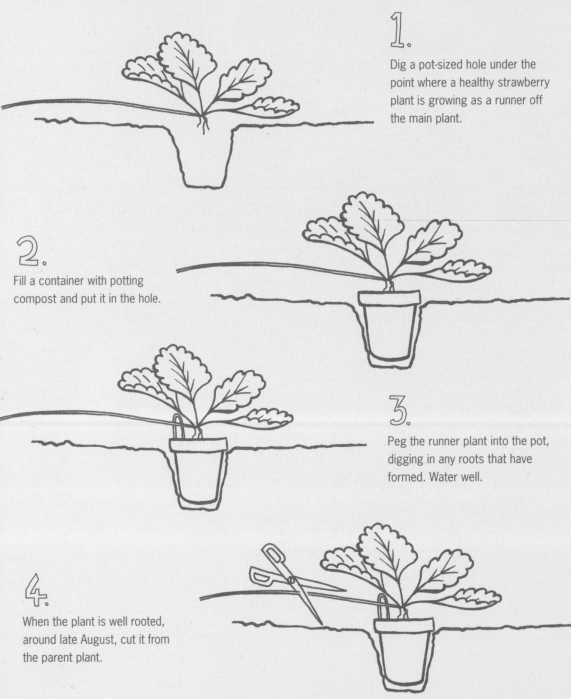

1.

Dig a pot-sized hole under the point where a healthy strawberry plant is growing as a runner off the main plant.

2.

Fill a container with potting compost and put it in the hole.

3.

Peg the runner plant into the pot, digging in any roots that have formed. Water well.

4.

When the plant is well rooted, around late August, cut it from the parent plant.

Potting up a young strawberry plant that has propagated by runners.

GROWING HERBS

We're great herb fans and between us have three herb gardens – one on each allotment and the other in Andy's concrete backyard, consisting of a few tyres filled with compost and some containers. The potent aromas exuded by the herbs – particularly lavender and chamomile – have a tremendously relaxing effect on us while we work and attract bees and other beneficial insects to our vegetable plots, aiding pollination. But the most enticing reason for growing herbs has to be for the piquant flavours they bring to our cooking, enlivening even the blandest of foods. Herbs also have powerful medicinal qualities; from the earliest times humans have grown plants to cure illness or relieve pain, and in the modern age they continue to be vital for our health and wellbeing (see pages 271–87).

Technically speaking, the term 'herb' means a plant that dies down over winter. However, the more popular definition of a herb is an aromatic plant grown for its culinary or medicinal properties and includes some woody plants such as rosemary and lavender.

Many of our friends say that they don't grow anything 'except for a few herbs', in an almost apologetic way. But we think that this is an excellent start to growing your own produce, and it's how many self-sufficientish gardeners first begin – inspired by eating something they've nurtured themselves, they often move on to the greater challenge of growing vegetables, and never look back. Herbs are surprisingly easy to grow, and even if you don't have the space for a proper herb garden they're happy in pots on the patio or on a windowsill, or even indoors – we've seen bedsits, studio flats and small offices brimming with herbs.

CREATING A HERB GARDEN

Humans have been cultivating herbs in small gardens for centuries, and many of the herbs that have been naturalized on our shores, such as thyme and sage, were escapees from Roman herb gardens. Most herbs will grow in even the poorest soil (in fact some actually dislike a nutrient-rich soil), so you don't need to spend much time preparing an area before growing them. Drainage is important, though, and a clay soil is not really suitable for this reason. The wonderful thing about herbs is that you don't necessarily need a garden to grow them. Your herb garden could consist of a few pots or a selection of less conventional, recycled containers.

Whatever the style or size of your herb garden, it's a good idea to divide herbs into separate growing areas. One method uses an old cartwheel to keep the herbs divided; alternatively, a ladder would work in just the same way. To create a cartwheel or ladder herb garden, dig over the patch where you wish to have your herbs and place the cartwheel or ladder over the area. Plant your herbs or sow seeds in between the spokes or rungs and write the names of the seeds on the spokes or rungs so that you know what they are when they come up. If some of the seeds don't germinate, don't worry – just sow some more.

A friend of ours has planted an attractive herb garden in the shape of a cartwheel, but using rows of carrots to divide the herbs. Use your imagination to come up with dividing lines – copper pipe could be a consideration, the beauty being that the slugs get a little electric shock when they touch copper and so leave your seedlings alone.

Andy decided to make a herb garden out of several old tyres, filling them with soil and sowing the seeds inside,

using a different tyre for each herb. The advantage of this is you can recycle old tyres and create a herb garden on a concrete surface. He tried a variety of herbs using this method, and the sage and parsley are doing pretty well but the coriander has suddenly gone to seed. This is perhaps because the drainage is not very good when tyres are placed on a concrete surface.

To make a tyre herb garden, fill a tyre with soil, ensuring that the whole inner area is packed full, including the rim, to prevent the 'container' from moving around. As nothing grows at the sides, stones or bricks can be used to pack them out. Sow your seeds or plant your seedlings in the soil.

The biggest pest in this type of herb garden has been the local cats. The earth-filled tyres must remind them of a litter tray and they keep digging up the seedlings. To keep cats at bay, push 40cm (16in) sticks around the edge of the soil. On more established plants, holly leaves can be used – a cat won't sit down where it thinks it will be prickled.

Planting herbs with vegetables

Herbs and vegetables not only taste good together but there are also benefits to planting them in the same plot. Some herbs act as companion plants – their aromas and secretions seem to deter pests and certain herbs are thought to improve the flavour of particular vegetables. For example, sage is good planted with cabbages and carrots, because it is thought to repel cabbage moths and carrot flies; similarly, chives and coriander are believed to repel aphids, and garlic keeps Japanese beetles at bay; basil is thought by many gardeners to enhance the flavour of tomatoes. However, be aware that not all plants work well together and certain combinations can actually be harmful: a good example is dill and tomatoes, as dill can attract the tomato horn worm, which can destroy your crop of tomatoes. In addition, avoid growing Florence fennel and coriander together. (For more details on companion planting with vegetables, see pages 105–6.)

Herb garden made out of an old cartwheel.

Dill growing in Andy's tyre herb garden.

Some herbs are known as 'garden thugs' – they don't like to stay where you put them and will invade other parts of your plot, suppressing any plants in the vicinity. Mint (tiger mint is shown left) is a prime example. Andy planted some mint on his first allotment, ignoring all advice that it would become a nuisance. It was contained in the first year, but by the second year it was spreading all across his herb garden, pushing out the other herbs. Fennel can also be troublesome, because it tends to scatter seed across a wide area, colonizing bare earth and popping up where you don't want it to appear. Before planting herbs, do a little research to ensure you don't make the same mistakes as us.

OUR TOP HERBS

One of the main reasons we first started growing herbs is that they're very easy to grow; even if many of your vegetables fail, there will always be some herbs to pick. The herbs that follow are ones that we both grow every year, and some of the perennials (ones that live for longer than three years, such as sage or rosemary) are like old friends greeting us every time we visit our allotments. We use all of the herbs mentioned on a regular basis, primarily in the kitchen but also as medicines (see pages 271–87).

Basil

Basil will be familiar to most people, as it's one of the herbs sold in supermarkets in pots. Although you can grow it on from supermarket plants, these have a relatively weak root structure because they've been forced (made to grow quickly), so it's far better to grow your own from seed and have a stronger plant right from the start.

Sow three seeds per pot in a good, peat-free organic potting compost. When the plants have grown to about 3cm (1¼in) tall, pull out the weakest two plants. Basil will not survive frost and should therefore be grown indoors until around June, when the risk of frost has passed. Pinch off the top leaves to create a more bushy plant. In autumn, dig up your basil plants and place them in containers for your windowsill.

Bay

Bay is used to add flavour to many dishes, and it's a familiar sight outside hotels and restaurants, often shaped like a big lollypop. Growing bay from seed is not for the impatient, as germination can be unpredictable, taking anything from 10 days to 6 months. It needs to be kept at a constant temperature of 21°C (70°F) and too much water can cause the seeds to rot. It's not easy to grow from a cutting either. For these reasons, we suggest you buy your plant from a garden centre.

Position the plant in full sun, in rich, well-drained soil, and shield it from high winds. In spring, cut back your tree to maintain a good shape and give it a good liquid feed; it will also benefit from a mulch (put hay or leaves around the base) to ensure it retains moisture in summer. In very hot weather, water well to ensure that young plants don't dry out. Bay should be protected from temperatures below –14°C (7°F), so cover it with straw or bracken on very cold winter nights. If it gets too cold the leaves may turn brown and fall off, but don't panic – new shoots should grow back in spring.

If growing bay in the open ground, be aware that although rather slow-growing it can reach up to 9m (28ft). Once established, it can sometimes look after itself. Our friend inherited a half-dead bay tree and planted it out next to his compost bin. He did nothing to it and it's happily growing away 3 years later.

Bay can also be grown indoors in a pot, preferably in a sunny position. Ensure that it doesn't dry out in summer. In winter it will grow at a slower rate and needs watering only occasionally – you should let the compost almost totally dry out.

Chamomile

There are two main types of chamomile that the herb gardener needs to know about: the type that you grow for the flowers and the one you grow as a lawn. Roman chamomile is the plant you grow as a lawn (although it does flower) and German chamomile, which is much taller, is grown specifically for the flowers, which are used in infusions.

German chamomile

Sow German chamomile in early spring or autumn in a spot that gets good sunlight. It will tolerate most soil types, but to help it establish work the soil so that it's very fine and not thick and clumpy. You can also buy chamomile plants that are already established, as Andy did; over the space of a year one plant has spread to cover an area of around 1m (3ft) square. Although it's an annual it will reseed itself. Plant it in an area that you don't mind it spreading over as the seeds can go everywhere.

Roman chamomile

This can be sown in the same way as German chamomile, although it prefers good, well-drained soil conditions. It's a perennial herb and will need to be divided and replanted about every 3 years. To keep growth in check, mow it like a lawn.

Lemon and lime chamomile shortbread

It's quite easy to end up with a glut of chamomile flowers, especially if you're growing German chamomile. Andy makes this shortbread to use up some of his extra flowers.

5 or 6 chamomile flowerheads
125g (4oz) sugar
250g (8oz) butter
375g (12oz) plain flour
Grated zest of ½ lemon
Grated zest of 1 lime

1. Cut the bottom stem and the petals off your chamomile flowers so that you're left with the bud. This might disintegrate but that doesn't matter. Cream the sugar and butter together, then add the flour, the chamomile buds and the lemon and lime zest.
2. Combine all the ingredients with your hands until you have one big ball. Put the ball on a greased baking round, about 30cm (12in) across. Flatten with a rolling pin.
3. Cut your circle into triangles and decorate using a fork. Use your imagination or copy the traditional shortbread design (lots of little dimples and a small border).
4. Bake in the oven at 160°C (325°F, Gas mark 3), or 140°C (275°F) for a fan-assisted oven, for 30 minutes or until golden brown. Remove the triangles with a fish slice and leave on a wire cooling rack.

Chives

Chives will take up only a small area of your garden initially, but do be aware that they can spread once they go to seed. Andy's first allotment in Bath was covered in chives. Since then, he's grown them in an old wooden fruit box packed with compost; now in their second year, they're still thriving.

Chives can be grown from seed. Start them off indoors in spring on a warm, bright windowsill and put a see-through plastic bag sealed with an elastic band over the top to help keep the heat in. Plant them out in a sunny spot in early summer (they're not fussy about soil). You could also sow seed outdoors in late spring, but sowing indoors is preferable as germination rates will be higher. Water in dry weather and cut back after they've flowered to promote growth.

In the autumn of the second year of growth, lift clumps of chives and divide up the bulbs to replant slightly further apart.

Comfrey

We grow comfrey for a plant feed (see page 83), which is particularly good for tomatoes, and put comfrey leaves into the planting holes before planting potatoes; the leaves rot down and provide useful nutrients.

Comfrey is very easy to cultivate and can overtake a plot if you're not careful, so we wouldn't recommend it if you have only a small growing area. Ask around for plants – Andy's comfrey was grown from roots that were given to him by someone on www.freecycle.org. Ideally, plant comfrey in spring or early autumn, in dampish soil in partial shade, at about 10–20cm (4–8in) deep and spaced at least 1m (3ft) away from other plants. It will tolerate most soils and dies back in winter.

Coriander

Coriander is the most popular herb in the world. As we're big fans of Mexican and Indian food, it's the herb most used by us too.

When Andy first grew coriander, he made the mistake of planting out a shop-bought plant. What he didn't know is that coriander doesn't like to have its roots disturbed and will react by suddenly growing very quickly and producing seeds (this is known as 'bolting'). The herb is also prone to bolting during particularly damp periods. It's much better to grow coriander from seed directly into the ground, or in the container you want the plant to remain in. Pots made from newspaper are ideal for coriander, as you don't have to transplant them (see pages 168–9).

Growing coriander in containers
Andy has two separate lots of coriander growing in his backyard: one in a tyre filled with soil (see page 154) and the other in a window box. Despite the backyard being north-facing, both batches are flourishing. The coriander in the window box has self-seeded and is now in its third year after surviving two winters.

To sow coriander indoors, line the base of a window box or other container with broken crocks for drainage and fill it with organic, peat-free compost. Spread the seeds over the surface of the compost then press them in with your thumb. Give them a little water in very dry weather and at other times water them only very occasionally.

Growing coriander outdoors
Coriander grows best in light, well-drained soil in a sunny position and in a dry atmosphere. It does not really respond well to high humidity or damp, so be careful not to over-water the plants.

Sow seeds directly in the soil in spring, after the danger of frost has passed (you're normally safe by June wherever you live in Britain). Coriander seed should be thinly sown, in shallow drills, then covered with a fine layer of compost. If you're growing the plants for seed they should be spaced about 23cm (9in) apart; if you're growing them for the leaves a distance of 5cm (2in) will be sufficient.

Keep picking the leaves as you need them – this will actually help the plants grow stronger, but try to leave about one-third of the leaves on each plant at any one time.

Dill

Dill is one of the lesser-used culinary herbs, and it's relatively rare to find fresh dill for sale. Like most herbs, it's best used fresh and it's very easy to grow. It goes well with most meats and is especially good with fish.

Choose the site where you're going to plant dill carefully – it can cross-pollinate with fennel, giving you a strange hybrid that won't be much like either herb. When dill goes to seed, ensure that you collect all the seeds or you'll find yourself digging it up all over the place. Collect the seeds in the same way as you would fennel (see right).

Dill is a sun-lover and too much shade will inhibit growth. Plant four seeds at a time, spaced at about 23cm (9in) apart. Dill benefits from well-drained soil and suffers in compacted ground, because the long taproot needs to grow freely. Sow seeds when you can be sure that the soil temperature will not go below −4°C (25°F), ideally in late spring.

Dill doesn't need any plant feed; in fact extra nutrients will actually hinder the plant because it doesn't grow as bushy and will make it susceptible to insect attack. It does need watering in dry weather, particularly when young; once it's established, dill can tolerate a little neglect.

We've grown dill in a tyre filled with earth (see pages 154–5), but it can also be grown in deep containers (at least 30cm/12in deep). Keep it on a bright windowsill out of direct sunlight and stake it if necessary.

Fennel

Andy decided to plant some bronze fennel a year ago; the seed was 2 years out of date and so he expected no results. However, it all came up and this year he's finding it growing across the whole allotment.

Broadly speaking, there are two types of fennel: common fennel (including bronze fennel), which is a perennial that grows wild but is also cultivated for its seeds and leaves; and Florence fennel, which is an annual, grown for its bulb-like root that is used as a vegetable (see page 116). All parts of fennel are aromatic, with a taste reminiscent of aniseed. The feathery leaves complement fish dishes and the seeds are considered good for digestion.

Common fennel will grow in poor soil conditions and is fairly drought-resistant once established. Plant four seeds together, about 28cm (11in) apart and 2.5cm (1in) deep. Thin out the weaker plants and water in dry conditions. Three plants should be sufficient – they can grow very high.

As soon as the seeds turn from green to brown, tie a brown paper bag to each plant so that the seeds don't distribute themselves everywhere. We cut our plants back each year in autumn, leaving about 6cm (2½in) of growth. You can also divide them in spring and give the extra plants out to friends.

German chamomile flowers are dried and
used in calming infusions.

Garlic

Ideally when cultivating garlic you should use seed garlic bought from a garden centre, as this will reduce the chance of any disease. Andy has grown garlic from the bulbs that he bought at his local greengrocer, but the results can be disappointing, particularly if the garlic has been grown in a different climate (it may, for example, be an import from China).

Plant each clove about 5cm (2in) deep and 15cm (6in) apart. There's no need to peel it. Plant the garlic out either in late October/early November or in January/February, because it benefits from a cold snap; alternatively, if the winter is mild, you could put it in the freezer for a couple of days. Keep the planting area weed-free and water in hot, dry weather.

Garlic will tell you when it's ready – the top of the plant will die down and turn yellow. To lift garlic, put a fork underneath to prevent damaging the bulb. After harvesting, dry it in the sun before plaiting the tops together (see page 247) and then hang it in a shaded, dry area in the kitchen or a well-ventilated cupboard, shed or outbuilding. If none of your garlic grows, don't despair – on two occasions, Andy has planted garlic cloves to find that they've decided to wait a year until they grow.

Apparently it's possible to grow garlic in containers using a deep 30cm (12in) pot. We know of people who've done this successfully but every time we've tried the bulb has gone rotten. (For wild garlic or ramsons, see page 225.)

Marjoram

Many adult butterflies and bees are attracted to marjoram flowers, and as with many herbs you could consider growing it to aid pollination. It also makes a great addition to pizzas and if you put the stems on barbecue embers they will infuse your food with their flavour. Three types of marjoram are commonly grown for culinary use: wild marjoram (common oregano), sweet or knotted marjoram and pot-grown marjoram.

Sow wild marjoram from seed in containers in March or directly outside in April. Other marjorams, such as sweet marjoram, are frost tender when young and seedlings should be hardened off before planting out. Plant in well-drained, nutrient-rich soil for best results. In autumn, cut back the top two-thirds of the plant; you can dry out these 'offcuts' by hanging them in a well-ventilated room and use them over the winter months when fresh herbs aren't available.

Marjoram can also be grown in a 30cm (12in) container. Sow seed in spring in rich compost, water occasionally to ensure that it doesn't dry out and give a liquid feed 2 or 3 times a year.

Mint

Mint has to be one of the easiest plants to cultivate and it tends to grow in abundance. The leaves are delicious for making mint tea and in gin and tonics, and a handful of mint leaves added to your boiled potatoes while they're cooking infuses them with a delicate mint flavour.

We wouldn't recommend growing mint from seed. By far the easiest way to grow it is from the roots of an established plant. Ask your friends, family and on www.freecycle.org if they have any spare. As mint can be invasive, most growers will be happy to give you some, but if you can't obtain it this way, plants can easily be bought from a garden centre or even some local greengrocers.

To stop mint from spreading all over your plot, cut the bottom out of a deep bucket and dig it into the ground with a bit of a 'lip' sticking out. Plant the mint root into the bucket. It may try to set roots over the top of the lip; cut these back before they take to stop it from spreading.

Mint will generally endure a bit of neglect, although it benefits from watering in dry weather. As you might have gathered, mint loves to spread itself around and doesn't like being made to grow in one area for too long, so after 2 or 3 years dig up the roots and plant them elsewhere.

Mint will grow pretty well in a container for a season. Give it a largish pot to promote healthy growth, place it on a sunny windowsill and keep it moist (almost any compost will do). We've also grown mint by taking a 20cm (8in) sprig off an established plant, removing the bottom 15cm (6in) of leaves (and making tea with them) and putting the sprig into a glass of water. Then we waited until it started to grow roots and those roots began to grow more roots. It was then ready to plant.

Parsley

In Britain, parsley is frequently used as no more than a garnish. Andy was made fully aware of this when he was 15 years old and took a job that involved putting two small bits of parsley on hundreds of plates a day – it was as interesting as it sounds. Mediterranean and Middle-eastern cooks use it for much more than this, as it tastes delicious and is vitamin- and nutrient-rich. In one cup of parsley there is twice as much vitamin C as in an orange, 20 times more iron than in liver and more calcium than in a cup of milk. There are two main types: curled and Italian flat-leaf parsley.

We've grown parsley in window boxes and directly onto our plots. It's a relatively easy plant to cultivate and

Parsley is full of vitamins, iron and calcium.

with a bit of forward planning it can be enjoyed all year round. Although parsley can take up to 8 weeks to germinate, either indoors or outdoors, it generally starts to come up within about 4 weeks.

You can sow parsley all year round in containers, although it's better to sow it from spring to the end of summer. It needs between 6 and 8 hours of sunlight a day but tolerates a bit of shade. We tend not to be terribly precise when it comes to growing parsley in containers – empty half a packet evenly in a container, with some broken bits of crockery at the bottom and some compost. Cover the seeds with about 1cm (½in) more of compost. Thin out the weaker seedlings and don't let it dry out.

To grow parsley outside, plant in rows about a hand's width apart, three or four seeds at a time, between May and July or when there's little risk of frost. About four or five plants should be enough for most households. Advice often states that the soil should be well drained, but Andy has grown parsley successfully in thick, clay soil. Parsley will survive most winters but may well benefit from a little protection. Either cover plants with hay on colder nights or grow under glass. Those big plastic water bottles with the bottom cut off will also work as makeshift protection (see page 88).

Rosemary

Rosemary is an excellent herb for the kitchen and it's also a beneficial medicinal plant.

Rosemary seeds can take up to 3 months to germinate, and for us sometimes-impatient gardeners this is too long. However, if you do wish to grow rosemary from seed, start it off indoors in a dark room, because this will aid germination. Sow a liberal number of seeds in a pot, then cover them lightly with compost. The optimum soil temperature is around 15°C (59°F). When you have shoots that are about 10cm (4in) high, plant them out.

For faster results, take a semi-hardwood cutting from an existing 2- or 3-year-old plant between May and July. Cut a 10cm (4in) sprig of soft, new growth, and remove all the leaves from the bottom half of the sprig. Now make your choice as to how organic you wish to be. Some gardeners will say that using rooting hormone (available from most garden centres) is within the organic standards, while others consider it is not organic enough, but an excellent alternative to hormone rooting powder is willow tea (see box, left).

Sage

Homemade sage and onion stuffing is reason alone for growing this herb. Another good reason is that when sage is in full flower you'll see bees climbing all over the plant, so even if you don't like the taste you might consider growing it simply to help pollinate your vegetables.

Sage grows well from seed. Sow three or four seeds in a small container filled with multipurpose compost in early spring. Place it where there's plenty of sun and a constant temperature of 15–21°C (59–70°F). This is around normal room temperature, so anywhere that isn't too draughty will be fine. Water plants to stop them from drying out.

We tend to wait until June before planting out, as a late frost has killed off a few of our plants in the past. Plant on poor soil, on a patch that gets the sun and does not become waterlogged. Prune in spring and wrap straw around plants on very cold nights; better still, dig the plants up and bring them indoors.

Sage can be grown in a container but it won't reach its full potential. Keep changing the container to a bigger one as the plant grows – as a rule of thumb, it's time to repot as soon as the roots are peeking out of the bottom of the container.

WILLOW TEA

Willow tea is an ideal organic alternative to hormone rooting powder, used when propagating plants by cuttings.

To make the tea, get a handful of willow twigs (discard the leaves), cut them into 10cm (4in) pieces, put the twigs in a bowl and pour boiling water over them. Stand the cut end of your cutting overnight in the tea and transplant it to a pot filled with multipurpose compost, then water with the tea for a couple of days. Fresh cuttings should be kept inside for the first few weeks so that the roots have time to grow before they're either planted straight out or hardened off gradually.

Rosemary is easy to propagate from cuttings.

Sage and onion stuffing

This is a slight take on a classic recipe and is a great addition to a traditional Sunday lunch. The quantities below make enough stuffing for a large chicken. Or, if you're vegetarian or fancy a little accompaniment on your plate, you can work the mixture into stuffing balls, baking them until they're golden brown.

5 onions
10 sage leaves
3 slices of stale bread
1 tsp chopped chives
1 tsp chopped parsley
40g (1½oz) unsalted butter
1 egg yolk
Salt and pepper, to taste

1. Peel the onions and put them whole into a pan of boiling water. Simmer for about 5–10 minutes or until they start to soften. Throw in the sage leaves in the last 2 minutes.
2. Take the onions and sage out of the pan, chop them both finely and put them into a mixing bowl. Grate the stale bread and add the breadcrumbs, chives, parsley, butter, egg yolk and seasoning to the mixture.

Savory

Of the 30 different types of savory there are two that interest herb gardeners and chefs, namely winter and summer savory. Winter savory is a perennial and has a stronger, more peppery taste than summer savory, which is an annual with a sweeter, milder flavour. Use both to flavour dishes as you would with pepper.

Summer savory should be sown indoors from late winter to spring, in 9cm (3½in) pots filled with peat-free, multipurpose compost. Seedlings should be kept at around 18–20°C (64–68°F) for 3 weeks in order for

them to germinate. Harden off when plants are large enough to handle and plant out in well-drained, fertile soil in full sun.

For winter savory, sow seed in a greenhouse or under cover in April in 9cm (3½in) pots and don't allow the compost to dry out. In early summer, plant them out in a well-drained soil in full sun.

Sorrel

Sorrel leaves have a strong, tangy, sour taste. In days gone by, hay-makers would eat wild sorrel to quench their thirst. There are several varieties of sorrel, most of which grow wild, but the variety known as French sorrel is milder and is the type grown for culinary use.

Sorrel is sometimes eaten like spinach, with the addition of eggs, butter or cream to complement the sharp flavour. It's also delicious in soup, and a few young leaves will liven up a green salad, giving it zing.

Sorrel can be sown directly into the ground in spring. Sow seeds 2–3cm (¾–1¼in) deep and 15cm (6in) apart in well-drained, acidic, fertile soil. Andy sowed his 3 years ago and has pretty much neglected it, yet it continues to thrive; as with beet spinach, if you cut the leaves they will keep growing back (but don't strip the plant of all its leaves).

Tarragon

Tarragon was thought by the ancient Greeks to ward off dragon attack, but even if you don't have trouble with dragons tarragon is well worth growing as a culinary herb. It's best used fresh, and gives an excellent flavour to many recipes, especially chicken, fish and egg dishes. There are two main types of tarragon: French (sometimes known as German) tarragon and the weaker-tasting but

easier-to-grow Russian tarragon. Tarragon requires well-drained soil and prefers full sun or partial shade. To grow French tarragon, we'd suggest you buy a small plant or plant a cutting, as it cannot be grown successfully from seed. Russian tarragon can be grown from seed planted in pots of multipurpose compost on a windowsill in the spring. Plant tarragon outdoors when the risk of frost has passed. The leaves can be harvested after it's been growing outdoors for about 2 months.

Thyme

Thyme goes with almost everything, and as it doesn't mind being walked on it can be grown in the cracks of paving slabs or in gravel. We've raised thyme successfully from seed, and as creeping and common thyme have a better germination rate we'd suggest growing one of these two varieties rather than any others. Sow the seeds in multipurpose compost in early spring indoors, at around 15–21°C (59–70°F). Don't over-water, as seedlings are prone to damping off (mould), and leave them uncovered. Get the plants used to the outdoors before planting them out by leaving them outside during the day for 2 weeks and taking them in at night. Plant out when the danger of frost has passed.

Thyme actually prefers a poor soil to one that is rich in nutrients. It also thrives in dry conditions and is an excellent drought-resistant plant. It benefits from a sunny position. A few plants spaced about 20cm (8in) apart will ensure ground cover for the following year, keeping weeds away.

If sowing thyme involves too much work, it can be bought from a garden centre. Instead of getting one big plant, try for a few different varieties, such as the mild-tasting lemon thyme.

Sage is grown for cooking and for its medicinal properties.

10 WILD HERBS TO GROW AT HOME FOR ONE SEASON

Agrimony
Alexanders
Chervil
Good King Henry
Great burnet
Horseradish
Sorrel
Sweet Cicely
Tansy
Yarrow

Seeds of most of these herbs are difficult to come by and you'll be unlikely to find them at your local garden centre. Instead, you'll need to find specialist seed merchants. We buy from Nicky's Nursery (www.nickys-nursery.co.uk) and Suffolk Herbs (www.suffolkherbs.com).

Wild herbs

There are numerous herbs that are not commonly grown in the herb garden because they grow prolifically in the wild. Our ancestors used some of these herbs regularly, for cooking or for medicinal reasons, but these days we seem to have lost the art of identifying some of the most common plants in our country.

Whenever we look up a wild herb we've found on the internet or in a book, it's not always clear if the plant that we've found fits the description. For this reason, we decided to grow at least two different wild herbs each year, so we could become familiar with the native plants that grow around us. When you grow a plant you can see what it looks like at every stage of its growth, from seedling to full flower. Armed with this knowledge, it's far easier to distinguish a poisonous plant from an edible one.

The best example of a herb that grows prolifically in the wild is chervil. It's a versatile herb that gives a kick to salads and it grows in abundance in the British Isles. The delights of chervil were unknown to us until this year, because we were too scared to pick it as it can be mistaken for fool's parsley or hemlock, both of which are poisonous (Socrates was reported to have been poisoned by hemlock).

Pick herbs only if you can be absolutely certain of their identity and never pick very young plants, because at this stage in their growth it can be hard to distinguish whether they're poisonous or non-poisonous plants. Also avoid picking wild herbs that might have been sprayed or are close to busy roads.

FREEZING HERBS

The easiest way to preserve herbs is to freeze them. First, plunge them into hot water for 5 seconds (you don't need to do this with chives, dill and parsley). Then get an ice-cube tray, put a few leaves of your selected herbs in, fill with water and freeze. Drop the cubes into soups or stews or defrost the herbs if using for a salad dressing.

Ten herbs that can be frozen

Bay
Chervil
Coriander
Dill
Fennel (leaves)
Mint
Parsley
Salad burnet
Tarragon
Thyme

Wild yarrow makes a good herbal infusion.

MAKING NEWSPAPER POTS

Newspaper pots are one of the self-sufficientish basics, as they make use of an item that might otherwise be thrown away. Anyone who uses public transport in a major British city will never be short of finding the materials as free papers seem to carpet every bus and train. Newspaper pots are excellent for plants that do not like having their roots disturbed, such as coriander or parsley, as the whole pot can be planted into the ground. Newspaper ink is generally made with vegetable dyes, so the whole pot biodegrades into the soil.

1. Fold one double sheet of newspaper down the centre fold, then fold in half again so that you have a long, narrow piece.

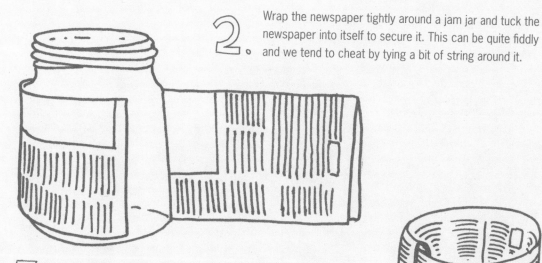

2. Wrap the newspaper tightly around a jam jar and tuck the newspaper into itself to secure it. This can be quite fiddly and we tend to cheat by tying a bit of string around it.

3. Slip the jar out from the paper covering and you'll be left with a cylindrical paper tube.

4. To make the base of the pot, take another page of a broadsheet or a full double-page spread of a tabloid newspaper and screw it up into a ball. Put the ball inside the cylindrical tube and press down with the jar to pack it in firmly. Repeatedly press down if the pot seems to wobble when left standing. For added strength, tie a piece of string around the pot and pack a few tightly together on a tray so they support each other.

5. Fill with potting compost and plant seeds, as you would with a normal pot. Place on a saucer or tray if you've made a number of pots. The pots will not withstand over-watering, so avoid planting anything that requires a lot of water in its early stages.

6. When the seedlings are ready they can be planted out. When planting, line up the soil in the pot with the outside soil and cut off the remaining 'lip'. The newspaper will rot away and the root need not be disturbed.

SMALL-SPACE KITCHEN GARDENS

Many people in towns and cities are keen to grow their own organic produce, but with land at a premium a garden is a luxury rather than the norm and allotments can be extremely hard to come by. However, the lack of a garden or an allotment doesn't mean that you won't be able to grow your own food. With a bit of ingenuity and careful planning, even the most unlikely areas can become productive growing spaces. All a plant really needs is soil or compost to grow in (whether in the ground or a container), sunlight and water.

There are plenty of spaces in and around our house or block of flats that we often forget about – the less obvious areas where, with a bit of imagination, you could consider growing vegetables. Dave worked as a postman for a time in Oxford, and during his rounds he was frequently amazed by the number of different ways people found to grow their vegetables in the town – he remembers looking up at a flat where French beans snaked their way up the supports of a balcony, and surrounding the beans were pots and pots of

tomatoes, lettuces and all kinds of vegetables shoe-horned into an area no bigger than the average bath. Once you're determined to grow your own, you'll discover you start thinking quite differently about your living space – the container full of cooking utensils will find a new home as you squeeze basil and chilli plants onto the sunny window ledge in the kitchen, you'll clear tables to accommodate a small potted herb garden, and the fire escape at the back of your flat now seems the perfect place to grow tomatoes.

As well as being an inexpensive way of producing organic food, growing your own vegetables will bring cheer to even the gloomiest of places – there are few people who wouldn't rather see a bee pollinating their home-grown beans than a grey, lifeless patch of concrete. There's also the satisfaction factor: we've both found that growing vegetables or fruit in what can seem like adverse circumstances is infinitely more rewarding than harvesting produce from a well-tended garden or allotment, and the look on guests' faces when you tell them that the salad they're tucking into was grown from scratch in a window box can be priceless.

Metal balconies can make ideal growing places, the balcony supports providing an excellent substitute for traditional bamboo poles. On larger balconies or roof terraces you can erect a mini-greenhouse. These are very inexpensive to buy nowadays and consist simply of a stack of metal shelves with a plastic covering. They do have a tendency to fall over, so try to secure them to the wall, particularly if you're high up or in areas that lack shelter from strong winds. Hanging baskets are also a good choice for balconies, because they don't take up much room and the balcony can still be used to enjoy the summer sun.

Stairwells can be ideal places for growing vegetables – the bonus is that there's no need for guide wires or a trellis, because the banisters or railings provide the structure the plants need. Many outdoor stairwells are ideal for vigorous climbers such as grapes and kiwis, and figs and citrus fruit could be grown in a sunny indoor stairwell. Bear in mind people's safety and don't block the stairs.

If you're fortunate enough to own a porch, make the most of it by growing fruit and vegetables there: in the height of summer, a porch can be hotter than many purpose-built greenhouses, especially if it's south-facing and has glass doors. Herbs and compact-growing vegetables in pots, such as a few tomato plants, are ideal for this small area. A porch can also be a prime spot for starting off seedlings. The temperature can drop overnight, so be careful with more tender plants.

GROWING IN CONTAINERS

Just about any plant can be grown in a container, provided its roots are given enough space and it is adequately watered and fed. Often the only outdoor space available for flat dwellers is a window box or windowsill, or for those in a town house just a patch of concrete or a tiny patio at the back. It's in these situations that containers really come into their own. Containers can also be used indoors, which makes them ideal for people in flats without any outdoor space at all.

Herbs and tomatoes do particularly well indoors. You may have to self-pollinate the tomatoes, taking pollen from a friend's outdoor-grown tomato plant. You do this simply by rubbing a small cotton bud in the flower of the outdoor tomato and then rubbing the inside of the indoor tomato with the same cotton bud. Alternatively, if you place tomato plants by an open window a passing bee might do the job for you, as it did for Andy's plants once.

Another great bonus of container gardening is that you can move the pots around. You can place them where the plants will catch the sun at different times of the day and bring them indoors over winter if necessary. Also, if you're on a short lease somewhere, you can simply pick up your 'vegetable garden' and take it to your new place. There's a regular visitor to our website whose entire 'allotment' is made up of nothing but fruit and vegetables grown inside 2-litre milk cartons he's cut into pots. We've seen the results of this and for certain crops it's very impressive –

some of the root vegetables, such as carrots, could perhaps do with larger containers but his leafier, more shallow-rooted vegetables, such as lettuces, fare extremely well using this method, and the great thing is his allotment is completely portable.

Recycled containers

Garden centres nowadays sell a vast range of pots, window boxes, tubs and troughs of all shapes and sizes and made from a variety of materials. They can be highly decorative and are usually frost-proof, but attractive as these pots often are they're frequently imported and can be costly. There's no reason why you can't grow plants in any number of containers you have lying around in your house or garage. Almost any kind of container possessing adequate drainage holes can be used for planting – we've seen sunflowers growing out of a car engine and a lettuce thriving in a discarded old shoe.

Growing in containers other than flowerpots not only saves you money, it also has the advantage of preventing more containers from ending up in landfill sites. It seems extraordinary to us that people buy products almost identical to those that they throw away – yogurt pots, for example, are of comparable size to the majority of flowerpots, and with the addition of a few drainage holes they are practically identical, yet thousands of yogurt pots are discarded every year and thousands of plastic flowerpots are bought. Some other examples of containers that can be used for growing vegetables and herbs are Tetra Pak and milk cartons and plastic bottles – if cut in half, these are all ideal for growing seedlings and small plants. If you're planning a herb garden you could use half-barrels, wooden fruit-packing crates, Belfast sinks and old tyres (see pages 154–5), as well as window boxes or small pots on the windowsill. For larger plants, such as courgettes and squash, half-barrels and old baby baths are ideal. Remember to make drainage holes in the base of whatever container you intend to use.

Courgettes grow happily in large tubs, sinks and baths.

Where to find containers

🌶 A good place to start looking for containers is in a local skip, but do ensure you ask the owner of the skip first. Dave successfully cultivated a herb garden in an old Belfast sink that had been discarded this way.

🌶 www.freecycle.org is another good place to start. Freecycle is an online community in which people advertise items they no longer need, or ask for items that would otherwise be destined to end up in a landfill site. With members now reaching their thousands, it's well worth checking this out before you decide to buy anything.

🌶 There are websites such as eBay that sell items such as half-barrels. Also, if you live near a distillery it's always worth asking if they have barrels they're willing to give away or sell to you.

🌶 Some local tips offer cheap discarded items. There's one near where we grew up in Northampton, where the owner of the yard used to deliberate for ages over the cost and value of the item and then in a broad Northamptonian accent would scratch his chin and say, 'That will be £5, me ducks.'

🌶 Reclamation yards more often than not sell half-barrels. However, these places are usually at the top end of the recycled-goods chain, so the quality of their merchandise is often excellent but they will sell to you at a premium.

🌶 You can make your own pots out of old newspaper (see pages 168–9). These are ideal for plants that dislike having their roots disturbed. Seed is sown in the newspaper pot and then the seedlings are transferred to the open soil. The pot rots down over time, leaving the plant's roots intact.

Container-growing tips

Provided you stick to the following tips you can grow plants in nearly any available container.

🌶 Ensure you clean the pot or container thoroughly before planting. This is because unwashed pots can carry diseases and transmit fungi from previous occupants.

🌶 Make sure there's adequate drainage by cutting a hole in the base of the pot if it doesn't already have one. For a small pot, this should be around the size of a 10p piece, but for anything bigger (i.e. a dinner-plate-sized container or larger) cut four or so holes at regular intervals.

🌶 For larger pots, some plants will do better with added ballast to aid drainage. Line the base of the container with broken crockery or small stones before filling it with potting compost. This will stop the roots from becoming sodden and reduce the likelihood of rotting.

🌶 Choose varieties that won't outgrow the container. Check the seed packet or gardening books to ensure you pick the right variety. The seed packet should give you an idea of how far apart to sow or plant the vegetable outdoors, so use this as a guideline to the size of the pot.

🌶 Water regularly to ensure the plant doesn't dry out. Container-grown vegetables need a bit more attention in terms of watering than their open-ground counterparts. If you're going away, try to get a friend or neighbour to water them for you. Or, as a very last resort, insert a full inverted plastic water bottle with the lid removed into the soil – the water should slowly seep into the pot over time, keeping the water level in the pot topped up. To check if this is working, see if air bubbles are slowly being released into the bottle – if they are, this means air is being released from the soil into the bottle and being exchanged for water.

🌶 Pot-grown plants will need an extra feed from time to time, so apply a homemade liquid feed of seaweed, comfrey or nettle (see page 83), liquid from a wormery (see pages 57–8) or organic liquid feed from the garden centre. Comfrey feed is a little pongy, so it's not ideal for vegetables grown on balconies or windowsills.

🌶 Choose vegetables that you really like to eat – it may seem an obvious statement, but you'd be amazed at how many people grow vegetables that are easy to grow but they can't stand the taste of.

Windowsill plots

Every year we start our seedlings off on all the available windowsills in the house. To germinate, seeds need to be fooled into believing the soil is warming up and the sunlight is returning, just as it would outside in spring. Often there's a radiator under the windowsill, which will heat the soil, but even if there isn't, the soil temperature in the pots will still be considerably warmer than if they were outside, especially if they were planted in the ground. Sunlight coming in through the window will heat the soil and as the seedlings are pre-programmed to head towards the light they will do the rest for you. To prevent lots of mess, place newspaper under the pots and put a tray beneath for the water to drain into. It might also be worth slightly under-filling the pots to keep spillages to a minimum.

We've started off corn, cucumbers, beans, tomatoes, courgettes, pumpkins and numerous other vegetables on a windowsill. Ideally, place a table in front of the sill, so you have space for a number of seed trays. If you have a long, narrow windowsill you could use a length of guttering for sowing seeds – we've seen carrots grown like this, simply sown in regular potting compost down the length of the pipe. Once the foliage reaches about 5cm (2in) high, the guttering is lifted from the windowsill and the plants can be placed in an equal-sized 'groove' on an outside plot. Some varieties of chilli peppers also do very well on a windowsill. As with other vegetables, check the packet first to see the eventual size of the plant. Some varieties will grow no bigger than the average pot plant but others can shoot up and range above the height of the window.

An outdoor or indoor windowsill can also make an excellent herb garden. Depending on the width of the sill, this can be a large trough with a mixture of herbs or a series of individual pots. The trough or pot should be 15–30cm (6–12in) deep and a mixture of herbs can be grown quite easily – basil, parsley, chives, French tarragon and marjoram will all do well together and give you a good selection for cooking. You'll need to repot herbs at least once a year if you're to be sure of a continuous supply (except for parsley and coriander, which don't repot well). Many are annuals, so will die off anyway, and the perennials, such as sage and rosemary, are best replaced with new plants as they'll grow too big for a windowsill, although they'd be happy growing on outside. Unlike the more sun-worshipping herbs, such as basil and marjoram, sage and rosemary can tolerate a shady or north-facing windowsill.

A bright windowsill is an ideal place for growing lettuces and herbs.

VERTICAL GARDENING

There are many ways to get round the problem of having very little outdoor space – you just have to be slightly more inventive and use all the dimensions available. By this we don't mean using a strange sci-fi method of growing in a wormhole, we're talking about growing vertically – up walls, fences, wigwams, pergolas, arches and arbours, rather than growing horizontally along the ground in beds and borders.

Vertical gardening is a trick that gardeners with limited space have used for years and it can be extremely effective. Plants can either be grown in pots with a wigwam (three canes dug into a pot and tied together at the top), or they can be planted in a patch of soil and trained up a wire mesh or a framework of training wires.

Growing against a wall

A wall provides excellent support for climbing plants, which can be attached using training wires, netting or trellis. Fruit is often grown against a wall, attached to wires and sometimes trained as cordons, espaliers or in a fan shape. Tree fruit, soft-fruit bushes, vines and some vegetables can all be trained against a vertical surface. Walls are particularly useful for growing slightly tender plants that originate from a warmer climate, such as a peach, because the wall absorbs heat from the sun during the day and releases warmth at night, providing shelter for the plant and helping to ripen the fruit. Vertical growing like this will also cover up any unsightly brickwork or fencing and is a highly decorative way to display plants.

The height at which you fix training wires, trellis and netting depends on what you're planting. Many plants, for example cucumbers, grow up to about 30cm (12in) or so before they need to attach to something. Some training might be needed to attach them to the wires initially, and you can always put in more wires above the first as the plant grows. Trellis and netting are good alternatives to training wires and they can be used year after year for most climbing plants. For peas and runner beans, a wire mesh might be better than training wires.

Wall-mounted training wires are very simple to fix and you can use the same method to put up a net or trellis for your climbing plants. First, drill a hole in the wall using a masonry drill big enough to put a screw-plug into, then hammer in the screw-plug and insert the screw. For trellis and netting, insert a small block between the wall and the trellis to allow the plant to 'breathe'. Attach the training wire/netting/trellis to the screws and trim any loose ends once you're sure the support is in place.

BAMBOO CANES + ALTERNATIVES

Plant-support canes are usually made of bamboo, which is a renewable crop because it grows back quickly when cut, but there are environmental issues to consider (see Furniture, page 16). Make sure you buy it from a reputable company, such as www.ukbamboosupplies.com, which sells bamboo from a sustainable source.

For a more environmentally friendly and sturdy alternative, you may want to use local hazel poles (simply long, straight poles made from coppiced hazel trees). They can be harder to source, but have the benefit of having been grown in Britain. For a first port of call, you could try your local wildlife trust or woodland estate manager. Also try www.allotmentforestry.com, as they have a list of over 250 different regional organizations that sell products from managed woodland, including hazel poles which are ideal for bean sticks (see page 97).

FRUIT + VEGETABLES FOR SMALL SPACES

Certain types of fruit and vegetables are more suitable than others for growing in containers or vertically. We've tried growing a number in this way and have had success with the ones described below. Some are actually better grown in containers, because you can move them indoors or under glass before frost strikes, while others are more suited to the open ground, climbing up a wall or fence.

Beans

French beans, runner beans

Runner beans and French beans are good plants for growing vertically, either in pots with a wigwam-style support or against a wall, provided there is some kind of guide wire, trellis or netting. They're also ideal for growing up and over arbours, pergolas and arches. Beans benefit from sowing indoors; leave them on a windowsill and plant them out in May or June. They should be ready to harvest by July or August (sometimes June in the case of French beans) and can be harvested right up until early October in some cases. (See also pages 116 and 122.)

Beetroot

The shallow roots of beetroot make it suitable for growing in containers, although it won't grow as large as its ground-grown counterpart. The leaves can be used for salads and the roots can be harvested while they're still young and tender. Sow under cover in February or March, about 10cm (4in) apart. Harvest the roots from June to October and the tops for salads as soon as they're large enough. It may seem an obvious point, but if you want to have salad leaves and roots don't remove all the leaves – the plant still needs them to grow. (See also page 110.)

Carrots

Carrots can be grown in pots on patios, balconies or even windowsills in full sun or partial shade. They will do best in deep pots; if planting in a relatively shallow container, use the rounded, 'globe' types, which are more like a beetroot in shape, because they have shallower roots than traditional carrots.

Carrots can be sown from February up until June depending on the variety, so check the packets to see when is best. Sow them either in the pot at 2.5cm (1in) intervals or broadcast across the pot. For both methods, thin out the seedlings, leaving 5–7.5cm (2–3in) between them. The compost should be kept moist, so water regularly and apply a mulch. Carrots are ready to harvest between July and December; you could harvest them young for a sweet crop of baby carrots, ideal for salads and stir fries. (See also page 112.)

Courgettes

For a long time, we were under the impression that courgettes and other squash needed a lot of soil and it would be impossible to grow them in containers, but we changed our point of view when we saw courgettes growing happily in old baby baths. Courgettes can be quite shallow-rooted plants and as long as they

have enough room to spread, lots of water and sunshine and are well fed there's no reason why they can't be grown in a container. For a regular supply, don't let the courgettes grow too big, as the plant will put its energy into that one fruit rather than producing more, and it will become a marrow. Several varieties of courgette can be grown vertically and require some form of support such as a trellis or wire fence. Courgettes are sown indoors in April or outdoors between mid-May and early June; harvest fruits between July and September or even October in some cases. (See also page 115.)

Cucumbers

Dave planted some outdoor cucumbers (also known as ridge cucumbers) in pots on the patio one year and others in a bed at the back of the vegetable garden. The ones in pots had room to grow horizontally, spilling out from the pots and trailing across the ground, and those planted in the bed were trained up the wall, using guide wires and chicken wire that were already in place for an established grapevine. The two plants seemed to co-exist quite happily, with the cucumber snaking around the grapevine. Cucumbers may need to be tied before they can be encouraged to grow upwards, but

Squash growing up a bamboo wigwam.

once they're established the tendrils will cling on to most things and they make for a very sturdy climber. The cucumbers planted in the open ground did slightly better than the pot-grown ones, but there was a good crop from both. Cucumbers do need a lot of water, so water regularly and apply a liquid feed fortnightly, whether growing in pots or in the ground. They may take a while to start fruiting but should be ready to harvest from July or August until October. (See also page 116.)

Figs

Figs can be bought as established, container-grown plants at any time of year. For best results and more fruit, place containers next to a sunny, south-facing wall, and during the coldest months bring them indoors if you can. Grow them in well-drained compost that is not over-rich, as this will just promote leaf growth rather than fruit. (See also page 139.)

Lemons

Lemons are the easiest of all citrus fruits to grow. Although frost tender, they can be grown outdoors in Britain in containers, provided they're brought indoors over winter in frost-prone areas, or have some other form of frost protection. They need a warm, sunny, sheltered spot to thrive, a large container, at least 60cm (24in) in diameter, and well-drained, slightly acidic compost.

Regular feeding with a specialist citrus feed will encourage more fruit. Sow seed in spring or invest in an already-established plant in spring. The downside of sowing seed is that you can't determine the size of the tree – some lemon trees can grow to 6m (20ft) or more. Also, it can take up to 12 years before they bear fruit. Lemons are usually ready to harvest in January or February.

Melons

Melons are generally quite large plants, but there are compact varieties available such as 'Minnesota Midget' or 'Musketeer' that can be grown in large pots (the containers must be at least 60cm/24in deep). Other varieties of melon are ideal for growing up a south-facing wall. Melons benefit from being sown indoors around April, then being hardened off before planting outdoors. If putting them in the open ground, plant seedlings in a soil mound about 30cm (12in) high.

As with cucumbers, melons use tendrils to cling to a surface once established, but they need tying in and some form of support when young. Melons will trail, but if you're growing them vertically the fruits sometimes need additional support. Smaller varieties are usually fine, but many gardeners use a melon net for larger types, to support the fruit and stop it from falling before it's fully ripe. You can make your own melon net out of recycled materials, using a mesh onion or orange bag wrapped around the fruit and tied on to the trellis or wire.

The fruit should start to appear in August and September, but don't be tempted to harvest it until it's fully ripe. To test for ripeness, lightly push on the top: if it gives a little, the melon should be ready. An early frost can damage the fruit, so try to harvest before this or cover with horticultural fleece at the first sign of cold weather.

Onions and shallots

Onions can be sown from seed, but it's considerably quicker (although slightly more expensive) to grow them from sets (small immature bulbs, already grown from seed). Plant sets 10cm (4in) apart in containers of

well-drained, enriched compost (preferably well-rotted garden compost from your bin, though most potting compost should suffice) and position them in full sun. For smaller containers, shallots are ideal.

There are two main growing seasons for onions: most are planted in spring for late summer or autumn harvest and others can be planted in autumn, which will be ready in the spring. Autumn-planted varieties are commonly the larger Japanese onion, but there's also a first early variety. If you prefer to grow onions from seed, sow them in small pots indoors from midwinter and transfer seedlings to larger pots in early spring. (See also page 118.)

Peas

Peas are happy in the open ground or in containers, but as they climb they need a form of support, such as chicken wire, a wigwam, a specialist pea net or pea sticks. Pea sticks are just deadwood branches with many side branches or shoots coming off them to allow the pea plant to cling on to something as it grows. Peas prefer full sun but will grow in partial shade.

Some pea varieties can be sown as early as March or April for an early June or July crop – these are known as first early varieties; after these, in April, the second earlies are sown for harvesting in July, then the maincrops are sown in May and are ready in August. Rather confusingly, the first earlies can be sown again in June for a crop in September or October.

It's worth starting peas off in what is known as a pea collar (see overleaf), because peas don't like their roots to be disturbed. You can buy specially made pea collars, but they're very easily made from Tetra Pak juice cartons or plastic milk bottles. (See also page 121.)

HOW TO MAKE A PEA COLLAR

Peas benefit from sowing in a pea collar: it makes transplanting easier and protects against pests.

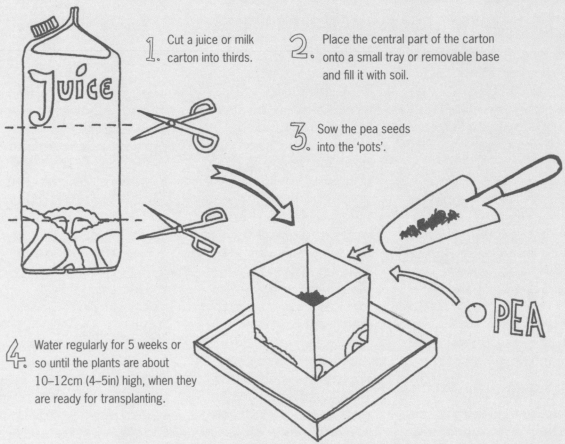

1. Cut a juice or milk carton into thirds.

2. Place the central part of the carton onto a small tray or removable base and fill it with soil.

3. Sow the pea seeds into the 'pots'.

PEA

4. Water regularly for 5 weeks or so until the plants are about 10–12cm (4–5in) high, when they are ready for transplanting.

5. Dig a hole in the soil or compost if transplanting to a container – the size of the hole should be the same size as the pea collar. Lift the plant (in its collar) from the tray and place it in the hole.

6. Ease the collar up over the plant. Don't remove it completely, as it can double up as protection against the pea and bean weevil. This should be left on for the whole of the pea plant's life.

The tendrils of peas will twine around wire mesh or other support as they grow.

Peppers
Chilli peppers, bell peppers
Although chilli peppers are often classed as a spice, they're really a fruit and, together with bell peppers, belong to the *Capsicum* genus of the Solanaceae family. Both chilli peppers and bell peppers grow well in containers, in well-watered, enriched compost in a sheltered, warm spot. Put them outside in May or June (if you start them off on an indoor windowsill you'll extend the season) and bring the plants indoors when the weather gets colder. On one rare occasion, Dave had a chilli plant that survived the winter on an outdoor, south-facing windowsill. Harvest in late summer to mid-autumn.

Pumpkins
and squash
Pumpkins and squash are very hungry plants, so they're not ideal for container growing. However, they can be grown vertically. On Dave's old allotment in Oxford, he made a trellis fence one year and had a trailing pumpkin plant growing up it quite happily. As with melons, the bigger pumpkin fruits need some support while growing (see page 179). Sow pumpkin seeds indoors in April, May or June, to plant out in June or July. Harvest in August, September or early October. (See also page 124.)

Radishes
Radishes are very fast croppers that are ready in just 10 weeks, so they're excellent for first-time growers. They grow well in most compost types and can even do well in ordinary, unenriched garden soil. Sow in pots (inside or out) from March and then plant continually every few weeks until late summer for successive crops. (See also page 122.)

Salad leaves
A mix of salad leaves can be grown in a hanging basket or window box, and having some physical distance from the ground should go some way in preventing attack from slugs. Once they're established, very little care is needed. There's such a wide choice of salad leaves, including winter varieties. Most can be planted in spring but check the seed packet for the particular variety you wish to grow. For best results, sow them indoors and take the containers outside after the danger of frost has passed. Alternatively, leave them to grow on a windowsill. Dave has successfully grown lettuces on the windowsill of a third-floor flat using a largish flowerpot for each lettuce. (See also page 118.)

Strawberries
Strawberries are best grown from established plants and can be placed in a strawberry planter to protect the fruit from slugs. They tolerate full sun and full shade but need adequate organic matter. Strawberries will propagate from runners in a similar way to spider plants. Hold down the daughter plants sent off by the runners with a hairpin or twist of wire into a compost-filled pot. Once the roots are established, the runner can be severed. It's best to propagate strawberries after they've fruited. Plant new strawberry plants between March and May. (See also pages 148, 150–1.)

Tomatoes
Tomatoes don't take up much space and can be grown against a wall or in containers in a sunny spot on a balcony, garden or patio. Seeds can be started indoors as early as January if the temperature stays relatively high

and constant, although March is a more usual sowing time. Ideally, maintain a temperature of around 18–20°C (64–68°F). Sow tomatoes in a seed tray filled with multipurpose (peat-free) compost at around 1cm (½in) apart, then thin out individually into bigger pots or old yogurt pots with five small holes in the bottom. Wait until they look like they're outgrowing their pots before transferring them to their final spot.

Tomatoes can be grown in containers outdoors or indoors, although you'll need to pollinate them if they're grown indoors. They'll have a longer growing period indoors and if you started them off in January you could have crops throughout the summer into autumn. If you have very little space you may wish to consider planting determinate varieties of cherry tomatoes, which are perfect for hanging baskets. Alternatively, you could grow tomatoes in grow bags on a balcony. Each grow bag will support two or three plants.

If growing tomatoes in containers, ensure you water them regularly and feed the plants at least once a week with comfrey feed (see page 83), organic tomato feed or liquid feed obtained from a wormery (see pages 57–8). (See also page 125.)

Strategically placed mirrors will reflect light onto plants and make small spaces appear larger.

3.
FOOD

SEASONAL COOKING

Food in season always tastes far superior to the offerings available year round in the supermarket. These out-of-season, imported fruit and vegetables – whether an under-ripe, polytunnel-grown Spanish tomato in spring, a bland New Zealand apple in summer or an insipid Egyptian strawberry at Christmas – are disappointing at best, and lack not only taste but also nutritional value. Importing foods across the globe also makes no sense when you consider the impact of carbon emissions and ever-depleting oil reserves. Fortunately, the growing number of farmers' markets indicates that the benefits of locally produced, seasonal foods are gradually beginning to enter the mainstream.

It's testament to our growing awareness of food that many people are choosing to eat meat and fish in season. Year-round, battery-farmed frozen imports simply cannot compare in flavour with fresh meat that is sourced locally, such as an organic free-range turkey allowed to reach maturity as nature intended, or the first lamb of the season in spring. It does seem extraordinary that we continue to fly lamb all the way from New Zealand to serve at our dinner tables when a country such as Wales contains more sheep than human inhabitants. Fresh fish is also infinitely

better than frozen and we should source locally caught fish whenever possible, avoiding the spawning season in order to give the stocks time to recover.

In this chapter we've provided a selection of our favourite seasonal recipes for every month of the year. Vegetables and fruit are the main ingredients, because we grow these on our allotment and we're frequently experimenting with new ways of using up a glut of one particular vegetable. However, some of our recipes include meat or fish (Andy's additions, as Dave's a vegetarian).

RECIPES FOR SPRING

MARCH

In season

Beet spinach

Broccoli (sprouting)

Brussels sprouts

Cabbages

Cauliflowers

Celeriac

Kale

Leeks

Rhubarb

Swedes

Kale and leek with tagliatelle

A well-managed vegetable plot or organic veg-box scheme will no doubt have two vegetables in common during the early part of the year – leeks and kale. Thankfully, they do go together quite well and can be very easy to prepare. For a meaty option, add a little chopped ham.

Serves 3–4 as a light meal

300g (10oz) tagliatelle (preferably green)

Knob of butter

2 medium leeks, chopped

200–250g (7–8oz) young tender kale, shredded

Large pinch of nutmeg

Twist of black pepper

Shavings of Parmesan cheese

1. Cook the tagliatelle as per the packet instructions.
2. On a moderate heat, melt the butter and fry the chopped leeks.
3. Add the shredded kale and cook over a low heat, stirring well, until it is wilted but still retains a little crunch. Add the nutmeg and pepper.
4. Serve with the shavings of Parmesan cheese.

Steamed sprouting broccoli
with lemon dressing

Fresh purple or white sprouting broccoli needs little adding in the way of flavourings and we often put small amounts in salads to give them extra crunch. The simple dressing in this recipe lends itself to all kinds of tender vegetables. As well as sprouting broccoli it complements new potatoes, French beans and asparagus. You can make it with butter for a richer sauce or olive oil as a healthier alternative.

Serves 4 as a starter or side dish

750g (1½lb) purple or white sprouting broccoli

2 tbsp olive oil or a large knob of butter

1 tbsp lemon juice

Twist of black pepper

1. Steam the broccoli or cook it in a little water for about 3 minutes until tender but still slightly crisp.
2. If using olive oil, mix it with the lemon juice and black pepper. If using butter, first melt it, then add the lemon juice and pepper.
3. Drizzle the butter or olive oil dressing over the broccoli.

APRIL

In season

Broccoli (sprouting)

Cabbages

Kale

Lettuces

Onions

Radishes

Rhubarb

Wild garlic (ramsons)

Spring salad

A crisp spring salad can be the perfect antidote to all those heavy winter meals. Any available leaves can be mixed together and April is the perfect time to start adding wild leaves such as sorrel, wild garlic or hairy bittercress (see pages 222–5). If you've managed to store some carrots they make an excellent addition to this recipe, grated, providing an added boost of beta-carotene.

Serves 2–4 as a side dish

½ small lettuce or equivalent in mixed leaves

Bunch of American land cress

Mustard cress or hairy bittercress

2–3 wild garlic leaves (optional)

½ red onion

For the dressing

1 tsp mustard

1 tbsp olive oil

½ tbsp white wine/cider vinegar
**   (or malt vinegar with a pinch of sugar)**

Purple sprouting broccoli is delicious with a buttery lemon dressing.

1. Chop the lettuce, chop or snip the cress with scissors, and shred the wild garlic leaves, if using.
2. Finely slice the red onion.
3. Put all the vegetables into a salad bowl and mix together thoroughly.
4. In a small bowl, make the dressing: mix the mustard, olive oil and vinegar together with a fork. Pour the dressing over the salad and serve.

Crunchy cabbage stir fry

If you've got a vegetable patch or an allotment or are getting a veg box delivered, the chances are by April you'll be crying out for new ways of cooking cabbage. Fortunately, it's quite a versatile vegetable. Among other things it can be made into soup, cooked with spices and vinegar as a tasty side dish, or it can be stuffed or used as a substitute for vine leaves in Greek dolmas.

This cabbage stir fry can be a complete meal with rice or noodles, or you could add other vegetables, meat or tofu. The toasted sesame seeds make an excellent garnish for all sorts of stir-fried dishes.

Serves 2
¼ head of spring cabbage
2 carrots
1 red onion
A little rapeseed oil, for frying
1 tbsp sesame seeds
2–3 tsp light soy sauce
Splash of Tabasco

1. Shred the cabbage, removing the hard stems and saving them for the compost or making vegetable stock. Slice the carrots and red onion into thin strips.
2. Fry the vegetables in a little oil until softened but still slightly crunchy (around 5 minutes).
3. To toast the sesame seeds, place them in a dry frying pan set over a moderate heat, cover the pan with a lid or plate (the seeds sometimes pop everywhere, like popcorn) and keep shaking the pan so they don't burn. Toast the seeds until they're golden brown (this usually takes a few minutes).
4. Add the soy sauce and Tabasco to the vegetables, then sprinkle on the toasted sesame seeds before serving.

MAY

In season

Asparagus	Lettuces
Broad beans	Mint
Cabbages	Rhubarb
Cauliflowers	Spinach

Grilled lamb with broad beans and rice

This is a good dish for the end of May, when broad beans are just coming into season.

Serves 4
1 onion
Vegetable oil, for frying
2–3 cloves of garlic, finely chopped
250g (8oz) basmati rice, rinsed and drained
750ml (1¼ pints) water
8 lean lamb chops
500g (1lb) fresh broad beans, shelled and cooked
    (soak dried beans overnight before cooking)
1 tbsp chopped fresh mint or 2 tsp dried mint
Twist of black pepper

1. Chop the onion, put it into a pan with a little oil and cook until soft. Add the garlic and cook for a further minute.
2. Add the rice and water. Bring to the boil, turn the heat down to low, cover and simmer for approximately 15–20 minutes or until the rice is tender.
3. As the rice is cooking, place the lamb under a preheated grill for 15–20 minutes until browned, turning halfway through the cooking time.
4. Add the beans, mint and pepper to the rice, cook for a further minute and serve with the lamb.

Moroccan mint tea

You can't go anywhere in Morocco without coming across its national drink, mint tea. Mint often grows like a weed if left unchecked, and it can spread all over your garden or vegetable plot. This drink is a useful way of keeping its growth in check.

2 tsp gunpowder green tea or 2 green tea bags
3 large sprigs of fresh mint
Honey or sugar

In a teapot large enough to hold four cups of tea, add the gunpowder green tea or green tea bags. Top up with about three large mint sprigs. Serve in small shot glasses, adding honey or sugar to taste.

Quinoa and asparagus salad

For centuries quinoa (together with maize) was one of the staple foods of the ancient Aztecs. It's an extremely nutritious grain and very high in protein. Quinoa can be grown in Britain and is available from many specialist seed outlets, healthfood shops and some larger supermarkets.

Serves 4 as a light lunch
300g (10oz) quinoa
500ml (17fl oz) vegetable stock
125g (4oz) fresh broad beans, shelled
    (if using dried, soak them overnight)
5 asparagus spears
125g (4oz) baby spinach leaves or other
    salad leaves, shredded
1 stick of celery, finely chopped
½ large red onion, finely chopped
Salad dressing (see Spring salad, pages 188–9)

1. Cook the quinoa for about 5–10 minutes in the vegetable stock until it's all absorbed. Quinoa cooks in a very similar way to cous-cous, and once cooked it will become translucent around the edges. If in doubt, try a little from the pan and if it's still very crunchy add a little more stock and cook for a while longer.
2. Blanch the broad beans and asparagus in a little water for around 4–5 minutes or until soft and tender.
3. Combine all the ingredients in a salad bowl, drizzle over the salad dressing and serve.

Grilled lamb with broad beans and rice.

Summer berry fruit salad.

RECIPES FOR SUMMER

JUNE

In season

Asparagus	Lettuces
Beetroot	New potatoes
Broad beans	Onions
Broccoli (calabrese)	Peas
Cabbages	Radishes
Cauliflowers	Rhubarb
Cherries	Spinach
French beans	Strawberries
Gooseberries	Turnips

Summer berry fruit salad

For this recipe we use a mix of foraged, grown and bought berries. Once they come into season in late June and early July there is really no reason to buy blackberries. In Bristol, like many other cities, they seem to grow on every street corner and on every bit of wasteland. This recipe can be adapted to what's in season, so later in the summer it can include more blackberries and in June you could include home-grown redcurrants.

Take a mix of any of the following and allow about a bowlful or 200–250g (7–8oz) for each person.

Blackberries
Blueberries
Raspberries
Redcurrants
Strawberries
Honey or sugar to taste, if necessary
1 tbsp low-fat crème fraîche or low-fat yogurt per person, to serve

1. Remove any stalks or leaves remaining on the berries. Halve any large strawberries.
2. Mix the berries together and divide between individual serving bowls.
3. Add honey or sugar if the berries are a little tart and serve with crème fraîche or yogurt.

Chicken and asparagus stir fry

The Chinese method of stir frying vegetables is quick and healthy and retains many of the vitamins and minerals that are often lost through the cooking process.

Serves 3–4
1 bunch of asparagus
1 red onion
3 medium cloves of garlic
1 fresh small green chilli or pinch of chilli powder
625g (1¼lb) chicken breast, skinned and boned
A little rapeseed oil, for frying
1 tbsp grated fresh ginger
2 tbsp light soy sauce
1 tbsp rice vinegar or cider/white wine vinegar or cooking sherry
1 tsp honey
1 tbsp toasted sesame seeds (see Crunchy cabbage stir fry, step 3, page 189)

1. Prepare the asparagus. It usually comes with a hard, inedible base to its stalk. To remove this, simply take a single stalk, put one hand in the middle and one at the base and bend until it naturally snaps, then compost the base or save it for vegetable stock. Chop the rest of the stalk into 2.5cm (1in) pieces.
2. Prepare the remaining vegetables: chop the onion, finely chop the garlic and deseed and finely chop the chilli. Slice the chicken into strips.
3. Heat the oil in a large pan or wok on a moderate to high heat. Add the onion to the pan and cook for about 2 minutes, stirring constantly.
4. Add the asparagus. Cook for about 2–4 minutes, depending on its thickness.
5. Add the ginger, garlic, chilli and chicken. Cook for another 2–4 minutes.
6. Add the soy sauce, vinegar and honey. Stir fry for a further 2–3 minutes.
7. Serve on a bed of rice or noodles with toasted sesame seeds sprinkled on top.

JULY

In season

Beans	Lettuces
Beetroot	Peas
Blackberries	Peppers
Broccoli (calabrese)	Potatoes
Carrots	Radishes
Courgettes	Raspberries
Florence fennel	Tomatoes

Trout baked with fennel and herbs

Both fennel and trout are very healthy foods. Trout is high in omega oils and can count as one of our two helpings of oily fish that nutritionists recommend we eat every week. Fennel is an often-overlooked vegetable that has a highly distinctive taste and contains many beneficial compounds, some of which have anti-carcinogenic properties.

Serves 4
4 small or 2 large trout
Olive oil
1 large fennel bulb
4 sprigs of fresh tarragon or 4 tsp dried tarragon
2 tsp chopped fresh dill or 1 tsp dried dill

1. Heat the oven to 200°C (400°F, Gas mark 6). Place each trout on an individual sheet of tin foil and brush lightly with olive oil.
2. Slice the fennel bulb and divide it between the foil parcels together with the tarragon and dill. Seal the parcels to ensure the juices are retained.
3. Bake the fish in their foil parcels for about 20 minutes. The fish is ready to eat when the flesh is firm and the eyes are white.
4. Unwrap the fish and serve it with the fennel and herbs and the juices from the foil poured over. New potatoes and peas make good accompaniments. NB If washed thoroughly, the foil can be recycled after use.

Trout baked with fennel and herbs.

Blackberry fool-ish

Some call them blackberries and others call them brambles, but whatever you call them they're always a welcome and easily identifiable wild food. They're best picked away from busy roadsides, because car fumes can contaminate the fruit.

Serves 2
500g (1lb) blackberries
200g (7oz) low-fat set yogurt

Wash the blackberries, then purée them with the yogurt. Place into individual bowls and put them into the fridge for about 1–2 hours until the fool has set a little.

AUGUST

In season

Artichokes (globe)	**Loganberries**
Aubergines	**Onions**
Beetroot	**Pears**
Blueberries	**Peas**
Broad beans	**Peppers**
Broccoli (calabrese)	**Plums**
Celery	**Potatoes**
Courgettes	**Radishes**
Cucumbers	**Runner beans**
Currants	**Shallots**
(red, white and black)	**Spinach**
Florence fennel	**Sweetcorn**
French beans	**Tomatoes**
Lettuces	**Turnips**

Summer salad

This seasonal salad is delicious served as an accompaniment with grilled chicken or fish or, for a vegetarian/vegan option, with rice or pasta or crusty wholemeal bread as a light lunch.

Serves 4
100g (3½oz) French beans
½ lettuce or equivalent in mixed leaves
4 medium or 8 cherry tomatoes
¼–½ cucumber
2 sticks of celery
Salad dressing (see Spring salad, pages 188–9)

1. Top and tail the French beans and cut them into quarters. Steam or blanch them in a little water for 6–8 minutes until soft.
2. Shred the lettuce, quarter the tomatoes (use cherry tomatoes whole) and cut the cucumber and celery into 1cm (½in) pieces (peel the cucumber if using home-grown ridge cucumber).
3. Combine all the ingredients in a salad bowl and pour over the dressing.

Stuffed courgettes

At the height of summer a few courgette plants can deliver their fruit day after day. They make a great addition to salads and soups and add texture to most vegetable dishes. In the recipe below they're the main focus of the dish and are delicious served on a bed of rice and peas or with pasta and a fresh tomato sauce. If you're growing your own courgettes, make sure you pick them young, before they turn into marrows.

Serves 2
2 large courgettes
8 tomatoes
Bunch of basil leaves
2 tbsp dried breadcrumbs
2 tbsp crushed mixed nuts
Salt and black pepper
30g (1oz) Cheddar cheese

1. Cut the courgettes in half lengthways. Using a teaspoon, carefully scoop out most of the insides, leaving a little of the flesh on either side. The courgettes should each resemble a long boat. Put half of the courgette flesh into a small bowl (the rest can be used in another recipe, such as soup or vegetable burgers).
2. Chop the tomatoes and shred the basil and add them to the bowl with the breadcrumbs and crushed mixed nuts. Season to taste and ensure the ingredients are combined thoroughly.
3. Using the teaspoon, carefully fill the courgette casings with the tomato/basil/breadcrumb/nut mixture and firm it in place.
4. Place the stuffed courgettes in a lightly oiled baking dish and cook in a warm oven at 200°C (400°F, Gas mark 6) for about 20–30 minutes.
5. Take the courgettes out of the oven, sprinkle on the Cheddar and return them to the oven until the cheese has browned and is bubbling.

RECIPES FOR AUTUMN

SEPTEMBER

In season

Apples
Artichokes (globe)
Aubergines
Beetroot
Cabbages
Carrots
Cauliflowers
Courgettes
Cucumbers
Florence fennel
French beans
Lettuces
Marrows

Melons
Mushrooms
Pears
Peas
Peppers
Potatoes
Pumpkins & squash
Radishes
Spinach
Swedes
Sweetcorn
Tomatoes
Turnips

Butternut squash and apple soup

It may seem unusual to have apples in a savoury dish but it works really well here with the butternut squash. This soup can also be made with pumpkin if you don't have any squash to hand. It does need the robust flavour of a winter rather than summer squash.

Serves 4
2 onions
2 cloves of garlic
A little oil, for frying
500g (1lb) butternut squash, peeled and deseeded
1 medium cooking apple (preferably Bramley), cored and peeled
200g (7oz) potatoes, peeled and chopped
900ml (1½ pints) vegetable stock
Fresh sage leaves and thyme sprigs, chopped
Salt and black pepper

1. Chop the onions and garlic. Put the onions into a pan with the oil. Cook gently over a medium heat for about 3–6 minutes without browning. Add the garlic and cook for a further minute.
2. Chop the squash and apple and add to the pan with the potatoes.

3. Cook for a couple of minutes, then add the stock and chopped herbs.
4. Continue to cook over a medium heat for around 20–25 minutes or until the potatoes are soft.
5. For a chunky soup put half of it into a blender, then return it to the pan, or for a smoother soup liquidize the whole lot. Use a potato masher if you don't have a blender.
6. Check the seasoning and serve with crusty bread.

Autumn salad

Salads needn't be just a summer food. The addition of walnuts and apple can make this just as much of a comfort food as a hot soup or a warm pie. It can be used as a side dish or as a vegetarian main course or light lunch.

Serves 4
300g (10oz) rice (white or brown)
100g (3½oz) mixed salad leaves (e.g. baby spinach, lettuce, nasturtium leaves, rocket)
1 apple, cored and diced
1 uncooked beetroot, peeled and grated
Handful of shelled walnuts
1 courgette, cut into 1cm (½in) cubes
Salad dressing (see Spring salad, pages 188–9)

1. Cook the rice according to the packet instructions. Rinse and allow to cool to room temperature.
2. Shred the salad leaves and put them into a large bowl with the apple and beetroot.
3. Add the walnuts and the raw courgette (you can lightly fry it in a little butter if preferred).
4. Add the rice to the vegetables, pour on some salad dressing and mix well.

Autumn salad.

OCTOBER

In season

Apples	Pears
Beetroot	Peas
Cabbages	Peppers
Carrots	Plums (wild)
Cauliflowers	Potatoes
Chestnuts	Pumpkins & squash
Courgettes	Radishes
Crab apples	Sloes
Cucumbers	Spinach
Lettuces	Swedes
Marrows	Sweetcorn
Melons	Tomatoes
Mushrooms	Turnips

Mushroom soup

By far the simplest way to serve mushrooms is in a soup. If you're used to the brilliant white colour of a tinned soup you may be put off by the more natural grey shade of this homemade version, but the taste is far superior to anything you might serve out of a can. Serve it with crusty brown bread as a starter or a light lunch.

Serves 4
Vegetable oil, for frying
1 onion, chopped
3 cloves of garlic, crushed
300g (10oz) mixed wild mushrooms (or button mushrooms if wild are not available), sliced
300ml (½ pint) vegetable or chicken stock
300ml (½ pint) semi-skimmed milk
1 tsp wholegrain mustard
Salt and black pepper

1. Heat the oil in a large saucepan and add the chopped onion. Cook gently in the hot oil until the onion is translucent. Add the garlic and cook for a further minute.
2. Add the mushrooms to the pan, stirring for around 2 or 3 minutes until they're softened.
3. Slowly add the stock and the milk and stir in the mustard.
4. Cook uncovered on a low heat for 15–20 minutes, making sure that the soup doesn't boil. Check the seasoning and adjust to taste.

Stuffed marrow

Marrows are delicious stuffed, and are particularly useful when you're having a combination of vegetarians and meat-eaters to supper, as you can add meat such as ham or cooked bacon to the recipe below for those who'd like it. For variety, the same filling could be used to stuff large flat mushrooms (omit the boiling stage in step 2).

Serves 2
About 15cm (6in) end of a marrow
425g (14oz) tin tomatoes (or equivalent of frozen homemade tomato sauce)
2–3 oyster or button mushrooms, chopped
1 tbsp rolled oats
1 tbsp dried breadcrumbs (or more if necessary)
1 tsp light soy sauce
Large pinch of dried basil
Black pepper
100g (3½oz) grated Cheddar cheese or crumbled feta cheese
Pine nuts (optional)

1. Cut the marrow in half lengthways, deseed and scoop out about 1cm (½in) of the flesh (you can use this in another recipe, such as soup).
2. Lightly boil the marrow halves for 10–15 minutes to soften the skin.
3. Chop the tinned tomatoes and put them into a bowl. Add the mushrooms, oats, breadcrumbs, soy sauce, basil and pepper. The mixture should not be too sloppy; if it is, add more breadcrumbs.
4. Spoon the mixture into the marrow halves and bake in the oven at 220°C (425°F, Gas mark 7) for about 25–30 minutes.
5. Sprinkle the grated or crumbled cheese and pine nuts, if using, over the surface of the marrow.
6. Cook in the oven for a further 5 minutes until the cheese turns golden brown and is bubbling.

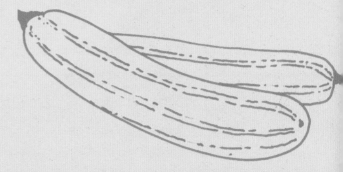

NOVEMBER

In season

Beet spinach
Brussels sprouts
Cabbages
Carrots
Cauliflowers
Celeriac
Celery
Chestnuts

Jerusalem artichokes
Kale
Leeks
Lettuces
Parsnips
Pumpkins & squash
Swedes
Turnips

Roasted chestnuts

Once roasted, chestnuts are among the tastiest nuts you can eat. They grow wild all over the place – they look a little like conkers or horse chestnuts, but have a slightly softer shell and the outer casing has more spikes and is a paler green. You can find them in the wild (see page 226) or buy them in markets or some greengrocers. Roasted chestnuts are delicious as a snack and work well in recipes such as risotto.

To roast chestnuts, score a diagonal cross on the flat side of each one and put them in the oven at about 200°C (400°F, Gas mark 6) for around 20 minutes. The chestnuts will be ready when you can easily poke a knife or fork into the soft flesh.

Pumpkin and chestnut risotto

This comforting risotto is a hearty, warming dish that is perfect for chilly autumn nights.

Serves 4
1 onion
1 small carrot
2 cloves of garlic
275g (9oz) pumpkin or butternut squash
12 roasted chestnuts (see above)
600ml (1 pint) vegetable or chicken stock
2 tbsp olive oil
175g (6oz) arborio (risotto) rice
Sprig of fresh thyme
60g (2oz) butter
Salt and black pepper
Strong Cheddar cheese, grated, to serve

1. First, prepare the vegetables: peel and finely chop the onion, carrot and garlic, peel and dice the pumpkin or butternut squash and peel and roughly chop the chestnuts.
2. Heat the vegetable or chicken stock in a small pan until almost boiling, then place it over a very low heat. Leave it to simmer gently.
3. In a separate, heavy-based saucepan, heat the oil and sweat the onion and carrot until soft. Add the garlic and cook for a further minute.
4. Add the rice and stir for 1 minute until the grains are coated with oil.
5. Add one-third of the simmering stock and stir until almost all the stock is absorbed.
6. Add the pumpkin or squash and the fresh thyme and a little more stock. Continue to simmer gently until the stock is almost completely absorbed.
7. Add more stock, a little at a time, until the pumpkin is soft and the rice is cooked but still has 'bite'.
8. When the risotto is almost ready, add the chopped chestnuts and stir in the butter. Season with salt and pepper and serve with grated cheese, to taste.

Pumpkin and chestnut risotto.

RECIPES FOR WINTER

DECEMBER

In season

Brussels sprouts	Leeks
Cabbages	Lettuces
Carrots	Parsnips
Celery	Spinach
Jerusalem artichokes	Swedes
Kale	Turnips

Christmas red cabbage

This is a colourful, healthy side dish to have with your Christmas meal.

Serves 4–5 as a side dish
½ large or 1 small red cabbage
½ glass of red wine or apple juice
Large pinch of grated nutmeg
Black pepper
1 tbsp olive oil or low-fat margarine

1. Shred the cabbage and put it into a saucepan with the wine or apple juice.
2. Simmer on a low heat for around 15 minutes, uncovered, until the cabbage is soft, adding a little water if necessary to prevent it drying out.
3. Add the nutmeg, pepper and oil or margarine and cook for a further minute.

Healthy roast potatoes

It's hard to gauge quantities with roast potatoes, as it depends on what else you're having and how many people there are. However, as a rule of thumb we'd say 1½ quartered 'jacket'-sized potatoes or 6 new potatoes would be more than enough per person. You can always throw a few cloves of garlic into the roasting tin. Not only will they enhance the potatoes but they're also very tasty in their own right. When garlic cloves are roasted in their skins the flavour is much more subtle and even sweet. Squeeze the base of each clove to skin it before eating.

Potatoes (use a floury variety such as Maris Piper, Wilja or Desiree)
Olive oil
Sprigs of fresh rosemary (if available)

1. Scrub the potatoes, leaving their skins on, and cut them into manageable-sized pieces.
2. Heat the oven to 220°C (425°F, Gas mark 7).
3. Parboil the potatoes in water for about 5–10 minutes until slightly soft but not crumbly. Drain well.
4. Shake the potatoes around in the pan to roughen up the edges.
5. Put the potatoes into a large roasting tin and drizzle over enough olive oil to coat them; they should just be 'shiny' with the oil and not soaking.
6. Place the rosemary on top of the potatoes. Roast in the oven for about 35 minutes, until tender. (If you don't have a roasting tin, this dish can be made by wrapping the potatoes in foil on a baking tray.)

Brussels sprouts with satay sauce

If you're a fan of Brussels sprouts, as we are, you could just make this recipe up to step 2 – they're delicious just as they are, lightly steamed. However, for those who still need convincing, or prefer to disguise sprouts' distinctive flavour, try serving them with a simple satay sauce. Alternatively, you could stir fry them.

Serves 4
750g (1½lb) Brussels sprouts
8 tsp peanut butter
2 tsp light soy sauce
8 drops Tabasco
4 tsp hot water

1. Trim the sprouts and halve them lengthways.
2. Steam the sprouts for no longer than 10 minutes or blanch them in a little water for 5–6 minutes.
3. For the sauce, mix the peanut butter with the soy sauce, Tabasco and hot water. Drizzle the sauce over the sprouts while they're still warm and serve immediately.

Stuffed cabbage

Cabbage is one of those vegetables that we all know is incredibly good for us but can be very difficult to get right. So often it's stewed to within an inch of its life and any nutrients and flavour are completely boiled out. In this recipe the cabbage is either steamed first or the rice is cooked in the cabbage water, retaining a lot of the goodness of the cabbage that would otherwise be poured down the sink. It's an excellent option for a vegetarian on Christmas Day.

Serves 2–3
4 large cabbage leaves (preferably Savoy)
250g (8oz) brown rice
1 onion
3 cloves of garlic
A little rapeseed oil, for frying
125g (4oz) chopped nuts (such as hazelnuts)
125ml (4fl oz) vegetable stock

1. Steam the cabbage leaves for about 5–10 minutes until they're pliable – they need to bend easily without breaking. Alternatively, boil in a little water, setting the water aside to cook the rice in.
2. Cook the rice as per the packet instructions, using the reserved cabbage water if desired.
3. Chop the onion and garlic. Put the onion in a pan with the oil over a moderate heat and cook until it is soft and translucent. Add the garlic and cook for a further minute.
4. Stir in the cooked rice and nuts and keep on the heat for about 1 minute.
5. Spoon some of the mixture into the centre of each cabbage leaf and roll them into sealed parcels, tucking the 'join' underneath.
6. Place the parcels in a casserole, surround with leftover rice and pour over the vegetable stock.
7. Cover the casserole with a lid or tin foil and bake in the oven at 200°C (400°F, Gas mark 6) for approximately 35 minutes.

JANUARY

In season

Brussels sprouts	**Kale**
Cabbages	**Leeks**
Celeriac	**Parsnips**
Celery	**Swedes**
Jerusalem artichokes	**Turnips**

Winter warming soup

Celery, leeks and parsnips all have complex flavours of their own. Sometimes it's best not to over-flavour a vegetable soup and let the ingredients do the talking by themselves.

Serves 2–3
1 onion
3 sticks of celery
2 leeks
2 cloves of garlic
Knob of butter, for frying (vegans can use a suitable margarine or sunflower/rapeseed oil)
1 medium to large parsnip
750ml (1¼ pints) vegetable stock
Black pepper
1 rosemary sprig, chopped, or ½ tsp dried rosemary

1. Chop the onion, celery and leeks. Put them in a pan with the butter or oil and cook gently for about 5 minutes, until the onion is translucent. Crush the garlic, add to the pan and cook for a further minute.
2. Wash the parsnip and trim the top, but do not peel. Cut it in half along the middle then, with the flat side down, chop into 1cm (½in) pieces.
3. Add the parsnip to the pan and pour in the stock to cover the vegetables. Bring to the boil and simmer for 15 minutes, until the parsnip is soft, stirring occasionally.
4. Add the pepper and rosemary and serve with crusty homemade bread.

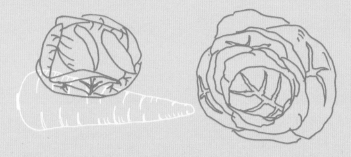

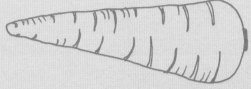

Winter warming soup.

Jerusalem artichoke crisps

The quantities for this recipe depend on how many artichokes you have and how many crisps you want. We've found that three or four small artichokes make enough crisps for a reasonable snack for one person.

Jerusalem artichokes
Rapeseed or vegetable oil, for deep frying
Pinch of salt or spices (such as ground coriander, chilli and cumin) per artichoke

1. Scrub the artichokes thoroughly – it may help to soak them in water for a few minutes first.
2. Cut the artichokes into small, crisp-sized pieces using a very sharp knife or the slicing part of a cheese grater.
3. Heat the oil. Meanwhile, wet the artichoke pieces and coat them in the spice mix. Drop them into the hot oil, ensuring they are completely covered, and turn when one side is cooked. They take only a couple of minutes and should start to turn golden brown when cooked thoroughly.

FEBRUARY

In season

Beet spinach	Celery
Broccoli (sprouting)	Jerusalem artichokes
Brussels sprouts	Kale
Cabbages	Leeks
Cauliflowers	Parsnips
Celeriac	Swedes

Creamy roasted vegetable soup

This creamy soup can be adapted to use whatever vegetables are in season. It works best with root crops.

Serves 4–5
1 small or ½ large celeriac
1 small or ½ large swede
1 large parsnip
2 onions
4 large cloves of garlic
Olive oil
1.25 litres (2 pints) vegetable stock
150ml (5fl oz) double cream
Salt and black pepper
Pinch of grated nutmeg (optional)

1. Peel the celeriac, swede, parsnip and onions and cut them into reasonably large chunks.
2. Throw all the chopped vegetables plus the garlic cloves (whole and unpeeled) into a roasting dish and cover generously in olive oil.
3. Roast in the oven for about 45 minutes at 190°C (375°F, Gas mark 5).
4. Leave the roasted vegetables to cool slightly, squeeze the garlic cloves out of their skins (throw the skins onto the compost), then liquidize the vegetables in a blender.
5. Put the liquidized vegetables into a pan with the stock and heat through, stirring, for about 5 minutes.
6. Add the cream and season to taste with the salt, pepper and nutmeg, if using.

Chinese winter salad

This recipe is good almost any time of year. It is kept simple so it can be adapted to include whatever is in season. Early in the year spring greens can take the place of winter leaves, and as the year progresses steamed carrots and/or courgettes can be added. Serve this salad as a main dish on its own with fish or cooked tofu.

Serves 2
2 eggs
150g (5oz) dried Chinese egg noodles (2 blocks)
150g (5oz) green leaves (cabbage, beet spinach, Chinese cabbage)
100g (3½oz) broccoli

For the dressing
2 tbsp olive oil
Pinch of grated nutmeg
Black pepper

1. Hardboil the eggs in water for about 7 minutes.
2. Cook the noodles as per the packet instructions.
3. Shred the green leaves, then steam or boil them in a little water with the broccoli for about 7 minutes.
4. Shell and quarter the hardboiled eggs. Combine all the salad ingredients in a large bowl.
5. Mix the dressing ingredients together in a small bowl and pour over the salad.

WILD FOOD

We're quite confident that very few people reading this can say they've never picked any wild food. Granted, not everyone would have gathered a sufficient number of edible mushrooms to make a soup or picked an entire mixed-leaf salad from a hedgerow. However, most would have plucked at least one blackberry off a bush or an apple off a tree at some point in their life.

Our journey into wild food started very simply, picking fruit we could recognize easily – apples, cherries and blackberries – and leaves that we'd known since childhood, such as nettles and dandelion leaves. From quite a young age, Dave became a bit of a dab hand at making nettle soup from plants growing in the back garden. There's no doubt that the idea of getting something for nothing has always appealed to us and that was a great incentive to start with, but we grew increasingly interested in wild plants, and foraging has now become a way of life.

We started to read up on wild foods and discovered a great number of people with a similar interest who could teach us more. We were amazed by the variety of plants in our locality that were not only edible but also easy to identify – elder (flowers and berries), rosehips, crab apples

and chestnuts are all unmistakable once you know what you're looking for. Wild food needn't be all about constantly checking with a reference book if the plant (or fungus) you have in your hand is deadly or fine to eat. It should also be about becoming familiar with food plants, particularly those in your local area, so you can find food quickly and safely, and in so doing greatly reduce the number of miles the food has travelled to reach your plate. We always keep an eye out for edibles on a walk, and whether in a town or in the countryside we're usually rewarded for doing so.

There are over 7000 wild food plants in Britain alone, so we can't possibly give a comprehensive list of what is available in this book. We've just included the plants, fruit and fungi that we consider both easy to find and among the most delicious foods that nature has to offer.

WILD MUSHROOMS

The idea of picking mushrooms for the dinner table from woodlands or grasslands can be a scary concept for some people. It's not surprising, as there is a bewildering array of fungi just in Britain alone and many of them are poisonous. On the other hand, a number are perfectly safe to eat and absolutely delicious, with a unique flavour far from that of the ordinary button or cultivated field mushrooms found in our supermarkets.

Between these choice and poisonous types there are great numbers of mushrooms that are deemed 'edible' but are not really worth going out of your way for. We found a good example of this 'edible' category a few years ago: it was a huge bracket fungus called the dryad's saddle. After removing the maggots by leaving it upturned on a piece of newspaper overnight, we painstakingly tried every way possible to cook this mushroom and make it palatable. We fried it, boiled it, marinated it, baked it, coated it in soy sauce and even left it overnight in some vinegar to see if strong acid would have an effect on it, but despite all this the mushroom just ended up tasting like a pair of old boots.

We've been picking mushrooms for a number of years and have found there are arguably between 10 and 20 different fungi that are very good to eat in Britain. Being somewhat limited for space, we've decided to concentrate mainly on seven of these in this book. It may not seem like many, but they've been carefully selected on the basis of their delicious flavour and the fact that they don't have too many poisonous look-alikes.

When foraging for mushrooms, always make sure you consult a good, reliable field guide before picking to ensure correct identification of edible mushrooms and in order to avoid the poisonous ones.

Giant puffball

Appearance	A large, round, almost spherical fungus of 10–30cm (8–12in). It has white skin and flesh and no stem. The flesh will change colour to yellow or dirty green/grey as it ages, and the mushroom should not be eaten at this stage.
When to look	July to November
Where to look	Grassland, hedges, meadows
Availability	Takes a bit of looking

Despite its size, we've found the giant puffball (see page 212) somewhat elusive in the past. As is the case with many mushrooms, if you go out with the intention of finding one you never will. However, once you spot a giant puffball it's unmistakable. From a distance, it looks as if someone has left a football lying around – perhaps it's because one single mushroom can be so vast and heavy that the giant puffball is so many people's favourite fungus.

Dave found his first puffball on an industrial estate in Northampton, while doing a day's work as a lorry driver's mate. He was over the moon and must have seemed like a schoolboy with a new toy. The lorry driver failed to share Dave's enthusiasm as he sliced off pieces to try with his lunch. Since raw puffball didn't hold a lot of appeal, he cooked it later in the day with some risotto rice, cream and a little pepper, happily feeding four people with the morning's find.

Cooking giant puffballs Puffballs taste delicious stuffed. Cut off the top, like a lid, and remove the flesh inside. Mix some of the flesh with cooked bacon or ham, tomatoes, basil, balsamic vinegar, thyme and coarse breadcrumbs, put the stuffing into the puffball, then bake at 180°C (375°F, Gas mark 5) for about 40 minutes on a large baking tray. If you're vegetarian, you could use tofu and a mix of mushrooms for the stuffing, and oatmeal or ground nuts will work just as well as breadcrumbs. You can really use anything that's available – we've found that with any recipe like this it's important to have a mixture of wet and dry ingredients and include strong flavours such as thyme, rosemary and black pepper.

Cep/penny bun

Appearance	An interesting-looking mushroom with a light reddish-brown cap, which becomes darker brown with age and can turn white towards the edges. The cap is round or bun-shaped, around 5–30cm (2–12in) across (sometimes bigger), and it has a bulging white stem, 7.5–25cm (3–10in) high and up to 7.5cm (3in) thick. The stem has brown markings, often making the mushroom look as though a child has drawn on it, but no ring. The inside of the mushroom is white. It has pores rather than gills and a rather pleasant aroma.
When to look	August to November
Where to look	Near oak, chestnut, beech and pine trees
Availability	Takes a bit of looking

Ceps (see opposite and page 214) are one of the favourites of the mushroom collector. They can reach high prices when sold commercially, as their taste is far superior to that of the majority of shop-bought mushrooms. The name penny bun comes from a time when bread rolls were sold at a penny a time and the brown bun-shaped cap of the mushroom was seen to resemble these bread rolls.

Cooking ceps The smaller, younger specimens have the most pleasant taste and can be eaten raw or cooked; the larger, older mushrooms are much better cooked, particularly in a hearty mushroom soup (see page 198). We often have a breakfast of eggs and ceps on toast, and simply fry them in butter. They're also fantastic in risotto (see page 216) or the larger ones can be stuffed and baked.

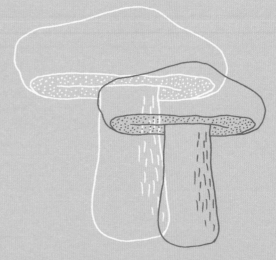

Chanterelles (foreground) and ceps (background) can both be found in late summer and throughout autumn.

Oyster mushroom

Appearance   A white to grey bracket mushroom, 5–25cm (2–10in) in diameter, with gills rather than pores. Oyster mushrooms are often sold commercially, so examine them at the greengrocer or supermarket before you go foraging.

When to look   All year round, but the best time to look is October to March

Where to look   On dead wood, often beech and ash, and sometimes on fence posts

Availability   Takes a bit of looking

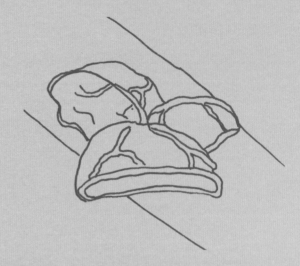

Oyster mushrooms (see opposite) are unusual because they can often be found throughout winter. They're particularly special to us, as they were our first-ever major mushroom haul. We found a cluster of them a stone's throw away from Andy's house in East Bristol – we ate a lot of them fresh and then dried the others on a rack suspended from a radiator (see page 248). The dried mushrooms filled a very large jar and lasted several months.

Cooking oyster mushrooms
Oyster mushrooms aren't very strong-tasting and are therefore useful in recipes where mushroom is not intended to be the overriding flavour or where they can bulk out dishes that contain other mushroom varieties. They come at a time of year when not much else is around and we often mix them with what's available. They go well in a curry with home-grown beet spinach or foraged sea beet and they also make a good pâté (see page 216).

Jew's ear/wood ear

Appearance   A lightish brown tree fungus, with a sometimes pinkish underside, slimy/velvety to the touch and with an irregular shape. The form and texture can resemble a human ear.

When to look   Most of the year round

Where to look   On living trees, mainly elder

Availability   Easy to find

Today, this mushroom is often referred to by its more PC name of wood ear. However, the name Jew's ear isn't necessarily anti-semitic. Some think it derives from a shortened version of Judas, because this fungus is often found on the elder tree, which is sometimes known as the Judas tree as Judas Iscariot is thought to have hanged himself from an elder after giving Jesus up to the Romans. An alternative theory is that in the Middle Ages fungi were often referred to as 'Jew meat', possibly a reference to the Jewish practice of abstaining from meat on certain days.

This mushroom is included here because it's very easy to identify, has no poisonous look-alikes and is available most of the year. It has a gelatinous, slimy texture that can be off-putting, and its somewhat eerie resemblance to a human ear means it takes a leap of faith to consider it as food. However, the taste is really quite agreeable.

Cooking Jew's ears
These fungi are very good in Chinese and Thai dishes, especially in soups and stir fries, possibly cooked with tofu, broccoli and carrots for a mixture of textures.

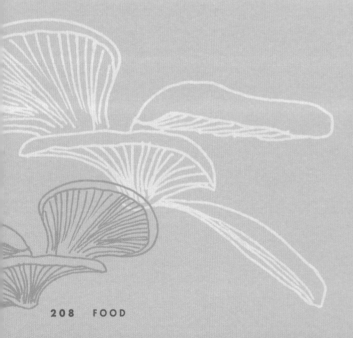

Oyster mushrooms are useful in the kitchen as they're found throughout winter.

Morel

Appearance	An upright, light to dark brown cap resembling a honeycomb or sponge.
When to look	March to May
Where to look	Waste ground, chalkland and sandy woodland, often in places where there has been a recent fire
Availability	Takes a bit of looking

Morels appear just as the winter crops are running out and the spring crops are emerging. They should never be eaten raw, because they contain a toxin that is harmful to humans unless cooked. There are higher levels of this toxin in the similar-looking poisonous mushroom, the false morel. It's important to know the differences between the two, because the false morel can be deadly poisonous, causing liver damage. The true morel has a much tighter, more upright shape, more like a closed pinecone, while the false morel is a lot looser in structure, looking more like brown brain. This looser structure is reflected in the cap, which hangs more freely around the stem on the false morel. The bottom of the cap is attached to the stem on a true morel.

Cooking morels Always wash morels thoroughly before cooking. Their hollow structure means they're good stuffed, perhaps with a mixture of nettles, cream cheese, chives and nutmeg, and baked for 15–20 minutes in the oven at 200°C (400°F, Gas mark 6). They also complement dairy products and eggs, particularly as an addition to scrambled egg with a little tarragon, black pepper and a small pinch of cayenne pepper (fry the mushrooms in a little butter before adding them to the eggs). We've also heard they go very well with duck.

Field blewit and wood blewit

Appearance	Field blewit – pale brown to grey with a rounded base and a purple to blue stem; the gills are greyish pink or white. Wood blewit – brown to red cap (sometimes pinkish to violet) with a swollen base and a pink to violet stem.
When to look	September to December
Where to look	Field blewit – in fields or grassland Wood blewit – in woodland, growing among dead leaves
Availability	Takes a bit of looking

On first picking, the wood blewit looks like a very poisonous mushroom indeed. It can be blue or pink in colour and is one of the most alien-looking of all edible mushrooms. You need to cook both field blewits (see opposite) and wood blewits, as they can be slightly toxic unless properly prepared. For this reason, it's probably best to leave these until you've been on a few mushroom forays and have gained a little confidence in identification and preparation. However, it's definitely worth persevering with blewits.

Cooking blewits Blewits make an excellent mushroom pâté (see page 216). They're also great just lightly fried on some toasted wholemeal bread.

Chanterelle

Appearance	A trumpet-shaped fungus, egg-yolk yellow in colour, with a smell similar to that of apricots and with gills but no ring.
When to look	August to December
Where to look	In woodland, especially under beech (but not directly on it)
Availability	Takes bit of looking

The chanterelle (see pages 206 and 212) has a couple of poisonous look-alikes, the false chanterelle and the jack o' lantern. The false chanterelle is orange in colour rather than yellow and the jack o' lantern grows directly on wood.

Chanterelles, together with shitake mushrooms, are high in vitamin D and are one of the only non-animal food sources of this vitamin. Synthesized from sunlight and absorbed by the skin, vitamin D is stored in the liver and is particularly important over the winter months, when sunlight is less intense.

Cooking chanterelles These mushrooms have a strong flavour and need very little adding to them. They make a great pizza topping and go very well with chicken or fish. They also lend themselves to dairy quite well, so are good in a white sauce with some pasta or lightly fried and then mixed with a little cream cheese on toast.

Field blewits are found in fields or grassland from early autumn to early winter.

Other edible mushrooms

In addition to the mushrooms described earlier, there are many other edible mushrooms and fungi found in British woodlands, gardens, parks and meadows.

Chicken of the woods – A large fungus found on tree stumps and decaying logs. As its name suggests, it isn't dissimilar in taste to chicken. It can be found from spring to autumn, and when at its best it looks bright yellow or even orange. Parboil before frying it in a little butter.

St George's mushroom – A tasty spring mushroom found on roadsides, on grassland and on the margins of woods. We've even found this growing on the edge of a retail estate in Bristol. It's found from around St George's Day (23 April) until June. It has a creamy white stalk, gills and cap, although the cap can have slightly darker patches.

Hedgehog fungus – Found in woodland from late summer to autumn, this distinctive mushroom has tiny teeth-like spikes instead of gills. The cap is irregular in shape and can be brown to nearly pink. It's full of flavour; some people prefer to parboil it before cooking.

Small puffball – We've found these in woodland and around the edges of woods in autumn, but they're also common on grassland and in gardens. Most small puffballs are edible when young, unless they're grey or black inside rather than white, or rather strangely have what appears to be another mushroom on the inside. They're light brown to white and sometimes have a small stalk under the completely spherical cap.

Field or horse mushroom – This is the mushroom found all over Britain in markets and shops, often referred to as a button mushroom, field mushroom or Portobello mushroom, depending on the size. They're available from July to November but do take real care when harvesting them as they have many poisonous look-alikes – the wild food expert Richard Mabey advises harvesting only the younger, pink-gilled specimens.

Giant puffballs, chanterelles and field blewits are all available in autumn.

Poisonous mushrooms

It's vital to recognize poisonous mushrooms as well as edible ones, and anyone going out foraging should learn to identify the deadliest varieties. If at any point you are less than 100 per cent certain of the identification of a mushroom do not eat it! Always take a reliable book with you on your expeditions.

The destroying angel, the death cap and the fly agaric all belong to the *Amanita* genus of mushrooms. As a group, amanitas account for 95 per cent of all known mushroom poisonings. The compound responsible, alpha-amanitin, is a slow-acting poison that takes up to 10 days to kill by shutting down both liver and kidney function. It's the slow action of the poison in these mushrooms that makes them not only hard to detect but also very hard to treat. A stomach pump is ineffective in these cases, because by the time the patient starts to get the first symptoms of the poisoning it can be anything between 10 and 24 hours after ingestion. Interestingly, the fly agaric is poisonous but not always deadly and it was often used by tribes in northern Europe, such as the Sámi, for religious purposes as it induces visions.

Tragically, every year many Asian immigrants die in North America as a result of the similarities between the deadly deathcap mushroom and the paddy-straw mushroom, which is native to many parts of Asia. The paddy-straw mushroom is a common ingredient in Asian cooking and there is no dangerous look-alike in China and the Far East. Thinking they've picked their own native mushroom, even experienced mushroom foragers can make this fatal mistake.

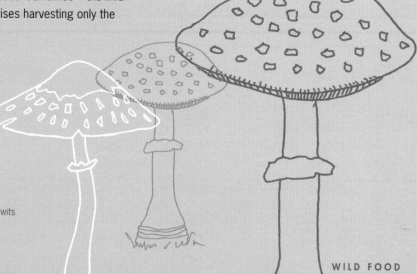

Ceps are highly prized by chefs and are available from late summer to autumn.

MUSHROOM RECIPES

Mushroom and bean burgers

This makes around six full-size burgers or about 12 'falafel'-sized burgers. It's essential to squeeze the mixture into tight shapes, or it can be too crumbly and the burgers may fall apart.

Serves 4–6
200g (7oz) chickpeas or red kidney beans (if using tinned, skip step 1)
½ slice bread (preferably wholemeal)
1 carrot, grated
100g (3½oz) wild mushrooms (preferably ceps or chanterelles), finely chopped
Pinch of chilli powder or ground turmeric, or herbs (such as basil or mixed herbs)
Black pepper
A little flour (preferably wholemeal)

1. If using dried chickpeas or kidney beans, put them in a bowl, cover with cold water and soak for at least 10 hours. Rinse and drain, place them in a large pan and cover with fresh water. Boil vigorously for 10 minutes, then simmer for a further 45 minutes–1 hour.
2. Rub the bread together between your fingers to make fresh breadcrumbs.
3. Mash the chickpeas or beans with a fork or potato masher and put them into a large mixing bowl with the grated carrot, chopped mushrooms, breadcrumbs and spices. If you don't like chilli or turmeric, you can use a large pinch of basil or mixed herbs. Add pepper to taste. If you have a food processor, combine the ingredients until the mixture forms a firm consistency.
4. Lightly flour a worksurface.
5. Take a small amount of the mixture in your hands, about the size of a golf ball, and squeeze it until it forms a tight, burger-like shape. If it remains too crumbly, put it back in the mix and add a tablespoon of flour and a drop of water. Press the burger down on the floured surface until lightly covered in flour on both sides. Continue in this way until you have used all the mixture.
6. Place the burgers under a grill until browned on both sides (about 5–10 minutes a side). Serve in a roll with salad or in place of the meat part of a traditional meat-and-two-veg dinner.

Mushroom and nettle lasagne

This recipe can be cooked all year round with whatever mushrooms are in season. Strong-flavoured fungi, such as ceps, chanterelles or blewits, give the best result but any wild mushrooms will work well. It is by no means as healthy as some of the other recipes, with a large quantity of cheese, but you can use low-fat ricotta and mozzarella for a slightly healthier alternative.

Serves 4
Couple of knobs of butter, for frying
500g (1lb) young nettle tops
Black pepper
Generous pinch of grated nutmeg
Dash of light soy sauce (optional)
200g (7oz) ricotta cheese
300g (10oz) wild mushrooms, roughly chopped
200ml (7fl oz) vegetable stock
Few large sprigs of tarragon or 1 tsp dried tarragon
1 pack of no-pre-cook lasagne
1 small ball of mozzarella cheese, grated or finely sliced

1. Put a knob of butter in a pan and cook the nettles on a moderate to low heat until wilted, then remove from the heat.
2. Allow the nettles to cool and chop the leaves finely (by this stage they should have lost their sting and you'll be able to handle them).
3. Return the chopped nettles to the heat and add the pepper and nutmeg; check the flavour, and if you feel you need it add a dash of soy sauce.
4. Remove from the heat and add the ricotta cheese, mixing it in well.
5. In another pan, heat a knob of butter and sweat the chopped mushrooms on a moderate heat until soft.
6. Add the stock to the mushrooms and stir well. Bring to the boil and cook until the stock has reduced by about half.
7. Purée the mushroom mix in a blender or with a potato masher, adding the tarragon as you do so.
8. Take approximately half the nettle mix and spread a layer in a large greased ovenproof dish. Arrange the lasagne sheets on the nettle mix to cover and then smooth over half the mushroom purée. Repeat the layers until the nettle mix and mushroom purée are used up.
9. Finish off with the mozzarella and bake in the oven at 200°C (400°F, Gas mark 6) for 35–45 minutes.

Mushroom risotto

Mushrooms and rice are quite natural partners and our first instinct when finding a glut of mushrooms is to make a risotto. After a cold autumn day in the woods, nothing beats the comfort of this warming, wholesome dish.

Serves 4
2 leeks or onions
4 cloves of garlic
250g (8oz) wild mushrooms
A little oil for frying
300g (10oz) risotto rice (such as arborio, carnaroli)
Few sprigs of fresh thyme or 1 tsp dried thyme
1 bay leaf
500ml (17fl oz) vegetable or mushroom stock
Black pepper
½ tsp grated nutmeg
½ small tub of single cream or low-fat crème fraîche

1. Chop the leeks or onions and the garlic and mushrooms. Place the leeks or onions and garlic in a large saucepan with the oil and cook over a moderate heat for about 2–3 minutes.
2. Add the mushrooms and after 2–3 minutes, once they have softened, add the rice and cook for a further minute. Add the thyme and bay leaf.
3. Meanwhile, in a separate pan, heat the stock until it reaches a simmer. Add a ladleful of stock to the rice and stir continuously until the stock has been absorbed. Add another ladleful of stock and again reduce until all the stock has evaporated. Continue this process until the rice is just cooked (about 15–20 minutes).
4. Take the risotto off the heat, remove the bay leaf and stir in the nutmeg, black pepper and cream or crème fraîche. Serve as a main course with crusty bread.

Wild mushroom pâté

The main bonus of mushroom foraging is you can experiment with your haul once you get it home, knowing it hasn't cost an arm and a leg. This is one such recipe made after a successful trip foraging in Oxfordshire with mushroom expert and old friend Antony Armitage.

Serves 4–6
300g (10oz) wild mushrooms (preferably blewits, puffballs, chanterelles, ceps, oyster mushrooms)
3 tbsp olive oil
1 tsp mustard (preferably wholegrain)
Black pepper
1 onion
3 cloves of garlic
30g (1oz) butter
200ml (7fl oz) single cream

1. Sweat the mushrooms in some olive oil and add the mustard and black pepper. Most mushrooms need only to be softened but if using morels you should cook them thoroughly in a well-ventilated area to destroy toxins.
2. Chop the onion and garlic. In a second pan, gently brown the onion in some butter and a little olive oil for 5–10 minutes until the onion is soft. Add the garlic for the final minute, then add the sweated mushrooms and heat through for 5 minutes or so to infuse the flavours.
3. Put the mushroom and onion mixture in the blender and liquidize. Alternatively, use a potato masher.
4. Return the mushroom mixture to the pan, add the cream and heat, without letting the liquid boil, for about 5 minutes until it has reduced. Season to taste.
5. Once the pâté is thick and creamy it's ready to serve. It can be eaten warm or allowed to cool, and should be consumed within 24 hours.

Wild mushroom pâté.

WILD FRUIT

Wild fruit is perhaps the most easily identifiable and ready-to-eat of all wild foods – blackberries, wild cherries and plums can all be eaten straight off the tree or bush. In our ancestral past, wild fruit would have been a very important food source, providing nutrients, such as vitamin C, which are in very short supply in a mainly meat-based diet. Today, wild fruit is still available in all parts of Britain; you may find a wild cherry tree growing on a council estate or a mulberry tree spreading over the wall of a large private house. As with mushrooms, use a good illustrated guide to help identify the less familiar berries.

Wild cherry

Appearance	Small, round, red to purple fruits with a stalk (like smaller versions of cultivated cherries)
Where to look	On trees (often found on council estates)
When to look	June to July
Availability	Very easy to find

Wild cherries (see page 204) look almost identical to their domestic cousins but the fruits are much smaller in size, about the size of a marble. We've noticed that both in Oxford and in Bristol wild cherry trees are often found in abundance on council estates. Avoid any very bitter cherries, as they can contain tiny amounts of cyanide, especially the pips. One of the best ways of eating them is to remove the pips and bake them in a tarte tatin, together with other fruit, or add them to brandy to make sweet cherry brandy liquor. They can also be used in summer fruit puddings together with early raspberries.

Blackberry

Appearance	Black or purple, glossy, berry-like fruits
Where to look	On brambles on waste ground, in woods, gardens, allotments – just about anywhere
When to look	June to September
Availability	Very easy to find

There's no mistaking the blackberry or bramble – it grows anywhere and everywhere. It's often the first wild food that anyone picks, and quite rightly so – it is delicious. It's worth looking for a good blackberry-picking spot away from any major roads or other sources of pollution. We tend to pick them in woodland, where pollution is at a minimum, and they do seem to taste much better than their city cousins (although this might just be in our imagination).

Blackberries are a very versatile fruit and can be made into pies, jams, chutneys, sauces, puddings, smoothies and all manner of desserts. Combining blackberries, yogurt, apple juice and a banana in a blender can make a refreshing morning drink. It's the perfect pick-me-up for a hungover Sunday morning.
• See Blackberry fool-ish, page 195; Blackberry and elderberry jam, page 255.

Sloe

Appearance	Small, round, dark, purple-black fruits
Where to look	On blackthorn trees or bushes
When to look	Late September to November
Availability	Very easy to find

If you're ever curious to taste sloes fresh from the bush, remember the saying 'Curiosity killed the cat'. Sloes have such an astringent taste you feel all the moisture leave your mouth after the first bite. However, when they're added to gin their flavour comes into its own (see page 220).

Sloes are the fruit of the blackthorn bush. They grow throughout the British countryside and urban areas (but avoid fruits growing near busy, polluted roads). The best season for picking is late September to November. Some people who make sloe gin say it's best to pick them after the first frost because this softens the fruit and skins, enabling the flavour to mix more easily with the gin.

Blackthorn bushes have large, sharp thorns, so you may want to wear gloves when picking. We use a crooked stick to pull down high branches gently, as this is where you'll find a lot of fruit – just out of reach! After picking, remove any twigs and leaves and wash the sloes in clean water. If you've found any maggots while washing, leave the sloes in a bowl of water and the maggots should float to the top.

Crab apples are in season from
late summer to mid-autumn.

Sloe gin

Here is a recipe for sloe gin, taken from our website and written by an old friend of ours called Simon Smith (or 'Smit' as we call him). Sloe gin does require gin – it isn't a cheap moonshine alternative – but it isn't worth buying a brand-name product as sloe gin doesn't retain any gin flavour, so super-cheap, bargain-bin stuff will do fine.

500g (1lb) sloes
1 litre (1¾ pints) gin
250g (8oz) sugar
Few drops of almond essence

1. Wash the sloes thoroughly and prick them with a fork, the sharp point of a knife or a darning needle.
2. Place the sloes into a sterilized bottle, such as a demijohn, with the gin, sugar and almond essence. Put in the stopper and shake to mix the contents.
3. Swill the contents around every day to help the sugar to dissolve. After 6 weeks, taste to check the sweetness. Add more sugar if needed. Your sloe gin should be ready in 8–12 weeks, just in time for Crimbo.

Elderberry

Appearance	Small, round, black berries growing in clusters from a central stem
Where to look	On elder trees or bushes
When to look	August to September
Availability	Very common and easy to find

Just as the elderflower marks the end of spring/start of summer, the elderberry signals the close of summer. It's a very useful berry and is also easy to identify. Elderberries can be used to bulk out apple or blackberry pies and are good in jams and pickles; they were even used in an old-fashioned ketchup, known as poulac, which was made before the introduction of the tomato. Poulac was made in a similar way to tomato ketchup – the fruit being reduced in a little vinegar and combined with spices and sometimes honey. It was traditionally served with meat, just as we use tomato ketchup today. After picking the berries, wash them thoroughly and take them off the stalks with a fork.
• See Blackberry and elderberry jam, page 255; Elderberry wine, page 268.

Crab apple

Appearance	Very small, yellow to reddish apples
Where to look	On crab apple trees, common in gardens and on waste ground
When to look	August to October
Availability	Very easy to find

The crab apple (see page 219) is the wild ancestor of our modern domesticated apple. Most apple-growers will grow from grafting, as apples have a tendency to revert to this more ancient form if grown from seed. If you look at it in botanical terms, the tree is more likely to produce the next generation by having lots and lots of small fruit rather than just a few larger fruits. Crab apples are often planted as pollinators for domestic apples within an orchard. One of the best things to do with crab apples is to make a chutney out of them. You can also make crab-apple jelly.

Mulberry

Appearance	A tree fruit resembling a dark raspberry, although it can be more uneven, a little hairy in texture and lacks the central core of a raspberry
Where to look	On mulberry trees, usually found in parks and gardens but sometimes growing wild
When to look	July to September
Availability	Takes a bit of looking

We've never felt more urban than the time when we came across our first mulberry tree. We were walking along the river in Bristol and saw on the ground what looked like misshapen raspberries. We had no idea what this strange fruit was, and despite it looking edible we didn't trust our judgement and left it to rot. Weeks later, Andy described the fruit to a friend, who informed him it was a mulberry. By then the season was over and the fruit was finished, but the following year we returned to the tree and were treated to one of the best examples of wild food we've ever experienced.

Mulberries tend to be hard to pick, as they fall off the branch before you even get a chance to grab them, but it's worth persevering, as they are really delicious. One of the best ways we've heard to pick them is to put a sheet underneath and shake the tree. They're usually ready around late July and the season can sometimes last until September. They can be eaten raw or made into wine or jam. The leaves are sometimes made into a juice using a wheatgrass juicer (if you're one of the rare people who has one of these) or they can be dried and made into tea.

Plum and damson

Appearance	Large purple fruit
Where to look	On trees in parks and gardens and in some woodland
When to look	July to September (cultivated varieties), September to October (wild varieties)
Availability	Very easy to find

Plum or damson trees are always a welcome bonus on any wild walk. Some years the fruit can be found as early as June, but in our experience August is one of the best months to go foraging for it. Plums and damsons can be eaten straight off the tree or made into jam or chutney (see pages 254–6). Both fruits are also very useful in winemaking. This year, with his home-brewing co-op dubbed 'The Musty Men', Dave has made a plum and elderberry wine, which he's hoping to start drinking around the time of this book's release. Damsons can be ready a little later than plums and are often around until September. (For information on growing plums, see page 141.)

Mulberries are delicious fruits, found in late summer and sometimes into early autumn.

LEAVES & SHOOTS

Leaves gathered from the wild can make a great addition to salads or an extra element in curries, soups and stews. When harvested fresh from the plant they retain a lot of their nutritive content – all too often lacking in the plastic-packed green leaves bought from the supermarket. The taste of fresh nettles gently cooked in a pan with a little butter or fresh sorrel or rocket leaves in a salad can really bring home how choice has been limited rather than improved with modern food practices. If you haven't tried any of the leaves we've described below, we suggest you get looking in your garden right now and try them for yourself.

Nettle

Appearance	Green, spiky leaves covered in tiny hairs – will sting when touched
Where to look	Just about everywhere
When to look	All year round but best picked in spring when young
Availability	Very easy to find

Nettles are one of the wild foods that people often need to be convinced are fine to eat. The main concern seems to be whether the leaves will sting your mouth when you eat them. Anyone who's eaten a delicious fresh nettle soup will tell you that they certainly won't. The sting from a nettle is administered by a hollow hair, which has a swollen base containing a small pool of chemicals including formic acid and histamines. When touched, the hair pierces the skin like a miniature hypodermic needle injecting its unfortunate victim with a dose of nettle venom. However, when the nettle is heated or dried the hairs are disabled and the venom is neutralized, making the leaves fit to eat without any risk of being stung.

We find the taste of nettles far superior to that of spinach, and nutritionally speaking they're more than comparable. Nettles are rich in minerals, including iron, and contain high amounts of the antioxidant vitamins A, C and E. They also contain serotonin, which has been found to be useful for people suffering from depression.

Most wild-food books tell you to eat only the young or tender tops of nettles. This is because older leaves can become gritty in taste and will act as a laxative and kidney irritant. The tender tops usually refer to just the top four leaves of the nettle, and they're best picked using gardening gloves (if we don't have any gloves to hand we sometimes put a couple of plastic carrier bags on our hands for protection against stings).

Nettles can be used as a substitute for cooked spinach in recipes. If you've not tried this before, have a go at cooking nettle and ricotta cannelloni, or replace the spinach with nettles in any of your favourite spinach recipes.
• See Mushroom and nettle lasagne, page 215; Nettle beer, page 265.

Chickweed

Appearance	Small, creeping plant with a hairy stem, small white flowers and leaves that grow opposite one another
Where to look	Gardens and on waste ground – just about everywhere
When to look	All year round but best in spring
Availability	Very common and easy to find

Chickweed, also known as chickwittles, mischievous Jack, starweed, starwort and winterweed, is common in most gardens and grows throughout the year. It has quite a crisp taste rather than a bitter flavour like some wild leaves and is therefore very useful in a salad. We like to add a bit of it, along with some mint and black pepper, to yogurt as a dip or as a topping for soup. It also makes a delicious sandwich with mayonnaise, tomatoes and mixed leaves.

Fat hen/goosefoot

Appearance	Upright plant with diamond-shaped, spiky leaves
Where to look	Grows as a weed on cultivated land, often found by the coast
When to look	May to October
Availability	Fairly easy to find

Fat hen is a common weed that often grows in freshly worked land. We both have this growing on our allotments and we haven't had anything to do with its propagation.

Harvesting fat hen for a summer mixed-leaf salad.

The spiky green-grey leaves appear from spring onwards and can be put into salads or cooked in the same way as spinach. White flowers give way to seed that can be ground and made into bread, although yields are small so really it's just a case of adding it to ordinary wheat flour as a supplement. Fat hen often grows by the sea, where it can adopt a salty taste.

Sea beet

Appearance	Thick, shiny, green leaves on robust stems
Where to look	By the sea
When to look	All year round but best in spring
Availability	Very easy to find

The thick leaves of sea beet resemble those of beet spinach and the stems are stout, also making it look a little like a mini rhubarb plant. It grows wild by the coast, where it has a saltier flavour than if it's growing inland. Although it's not a true wild plant away from the coast, it often 'escapes' from allotments as it bolts and self-seeds very easily. Pick only the young leaves (small ones) for salads, as the older ones are quite bitter. The older leaves can be cooked as you would spinach or cabbage, and like that of spinach their taste goes very well with nutmeg.

Sorrel

Appearance	Small, spear-like leaves coming from a central stem and clusters of red flowers (the cultivated variety has white flowers)
Where to look	Mainly found in meadowland which hasn't been mowed, and often found on waste ground and occasionally in parks
When to look	Late March until August, occasionally as late as September or October
Availability	Takes a bit of looking

Sorrel belongs to the dock family, so it looks similar to many other docks. Found mainly in grassland and undisturbed meadows, it's identifiable by its clusters of red flowers and spiky leaves, and it grows about 60cm (24in) high. It has a tart, lemony taste and is excellent in a salad or with a strong cheese in a sandwich. It will keep in the fridge for a couple of days but will start to wilt after that. We sometimes add it to meals just before the end of cooking to give extra texture and flavour to a dish.

Mallow

Appearance	Large, green, crinkly, divided leaves (almost heart-shaped) and large, pinkish flowers
Where to look	Gardens, parkland, roadsides, waste ground
When to look	Leaves come early but best identified when it flowers, between June and October
Availability	Very common and easy to find

By early summer the mallow is usually in full flower and the plant is therefore quite easy to identify. This is also the time when elder starts to bloom, reminding us that summer is just around the corner. To mark the occasion we usually make delicious fritters using elderflowers and mallow – the leaves of mallow make an excellent egg substitute.

Mallow and elderflower fritters

3 mallow leaves
3 tbsp water
100ml (3½fl oz) milk (substitute rice milk for vegans)
60g (2oz) flour
Pinch of ground cinnamon
5 elderflower heads
Vegetable oil, for deep frying

1. Boil the mallow in the water until it becomes gloopy, resembling the consistency of raw egg.
2. Make a batter by combining the milk, flour, cinnamon and mallow water. Stir well until smooth.
3. Dip the elderflowers into the batter mix and deep fry in hot oil until brown and crispy.

Dandelion

Appearance	Spear-shaped leaves, which become 'toothed' with age, and yellow flowers
Where to look	Everywhere
When to look	All year round, although the leaves are best in spring and the roots in autumn
Availability	Very easy to find

Despite its being a pernicious weed, almost all of the dandelion plant is useful. The flowers can be boiled with sugar or honey and made into a cough mixture, the young leaves can be eaten raw, older leaves can be cooked, and the roots can be roasted, ground and made into coffee. Personally, we find the leaves a little bitter-tasting, particularly the older ones, and prefer to add young leaves to cooked dishes rather than eat them raw. (To remove the bitterness, the leaves can be blanched in a similar way to forcing rhubarb, by excluding light with an upturned pot. However, the nutritional value will be compromised.) After a little experimentation, we found dandelion leaves go well with strong-flavoured vegetables such as celery, beetroot and parsnips.

• See Dandelion wine, page 266; Dandelion cough syrup, page 275; Dandelion coffee, page 277.

Wild garlic/ramsons

Appearance	Leaves similar to those of bluebells but broader and lighter green and emerging from a central white flowering stem
Where to look	Woodland
When to look	February to May
Availability	Very easy to find

Every year the sight of wild garlic emerging on a woodland floor never fails to put a smile on our faces. It marks the end of long, dark winter nights and the start of spring, appearing in great numbers around the spring equinox. Wild garlic is best picked where it grows in abundance, as thinning it will actually aid its growth rather than hinder it. Pick just a few leaves from many plants rather than decimating one single specimen. For the same reason it's best not to take the bulb – it's only the size of a single garlic clove and therefore quite labour-intensive to gather enough bulbs of any use anyway. Wild garlic can be added to soups and stews to give a garlic flavour. We often use it in curries, or it can make an excellent pesto used in the place of basil.

Another useful, garlic-flavoured plant that appears this time of year is Jack-by-the-hedge, or garlic mustard. Unlike the true wild garlic, garlic mustard does not belong to the *Allium* (onion) genus but is closer to mint.

Hairy bittercress

Appearance	Main central stem with white flowers and mustard-like seedpods, and watercress-like leaves emanating from a central stem
Where to look	Often found on wasteland and in flower or vegetable beds that have recently been worked over
When to look	All year round but best in spring
Availability	Very common and easy to find

Hairy bittercress is so widespread during spring that we often pick a mixture of salad leaves growing on patches of land by the pavement on our way home. (If you pick it from the roadside, wash it thoroughly before use.)

Hairy bittercress is slightly peppery in taste and can be used in place of watercress in many recipes. It is good in soups if added towards the end of cooking; if it's over-cooked, the flavour and the nutritional value of the plant are greatly impaired. Bittercress also goes very well in salads, with cheese and in sandwiches. It is most prominent early in the year and sends up its little white flowers as early as March right through to September. We've found it out of the flowering season but it seems to get overtaken by other weeds after May.

Rocket

Appearance	Darkish green, toothed leaves that grow from a central stem; it can be low-lying at first but will bolt later, sending up a tall central stem with yellow flowers
Where to look	Mainly by the riverside but will grow in parks, gardens and on waste ground
When to look	May to September (mainly in summer)
Availability	Fairly easy to find

The spicy, tangy taste of rocket makes it one of the most choice salad greens of all wild leaves. It goes well in salads or with any savoury dishes using cream or cheese (risotto is especially good) and combines beautifully with Parmesan cheese.

Wild rocket differs slightly from cultivated rocket in that it has a stronger flavour and yellow rather than white flowers. The leaves are pointed and fairly distinctive. You could check out wild rocket at the greengrocer to make sure you know what it looks like before picking it in the wild, but once you're familiar with the plant you'll see it everywhere. Canal towpaths and riverbanks seem to be good places to find rocket, but we've also seen it growing by roadsides. White scale insects like to live on the underside of rocket leaves, so you need to wash them thoroughly before eating.

NUTS & FLOWERS

Nuts are another one of those wild foods that are often neglected. However, they're easily identifiable, very nutritious and of course extremely delicious. Flowers are usually overlooked as a food source but they can make a useful addition to the dinner table or as an infusion such as chamomile tea. Both flowers and nuts are readily available in the countryside and the town. We've found all of the ones described here while foraging within the city limits of Bristol and most within London.

Chestnuts

Appearance	A brown, conker-like nut, usually in pairs, in a spiky, light green shell
Where to look	On sweet chestnut trees in parks and woodland
When to look	September to November
Availability	Very easy to find

Chestnuts are one of the crowning glories of the wild-food year. Roasted chestnuts have a rich, starchy taste and have been used in the past as a staple food when other starch-rich foods were in short supply. In many ways they resemble the horse chestnut, but they're much softer and usually form more of a point at the base of the nut. It's important not to get the two mixed up, as the horse chestnut is poisonous. Chestnuts can sometimes be quite hard to harvest because of their prickly outer shell. A pair of good gardening gloves and walking boots can be the best way of opening these prickly casings. Just gently squeeze the spiky green shell underfoot until the nuts pop out. In the past, we've found chestnuts that just litter the forest floor with no need to take them out of the shell, but this is quite rare. Chestnuts will keep for a few months if you allow them to dry properly.

Chestnuts go really well with all types of mushroom. Adding ground-roasted chestnuts to ordinary flour can make chestnut flour, which is excellent for making pancakes as well as many other savoury dishes. Roasted chestnuts can also be used in the place of other nuts in most recipes.
• See Roasted chestnuts and Pumpkin and chestnut risotto, page 199.

Walnuts

Appearance	Hard, green fruit that opens to show the familiar walnut seed
Where to look	On walnut trees in woodland, parks and gardens
When to look	September to October
Availability	Quite rare in the wild

Ripe walnuts are a rare find but delicious if you do manage to beat the squirrels to them. Their outer casing gives them an appearance almost like hard, smallish apples. They do exist in the wild but are much more common in parks and gardens. Walnuts may be harvested in autumn, or they can be harvested immature in spring and pickled in a little vinegar.

Hazelnuts

Appearance	Small, brown nuts growing in a casing, usually in pairs
Where to look	On hazel trees, common in hedgerows woodland, parks and gardens
When to look	August to October
Availability	Very easy to find in some areas

Hazelnuts – which include cobnuts and filberts – should start to ripen around the end of August. The cobnut is rounded and only partly covered by its husk, while the filbert is longer and more pointed, and enclosed completely by the husk. Some years hazelnuts can be around right until October, and very occasionally into November on the ground, but this largely depends on the squirrel population. In some parts of the country you have to fight a battle with them to get to the hazelnuts first – they will strip a tree, often before the nuts have even had a chance to ripen. In other places, they seem to leave them alone.

Hazelnuts can be dried for storage but are best eaten fresh. We've experimented with cooking these as a vegetable and they go very well in sweet and savoury dishes (they soften in cooking). Use them in muffins or risottos. They're also great in flapjacks, granola, muesli and on their own, roasted.

Yarrow

Appearance	Fern-shaped leaves with small, umbrella-shaped flowers
Where to look	Parkland, waste ground, roadsides
When to look	March to December
Availability	Very easy to find

It's hard to leave your house without spotting a yarrow plant, and once you discover what yarrow looks like you will see it everywhere. The leaves are feathery with an ordered, fern-like pattern and the white flowerheads are borne in small clusters on an upright stem (see page 167). The stems can be cooked as a vegetable but we have yet to try this, as we use it all up to make a delicious yarrow tea each time we pick it.

Chamomile

Appearance	Daisy-like flowers with a characteristic scent
Where to look	Waste ground, by hedgerows and roadsides
When to look	June to September
Availability	Easy to find but not always common

Chamomile has very distinctive, daisy-like flowers and you need only to have previously smelt a chamomile tea bag to distinguish this plant from other flowers in the daisy family. The leaves are feathery and it will flower in Britain between late June and September. It's well known for its soothing properties and is good as a herbal infusion (see page 272).

Elderflower

Appearance	Small, white flowers growing in clusters from a central stem
Where to look	On elder trees in hedgerows, parks, waste ground, just about anywhere
When to look	May to June
Availability	Very easy to find and common

Elderflower has always been a favourite on the Self-sufficientish website. The fragrant smell of elderflower is just as distinctive as the appearance of the small, delicate, white flowers. Elderflower fritters are a firm spring favourite, as is elderflower cordial. Elderflower is also good in any baked products – elderflower muffins are especially tasty: just add a few blossoms to your favourite muffin recipe. We've also made elderflower vinegar in the past simply by putting some blooms into a bottle of white wine vinegar and leaving it for a couple of months. We made lots when we were hard up one year and they were welcome presents to those celebrating birthdays over the summer.

• See Mallow and elderflower fritters, page 224; Elderflower wine, page 266.

Elderflower cordial

This is a very straightforward recipe and needs little preparation and no complicated ingredients like citric acid (this is sometimes used as a preservative but lemon juice will suffice for smallish batches of cordial).

20 elderflower heads
1.5kg (3lb) sugar
1.25 litres (2 pints) boiling water
Juice of 2 lemons and grated zest of 1 lemon
1 cinnamon stick (optional)

1. In a clean bucket or large bowl, place a layer of elderflowers and then cover with some of the sugar.
2. Repeat with another layer of elderflowers and another layer of sugar until the bucket or bowl is about three-quarters full.
3. Pour over the boiling water and add the lemon juice and the zest. Some people add a cinnamon stick at this stage to give extra flavour to the cordial.
4. Cover and leave overnight. Strain the liquid and bottle it in sterilized bottles the next day. It will keep for a few months in a cool place; once opened it will last 1 week.

WILD FOOD CALENDAR

The calendar below indicates when you can hope to find certain plants and fungi growing in the wild in Britain. Bear in mind these are approximate guidelines only – growing times vary depending on where you are in the country and the climatic conditions that year. Also, in many cases there may be an optimum time for foraging – for example, oyster mushrooms are available all year round but you're most likely to have success between October and March. All the foods listed here are described in more detail earlier in this chapter.

	DEC	JAN	FEB	MAR	APR	MAY	JUN	JUL	AUG	SEP	OCT	NOV
Mushrooms												
Cep									•	•	•	•
Chanterelle	•								•	•	•	•
Field blewit/wood blewit	•									•	•	•
Giant puffball								•	•	•	•	•
Jew's ear	•	•	•	•	•	•	•	•	•	•	•	•
Morel				•	•	•						
Oyster mushroom	•	•	•	•					•	•	•	•
Fruit												
Blackberry							•	•	•	•		
Crab apple									•	•	•	
Elderberry									•	•		
Mulberry								•	•	•		
Plum/damson									•	•	•	
Sloe										•	•	•
Wild cherry							•	•				
Leaves & shoots												
Chickweed	•	•	•	•	•	•	•	•	•	•	•	•
Dandelion	•	•	•		•	•	•	•	•	•	•	•
Fat hen							•	•	•	•	•	•
Hairy bittercress	•	•	•	•	•	•			•	•	•	
Mallow							•	•	•	•	•	
Nettle	•	•	•	•	•	•	•	•	•	•	•	•
Rocket							•	•	•	•	•	
Sea beet	•	•	•	•	•	•	•	•	•		•	•
Sorrel				•	•	•	•	•	•			
Wild garlic			•	•	•	•						
Nuts & flowers												
Chestnuts											•	•
Hazelnuts									•	•	•	
Walnuts										•	•	
Chamomile							•	•	•	•		
Elderflower						•	•					
Yarrow	•			•	•	•	•	•	•	•	•	•

LIVESTOCK

If you've ever seen pictures of a farm where animals are intensively reared, there's little doubt that you'll think twice before buying cheap meat again. It's well worth paying the extra to source animal products from a reliable, specialist supplier who has the animals' welfare and food quality at heart. Even better, you could raise livestock yourself if you have the space and the inclination to do so.

Smallholders take great joy in getting to know their livestock, and when you hand-rear animals yourself you can be sure that they're treated with the respect they deserve. In return, they'll reward you with great-tasting eggs, meat, milk or honey – as with all organic food, the produce tastes far superior to anything that you'll find in a supermarket.

The first consideration is whether you have sufficient space to accommodate livestock comfortably. Some animals, for instance chickens, are happy in fairly small spaces, and can cope with a town garden, while many larger animals such as cattle need acres of land on which

to graze. Time is also an important issue, as regular feeding is a major commitment. When keeping animals you should be aware of legislation, as there can be some paperwork involved, especially when it comes to raising larger animals.

To purchase livestock, check the local press, farm shows and markets, specialist magazines and the internet and ask local farmers in your area. Ensure that you're buying from a reputable dealer or from someone you trust – it has been known for some unscrupulous dealers to pass on sick and diseased animals.

KEEPING CHICKENS

In 2005 TV presenters Richard and Judy announced that keeping chickens was Britain's fastest-growing hobby. Most will agree that the main reason for this is probably the taste of the eggs. If you've yet to experience the taste of eggs laid within 24 hours of reaching your plate, we suggest that you find someone who keeps chickens or go to a farm shop and try them – the taste alone might be enough to convince you to get some egg-laying hens and build your own chicken ark.

Before you get carried away and rush out to buy your birds be aware that chickens require commitment, as is the case when caring for any animal. They need regular feeding twice a day, and even with an automatic feeder you can leave them for only a couple of days at a time.

Something else to bear in mind is that most chicken breeds will lay efficiently for the first 2 years and then start to slow down production by around 15–20 per cent in their third year. On average, chickens live for around 6 or 7 years (it has been known for some to live to over 15) and there will come a point when their feed will cost more than the eggs you receive (with the possible exception of breeds such as Black Rocks). You may also have to rehouse older chickens away from any younger ones to stop them from being picked on. Running a retirement home for chickens can be a rather costly business, but if you view them as pets it can be an experience that's worth paying for. Dave is considering getting some chickens purely for entertainment value, as he loves watching them and listening to their quirky noises.

Contrary to popular belief, you don't need to keep a cockerel if you want to get eggs from your chickens. It's only when you wish to fertilize the eggs to increase your stock of birds that you'll need the services of a cockerel. Cockerels are also useful if you have a bigger flock of birds because they can reduce 'pecking order' fights among the hens. However, the downside is they can be very noisy, and in a densely populated residential area you're likely to get complaints from neighbours. In fact, some councils don't permit the keeping of cockerels, so you'll need to check first whether or not you're allowed to before getting one. If you can't keep cockerels and still want to breed chickens, don't despair – you may be able to borrow one from another chicken keeper or farmer. Look on the internet forums and check chicken-keeping magazines.

Some people get chickens that are past their best cheaply from farmers, although this can cause problems if chickens are already resident, as they may pick on the newcomers. A noble way to obtain chickens is to get those that have been rescued from battery farms – visit the website www.thehenhouse.co.uk for more information. The conditions many commercial chickens are kept in are pretty barbaric, so if you have the space and time to rear some of your own it's worth giving them a better life.

Always go to pick up your birds so see what conditions they're kept in and how healthy their parents look. A healthy bird will have a glossy coat and will appear to be interested in its surroundings.

Housing chickens

If you intend to keep only two chickens at a time, not much space is needed (it's considered cruel to keep only one chicken). An area approximately 2 square metres (22 square feet) is just enough space, so most backyards are adequate. On rare occasions you see poultry on allotments, but you'll need to seek permission from your allotment rep and the council beforehand, as restrictions can apply in some areas. Our parents would like to keep chickens but the deeds of their house state that they're not allowed to, so do check your deeds or with your landlord before you buy your flock.

Chickens like grass, but if you don't have a lawn they can be kept on concrete, tarmac or paving; however, they need a thick layer of straw or wood chippings laid down to compensate and you'll need to keep the area clean to reduce the chance of disease.

All chickens need a hen hut. This has to be dry, draught-free and, most important, secure enough to keep out foxes and rats. Also, bear in mind that you'll have to visit the hut to fetch the eggs and to clean up, so consider roof ventilation (a flap that opens should suffice). An old converted shed will do the job, or you can check your local www.freecycle.org group, eBay and in the classified ads for second-hand hen huts. They're also available new online. Alternatively, you may consider making your own chicken ark (see overleaf).

Chickens are happy in smallish outdoor spaces but need company.

MAKING A CHICKEN ARK

A chicken ark is a triangular structure with one section for living accommodation (the shed) and the other half for the run. The whole ark can be moved around every few days or weeks, when the birds have scratched and pecked down to bare earth. As a rule of thumb, one chicken needs at least 1 square metre (11 square feet) of space. This ark will house two chickens, but you can obviously make it bigger if required. The back door is for inspecting the chickens to see if they've laid. Place a small nesting box full of straw inside and a tray that you can get out through the door, to save cleaning. Use sustainable outdoor-grade plywood and treated timber.

What you need
Set square and jigsaw
12 pieces of wood, 1m x 50mm x 50mm
    (3ft x 2in x 2in) (A)
Wood glue
Screws and small nails
2 planks of wood, 2m x 150mm x 20mm thick
    (6ft x 6in x ¾in) (B)
1 piece of wood, 2m x 50mm x 50mm
    (6½ft x 2in x 2in) (C)
1 sheet of plywood, 1 x 1.5m (3 x 5ft) (D)
4 sets of hinges and 1 door clasp
1 screw eye and length of twine, 1.5–2m (5–6½ft) long
1 sheet of plywood, 1 x 1m (3 x 3ft) (E)
2 sheets of plywood, 1m x 850mm (39in x 34in) (F)
Large nail or cleat
Chicken wire, 1 x 3m (3 x 10ft)
Industrial stapler and staples
1 door catch

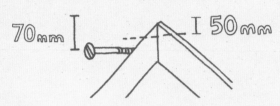

2. Glue the pieces of wood together to make four triangles and leave to dry. Measure 70mm (3in) from the corners, drill guide holes and insert screws. On one of the angles, 50mm (2in) from the tip, draw a line parallel with the bottom of the triangle and saw across the line so that the tips of the triangle are flat.

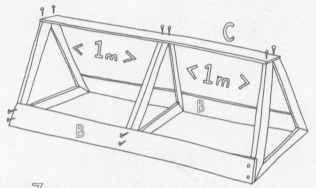

3. To make the basic frame of the ark, hold one of the triangles upright, place one plank (B) against its side and nail the plank in place so it lies flush against the triangle. Attach the second and the third triangles in the same way, spacing them 1m (3ft) apart. Attach the second plank (B) on the other side. Finally, screw the piece of wood (C) onto the flat tops of the triangles.

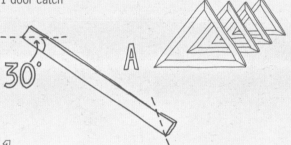

1. Use a set square to measure a 30-degree angle at the ends of the 12 bits of wood (A). Cut all the angles using a jigsaw. The angles must be exact so the triangles fit together. A mitre box is useful for this task.

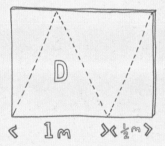

4. Cut the shapes for the doors out of the rectangular piece of plywood (D). Mark out triangles as shown. This will give you two equilateral triangles and two right-angled triangles. Saw along the drawn lines.

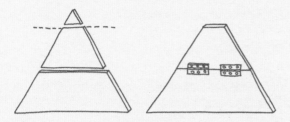

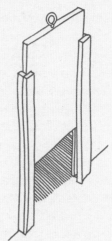

5. To make the back door, measure 50cm (20in) up from the base of one of the equilateral triangles. Saw across this line so the triangle cuts in half. As previously, saw off the tip of the triangle so that it's flat (it needs to be the same size as the other triangles). Join the two bottom sections of triangle by screwing in a pair of hinges and on the other side attach a clasp so the door can open and close.

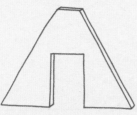

6. Use the second equilateral triangle to make the divider and door between the shed and the run. Cut out a rectangular aperture and make 'runners' by cutting the leftover pieces of plywood and attaching them around the opening so they create a lip of 20mm (¾in).

7. Use the cut-away piece of plywood to make the door. Attach a screw eye at the top of the door, feed the twine through the hole and tie to secure. Slide the door into place. Nail the triangle onto the shed frame.

8. To make the base of the shed area, screw the square of plywood (E) to the base of the triangles, on the back half of the ark. Nail the plywood pieces (F) to the sides of the triangles to make the shed walls. Hammer a large nail or cleat onto the shed roof (this is to keep the twine in place when the door is open).

9. Secure the chicken wire to the front half of the ark using industrial staples, ensuring that there are no gaps and that it's completely secure.

10. Use the fourth, remaining triangle to make a door for the front of the ark. Affix chicken wire around the triangle, stapling it in place, then attach the door on one side with two sets of hinges and attach a catch so you can open and close the door.

Feeding chickens

Chickens naturally forage and will eat grass, insects, grubs and even small mice if they have access to them. However, you still need to feed them regularly. Chickens have different dietary requirements depending on their age and what you're using them for: for example, brooding hens require very little feeding. The easiest way to know you're giving them the correct nutrients that they need is to buy commercial feed specific to your birds' requirements – for instance, brooding hen feed or chick feed. Chickens need a certain amount of grit to help them digest their food and also calcium for laying eggs (oyster shells can be bought for this purpose). Green leafy vegetables can be a great bonus to their diet, so throw some of your kitchen scraps in with your flock. It's also very important that you provide them with plenty of clean water, which should be changed every day.

Which type of chicken?

When choosing a breed of chicken, you have to ask yourself what you want from your birds – do you plan to have eggs, meat or both?

Good egg layers

Andalusian – Small bird with white eggs; not a good choice for breeding.
Black Rock – Produces good eggs and it has been known for 10-year-old birds still to be productive. Suitable for northern climates, because it's able to withstand very cold weather.
Bluebelle – Peaceful blue bird that lays brown eggs.
Isa Brown – Named after Institut de Sélection Animale, the company that first bred them for battery farms because of their high production of eggs (up to 300 in a year). If you rescue a battery hen you're likely to get an Isa Brown.
Warren – A very good layer, sometimes producing over 300 eggs a year.

Good for meat and eggs

Chantecler – First bred by a trappist monk, which is perhaps why this bird has such a friendly nature! Lays a reasonable number of eggs, often one a day.
Rhode Island Red – Good choice for a small flock, although males can be aggressive.
Silver Laced Wyandotte – Very attractive-looking, friendly and long-established American breed. Both the birds and their brown eggs reach a good size.
Sussex – A heavy bird that can lay about 250 eggs a year.
Welsummer – Many keep this bird for the eggs alone as it

is a great layer, and if crossed with a heavier breed it will supply a fair amount of meat too.

Meat only

Ross Cobb – The Ross part of this chicken's name comes from the frozen-food company that helped to develop it. It's a fast-growing bird.
Brahma – A slower-growing bird thought to originate from India. There is a number of varieties of Brahma and some are very beautiful specimens.
Cochin – Introduced to Britain from Vietnam and presented to Queen Victoria. A friendly bird that's particularly suited to a free-range environment.

BIRD FLU – H5N1

Bird flu is a highly contagious disease and the majority of birds contracting it will die. It is spread by migratory birds with the disease, or through illegally imported poultry, or even by contact with a person who's been to an infected area. Although it's possible for the H5N1 virus to infect humans, current thinking suggests that it will need to mutate twice, first infecting pigs that are kept near livestock and then passing to humans. There have been only a few isolated incidents where the infection has gone from person to person. Following these precautionary measures should help reduce the instances of bird flu:

- Avoid contact with wild birds, especially their faeces.
- If you've been to an area where there are wild birds, wash and disinfect yourself and change your clothes before handling your flock.
- Buy birds only from a reputable source.
- If any of your birds becomes ill contact your vet immediately.
- Wash down your vehicle if it's been in contact with wild birds or large poultry stock.

If your birds are within a 10-kilometre (6-mile) radius of any infected bird they may have to be destroyed along with any of their eggs. For more up-to-date information visit www.defra.gov.uk.

KEEPING DUCKS

Raising ducks is quite different from keeping chickens. One main difference is that they need a lot more room, including water, but to compensate you'll get more eggs and/or more meat. A duck bred for its meat will provide almost twice as much meat as a chicken and can lay anything up to 300 eggs a year. If you do intend to keep ducks for meat, be aware that they have more 'personality' than chickens – ducks can follow you round the garden or house, mistaking you for another duck. This attachment is an obvious downside when it comes to slaughtering them later.

Access to a stream is ideal for ducks. A pond is an option, but you do have to be careful that the water doesn't turn stagnant as this can cause disease. Also, because eggs can be laid in water they could be dangerous to eat as bacteria can pass through the shell. A pond that's fed by a spring or other source of running water helps to avoid the problem. However, a great number of duck owners who visit our web forum (www.selfsufficientish.com/forum) have used old bathtubs and paddling pools sunk into the ground and claim this provides sufficient water for their birds.

Newborn ducklings ingest the remaining yolk from their eggs, which keeps them nourished for 3 days. After that time you should feed them a starter ration of special pellets. If you can't find duckling feed, chick feed with added niacin will suffice. After about 3 weeks you can slowly introduce a grower's feed ration. Ducks will also eat the insects that you have around the garden, and you can feed them fresh kitchen scraps. Muscovy ducks are a particularly good breed – they're easy to look after, provide good meat and lay about 80 eggs per year.

Muskovy ducks are relatively easy to care for, resist disease and reproduce easily.

KEEPING PIGS

Those who remember the 1980s might also recall reports on pigs being kept as pets. Pigs are lovely animals, and we can quite understand wanting to have them around for their company alone. However, in this book we're going to concentrate on keeping them for meat, but in a humane way. Home-reared pigs will provide meat far tastier than you could possibly buy in any supermarket, and in addition they'll eat your scraps and fertilize the area in which you keep them.

Pigs farmed commercially for their meat are often kept in pretty appalling conditions, second only to those of poultry, and a strong reason for keeping your own is to give them a better life. If you have no experience with pigs it's well worth going on a pig-keeping course. Many towns and cities have a city farm that should be able give you some pointers or put you in touch with someone who can help.

It's actually illegal to slaughter your own pig, so you'll have to find a nearby abattoir to do it for you. You are allowed to butcher it yourself, but it's advisable to get a professional to do it on the first occasion.

Buying and choosing pigs

Local newspapers, the internet and specialist smallholding magazines are all good places to start looking for your first pigs. Start with a pair to begin with – pigs like company, so keeping a single pig is cruel, while two will help you get a feel for the animals to see if pig-keeping is for you without committing yourself to a great number.

When buying pigs, look for good pure breeds and check that the pigs have the following characteristics:

- Good shiny coat
- Skin that is not red or flaky
- Bright eyes
- Alert and not sullen look
- High-set tail, not dirty and wet
- Cold, moist nose
- No limp
- They should acknowledge humans in the area, making a beeline for you

If you decide to keep pigs, you'll need to contact DEFRA (Department for Environment, Food and Rural Affairs). They'll let you know what legislation to follow and may send someone to assess the area in which you wish to keep them.

Transporting pigs

You could transport smaller pigs in a large estate car and bigger ones in a four-wheeled trailer. In warm weather, try to travel in the evenings or mornings, when it's cooler, rather than in the middle of the day. The pigs will move around, so it's advisable to put them in a large dog cage to contain them. Generally, we would never suggest keeping livestock in cages, but as they're likely to sleep most of the way in any case it's simply easier for a short distance. Bed the area with straw and newspaper and keep windows open in hot weather. If your car gets particularly hot you might want to block out the back windows with cardboard to keep the pigs cool. Or, if they're kept in a cage, cover the cage with a blanket. You must wash your car or trailer out after transportation. Give them a drinking bowl but don't feed them before you travel, because pigs can be particularly prone to travel sickness.

Housing pigs

Ideally, you need an area of approximately 80 square metres (860 square feet) for two pigs; it should be a place that won't flood and is free of poisonous weeds such as ragwort. Pigs can be kept in smaller areas – indeed, at one time many people used to keep a pig in their backyard to fatten up for winter – but this isn't advisable as they really need more space to roam around and are also happier living in pairs.

Pigs also require shelter in bad weather. You could buy a second-hand pig ark relatively cheaply, although you may consider building your own. If you plan on keeping a lot of pigs, you may need planning permission before you build their home. Their shelter needs to be draught-free, warm, dry and airy. A wooden ark is ideal, as it's warm in winter and cooler in summer. It should have a door so that you can enclose your pigs if needs be. Also, give them a bed of straw to keep them comfortable.

People often use electric fencing to contain their pigs, because the animals soon learn that they can't get through it and it's far easier to move than conventional fencing.

Pigs need a warm, comfortable shelter in winter.

Feeding pigs

The easiest way to feed pigs is to give them pig pellets. Adults require approximately 1.75–2kg (3½–4lb) a day of pellets. They will also appreciate your scraps from the kitchen. However, be aware that it's illegal to feed pigs meat, so don't just scrape off your Sunday dinner leftovers into their trough. It's strongly advisable to let your pigs have access to grass; they will also benefit from valuable minerals in the soil.

Pigs need access to clean fresh water; metal troughs that fill automatically and are secured in concrete are ideal. They also require 1–8 litres (1¾–14 pints) of water a day, depending on their size.

KEEPING GOATS, SHEEP & CATTLE

If you're lucky enough to have a field or a very large garden you may consider keeping bigger animals such as goats, sheep or cattle. Andy visited a Romanian village in the early 1990s where keeping such animals was commonplace – sheep's cheese was swapped for goat's milk and cow's milk became almost a currency in itself. Cows were kept in back gardens and were walked across the village for pasture on common land every morning. Although it was like stepping back in time, we'd like to think that if the current interest in smallholdings continues, we could see a similar kind of bartering come into play in this country – we hope so, because it would result in better animal welfare, purer food and less waste.

Goats

Goats can provide you with delicious milk and cheese and offer a good alternative to cow's milk, particularly for those with certain food allergies. They're also a good source of meat. The problem with keeping goats is that they can be difficult to keep in one place. Tethering is an option, but this doesn't seem terribly humane. Good electric fencing or a 1.4m (4½ft) high fence will certainly help keep a goat within its set boundaries, and they'll soon learn to avoid an electric fence.

Goats need shelter in cold weather and at night – a ventilated shed that's slightly raised off the floor with some straw bedding is ideal. Given some woodland and meadowland, goats will happily forage for their own food, although it's advisable to give them supplementary feeds. They will eat kitchen scraps (organic matter) and leftovers from your vegetable garden. If you're keeping more than one goat, feed them individually, as they'll steal food from each other.

Sheep

There are many breeds of sheep that serve different purposes. Suffolks are suitable for fattening for meat, Jacobs produce good wool and almost any cross keeps the grass down. The inexperienced should consider buying only ewes and not rams, as they can become rather boisterous and injuries are not uncommon. A 2- or 3-year-old ewe will be a lot less problematic than a young lamb that will need bottle-feeding and will no doubt cost more than you planned for in expensive veterinary bills.

Sheep need a large area of pasture to graze in – around 4 hectares (10 acres) used on a rotation system should be enough to sustain about five to ten ewes. Pasture and hay make up most of their diet, although rams before the breeding season, lactating sheep and elderly sheep all benefit from a grain supplement. Sheep need about 2–4 litres (3½–7 pints) of water a day and should have access to a salt block. There are special feeds available, which are useful where the pasture is poor.

Cows

Cows keep you in dairy products and beef in return for some hay, grass and oats in winter (although high-protein food is advisable as a winter supplement). You'll also have to milk them every day. They're expensive to keep and two cows need about 140 square metres (1,500 square feet) of land, so they're for the more serious smallholder.

Cows can be kept outside all year round, but it's better to bring them indoors in the winter months. A shed of 4 x 10m (12 x 30ft) should suffice for two cows. Covering the floor in straw and cleaning it out every day will provide the cows with some comfort and will also give you excellent compost.

The field in which the cows live should contain various grasses and wildflowers and they need 30 litres (7 gallons) of water a day; a metal trough fitted with an automatic filling system is ideal. To prevent diseases, your animals should not be kept on the same pasture year after year, so make sure you have enough space to move them around.

Goats are friendly animals and will happily eat your vegetable leftovers.

BEE-KEEPING

Einstein is often quoted as saying, 'If the bee disappeared off the surface of the globe then man would only have four years of life left. No more bees, no more pollination, no more plants, no more animals, no more man.' Some people claim these words have been falsely attributed to Einstein, but whatever the case the vital role played by bees remains undisputed. Honeybees are essential for the pollination and production of agricultural food crops, and without bees there would be major food shortages across the world; indeed, one-third of all the food we eat has been pollinated by bees.

The bee population worldwide is in decline, and at the risk of being slightly melodramatic it is our duty to keep bees to ensure the survival of our own species. There is also the satisfaction factor in watching your bees going about their daily business with the knowledge that they're working to make you delicious honey. The bee-keepers we've met all seem unable to imagine a life without bees – it would appear that once 'stung' by the bee-keeping bug you'll never look back.

Taking up bee-keeping

Even the smallest gardens are suitable for bee-keeping, although it may be difficult to keep bees in densely populated areas as neighbours may object. Most allotments will allow holders to keep bees, so this can be a good compromise in cities. Using a rooftop may also be an option in an urban environment – there is a London-based honey producer who does just that.

Bees live in colonies of up to 75,000 during peak production times. Of this number there is just one queen and roughly 200 drones. The rest are female worker bees. The queen is capable of laying 2000 eggs a day. A hive provides just the right amount of space needed for bees to crawl and make their honey. The most popular hive is the National Hive. Second-hand ones are available, or experienced carpenters could make their own.

Bee-keeping can be very technical and there's a lot to learn. The best option is to enrol on a theory course over winter, then join a practical course in spring and summer. Your local bee-keeping association will recommend a suitable course in your area. Check out this website for details – www.bbka.org.uk.

The best place to look for bees is in specialist magazines, and the time to buy them is from mid-April onwards. Alternatively, you could ask at your local bee-keepers' society, as it may be possible to get a swarm of bees for free. However, it's important to make sure they don't have any diseases.

There are several things to look out for when buying bees:

- Make sure the combs are covered with bees; gaps could be a result of a high death rate and inferior bees.

- The bees should be returning to the hive with just enough pollen that you can see it.

- Bees should be flying from the hive in good weather.

- The queen should be young.

The bee-keeper's year

This is a rough month-by-month guide of the duties you must expect to perform over the course of a year. It's always worth keeping a log of what's going on with your hive.

December, January and February

This is a quiet time for the bee-keeper, and you shouldn't need to spend more than an hour a week at the very most. It's the perfect time for reading up about bees. As there are a few flowers starting to appear in February there will be some pollen about; consequently, the queen will start to lay eggs and a few bees will start to leave the hive.

- Check the outside of the hive once or twice a week or after particularly bad weather. Repair any old or damaged hives and check the mouse guard and insulation are intact.

- Lift up your hive and see how heavy it is; if it's really light the bees may need feeding with a candy block.

March

There is still little to do (about an hour a week).

- As soon as you have fine weather, check your hive to ensure that you still have a queen – no queen means no bees, no bees means no honey, and you will just have very expensive boxes sitting in your back garden. You can usually tell by judging the weight of your hive – it should start getting heavier now as the bees start to work.

● Check the candy block as the bees might need some more food: you could offer a syrup solution.

● Inspect the hive for diseases and pests: ants, mice, humans and woodpeckers can all be a problem.

April

This is the month that the bees really start work. There's a lot of tree pollen around at this time, so the bees should have plenty to eat, but it's worth making sure. Swarming can begin at the end of the month (although it's unlikely to happen in the first year), and occurs when a queen leaves a hive with a group of workers to form a new colony. You should put measures in place to prevent this (see below).

● Check the hive weight and make sure it's getting heavier. There might also be a need for a half-strength syrup: see if they've eaten last month's supply.

● Make sure that you still have a queen – the hive will hum restlessly if you don't and there will also be bee poo at the entrance to the hive.

● To control swarming, place bait hives around the existing colony to attract the swarm. Look out for queen cells, which will be elongated in the brood, as these are the likely culprits for swarming; you can either divide the colony or destroy these cells.

May

The colony will now be at almost full strength and it's the time the bees are most likely to swarm; as in April, consider a bait hive to catch them.

● Regularly inspect the brood combs. As the older brood combs might harbour diseases they'll need to be worked to the outside so they can be removed and replaced.

● The queen will need a little helping hand, so place new frames in the foundation area, either side of the brood nest, to give her more room to increase the nest. There may be a lot of pollen stored. If this is the case, you can remove a few combs and freeze them until autumn.

June

This is one of the greatest months for the bee-keeper, because you may be rewarded with some honey. It is also a good month for rearing new queens. Look out for the elongated queen cells at this time of year as they can be used to establish new colonies.

● There is still a danger of swarming (see April, left).

● Check the brood frames for disease.

● Harvest the honey.

July and August

Time to relax a little in mid-July – well, you need not worry so much about swarming anyway.

● Take precautions against wasp attacks by placing an excluder on the hive entrance.

● Combine the weaker colonies. One strong colony is better than two weak ones, so you should destroy the queen from the weaker colony and place the bees together in one hive.

● Harvest the honey.

September

The colonies are growing smaller now, because the bees aren't being replaced. You may still be able to harvest honey this month.

● Fit a mouse guard if there's a likelihood of attack.

● Feed the bees some sugar – they might need a little help for the coming winter months.

● Harvest the honey.

October and November

This is the time to prepare the hive for winter.

● In windy areas, strap the roof of the hive down.

● Give your hive a lick of paint to protect it further.

● Add some insulation if necessary.

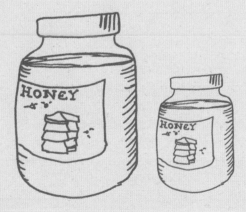

PRESERVING

Our Nan used to have cupboards and cupboards full of pickles, chutneys and jams. The fruit-laden plum tree in her garden and our Granddad's well-tended vegetable plot meant that there was always much more than they could possibly eat in a season, so they would preserve it for the less plentiful times ahead. This is a passion we've both certainly inherited, and some years the contents of our kitchen cupboards could rival the selection at any Women's Institute meeting.

When growing your own vegetables and fruit it's easy to produce more than you can eat before they get past their best. It helps if you manage your crops by planting in succession, several weeks apart, but however efficient you may be some things will do better than expected and others will fail miserably. At the height of the runner-bean season we've been so inundated with them that they've been on the table 7 days a week for a whole month. To make the most of these gluts, and to ensure that half your crops don't end up on the compost heap, it's well worth

getting a variety of preserving techniques under your belt – drying and freezing, as well as making jams, pickles and chutneys, are all fantastic ways of putting home-grown or foraged produce on the table every day of the year.

It's in the depths of winter that preserved food comes into its own. We've found that crackers with cheese, pickles and a home-brewed ale make the perfect snack on a cold winter's night, jams from foraged berries are a real treat for breakfast, and sweet homemade chutney enlivens the inevitable turkey sandwiches on Boxing Day.

The best way to store onions and garlic is to dry them, make a plait and hang the bunch in a cool, well-ventilated place.

DRY STORAGE

Before the fridge and freezer came into being, people preserved their fruit and vegetables for long-term keeping in a number of different ways. Many of the principles of food preservation used by our grandparents' generation and those before them can still be employed today, including various methods of drying food and burying it in pots of sand or in an underground trench known as a potato clamp.

Drying methods

Many vegetables, fruit, herbs and fungi can be dried easily. You don't need any specialist equipment – an oven, radiator or airing cupboard will often suffice, or you may thread them onto string and hang them up. We just leave French and runner beans to dry in their pods on the plant until the end of the season, then shell the beans and store them in an airtight container.

The drying process is best carried out somewhere warm and well ventilated; in Britain this means indoors, often under artificial heat. Any moisture in the air will hinder the evaporation of water from your produce and will spoil it – the more ventilated the drying space, the faster the food will dry. It's rather like drying clothes: on a warm, windy day your clothes will dry very quickly on the line, but they'll take ages if placed on a turned-off radiator in a damp flat.

Drying naturally Most members of the squash family can be stored by simply cutting them from the plant and leaving them out in the sun for around a week to harden the skin. You may need to turn them a couple of times to ensure all of the fruit hardens. Alternatively, if the weather is wet, you can bring them indoors and dry them on the windowsill. If the fruit has any blemishes or cuts in the skin it won't store well at all, so it's best just to eat those particular specimens fresh.

To dry onions and garlic, dig them up, then snap the tops close to the bulb but don't remove the stalks. Spread them out on the soil in dry weather or, if the soil is wet, on a concrete path or even in a shed, an outbuilding or on a windowsill: this could take up to 2 weeks. To store, plait the stalks or tie them together with string and hang the vegetables in a shed or other cool, well-ventilated place.

The oven method Apples, grapes, pears and apricots, as well as numerous other fruits and some vegetables, can be dried successfully using a conventional kitchen oven.

1. Remove the seeds or stalks and slice the fruit or vegetable into chip-sized pieces.

2. Dip the chopped fruit or vegetable in a little diluted lemon juice (juice of 1 lemon to 7 tablespoons of water) and arrange on a baking tray, allowing a gap of at least 1cm (½in) between the pieces.

3. Set the oven to the lowest possible temperature, about 60°C (140°F); some ovens have a slow-cook button.

4. Prop the door ajar and place the baking tray on the middle shelf. Check every half an hour or so to make sure the food isn't scorching. It needs to be completely dehydrated – this can take about 5 or 6 hours, if not longer. If you're lucky enough to have an Aga or Rayburn, many of these have a warming oven and fruit or vegetables can be left in this for 24 hours or so until dry.

Drying in an airing cupboard An airing cupboard is an ideal place to dry large gluts of vegetables, especially beans. You could either put the fruit and vegetables on baking trays, as for the oven method (see above), or use the string method of hanging (see below). Either way, in a warm airing cupboard it will take around 6 hours or sometimes longer until the food is completely dried.

The string method This is particularly suitable for mushrooms. Remove the stalks before drying (use them to make a stock or soup).

1. Cut large mushrooms into quarters and leave the smaller ones whole.

2. Thread a piece of string through a darning needle and carefully pull it through the centre of the mushroom. Tie a knot underneath the mushroom and repeat with the other mushrooms or mushroom pieces, leaving enough room between each one so they don't touch.

3. Put between 10 and 12 mushrooms on each string. Leave them to hang in an airing cupboard or a well-ventilated part of the house. They can take anything up to 3 days to dry completely.

The radiator method of drying mushrooms.

STORING & REHYDRATING MUSHROOMS

Store dried mushrooms in an airtight container, such as a glass jar or an old ice-cream tub. To rehydrate them, leave the mushrooms in a bowl of water for about an hour or two before using them. The remaining water can be used as a flavourful mushroom stock for soups and risottos. Before eating any mushrooms, peel them or wipe the surface with a clean damp cloth.

The radiator method This is particularly good for drying mushrooms and other vegetables with a low water content. It's very slow, so isn't suited to most fruit and vegetables, particularly larger items, but if you're faced with a big glut it would be worth experimenting. Either place a bowl containing your produce directly on the radiator, or for larger amounts of food use a wire rack suspended over the radiator. Leave for a couple of days, turning the produce as the underside dries.

Burying root vegetables
and potatoes

Traditionally, root vegetables such as beetroot, carrots, parsnips, swede, celeriac and turnips, as well as potatoes and Jerusalem artichokes, can all be stored in a bucket of sand. Brush the earth off the vegetables before storing (it's considerably easier if you lift them on a dry day). Discard any vegetables that look diseased, twist off the green tops carefully and place the roots in the sand, ensuring that they don't touch. The sand helps insulate each vegetable from the others in case of rot and also lets air circulate. The vegetables should last several weeks or in some cases months in the sand.

Another good burying method for many vegetables and some tree fruit is to make a potato clamp (see opposite).

THE POTATO CLAMP

Despite its name, a potato clamp can be used for storing more than just potatoes: you can use it for root vegetables, some fruit (apples and pears) and flower roots such as gladioli and dahlias.

1. Clear a patch of earth and dig a shallow hole (about 10cm/4in down). The area it takes up depends on how much you need to store.

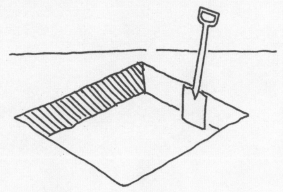

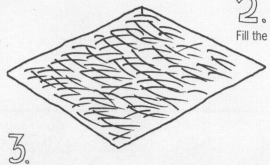

2. Fill the hole with straw.

3. Pile the potatoes, or whatever you're storing, up to half the width of the clamp, so if your clamp is 1m (3ft) across they should pile up to 50cm (20in).

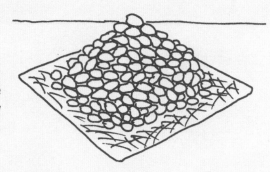

4. Cover your produce with another layer of straw, about 15cm (6in) thick.

5. Pile soil on top of the straw, covering the produce, and dig a trench (about a spade's depth) around the finished clamp to keep animals at bay. The earth covering should be about 15cm (6in) thick. Make a 15cm (6in) ventilation hole in the top of your clamp and fill it with straw.

This is a cutaway picture of how the finished clamp should look. The clamp should be able to store your produce over winter until the following spring.

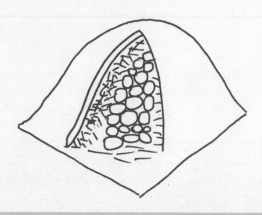

Freeze soft fruit on trays, making sure the individual
fruits aren't touching, and bag them up later.

FREEZING PRODUCE

By far the easiest way to preserve your produce is to deep freeze it. If frozen correctly, food will retain its colour, texture, taste and nutritional value and will still be safe to eat. Most vegetables will freeze, except for kale, radishes, the majority of salad leaves, swedes, potatoes and vegetables with a high water content such as cucumbers or tomatoes (unless cooked). The delicate cell structure of these vegetables can be damaged by the process, leaving you with a gooey mess when they are defrosted.

Freezing vegetables

Vegetables benefit from blanching before they're frozen, to help maintain their structure and colour. To blanch your vegetables, bring a pan of water to the boil and once it's boiling rapidly put in the required vegetables. The length of time depends on the thickness of the vegetable – carrots will need to be blanched for around 4 minutes, whereas courgettes need only a minute before they're ready to freeze. Beans come somewhere in between, requiring about 2 to 3 minutes, and broccoli and cauliflower a little over 3 minutes; cabbage needs only a minute and a half or so. Some softer vegetables, such as tomatoes (technically a fruit), will spoil if frozen, but making them into a sauce and freezing it gets around the problem.

To prevent the vegetables sticking together, and to enable you to defrost small quantities at a time, use the method of freezing them individually on trays and then putting them into bags or cartons once they're frozen (see opposite and right).

If faced with a glut of all sorts of vegetables, to save cooking them twice it might be worth making up a soup, curry or casserole and freezing the meals individually, to use at a later date. On those days when cooking seems too much of a chore it's a relief to know there's something healthy and delicious waiting for you in the freezer, and it's so much better than buying a ready-made meal.

Freezing soft fruit

Blackberries, blueberries, currants, raspberries and most other soft fruit can be dry frozen, which means freezing them without turning them into a purée or adding sugar. Strawberries become damaged in the process, so for this reason it's much better to use them in a recipe before freezing, such as ice-cream or sorbet; alternatively, turn them into jam (see pages 255–6). Freezing is the perfect way of storing a little bit of summer for the depths of winter – a homemade blackberry crumble is always a welcome addition to the table in the middle of January. In our early gardening days we froze a glut of blackberries by putting them straight into an old ice-cream tub and sticking them in the freezer. The result was, of course, a big block of blackberries the size and shape of the tub, and they all had to be defrosted at once. To avoid this, follow these guidelines –

1. Lay the fruit on a tray without any of the individual items touching. Freeze for between 1 and 2 hours, until the fruit is solid.

2. Place the fruit in a tub or freezer bag; the items will now remain separated. If you wish to use the fruit for pies, tarts or flans in the future, it's easy to defrost the appropriate quantity as and when you need it.

FREEZING TIPS

- The faster the food is frozen, the better its quality when thawed.
- Always write the date on anything you freeze so you don't store frozen foods for too long, because flavours and textures begin to deteriorate. Wrap food closely before freezing.
- Ideally store blanched vegetables and fruit for no longer than 12 months in the freezer.
- Cover food loosely while it's thawing.
- Defrost food in a cool place such as a larder or fridge.
- Never refreeze food once it's thawed, unless you've cooked it. For example, it's safe to thaw raw meat, use it to make a casserole and then refreeze it.
- If defrosting in a microwave oven, use only the defrost or low setting.
- Cook food as soon as possible after thawing.

PICKLES & CHUTNEYS

Chutneys and pickles preserve food by creating an environment that inhibits the growth of or kills micro-organisms. Vinegar is the preserver's choice when making both chutneys and pickles, because the high acid content means the majority of bacteria can't survive in it. The vinegar is often spiced, or sugar may be added to improve the flavour, although some foods such as boiled eggs or onions can be steeped straight in vinegar without the need for further flavouring. In pickles, the whole fruit is preserved and every effort is made to keep its shape, some of its texture and its colour. Chutneys are often a mix of ingredients pulped, mashed or cut into pieces.

Pickles

In many cases, all you have to do to pickle a food is to soak the vegetable or fruit in brine and put it in vinegar. You may like to add sugar to cauliflower or apples to sweeten them and aid the preservation. Below is a recipe for making the pickling vinegar a little more interesting.

Spiced vinegar for pickling

Ideally, you should make the spiced vinegar at least a month before pickling your fruit or vegetables so the flavours have time to settle. The spice mix can be tailored to the items you are pickling and to your particular tastes, so the quantities depend on what you have in the cupboard and how spicy you like your pickle or chutney. You can add ground spices to chutney because there isn't a need to maintain a clear liquid, but pickles can become cloudy and the appearance of the food may be impaired. To avoid cloudiness, use whole spices or steep a muslin bag full of spices in the vinegar.

1 litre (1¾ pints) white malt vinegar
50–100g (1½–3½oz) whole spices (such as bay leaves, caraway seeds, coriander seeds, chilli, cinnamon bark, cloves, cumin seeds, dill seeds, fennel seeds, fenugreek, garlic, ginger, horseradish, mace, mustard seeds, peppercorns) and/or herbs (such as rosemary, sage or thyme) or a ready-made muslin bag containing spices

1. Put the vinegar and spices, herbs or muslin bag into a non-corrosible pan, bring the mixture to the boil, then remove from the heat and leave to cool for 2 hours.
2. Strain the mixture or remove the muslin bag. Alternatively, you could leave the spices or herbs in for extra flavour (this works very well with a carrot chutney containing coriander seeds).

Pickled onions

This recipe is for one or two jars of pickled onions but can of course be scaled up if you have a glut of onions.

100g (3½oz) coarse salt
1 litre (1¾ pints) cold water
500g (1lb) pickling onions, peeled
150ml (¼ pint) spiced vinegar (see left)

1. Make a brine by combining the salt and the water.
2. Put the onions in a bowl and pour over the brine. Place a plate directly on top of the onions to make sure they're completely submerged and leave for 1½ days.
3. Rinse the onions after soaking, then pat dry. Put them in a sterilized jar and cover them with the spiced vinegar.
4. Ideally, leave the onions for at least 2 or 3 months so that the vinegar can soften them and the spices can infuse them fully.

TIPS FOR MAKING PICKLES & CHUTNEYS

- Make sure the jar is completely clean. Sterilize the jar by placing it in boiling water for about 10–15 minutes.
- Ensure the jar is airtight by placing a layer of greaseproof paper under the lid.
- Use fresh, blemish- and disease-free produce for pickles and wash thoroughly.
- Make sure the food to be pickled is completely covered with vinegar.
- Use sea, rock or coarse salt, not table salt, which will cloud and discolour produce.

Chutney is an excellent way to use up
surplus cooking apples.

Easy mustard recipe

It's not exactly a pickle but it does use the same basic techniques, preserving a food in sugar and vinegar. It goes well with a good strong cheese in a sandwich, and our Granddad used to smear it on cuts of pork or beef for an extra kick. It also works well in a salad dressing mixed with olive oil and balsamic vinegar. It's hard to make this with exact quantities and a specific list of ingredients, and we always make it in whatever jar we have to hand; it's a basic recipe that's open to lots of interpretation.

1. Put 1 teaspoon of demerara sugar to 2 teaspoons of mustard seed into a small jar until you've almost filled it.
2. Completely cover in a vinegar of your choice, or red wine, and leave overnight. For wholegrain mustard, leave the grains whole and for smooth mustard liquidize it.
3. If desired, you can add further ingredients such as horseradish or chilli to give it an extra kick.

Chutneys

Chutneys are easier to make than pickles. There's no need to keep fruit or vegetables whole and just about anything can be made into a chutney. We often make chutneys with no particular recipe, just using what has been picked that day and what spices are to hand in the kitchen. Leave all these chutneys for at least 2 months before eating.

Budget chutney

This is a useful recipe for using up over-ripe bananas, mangoes or anything else a greengrocer/market stall might be selling off inexpensively at the end of a day. Use any spices you have to hand, but it's particularly good with coriander seeds.

**1 ripe banana, mango or carrot per person
    (or other sweet fruit and vegetables)
Enough white malt vinegar to cover
1 tsp spices
2–3 tbsp sugar per person**

1. Peel, core and cut up the fruit or grate the carrot and put it in a non-corrosible pan with enough vinegar to cover. Add the spices and sugar.
2. Bring to the boil and simmer, stirring occasionally, until the chutney has a porridge-like consistency.
3. You can serve immediately, but for improved flavour put the mixture into a sterilized jar and leave to mature.

Basic, no-weigh chutney

This is an easy chutney recipe for those who prefer to cook by sight and taste rather than be restricted by ingredients lists and quantities. Try experimenting with a variety of different vegetables, fruit and spices each time you make it so you never tire of the results.

1. Peel, core and chop some fruit and/or vegetables, put them in a pan and cover them in a layer of brown sugar.
2. Add a couple of teaspoons of spices, cover with vinegar (any will do) and bring to the boil.
3. Simmer to reduce the mixture until it is not as runny as pasta sauce or as thick as peanut butter but somewhere in between. The best way to check this is to see if there is a little resistance when it is stirred with a wooden spoon and whether the bottom of the pan can be revealed without all the mixture filling up behind it straight away.
4. Bottle in sterilized jars. You could eat it straight away but for better flavour leave it to mature.

Apple chutney

This is a good way of using up any leftover apples. The sugar will counteract any tartness they might have. It's worth opening a window when you make this, as the house will start to smell strongly of boiling vinegar.

**2kg (4lb) cooking apples (such as Bramley), peeled,
    cored and chopped
300g (10oz) onions, chopped
500g (1lb) soft brown sugar
1 clove of garlic, crushed
250g (8oz) sultanas
2.5cm (1in) cube of fresh ginger, grated
1 litre (1¾ pints) white malt vinegar
    (or cider vinegar if available)
½ tsp cayenne pepper
2 small chillies, finely chopped, or ½ tsp chilli powder
Large pinch of salt**

1. Put all the ingredients together in a large, non-corrosible pan and bring to the boil.
2. As soon as the liquid starts to boil, stir the ingredients well and reduce the heat.
3. Simmer until the mixture is fully thickened. For a ketchup-style sauce this usually takes an hour but a good chutney can take up to an hour longer.
4. Store in sterilized jars and leave to mature.

MAKING JAM

Jam is one of the most effective and delicious ways of preserving fruit. It can be slightly messy and is more labour-intensive than other ways of preservation, such as drying and freezing, but the results are more satisfying and homemade jam is far superior to any supermarket-bought product.

The three 'rules' of jam-making are: the jam should have a higher sugar content than the fruit used (or equal if the fruit is already high in natural sugar); a little pectin should be added to help it set; and the fruit should be on the acidic side, which thankfully most fruit is. With jam it's often better to follow a recipe, tapping into centuries of trial and error. Improvised jams can be disappointing in our experience. One year, Dave tried making a low-sugar jam for a friend's diabetic father and the result was a pot of mould!

Most of the recipes here are traditional British jam recipes, except for the more unusual Marrow and ginger jam (overleaf), which was posted on the web forum by one of our original members, Diver from Merseyside. To give an idea of weight for these recipes, 3kg (6lb) of fruit will make approximately 5kg (10lb) of jam. There are three main steps to jam-making. Step A is to prepare and simmer the fruit, step B is to get the mixture to setting point and step C is potting the jam. Step A varies between recipes, and is described in each one below, but steps B and C are the same for all the recipes and are described overleaf.

A. Prepare and simmer the fruit

Blackcurrant jam

1kg (2lb) blackcurrants
750ml (1¼ pints) water
1.5kg (3lb) sugar

1. Remove the stems from the currants and wash and drain the berries. Put them in a pan with the water. Simmer until reduced by almost half, stirring frequently.
2. Stir in the sugar and boil the mixture until it reaches setting point. (Go to steps B and C, overleaf.)

Raspberry jam

1.5kg (3lb) raspberries (alternatively, use loganberries or a combination)
1.5kg (3lb) sugar

1. Clean the raspberries, put them in a pan and simmer over a very low heat for 15–20 minutes or until reduced to a pulp, stirring constantly to avoid burning.
2. Add the sugar, stirring until dissolved, then boil until setting point is reached. (Go to steps B and C, overleaf.)

Blackberry and elderberry jam

500g (1lb) elderberries
150ml (¼ pint) water
500g (1lb) blackberries (cultivated or wild)
1kg (2lb) sugar

1. Remove the stems from the elderberries, then wash and drain the berries. Put them into a pan with the water and simmer until they're soft.
2. Push the berries through a sieve to remove the seeds.
3. Return the elderberry pulp to the pan, add the rinsed blackberries, and simmer them until they're soft.
4. Add the sugar, stirring until it's dissolved, then boil the mixture until it has reached setting point. (Go to steps B and C, overleaf.)

Apple jam

1.5kg (3lb) tart cooking apples
600ml (1 pint) water
2 tbsp citric acid
12 cloves in a muslin bag
1.5kg (3lb) sugar

1. Slice and core the apples but leave the skins on. Put them into a pan with the water, citric acid and bag of cloves. Simmer until the apples are mushy, then remove the cloves.
2. Add the sugar to the pulp.
3. Stir until the sugar has dissolved and boil the mixture until it reaches setting point. (Go to steps B and C, right.)

Marrow and ginger jam

475g (15oz) marrow
    (weight when peeled and seeds removed)
3 tbsp chopped ginger (crystallized, preserved or
    fresh; use less if using fresh) or ground ginger
475g (15oz) sugar
2 tbsp lemon juice

1. Cut the marrow into 1cm (½in) dice, put it into a pan with the ginger and sugar and leave overnight.
2. Stir well, as this encourages the juices to run, then put the pan over a low heat, stirring constantly until the sugar has dissolved.
3. Add the lemon juice and boil steadily until setting point is reached. (Go to steps B and C, right.)

B. Setting point

To see whether or not your jam is at setting point, pour a little of the jam mixture onto a cold saucer and leave it to cool. Once it has cooled (after 30 seconds to a minute or two), run your finger across the top of the jam and if a skin has formed and the jam wrinkles it has reached setting point. If it stays runny and no skin is present, boil it for longer. If you're using a thermometer, the setting point should be around 104°C (220°F). This is the temperature at which the acid in the fruit and the pectin react with the sugar. Once setting point has been reached, leave the jam for 10–15 minutes without stirring before potting.

C. Potting jam

1. Sterilize and warm the jars by placing them in a pan of boiled water for 10–15 minutes or so.
2. Remove any scum that may have formed on the surface of the jam and allow the jam to cool slightly.
3. Dry the jars and pour the warm jam into them.
4. Cover the top of the jam with a wax disc (we use cut greaseproof paper).
5. Cover each pot with cellophane or greaseproof paper.
6. Secure the cellophane or greaseproof-paper lid with an elastic band and screw the cap on the jar.
7. Label and date the jam. This is important, because jam should not really be stored for more than a year as the colour, texture, aroma and flavour may deteriorate.
8. You can make personalized gifts with the jam: for example, create a printed label with 'This jam was exclusively bottled for [insert name]'.
9. Keep jam in the fridge once the jar has been opened.

JAM FACTS

- In Victorian England the main source of vitamin C was jam. This is quite an astonishing fact when you consider that vitamin C is destroyed by both heat and sunlight, yet jam is heated to 104°C (220°F) and is normally kept in clear glass jars.
- Pectin is a carbohydrate found to a greater or lesser degree in the cell walls of all fruits and vegetables. It is high in fruits such as apples and citrus fruits and lower in cherries, figs, peaches, strawberries and raspberries.
- The jam-making process allows some of the water to evaporate from the fruit. This water loss and the addition of sugar makes the pectin (added or already in the fruit) form a barrier, trapping the remaining water within the cells and making the characteristic jelly- or gel-like substance we call jam.

Dave potting homemade raspberry jam.

MAKING BEER, WINE & CIDER

The earliest archaeological evidence of home brewing dates back over 7000 years in Iran, where ancient pottery jars containing traces of beer were recently found. Ironically, buying, brewing and drinking alcohol in Iran is now illegal, punished with between 70 and 80 lashes, a hefty fine and a prison sentence of three months to a year. In Britain, home brewing was kept under government control from 1880 with the introduction of a 5-shilling (25p) home-brewing licence, but this legislation was lifted in 1963. Today you're allowed to make beer, wine and cider without a licence; however, as in almost every other country in the world, it's forbidden to make spirits at home because of the dangers of the alcohol causing blindness or even death.

There are three important factors that should persuade the self-sufficientish person to make their own beer, wine and cider. The first is cost – we've made red wine for less than 30p a bottle and nettle beer for about 5p a pint. The second factor is 'beer miles'. Despite the fact that many ingredients, such as hops, grow in Britain, 30 per cent of hops are imported from the United States and some breweries import them from as far away as New Zealand. Friends of the Earth suggests that a barrel of beer could have travelled over 38,500 kilometres (24,000 miles) by the time we buy it, taking into account the journey from the field to the off-licence via the brewery – a ridiculous figure when you can grow hops so easily on your allotment. Finally, if you make your own wine, beer or cider you can control what goes into it. You can use Fairtrade sugar, add local honey or other flavours to get the specific taste you're after, and the whole brew can be free of chemicals.

It can be difficult to judge the level of alcohol in home brew, so as a precaution don't drive or operate heavy machinery after drinking.

WHAT YOU NEED

It can be quite daunting when you first walk into a home-brew shop or surf the internet for equipment – there are so many different items for sale, and if you're not careful the start-up costs can spiral out of control. However, if you're new to making cider, beer or wine, don't worry about getting a vast array of kit – you need only a few basic items initially and can build up your equipment as and when you need it.

Containers

● **Fermentation bin** – A large bucket (usually food-grade plastic) with an airtight lid, used in making beer, wine and cider. Fermentation bins are available in various sizes and can be quite costly, so it's worth asking friends, checking in charity shops and on www.freecycle.org.

● **Beer barrels** – These are used instead of bottles when making beer and you can just turn on the tap and help yourself when it's ready. Generally, they're made of plastic and can hold up to 25 litres (43 pints). They can be expensive, although you may be lucky and find them in a charity shop or on a skip.

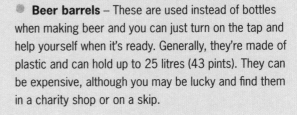

● **Demijohn** – A 4.5-litre (1-gallon) glass container, available from home-brew shops or online. Plastic demijohns are available, but they won't last as long and are frankly much less attractive than the traditional glass demijohn.

● **Bottles** – Although bottles are available from your home-brew shop, we really don't see the point in buying them as you can use recycled containers. Keep every screw-top glass bottle that you have (the thicker the glass, the better – thin glass can shatter or explode), and ask friends and family to set theirs aside for you. Grolsch bottles are among the best to use for beer making, and some home-brew shops may even sell you some if you're short of containers. We've also used jars to store wine in, although bottles are better.

Other equipment

● **Sterilizing solution** – Useful for quick and easy sterilizing of all equipment before beer, wine and cider making (see below and overleaf).

● **Siphon tube** – Used for siphoning liquid from one vessel to another. The liquid you wish to siphon is placed on a higher surface than the container you wish to siphon it into. The tap end is placed into the new container and the other end into the liquid.

● **Airlock** – A one-way valve in the form of a rubber bung and plastic tube, which allows carbon dioxide to escape when you're brewing. It's useful in the fermentation process to put in demijohns or just the plastic tube in a fermentation bin.

● **Hydrometer** – A useful but not essential piece of equipment that helps you determine the amount of sugar in your mix and the potential alcohol content of the final brew.

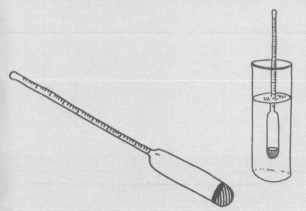

● **Funnel** – A plastic funnel is helpful to decant beer, wine and cider into a separate vessel – for example, when siphoning beer from the fermentation bin into bottles. It can be bought from a hardware shop very cheaply. Ensure that the end spout can fit into your bottles. It's wise to get two or more different sizes for different jobs.

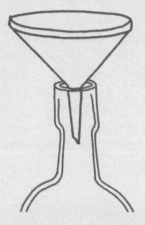

● **Muslin cloth** – A finely woven fabric used for straining, available from hardware stores.

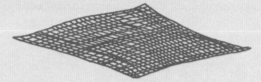

● **Nylon brush** – This is not essential but it does make it easier to clean visible dirt from your equipment. A 'cranked' or shaped brush will help clean out demijohns.

Cleaning and sterilizing

The key to making good beer, wine and cider is better-than-excellent hygiene. We've seen many a brew end up with mould floating on top of it or stinking to high heaven because of improper sterilization of equipment. It's certainly not very self-sufficientish to end up wasting brew after brew because of contamination.

We're not the tidiest of people, and we wouldn't say we clean our houses frequently. However, we have every good reason to dust and clean every few months when we make a new batch of home brew. Dust and dirt will contaminate a brew, rendering it undrinkable (we can't emphasize this enough), so keep all the areas that you use during brewing and bottling as clean and dust-free as possible and ideally keep animals away too.

As a rule of thumb, you should sterilize whatever you're going to touch when making beer, wine and cider, and sterilize in between every stage of a recipe. This is particularly vital when making home brew. The most common sterilization method is a chlorine-based sterilizing powder such as VWP, which is available from most home-brew shops. It kills harmful fungi, wild yeasts and active bacteria that might otherwise contaminate your batch. You'll need to rinse your equipment thoroughly after using chlorine-based sterilizing powder because it will kill your brewing yeast, making it impossible for the brewing process to begin.

A non-chemical method of sterilization that has been used for centuries is to boil your bottles and equipment in water for 20 minutes to an hour. We prefer to use natural methods, so we opt for this when appropriate: for example, when we're making wine for a party and it won't be around for long. However, when it comes to brewing we'd recommend using sterilizing powder (even though we're generally reluctant to use chemicals), as beer is very susceptible to contaminates. Also, because most brewing equipment is made from plastic, boiling it for hours is simply not practical as it will render each part unusable.

Some people burn their equipment in order to sterilize it. They cover the glass and stainless-steel equipment with a high-volume spirit, such as vodka, then in controlled conditions set light to it. This method obviously requires great caution and we suggest you read up on it thoroughly before trying it at home.

Hops are easy to grow on the allotment for home brewing.

HOME BREWING

When we were teenagers, there was always someone who was trying to make beer – their efforts ranged from the slightly palatable to the downright disgusting. In more recent years, we've found that it's not as difficult as we first thought to make a decent brew and we strongly suggest trying it for yourself. The main rule of successful home brewing is to sterilize all the equipment thoroughly (see opposite). Even dropping the hydrometer in the brew without sterilizing it can cause contamination and render the brew useless.

Pure beer

Germany has a rich beer culture. In 1516 a purity law, known as the *Reinheitsgebot*, was implemented to protect public health from harmful additives. Although this law is no longer in force, many German brewers still stick to the principles. The four ingredients allowed are water, hops, yeast and grain. This recipe upholds the *Reinheitsgebot* and makes an authentic, pure brew. It's vital that you take temperatures regularly using a brewing thermometer and use soft, unchlorinated water. If you live in a hard-water area, use filtered rainwater or add ¼ tsp salt to 9 litres (2 gallons) of water. To get rid of chlorine, boil the water.

10–11 litres (2¼–2½ gallons) water (see above)
1.5kg (3lb) crushed lager malt grains
2 drops of iodine (for testing)
28g (1oz) seedless hops (preferably Hallertau hops)
5g (¼oz) lager yeast

1. Pour 3.5 litres (6 pints) of the water into a large saucepan and stir in the crushed lager malt grains. Place the pan on a moderate heat, cover, and heat the mixture to 55°C (131°F). Maintain the temperature for 15 minutes.

2. Pour half of the mixture into a smaller saucepan. Bring it to the boil and simmer for 15 minutes, stirring occasionally. During this time, keep the mixture in the first pan at 55°C (131°F).

3. The mixture in the second pan should look a little darker and taste sweeter. Return it to the main brew, turn up the heat slightly and keep it at a constant temperature of 63–65°C (145–149°F) for 1 hour, stirring occasionally.

4. Repeat steps 2 and 3 – remove half of the mixture, bring it to the boil, simmer for 15 minutes, then stir it into the main mixture. Leave it on the heat at a constant temperature of 63–65°C (145–149°F) for 30 minutes.

5. Remove 30ml (1fl oz) of the mixture and place it in a small bowl. Add the iodine. If the mixture turns blue, leave the main mixture for another 30 minutes at the same constant temperature of 63–65°C (145–149°F). If it stays clear, move to the next step.

6. Strain the mixture into a very large pan (9-litre/2-gallon capacity) using a muslin cloth. It helps to have a second person at this stage. Set the muslin and grains to one side.

7. Place a further 1.25 litres (2 pints) of the water over a moderate heat and bring the temperature to 82°C (179°F). Pour the hot water over the grains in the muslin and into the mixture. Compost the grains and the muslin. Add the hops to the mixture and boil for 45 minutes, then strain and return the mixture to the large pan.

8. Top up with more water to make 9 litres (2 gallons) – you should need to add around 6 litres (1¼–1½ gallons). Leave the mixture to cool to less than 24°C (75°F), then remove 400ml (14fl oz) of the mixture (this is to be bottled in an airtight container and put in the fridge). Sprinkle the yeast over the remaining mixture in the pan.

9. Using a funnel, pour the mixture into demijohns, fit airlocks and leave in a place that gets a steady temperature of 11–24°C (52–75°F). After 2 days, skim off the top of the mixture in the demijohns and clean any ring that might have collected around the top. Shake the mixture and refit the airlock. Leave for a further week, repeating the skimming/cleaning process if necessary.

10. Using a siphoning tube, transfer the liquid from the demijohns into clean, sterilized demijohns. Leave for a few more days until the mixture is clear and bright.

11. Pour equal amounts of the mixture from the fridge into bottles, then siphon the brew from the demijohns into the bottles. Store for 3 months before drinking.

Nettle beer

This is an easy recipe and creates a delightful, unusual-tasting beer. It's very cheap to make and follows a traditional English recipe. Before hops were widely used in the 17th century, all sorts of plants were used to flavour ale including stinging nettles (*Urtica dioica*) and nettle beer was thought to help alleviate rheumatic pain, gout and asthma. Nettle beer is still available in the Czech Republic and in parts of northern England, where it's brewed with hops. A visitor to the Self-sufficientish website, Michael Kempster from Lisbon, couldn't get hold of any nettles so has made a variation of nettle beer using spinach leaves instead – he reports that it has very tasty results.

1kg (2lb) young nettle tops
4.5 litres (1 gallon) water
1 tsp ground ginger
250g (8oz) sugar (soft brown or demerara
**   works best)**
1 tsp fresh yeast
¼–½ slice of toasted bread

1. Boil the nettle tops in the water for half an hour.
2. Using a sieve or muslin cloth, strain the nettle-flavoured liquid into the fermentation bin.
3. Add the ginger and sugar, stirring to dissolve.
4. Spread the yeast onto the toast and float it on the surface of the nettle liquid. Cover and leave for about 3 days at room temperature. Do not allow the temperature to fluctuate too much, as this will ruin the fermentation process – somewhere between 18°C (64°F) and 24°C (75°F) is ideal.
5. Siphon and strain the liquid into bottles or a beer barrel; a funnel will help with this process. Nettle beer can be drunk after about 2 days, but the taste will be better if left for 7–28 days.

Making beer from a kit

Even the novice can make a decent home brew from a kit, but don't be fooled into thinking that all you need is that kit and a bag of sugar, because some basic equipment is required too (see pages 260–1).

A kit comes in a can and contains malted hop extract – a gloopy mixture that looks a lot like Marmite. When water is added to this it becomes the 'wort', or the beer before it's been brewed. Full brewing instructions are provided with all beer-making kits and these should be followed to the letter for your first attempts. When you start to feel a bit more confident you can experiment a little with the ingredients and quantities; Andy likes to add some honey when brewing ale as it gives it a more distinct flavour.

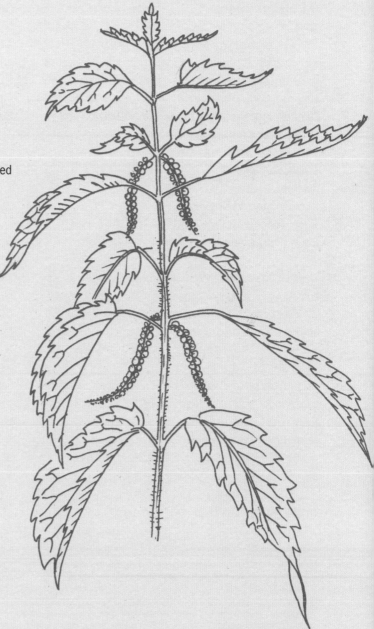

Nettles make a delicious, nutritious and inexpensive home brew.

WINE MAKING

If you embrace the self-sufficientish way of life there's no doubt that you'll have a glut of fruit or vegetables or an abundance of particular weeds at certain times of the year and you'll be wondering how you can make use of them. This is where wine making can really come into its own. It need not cost you much to make a palatable and alcoholic wine – we've tried making wines from various different plants, and while not exactly Pino Grigio they can taste very good indeed. Wines made from a fruit other than grapes are generally referred to as 'country wines' and they have been enjoyed for centuries, with good reason. Here are recipes for some of the wines we enjoy making – remember to sterilize all your equipment before you start (see pages 261–2). When it comes to fitting corks, it helps to soak them in boiling water first. We have a bit of kit that makes cork-fitting easier, but brute force and a rubber mallet will work too.

Dandelion wine

This wine tastes much better than it smells and is a perfect way of using up unwanted dandelions on the allotment or lawn. This makes enough wine for two wine bottles.

Dandelion flowerheads (up to the 500ml/17fl oz
mark in a measuring jug)
2 litres (3½ pints) hot water
1 satsuma, peeled
Juice of 1 lemon
½ tsp grated fresh ginger
1 tsp dried yeast
200g (7oz) granulated sugar

1. Wash the dandelion flowerheads, discard their stalks and put them into a demijohn.
2. Pour over the hot water, cover and leave for 3 days, stirring occasionally.
3. Strain the mixture through a fine sieve or muslin cloth into a second demijohn with an airlock.
4. Add the satsuma, piece by piece, along with the lemon juice, ginger, yeast and sugar. Leave for about 3 weeks at room temperature to ferment; try not to let the air temperature go below 15°C (59°F) or above 25°C (77°F).
5. Strain through a sieve into sterilized bottles. Leave for a further 3 weeks and drink within 6 weeks.

Elderflower wine

During June or July every year you'll see and smell elderflower in full blossom around towns, cities and in the countryside. It's very easy to identify (see page 228) and grows in abundance. Don't worry about picking too much, because the birds and insects that eat elderberries will happily feast from the out-of-reach branches, so there's always plenty left. Some home-brew shops sell dried elderflowers out of season, but fresh flowers make a better wine.

Elderflowers (up to the 500ml/17fl oz mark
in a measuring jug)
Grated zest and juice of 2 lemons
3.5 litres (6 pints) boiling water
1.5kg (3lb) granulated sugar
25g (¾oz) champagne yeast

1. Put the elderflowers and lemon zest into your demijohn. Be careful not to add any of the bitter green elderflower stems, as this will taint the overall flavour and can cause stomach upsets.
2. Pour over the boiling water. Cover and leave to stand for 4 days, stirring occasionally.
3. Strain through a fine sieve or muslin cloth into a second demijohn with an airlock. Stir in the sugar, lemon juice and yeast. Keep covered and at room temperature to ferment; try not to let the temperature go below 15°C (59°F) or above 25°C (77°F).
4. When you're sure all the bubbling has ceased, after about a week, stir the wine and allow to settle for 3 days.
5. Strain again carefully and decant into another demijohn. Leave for 3 months to mature, then put the wine into sterilized bottles. You could drink it now or, for best results, leave it for another 3 months or more, up to a year.

Elderberries for wine making are easy to
find in August and September.

Elderberry wine

Our parents, who are fortunate enough to have an elder tree at the bottom of their garden, have tried various different elderberry wine recipes over the years and they have now settled on this one as their favourite. This recipe makes six bottles. It is quite a dry wine, but we've found the taste varies from year to year, depending on the amount of sun and rain during summer.

1.5kg (3lb) elderberries
4.5 litres (1 gallon) water
1 tsp brewer's yeast
1.5kg (3lb) granulated sugar
7 tbsp warm water
2 yeast nutrient tablets, crushed

1. Take the berries off the stalks with a fork, as shown above. This is important, because the stalks are poisonous. You could put the berries in the freezer before making the wine – this is not essential, but they seem to be juicier as a result. When ready to make the wine, defrost the berries first.
2. Crush the berries into a fermentation bin.
3. In a large pan, bring the water to boiling point and pour it over the berries in the bin. Leave to rest until the water is lukewarm.
4. Mix the yeast, 1 tsp of the sugar and the warm water in a cup; leave for 15 minutes to activate.

5. Put the yeast mixture together with the crushed yeast nutrient tablets into the fermention bin. Stir well. Cover tightly and leave at room temperature for 3–5 days, stirring daily. Do not allow the temperature to go below 15°C (59°F) or over 25°C (77°F).
6. Put the rest of the sugar into a second fermentation bin and sieve the gunge (known as 'must') from the first bucket into the second. Combine the must thoroughly with the sugar until dissolved.
7. Using a funnel, fill a demijohn up to the shoulder with the mixture.
8. Fit the bung with the airlock attached and half fill the airlock with water.
9. Leave the mixture to ferment at room temperature – this can be quite a violent process. When all activity has ceased (that is when no bubbles are coming out of the airlock and sediment has formed at the bottom of the demijohn), the wine can be siphoned into sterilized bottles.
10. Leave the bottles stored on their side for a good 6 months before drinking.

Coffee wine

We were first made aware of this recipe for coffee wine when it was posted on the Self-sufficientish forum. It's a very strong wine, at around 19 per cent alcohol. We'd say that it's an acquired taste and some liken it to Tia Maria.

4 tbsp instant coffee
4.5 litres (1 gallon) water
1.5kg (3lb) granulated sugar
5g (¼oz) brewer's yeast

1. Put the coffee into a fermentation bin.
2. In a large pan, bring the water to boiling point and pour it over the coffee.
3. Add the sugar and stir to dissolve. Allow the mixture to cool until tepid.
4. Add the yeast. Cover the fermentation bin and leave in a draught-free area at room temperature, 18–23°C (64–73°F), for 5 days.
5. Using a funnel, transfer the mixture to a demijohn and leave for about 3 months.
6. Transfer to sterilized bottles and leave for a further 6 months to a year before drinking.

CIDER MAKING

We've both settled in the West Country – the area of Britain that's renowned for its cider. In fact, when we first got off the train at Bristol Temple Meads station one of the first things we saw was a huge placard advertising cider, stating, 'You are now in Blackthorn country,' and there was a photograph of Brunel's famous Clifton suspension bridge with the towers on either side replaced by two giant pints of cider.

In this area there's no shortage of apples to scrump, and rather than see the fruit rot on the tree we love to have a day out collecting as many apples as we can to make cider. It does take some work to make your own, but you can't beat putting your feet up on your allotment with a cool bottle of homemade cider, making the whole process more than worthwhile. In the United States, apple juice is known as 'cider' and what we call cider is known as 'hard cider' in the States – this can cause considerable confusion, and we've seen Americans getting tipsy on what they think is pure, unadulterated apple juice.

Cheat's cider

Cider making can be a bit of chore, but there is a cheat's way of making it that doesn't rely on the seasonal nature of the main ingredient – apples – nor do you need a cider press or really have to put much effort in. Admittedly, the results aren't as good as you get using the traditional method, but it makes a surprisingly drinkable, dry cider.

4 litres (7 pints) unsweetened apple juice
5g (¼oz) champagne yeast
100g (3½oz) granulated sugar

1. Pour the apple juice into a demijohn with an airlock and add the sachet of yeast and a pinch of sugar. Put a piece of cotton wool in the airlock and leave for a couple of days.
2. Add some more sugar so that that whole brew fizzes up and replace the airlock, this time with a little water in it.
3. Keep adding sugar, pinch by pinch, so that the brew almost froths over. Repeat this process every few days over a period of a couple of weeks, until the airlock is no longer bubbling.
4. About 2 weeks after you've added the last bit of sugar, siphon off the cider into sterilized bottles and leave on a wine rack for a further 3 months before drinking.

Scrumpy cider

As we're West Country dwellers, this book wouldn't be complete without a scrumpy recipe. This is a traditional recipe adapted by a regular website visitor (Stoney) and will make a reasonably strong cider with only a little amount of effort.

Be aware that you mustn't use any metal when making cider because it can have an adverse effect on the yeast in the apples. Cut the apples with a plastic fish slice or ice scraper (it takes a bit of force to cut them without using a knife) and crush them with a plastic potato masher – although this can be tricky, it's not impossible.

3.5kg (7–8lb) cider apples
9 litres (2 gallons) boiling water, plus an additional 150ml (¼ pint)
30g (1oz) fresh ginger, bruised
Juice of 4 lemons

1. Cut up the unpeeled apples roughly with a non-metallic implement, such as a plastic fish slice.
2. Place the apples in a fermentation bin and cover with the 9 litres (2 gallons) of boiling water.
3. Leave the mixture for 2 weeks, returning to crush the apples thoroughly every 3 days using a potato masher.
4. Strain the liquid and add the bruised root ginger and lemon juice.
5. Add the 150ml (¼ pint) boiling water and leave the whole thing to stand again for just over 2 weeks, removing the scum off the top as it rises.
6. Strain into sterilized bottles and screw on the tops lightly, just to the point where they would need another half turn to close them fully.
7. After 2 days tighten the tops and store the bottles in a cool, dark, dry place for 2 months before drinking for best results.

NATURE'S MEDICINES

Peter Cook once said, 'I made a fortune selling dock leaves last week – I put a sign up next to a field of nettles saying "free mint".' Even if you don't laugh at that but get the joke, you're obviously aware of dock being a treatment for nettle stings – just one of thousands of natural remedies in existence. Plants have been valued for their pain-relieving and healing abilities since the earliest times, and about 80 per cent of the world's population still relies on medicinal herbs today.

There's evidence to suggest that herbs may have been used for their curative qualities as long as 60,000 years ago. The major ancient civilizations certainly understood the medicinal properties of plants – the ancient Greeks marched into battle with yarrow (known as the 'warrior's herb'), which they applied to wounds to reduce blood flow, and the Romans brought to Britain many of the herbs we grow today, for using in cooking and as medicines. Thyme, for example, was introduced to flavour food and was also thought to guard against food poisoning.

Although Western medicine has moved away from using whole plants, about 25 per cent of prescription drugs contain at least one active ingredient found in plants. The modern-day pharmaceutical industry owes much to white willow, which has been used for thousands of years around the world to relieve joint pain and to manage fevers. The active constituent salicin, found in the bark, was the first drug treatment to be synthesized and in 1899 this process was patented by the German company Bayer, resulting in the compound named aspirin.

USING NATURAL REMEDIES

There has been a resurgence of interest in herbs over the past few decades, and rightly so. They're particularly useful for treating minor ailments, such as coughs and colds, or easing the symptoms of chronic illness for which there is no cure, such as eczema or asthma. In addition, if used responsibly, nature's medicines are less likely to have as many side effects as conventional medicines – there's much evidence to suggest that preparations made using the whole plant are gentler and more effective than pharmaceutical drugs, which incorporate isolated plant chemicals.

Another bonus to growing, picking and making your own remedies is that it is considerably less expensive than buying traditional medicines; in addition, we feel that if you play an active role in your medicine's preparation you 'engage' with it, and that this is also part of the healing process.

In this chapter we look at some of the most common ailments and offer natural treatments that help to heal, ease pain and restore a sense of wellbeing. We've collected the remedies from a variety of sources and they're based on the traditional uses of herbs. You may have many of the herbs growing in your garden or allotment already and a great number of them grow in the wild.

These remedies aren't meant to replace a visit to your GP – they're really for minor ailments or to complement conventional medicine. Be aware that some herbs interact with pharmaceutical drugs, so if you're taking a prescribed drug you need to consult your doctor before taking a herb. Use the remedies until the symptoms disappear. If there's no improvement within a couple of weeks, or if the condition gets worse, consult a professional practitioner, and stop taking the remedy if it causes irritation.

Do not give babies under 6 months any internal herbal medicine without professional advice. Pregnant women should avoid using chamomile oil and thyme oil and the following herbs: aloe, arbour vitae, barberry, basil oil, bugleweed, devil's claw, feverfew, ginseng, golden seal, juniper, lady's mantle, liquorice, mistletoe, motherwort, mugwort, myrrh, pennyroyal, rue, shepherd's purse, vervain, yarrow, yellow dock and wormwood. They should also avoid medicinal doses of angelica, anise, cayenne, celery and sage.

Herbs need not be taken only when you're unwell. A great number of medicinal herbs can be used any time, to maintain health and prevent illness – tonics such as nettle or ginseng, or soothing herbs such as chamomile and mint, can be taken year-round. Together with a healthy balanced diet and plenty of exercise, these beneficial herbs will help to give energy, encourage sleep and strengthen the immune system.

Herbal infusions

Many of the remedies in this book involve making an infusion, and all work on the same principle. Plant material (usually leaves and flowers) is steeped in just-boiled water, which penetrates the plant and releases the active ingredients. Drink one cupful of infusion approximately 3 or 4 times a day.

How to make an infusion

You can make an infusion either in a cup using a tea ball or, if you want to make up a large batch in advance, in a warmed teapot.

● To make an infusion in a cup, put about 1 teaspoon of dried or 2 teaspoons of fresh herbs into a tea ball. Fill the cup with freshly boiled water, put in the tea ball and leave it to steep for about 4 minutes before removing the ball.

● If you're using a teapot, warm the pot and put in about 20g (¾oz) of dried herbs or 30g (1oz) of fresh herbs to every 500ml (17fl oz) of freshly boiled water. Replace the lid and infuse for at least 5 minutes. Strain some of the infusion into a cup to drink straight away or, if all the infusion is not to be used immediately, let it cool in the pot before straining it off. You can store infusions in the fridge and use within 24 hours.

Dried chamomile flowers are commonly used in infusions for their gentle sedative properties.

COUGHS, COLDS & FLU

We're all familiar with the symptoms of the common cold: running nose, a cough and mild aching. We've a few tried-and-tested methods to alleviate these symptoms and find that they help, certainly as much as the over-the-counter medicines will. Some people swear by the use of mega doses of vitamin C pills, but we've never found them to be particularly beneficial and they seem to have a laxative effect. Instead, try making smoothies with fruits that are high in vitamin C such as kiwi fruits, strawberries and oranges.

● **Echinacea** is a good preventive, but only if it is taken at the right time, as soon as the symptoms start to appear. The way it works is to stimulate white blood-cell activity, increasing production of anti-viral substances. Or, to put it another way, it 'tricks' your body into thinking it's ill, so your immune system starts to work harder. If you take it all the time, or when the illness is well under way, as many people mistakenly do, it won't help in the slightest and will very likely make you feel worse. Echinacea should not be taken by people with an autoimmune disease and should be avoided by those who are allergic to other members of the daisy family.

● **Liquorice root** is a powerful expectorant and is useful when you're suffering from a cough. It can be bought from many healthfood shops as a liquorice bar or in tea bags. Avoid using liquorice if you suffer from hypertension, heart or liver disease or if you're pregnant or diabetic, and don't take it in high doses for longer than 6 weeks.

● **Garlic** boosts the immune system, helping you fight against cough, cold and flu viruses. Raw garlic works much better than cooked, so add some crushed garlic to an olive-oil-based salad dressing. Garlic can cause gastrointestinal upset and adding the oil helps to counteract this. To make the smell of garlic on your breath less noticeable, chew on some fennel seeds or eat parsley afterwards.

● **Infusions** can help your recovery (see page 272 for how to make an infusion). Try taking them at least every hour when you're suffering; if nothing else, you'll aid flushing the virus out of your system. A sage infusion is good to alleviate a sore throat (three leaves infused in a cup of boiled water for 3 minutes should suffice) and a yarrow-leaf infusion should help with a chesty cold. A combination of peppermint, yarrow and elderflower, if taken just before you go to bed in the early stages of a cold, could keep it at bay. Sage should be avoided by pregnant women and breast-feeding mothers.

● **Herbal footbaths** can help reduce the heat and congestion you may feel in the rest of your body when you have a cold or flu. Put a couple of teaspoons of chopped fresh ginger in a bowl of hot water to draw blood away from the head to the feet, or add a teaspoon of mustard powder. As smells can be very calming, also consider using rose petals, hops, rosemary or lavender.

Rosemary and rose petal footbath.

COLD, COUGH + FLU REMEDIES

Dandelion cough syrup

Dandelion is one of the most useful and common European herbs. The leaves and roots are both used in medicines, and the flowers have antioxidant properties and are thought to help the immune system. A teaspoonful of this mixture should be taken when required to soothe a tickly cough. Try not to exceed 12 doses a day. The syrup will keep for 2–6 months in a cool place, occasionally longer, but check for spoilage before using.

250g (8oz) honey or 500g (1lb) soft brown sugar
25 dandelion flowerheads

1. Put the dandelion heads into a saucepan and add the honey or sugar.
2. Pour in enough cold water to cover the dandelion heads with about 2cm (¾in) above.
3. Bring to the boil and then lower the heat to a simmer, stirring frequently.
4. When the mixture begins to stiffen, remove the pan from the heat, pour the mixture through a sieve and leave it to cool.
5. Pour the cooled mixture into a sterilized jar.
6. Seal the jar tightly, particularly if you intend to keep the syrup for some time, because this will reduce the likelihood of mould forming.

Honey, lemon and ginger drink

The lemon in this healing hot drink has a high vitamin C content to help repel toxins and the honey will soothe your throat. The ginger helps stimulate digestion and circulation and also works as an expectorant (a polite way of saying it helps you cough up mucus). Drink this no more than twice a day.

Serves 1
Juice of 4 lemons
1½ tbsp honey
1 tsp grated fresh ginger or
**   ½ tsp ground ginger**

1. Put the lemon juice in a small saucepan over a medium heat.
2. Add the honey and stir.
3. Add the ginger and stir again. Pour into a cup and drink immediately.

Andy's magic remedy

Whenever Andy gets a cold, he always makes up this concoction and it seems to help.

Serves 1
2 cloves of garlic
1 tsp grated fresh ginger
2 lemons
1 cup water
2 tsp honey
1 cinnamon stick

1. Crush the garlic, grate the ginger and squeeze the lemons.
2. Boil the water and pour into a cup.
3. Add the garlic, ginger, lemon juice, honey and cinnamon stick.
4. After a couple of minutes, remove the cinnamon stick and drink while still hot.

Curry powder remedy

There's nothing like a curry to help alleviate the symptoms of colds and flu and ease congestion. It's actually the cayenne pepper in it that helps, as it stimulates secretions that help clear mucus and relieve stuffiness. Many of the ingredients in this curry powder will help if you're suffering from a cold or flu; it can be used as a base for many curry dishes or to spice up bland food.

2 tbsp whole cumin seeds
1 tbsp whole cardamom seeds
2 tbsp whole coriander seeds
2 tbsp ground turmeric
1 tbsp black mustard seeds
1 tsp cayenne pepper

1. Put a frying pan over a medium heat, without oil. When it's hot, add the cumin, cardamon and coriander seeds and cook for about 5–10 minutes, shaking the pan occasionally. Take care not to burn the seeds.
2. Put the roasted seeds into a small bowl and leave to cool. Add the turmeric, mustard seeds and cayenne pepper.
3. Mix well and decant the mixture into a jar.
4. When you wish to use the mixture, pound 1 or 2 teaspoons of it, using a pestle and mortar, until it's a fine powder. The spices are best when they're freshly ground.

ACHES & PAINS

Back pain

It's likely that at one time or another self-sufficientish folk will suffer from back problems because of all the digging they do, although it's not just gardeners who suffer – back pain is one of the most common reasons why people visit their doctor.

To help prevent back pain, try taking regular exercise to strengthen the back including swimming, yoga and t'ai chi. Shiatsu and Thai massages can also help alleviate the problem. Correcting your posture is a very important step in preventing recurring back pain – bend your knees and keep your back straight when lifting, and try not to slouch when sitting – sit on an upright chair rather than a squishy armchair you can sink into. Some doctors might recommend the highly regarded Alexander technique. If you do consider having treatment, ensure that you use a STAT accredited practitioner.

Ginger root can also help relieve back pain as it works as an anti-inflammatory. Grate a little into hot water and drink this every day; there are considered to be no side effects to this remedy.

T'ai chi helps ease aches and pains.

Muscle aches and strain

Muscle aches are usually a result of over-exertion during strenuous physical activity. After we finished writing this book, we both decided to go on a walking holiday. Having

been cooped up for weeks with little exercise, we were foolish enough to think that we were both as fit as when we started. As a result, our leg muscles ached for days. Avoidance is the key: don't overdo physical activity, know your limitations, and always stretch or limber up before undertaking any strenuous exercise.

Muscular aches and pains will ease over time, but you can bring some relief to the affected area by applying a bag of crushed ice 3 times a day for 10–20 minutes at a time. Anti-inflammatory herbs and spices, such as turmeric and ginger, will also help; these can be added to a spicy meal.

RSI

During the writing of this book, both of us have suffered from mild RSI (repetitive strain/stress injury). This is characterized by any abnormal and persistent pain, tightness or stiffness in the hand, wrist, arm, elbow and shoulder. RSI is the collective term for a variety of disorders including carpal tunnel syndrome, tennis elbow, gamekeeper's thumb and intersection syndrome. The first port of call should be your doctor if you're experiencing any of the symptoms described above.

Computer users should ensure that their working conditions are not contributing to the condition. Make sure that the top of your screen is at eye level, your arms are at right angles to the keyboard and your knees are at right angles, with your feet firmly on the floor. Try using an RSI hand rest (see page 331).

Deficiency of vitamin B complex can be a contributing factor and increasing the amount of wholefoods in your diet or using a vitamin B supplement can sometimes alleviate symptoms. Other helpful remedies include turmeric, which is an anti-inflammatory that you can add to meals, ginkgo (available in tea bags) and cod liver oil.

Headaches and migraines

Headaches and migraines can be extremely painful and debilitating. If your headaches are severe, and especially if they're coupled with vomiting or if you suffer from frequent chronic headaches, you should consult a professional practitioner. They may just be a result of eye strain, so it's worth having your eyes checked. If you spend prolonged periods in front of a computer screen, try to take a break every hour.

A herbal infusion made from a small sprig of rosemary, peppermint leaves and chamomile flowers will help treat the various elements of a headache. Rosemary contains several antioxidants, peppermint reduces pain and clears sinuses and chamomile relieves headaches caused by indigestion. (See page 272 for how to make an infusion.)

Migraines and headaches can be the result of a food allergy or intolerance. If symptoms persist, and your doctor is at a loss to find a cure, you could try cutting out foods that are likely to be the culprit for a couple of weeks and see if it makes a difference. Common causes, especially of migraines, are the four Cs: caffeine, chocolate, citrus fruit and cheese.

Earache

Ear infections and earache can be very sore, although often the pain will disappear within a couple of days. To relieve the symptoms of earache, place a few drops of St John's wort extract or lavender oil in the infected ear and plug it with cotton wool. A hot water bottle wrapped in a tea towel (to prevent the skin from burning) and held next to the ear can also help soothe the pain. Earache can be a symptom of a cold or flu, but it is more often than not caused by a local infection. It's important to see a doctor if pain persists for more than a couple of days.

Toothache

If you're suffering from toothache, it's usually a sign that something is wrong, so make an appointment with your dentist. While you're waiting to see the dentist there are some herbs that will help numb the pain.

Cloves work really well – you can either suck on them or apply clove oil to the affected area (this is available from most chemists). Yarrow root and leaves also have a numbing effect: you can either chew these or make an infusion with the leaves. A tea tree oil mouthwash (2 drops of tea tree oil to 250ml/8 fl oz water) works as an anaesthetic and an antiseptic, so it's good for gingivitis (inflammation of the gums) too. However, as it mustn't be swallowed it's best to avoid giving this to young children.

Be aware that toothache can also be caused by sinus problems, so you may not actually have anything wrong with your teeth or gums but may need to treat a cold instead (see pages 274–5).

HANGOVERS

Prevention is better than cure for most ailments, including hangovers. Before drinking try to have a large meal rich in carbohydrates, including rice or potatoes, and drink water between alcoholic drinks, finishing off the evening with a rosemary infusion and another glass of water. It's generally agreed that it's the dehydration brought about by excessive alcohol intake that's the biggest cause of a hangover.

Nettles are a good restorative to the liver and kidneys, so you could make your own nettle infusion (see page 272), perhaps adding honey to make it more palatable (alternatively, you can buy a commercially produced nettle tea). Drink one cup in the morning, one in the afternoon and one in the evening. Milk thistle seeds (which contain silymarin) are thought to help protect the liver from toxins including alcohol. Milk thistle is available in pill form from herbalists and healthfood shops and has been used in treating cirrhosis of the liver. Dandelion coffee is an excellent detox treatment for the morning after.

Dandelion coffee

Dandelion root is one of the most effective detoxifying herbs, so this dandelion coffee recipe is an ideal treatment for a hangover. It also has major therapeutic benefits for various other conditions, including skin problems such as acne and boils, constipation, eczema, high blood pressure and arthritis. It's an ideal way of using up all the dandelions that you weeded out of your vegetable patch. The roots take quite some time to roast, so to save energy carry out this task when the oven is in use to cook something else such as your Sunday dinner.

1. Ideally, gather dandelion roots in autumn, when they have their highest concentration of nutrients.
2. Clean the roots and dry them in hot sun, in a low oven or in an airing cupboard (see page 247).
3. Once they have dried, roast the roots at 240°C (475°F, Gas mark 9) for 2 hours or until they are brittle.
4. Allow the roots to cool, then grind them using a pestle and mortar. Make coffee with the resulting powder as you would with normal coffee.

DIGESTIVE DISORDERS

Indigestion

Difficulty in digesting food can be accompanied by various symptoms including stomach ache, heartburn, wind and too much acid production. Herbal infusions can often have a beneficial effect. A chamomile and peppermint mix will help rid the body of wind and relax the digestive tract – you can make this from scratch or buy tea bags. It might not sound that tasty but with a spoonful of honey it becomes an acceptable drink. Dandelion, ginger, lemon balm and thyme will also ease the symptoms.

Long-term sufferers should consider seeing a doctor, because indigestion can be a symptom of other problems, including gasto-intestinal reflux (or GIR), which needs to be treated by medication. Avoid acidic foods such as tomatoes and oranges and also red meat.

Constipation and diarrhoea

Constipation, the infrequency of bowel movements, often results from a low-fibre diet. If you suffer from constipation you'll need to increase your intake of fibre-rich foods such as wholegrain cereals, fresh fruit and pulses, but do this gradually, as ironically a sudden shift can exacerbate the problem. Dandelion root will help ease your movements – dandelion coffee is ideal (see page 277) – and chewing on a liquorice root will also help.

Diarrhoea is usually caused by intestinal infection or inflammation and can be fairly dangerous as it causes dehydration, so you should seek medical advice. Sufferers should ensure that they're drinking plenty of fluids. Eating apples can help – the pectin present in the peel will help add bulk to your stools – and black tea has also been used to treat diarrhoea. Agrimony and sage are astringent herbs that dry and tighten the bowel lining, but they should be taken for up to 3 days only.

Nausea and vomiting

Nausea can have many causes: for example, excessive alcohol intake, pregnancy (morning sickness), travel sickness, infections, eating too much, food poisoning, stress and emotional problems. If you've been vomiting periodically for over 24 hours you should seek medical advice. Dehydration is always associated with vomiting, so make sure you drink plenty of fluids.

Ginger is a common remedy for nausea, as it helps to settle the digestion. If it's impossible to keep anything down, make a ginger infusion, allow it to cool, pour it onto a flannel and place it on your stomach. You will absorb the ginger through your skin and it should help reduce vomiting. Drinking chamomile and peppermint infusions can also be soothing. If you're not in favour of herbal infusions you could try chewing on about 25 fennel seeds, which will work as a digestive aid. For sufferers of morning sickness, a ginger infusion before bed and one in the morning should provide some comfort. (For remedies for alcohol-induced nausea, see the box on page 277, but remember prevention is better than cure.)

Haemorrhoids

Also known as piles, haemorrhoids occur when the veins in the region of the anus become enlarged and inflamed. Symptoms include itching, bleeding and anal pain. One of the key culprits for aggravating haemorrhoids is constipation (see left), so try to maintain regular bowel movements and avoid straining.

Any anti-inflammatory herb will help alleviate the symptoms – try adding turmeric or root ginger to as many meals as you can. To relieve the itching you can use horse chestnut in capsule form (these are available from your local herbalist). You might also consider applying diluted witch hazel (1 tablespoon of witch hazel to 1 tablespoon of warm water); for best results, apply the mixture to an organic cotton wool ball and attach it in place overnight.

Fennel seeds and root ginger are both good for a variety of digestive disorders.

CIRCULATORY COMPLAINTS

High blood pressure

You might not be aware that you have high blood pressure (also known as hypertension) if you haven't had your blood pressure checked recently. Common symptoms include headaches, ringing in the ears, insomnia, visual disturbance, fatigue and breathlessness. If your natural parents or grandparents suffer you could be at risk and should consult your doctor.

High blood pressure is far more common in the developed world, mainly because of our lifestyle. Smoking, stress, high-fat foods, alcohol, salt, caffeine and lack of exercise are all contributing factors. Cycling to work could be the first step to changing this, as stress levels can be reduced if you exercise before work, thus immediately reducing two contributing factors.

A sprig of lavender in your pillowcase or a cup of chamomile tea before bedtime may help to induce sleep and lower stress levels. A daily infusion of yarrow and lime flowers will help widen constricted blood vessels, thus lowering the pressure in your arteries. (See page 272 for how to make an infusion.) Yoga and t'ai chi are also great ways to keep fit, relax and aid natural breathing.

The self-sufficientish diet will undoubtedly benefit blood pressure – lots of fresh fruit and vegetables, especially ones rich in beta carotene such as carrots – as will low-fat dairy produce, for example yogurt or cottage cheese. Eating raw garlic is also excellent – try a clove or two crushed and mixed into a salad. Don't exceed two cloves a day, as eating too much raw garlic can cause problems in the digestive tract; mixing crushed garlic with olive oil, rapeseed oil or sunflower oil will coat the stomach and will make the garlic more palatable. Omega-3 fatty acids, found in oily fish, are also reported to help reduce blood pressure.

Anaemia

Anaemia occurs when we have abnormally low levels of haemoglobin, which is more commonly known as a low red blood cell count. As red blood cells carry oxygen to blood tissue, this can be problematic. There are several types of anaemia, but the easiest to treat with herbs is iron-deficiency anaemia, which can be caused by insufficient iron in the diet or heavy menstrual bleeding.

Anaemics should increase dietary sources of iron by eating green, leafy vegetables or supplementing with iron tablets and/or adding vitamin C to their diet, as this will help absorb iron into the bloodstream. A nettle infusion will certainly be useful too. A yarrow infusion can be an aid when heavy menstrual bleeding is the cause of anaemia, as this herb can help to regulate your menstrual cycle.

Poor circulation and chilblains

We often change the old saying 'Cold hands, warm heart' to 'Cold hands, poor circulation'. It might not sound as kind but there's much more truth in it.

Poor blood flow can cause a lot of discomfort and may result in chilblains (inflamed sores) on the fingers and toes. These can be very painful. If you suffer from poor circulation and chilblains, you need to stimulate the circulation and 'warm up' the system. Try to eat more hot spices, such as cayenne pepper, and introduce more garlic and ginger to your diet. A herbal infusion of nettle and yarrow, taken first thing in the morning and last thing at night, will also help. Aerobic exercise to aid your circulation is often the key to improving this condition, because it increases blood flow to the hands and feet. If you suffer from numb fingers and toes, always seek professional advice as it may be an indication of other conditions.

MAKE CHANGES GRADUALLY

Many people try to change their ways drastically in January each year but this can be counter-productive. Try making just one change at a time and work gradually towards the goal of a healthier lifestyle. If you manage to replace coffee with herbal teas, for instance, keep this up for at least 2 months before contemplating giving up cigarettes. You're more likely to fail in your efforts at self-improvement if you try to renounce all your bad habits at once. Incidentally, an easier transition from caffeinated tea to herbal teas is rooibos tea, as you can still add milk.

Gel from the aloe vera plant has a soothing
effect on sunburn or minor burns.

SKIN, HAIR & NAILS

Minor burns and sunburn

Serious burns always require hospital treatment, so don't delay in contacting the emergency services and getting treatment. While you're waiting for the ambulance to arrive, or to treat minor burns, hold the burn under cold running water for 20 minutes to reduce pain and damage; if your clothing is stuck to the burn, don't attempt to remove it as this can cause further harm. If the burn is mild but bigger than a playing card, it should be considered serious and you must seek medical treatment.

After minor burns have been cooled by water, apply natural yogurt mixed with honey and cover with a clean bandage or rag. To help prevent scarring, lavender oil can also be used; place a few drops neat onto the affected area. Drink (or give the patient) plenty of water to replenish any lost fluids. If you're growing aloe vera, snap off one of the leaves and apply the gel to your wounds, as aloe vera helps to restore skin tissues. It's also anti-inflammatory and will help the body to heal. Some folk remedies mistakenly suggest that you should use butter on a burn, but never do this as it will worsen the burn if the skin is still hot and will serve only to infect it.

For sunburn, use aloe vera, as described above. Cider or white vinegar diluted with equal parts of water can also be applied to minor sunburn.

Minor cuts and bruises

Wash minor cuts thoroughly under a tap to reduce the chance of infection; if a cut doesn't stop bleeding, apply continuous direct pressure to it for up to 20 minutes using a clean dressing or cloth. Cuts will heal faster if left to breathe, so don't cover them with a sticking plaster and use a bandage only if you intend to garden or do anything that might cause the wound to get dirty. As in the case of burns, aloe vera can be beneficial (see above). Also, covering the wound with unprocessed honey (available from your local farmers' market) is effective as honey has antibacterial properties; place a gauze cloth over the top to stop insects from being attracted to your arm.

We all bruise from time to time. Arnica is the most common remedy for bruising and is available from healthfood shops and herbalists. A bag of crushed ice placed on the affected area for 10–20 minutes at a time will also help, as will wrapping wet comfrey leaves over the bruise and covering with a clean piece of cloth or bandage; the allantoin in the comfrey will aid the body's healing process. If you bruise for no apparent reason you should consult your doctor, as it could be a sign of kidney disease or diabetes.

Insect stings

If you have a bee sting, remove the sting with a pair of tweezers or a needle. This is a delicate job if you're to ensure no more poison is to be released.

For any type of insect sting, to relieve the pain make an infusion from chamomile flowers, elderflower or a sprig of lavender (see page 272 for how to make an infusion). Leave it to cool, preferably adding some ice. Pour this onto a flannel and apply to the sting. Repeat if necessary.

Warts

Warts are hard, lumpy patches of skin caused by the papilloma virus. There are various different types of warts, such as verucas and genital warts, but here we are focusing on common warts, such as those on your hands.

One of the old folk remedies for ridding yourself of warts is dandelion sap. Pick a fresh dandelion and break the stem; apply the milky substance inside onto your wart about 3 or 4 times a day and repeat every day until your wart disappears. Banana peel has also reportedly been used on warts. Wrap a bit of the peel around your wart (white side touching it) and leave it in place for a day, replacing it with a fresh piece daily. Aloe vera gel applied to the wart 2 or 3 times a day is also said to help.

Cold sores

Cold sores are caused by the herpes simplex virus and result in blistering of the infected area (usually around the lips and nose) and an unpleasant tingling sensation. A friend of ours always suffers from them after all-night partying or when he's feeling run down. The latter is a common cause, as is infection. Healthy eating and lots of sleep will help keep cold sores at bay. Also, try reducing stress levels: practising yoga and t'ai chi are beneficial.

The hypericin in St John's wort has been reported to help in the fight against the virus. Take one capsule a day until the cold sore starts to disappear. Garlic is also known to beat virusus and can be a great ally in the herpes war.

Fresh horseradish grated into a cup of hot milk and applied to the skin is a cure for acne and boils.

Acne and boils

It seems to be Murphy's law that a spot will appear right on the end of your nose when you least need it to – for instance, before an important date or a job interview. It's no surprise, though, because nervous tension is often a contributing factor. Faddy detox diets and binge drinking can also cause an outbreak, as the toxins are fighting to get out. Cleansing the skin regularly and eating a healthy diet will certainly help keep spots down.

Dandelion root is a good detoxifying herb, so make dandelion coffee out of plants found on your allotment or in your garden (see page 277) or buy it from a healthfood shop. (Please be warned that dandelion can have a mild laxative effect.) You could also make an infusion with red clover leaves and apply it to the affected area: red clover grows in many parks and open spaces and is identified by its purplish flowers. Alternatively, grate some horseradish into a cup of hot milk. Leave it to cool for about half an hour, then apply it to the skin.

Ringworm

Ringworm is a fungal infection that causes circular patches of red or scaly skin on the body or the scalp. Keep the infected areas cool, dry and clean and don't share towels, clothing, combs or brushes with anyone in your household. Ringworm can be transferred from animals, so check your pets and livestock if you've been infected. If you're infected, avoid scratching as this can cause secondary infection or spread the ringworm.

As with most fungal infections, vinegar will help. Make a solution of equal amounts of vinegar and water and dab it on the infected area. Alternatively, add 2 drops of tea tree oil to a glass of water and apply it to the infected area. With both treatments, apply once a day and continue for 2 weeks after the symptoms have disappeared (stop using immediately if they cause irritation).

A related condition, jock itch, or ringworm of the groin, is also aggravated by moisture and friction, so wash and dry your groin well and wear boxers instead of tight-fitting underpants. Garlic can be used in persistent cases – mash up a clove of garlic, mix it with a tablespoon of olive oil and apply it to your groin. Discontinue use if it causes irritation.

Athlete's foot

Athlete's foot is very common and can be spread in public swimming baths and shower areas. To prevent athlete's foot, allow your feet to breathe: wear sandals (without socks) or flip flops whenever possible. Otherwise, carry a spare pair of socks to change into if your feet become sweaty. You can even add baking powder to your shoes and socks to keep them dry.

If infected, make a footbath using a 50:50 ratio of white or cider vinegar to water. Soak your feet for 10 minutes a day for 10 consecutive days, and let them dry naturally in the air after application. Alternatively, add a few drops of tea tree oil to a 'carrier' oil, such as olive or almond oil, and apply it to your feet daily (stop using immediately if it causes irritation).

Nail infections

Nail infections typically form on the big toe, characterized by white or yellow patches of discoloration. After a period of infection, the nail can become thick, deformed and will have a slightly musty smell. Always keep your feet (or hand if infected) clean and dry, keep nails short and do not use nail varnish if you're prone to infections, because this will cause moisture to collect, which will exacerbate the problem. Nail infections often start right at the base of the nail, and for this reason they can be notoriously difficult to treat. However, you could apply some tea tree oil or mash up one clove of garlic with a tablespoon of olive oil and apply it to the infected area.

Head lice

Over-the-counter pesticides in the form of head lice shampoo and mousse frequently don't work, because the lice have become resistant to them. The best solution we've come up with is to wash your hair in normal shampoo, then use a conditioner with a couple of drops of tea tree oil added. Leave the conditioner on for an hour and then use a metal nit comb to work through the hair thoroughly. You'll need to comb very carefully, from the root to the tip across the whole head, and will need to wash the lice away after each comb. Sometimes a white apron comes with the comb, and you can dispose of the nits easily. Repeat the process once more. Even if you think you've got rid of all the nits, you'll need to repeat this method every 3 days to make sure that new lice haven't hatched.

Dandruff

Dandruff is an inflammation that causes itchy and flaky bits of skin on the scalp and in some cases other parts of the body such as the face. To lubricate the scalp, mix evening primrose oil with 2 drops of tea tree oil, apply it to your scalp at night and put on a shower cap to save your pillows from getting greasy. Wash the oil off in the morning. Always use a gentle shampoo if you have a dry, flaky scalp.

ANXIETY & DEPRESSION

Insomnia and nervous tension

Most of us at some time or another will be anxious and may suffer from insomnia, particularly at times of stress, such as moving house, overwork or emotional upsets. Sometimes just the thought of being unable to sleep can keep us up and, paradoxically, we become too tired to sleep. It's at these times we might need a little helping hand to take us to the land of nod.

Getting into good habits can help: cut out caffeinated drinks at least 3 hours before going to bed, don't smoke at least an hour before and try to get at least some exercise during the day. Don't rely on an alcoholic nightcap before bed, as it doesn't promote the right kind of sleep; if you're drinking more than three or four units a day on a regular basis, that in itself could be the cause of your insomnia. Yoga, t'ai chi and meditation will all help focus the mind and relieve the everyday stresses and strains that might be keeping you awake at night, and many people find that a hot bath helps them to relax before bedtime.

There are also many herbs that can encourage a good night's sleep by helping you to unwind and 'switch off'.

The following herbs can aid relaxation and help you to return to a normal sleep pattern:

- **Valerian root** – Take this soothing plant in the form of an infusion (see page 272) or capsules. Do not exceed the recommended dose or use with other sedatives.

- **Lavender** – Dried lavender flowers are widely recognized as having sedative properties.

- **Chamomile** – A dried chamomile flower infusion will relax you before bedtime.

- **Basil** – Whether it's eaten in food or taken as an infusion, basil has a calming effect on the nervous system.

- **Hops and rosemary** – you could make a restorative infusion for the bath by putting 30g (1oz) of rosemary or hops, or a combination of both, in a muslin bag and leaving it to soak in the bathwater for 5 minutes or so before getting in. The same can be done with chamomile and lavender.

Lavender can be slipped into a pillowcase to aid sleep.

Lavender nightcap

Lavender is rarely used in food and drink these days, which is a shame as it has a lovely, delicate flavour and is very calming. Orange flower water is widely available at many stores and can be found in the baking section.

125ml (4fl oz) water
3 tbsp fresh lavender leaves
1 tbsp honey
3 tbsp orange flower water

Put the water, lavender leaves and honey into a saucepan. Heat gently and stir until the honey has dissolved. Strain and add the orange flower water.

SAD and winter blues

Every winter many people in the northern hemisphere suffer from SAD (seasonal affective disorder). Sufferers can find it more difficult to get up in the morning, graze on unhealthy foods, have difficulty focusing on anything and will generally feel more down in the dumps during the winter months. True SAD is thought to affect about 2 per cent of the population, while the milder form, known as the 'winter blues', is thought to affect about 20 per cent. We both suffer from the winter blues to some extent, and Andy's final dissertation for his psychology degree was about SAD, so while he's by no means a medical professional he can suggest a variety of natural treatments and lifestyle changes that are well worth experimenting with to ease the symptoms. As with any form of depression, you should consult your doctor if you believe that you suffer from SAD.

According to popular research, light boxes can be worth their weight in gold to anyone who suffers from SAD, but we haven't yet tried them. By far the best herbal treatment that we've come across is St John's wort. Dave swears by it, and as soon as the winter months are upon us he starts to take two tablets of St John's wort a day, gradually cutting it out as the spring approaches. A study in the medical journal the *Lancet* in 1996 validates the use of this herb as an antidepressant. It's worth noting that St John's wort can make you sensitive to sunlight, which is one of the reasons to stop taking it in the spring. Other side effects can include nervousness and abdominal upset. The abdominal upsets can be controlled if you take the medication with food, but if you still experience side effects you should discontinue use immediately. It should also not be taken in conjunction with any other antidepressant.

Other beneficial herbs that are thought by many to help this debilitating condition include basil, lemon balm, rosemary and cinnamon.

The chief reason that people suffer from SAD or the winter blues is the lack of light during the winter months. One of the best remedies is to get out as much as possible – try to leave the house as often as you can and go to the nearest green area, even if only for half an hour during your lunch break. To make the most of the short daylight hours, open your curtains as early as possible in the morning and sit by a window if you can.

St John's wort

ALLERGIES

Hay fever

An old remedy for hay fever is to chew on natural honeycomb, although these days it's not cheap or easy to find. Instead, get some honey from your local farmers' market or farm shop, ensuring that it's local honey. This will help you build up a tolerance to the pollen in your area.

There are some foods that can aggravate hay fever and therefore should be avoided during times of high pollen counts. For example, dairy produce – eggs, milk, butter and cheese – all increase mucus. Consider cutting down on dairy intake, replacing part or all of it with soya milk, rice milk or hemp milk (see pages 344–6). Some groups of people, such as growing children and the elderly, need high levels of calcium, so replace dairy products with other calcium-rich foods such as spinach, okra, salmon, rhubarb, baked beans and peas. Sufferers whose hay fever is triggered by grass pollen should avoid sugar and wheat, as they're from the same botanical family and can cause allergic reactions.

There are also beneficial foods that help prevent hay fever, particularly those that boost the immune system: for example, zinc-rich foods such as cottage cheese, oatmeal, pork, peas, lentils, jacket potatoes (eat the skin) and oysters. As a possibly favourable side effect zinc also increases libido. Vitamin C, found in fresh fruit and vegetables, is also useful, as is vitamin B5, found in wholegrain cereals and eggs, which helps to control high levels of excess histamine. Magnesium is a natural anti-histamine and can help reduce the frequency and severity of hay-fever attacks; it's found in nuts, such as almonds and cashews, wholegrains, spinach and peanut butter.

It might seem strange to take a flower to reduce hay fever, but chamomile acts as an anti-inflammatory and an anti-allergic herb. The easiest way to take this would be to substitute one cup of tea or coffee a day with a chamomile infusion. Many herbs that are good for coughs and colds will also ease hay-fever symptoms (see pages 274–5).

Mild asthma and wheeziness

Asthma is usually triggered by an allergic reaction to substances such as dust, pollen, pets, smoky environments and certain foods, but it may also be a result of an infection. As asthma can be life-threatening, it's important that you talk with your doctor to find the cause of your asthma, and also to discuss the use of herbal treatments. Do not suddenly stop taking steroidal or other inhalants without professional advice.

Use your common sense and avoid things that could trigger an attack, and eat healthily – stay away from food colouring (especially tartrazine), fatty and sugary foods, and try to eat more garlic, onions, green vegetables and salads. Swimming can be beneficial to the asthma sufferer, as it helps to open up the airways and make the lungs stronger. There's much evidence to suggest that if children are fed milk other than their mother's in their first 4 months they're more likely to develop asthma, although some experts disagree.

There are several remedies that may ease breathing and reduce inflammation. A chamomile steam inhalation can bring great relief. Fill a large bowl with freshly boiled water, add 5–10 drops of chamomile oil and stir well. Cover your head and the bowl with a towel, close your eyes and inhale the steam for about 10 minutes, or until the preparation cools. Alternatively, a chest rub will have a similar effect. Combine a few drops of eucalyptus, menthol or thyme oil with a tablespoon of almond oil and massage it onto your chest and back.

A herbal infusion containing equal measures of comfrey leaves, thyme, hyssop, chamomile and skullcap can help. Comfrey leaves have been used as a folk remedy for asthma and other bronchial conditions for centuries, thyme and hyssop can loosen and expel mucus, chamomile helps to relax the airways and skullcap is anti-inflammatory.

Coffee can also help – yes, you have read it correctly, coffee – or any other caffeinated drink. Caffeine is similar structurally and pharmacologically to theophylline, which is used to treat asthma. It should not be used frequently but as a last resort when nothing else is available – three cups of coffee or six cups of tea might help to stop wheezing.

Eczema

In eczema sufferers the skin becomes red, inflamed, flaky and blistered, and it can be itchy and extremely sore. It's difficult to self-treat, but some of the ideas suggested here should help bring some relief.

It's very likely to be an allergic reaction that triggers your eczema. There are obvious culprits and easy solutions. Washing powder is a common irritant, so use eco-balls or soap pods instead (see page 55), as are many cosmetic soaps and perfumes – cut out the use of one of your products every 2 weeks to find the culprit. Other likely causes are nickel, so avoid cheap jewellery and any metal that might touch your skin, such as a watch strap. Many people are allergic to feathers, so buy hypo-allergenic pillows and duvets.

To bring some relief, place liquidized fresh green cabbage leaves on the infected area, secure with a bandage and leave in place for about 20 minutes. You can also use fresh comfrey or chickweed in the same way. There are a few herbs that can be taken as an infusion (see page 272) to help cleanse the body. These include nettle, red clover, burdock, cleavers and dandelion root.

Lifestyle can be a contributing factor when it comes to eczema, so try to control stress levels. Take up yoga or t'ai chi to help you relax. Eczema can be exacerbated by dairy foods, so some people may choose to limit their intake. Also, healthy skin cells need a supply of beneficial fats and oils, so eat plenty of nuts, seeds, fish and avocados.

Chewing on honeycomb is a traditional remedy for hay fever.

4.
LIFESTYLE

TRAVEL & HOLIDAYS

We tend to think nothing of travelling great distances nowadays. Consider how many miles you travelled over the last year – probably for even the least travelled of people this will amount to over 1600 kilometres (1000 miles). If you work just 4 kilometres (2½ miles) from your home, this journey alone brings your total to 1930 kilometres (1200 miles) a year. It's no wonder that more than one-third of most people's carbon footprint is attributed to travel.

Of course, the easiest way to cut down on your fuel consumption would be to avoid travelling entirely, but unless you live like a resident of Albert Square in *EastEnders*, where everything revolves around one tiny area with seemingly nothing beyond, this is going to be dull at best and more than likely darn near impossible. The most realistic way of making a difference is to change the way in which we travel – flying only when there is no other option, walking more instead of driving, taking more public transport for longer journeys rather than getting in the car (there are plenty of advantages of taking trains and buses), and using a bicycle for the daily commute and as a means of getting around your local area. If you must take your car, consider joining a car-share scheme.

MAKING THE JOURNEY

There was once a time when flying was the privilege of the wealthy, but in the past 30 years it's become an increasingly common form of travel and is often the only option that's considered when most people book a holiday. However, there are many other ways of getting to your holiday destination that can be far more comfortable and interesting, as well as less stressful and less damaging to the environment. With overland travel, the holiday can often start as soon as you get on board.

The true cost of flying

In recent years an ever-increasing number of cheap airlines has emerged and many people have decided to take to the air, even when travelling within the UK. We have to put our hands up and say we've taken our fair share of flights in the past, but as is the case with most people, we didn't realize the damage that could be caused by flying until recently.

The statistics of damage caused by air travel are certainly sobering: a 2003 study predicted a doubling of carbon emissions between 2003 and 2012 if the growth of the airline industry continues unabated at its current pace. This means that all homes and businesses need to become carbon neutral in order to reach the target of 60 per cent reduction in carbon dioxide emissions set by the government and recommended by scientists to stop dangerous climate change by 2050. A process known as 'radiative forcing' means that carbon dioxide released at altitude creates a greater greenhouse effect that is at least twice (some think 3 or 4 times) as damaging as the same amount of gas released at sea level. Even if you disregard the carbon contributions by aircraft, there is still the consideration of using up limited oil reserves, airport expansion ruining the countryside, reduced air quality and the noise of aircraft.

We're sure you're fully aware of the damage that air travel causes and don't wish to lecture you any further. However, we do suggest you consider alternative ways of travelling, many of which are considerably more civilized and romantic than flying, such as travelling on board a ship or by sleeper train. Think about it – when was the last time you read a romantic novel set on a Ryanair flight?

Travelling overland

We've always found the main bonus of travelling overland is that there isn't a hidden amount of time travelling from the airport to the city you wish to arrive in. Most train or bus stations are quite central and they don't claim to be in a town they're not, unlike some airports. A trip from London to Paris on Eurostar is the most straightforward city-to-city journey we've ever taken. Why anyone would still fly to Paris is a mystery to us.

Although at first glance it often seems cheaper and quicker to fly to your destination, once you take everything into consideration this isn't always the case, particularly when travelling within Britain. When flying, you have to build in travel time required to get to and from the airport at both ends (up to an hour in big cities), checking-in time (usually 2 or 3 hours) and waiting at baggage claim (about half an hour). So what appears to be a 1-hour flight can actually extend quite easily to being a 5- or 6-hour trip in total. In addition, you need to take into consideration the 'hidden' costs of flying – air tax is added on to what at first appears to be a very cheap ticket price, then you have the cost of travelling to and from the airport, not to mention the inflated prices you spend on food and drink while waiting around for your flight. Shop around for cheap rail and coach tickets in advance of your trip (it may well be worth getting a rail or coach card) and try to calculate the real time flying takes before making the decision to take the plane.

CAR SHARE

Next time you're about to drive a long distance, either for work or for a holiday, if you have room for an extra passenger consider offering someone that seat in exchange for a share of the fuel costs. Websites such as www.nationalcarshare.co.uk allow you to team up with people making similar trips as yourself. Even if you don't have a car it's possible to join a car-share network as a passenger and contribute to the fuel cost. (See also page 387.)

Taking the train

Some people may view the extra travelling hours of going by train or bus as a downside, but this is only if you don't think of them as part of the holiday. A train journey really can be an enjoyable part of the trip rather than simply a way of getting there. Many European trains have a bar area where you can sit, chat, play cards and meet new people from all over the world. It can be like sitting in a moving pub. Alternatively, you might want to use the time to catch up with your reading or, if you're not on holiday, your work. Some trains have mobile-phone boosters, so you can still stay in touch if you need to, as well as quiet carriages so you can get away from calls if you wish. Almost all longer-distance trains now have plug sockets on them so you can use your laptop computer should you wish to work.

Trains are also an advantage for people travelling with children. There's room to walk up and down the train, they don't need to be strapped into a tiny space with seatbelts and the window can be a great source of entertainment as the train passes through an array of different landscapes. The nappy-changing facilities are far better on trains than on planes, and babies are much more likely to sleep through the gentle rocking motion of a train than possible turbulence of an aircraft.

Ten reasons why the train is better than flying

1. Airports can be miles out of town, while train stations are either in the centre or within walking distance of the centre.
2. There are less obtrusive security checks.
3. There is generous baggage allowance.
4. You get to see the countryside you're travelling through and experience the world instead of just going over the top of it.
5. You can open the window.
6. The toilets are bigger and there are more of them.
7. More people survive train crashes than plane crashes.
8. There is no need for baggage retrieval and no chance of luggage ending up on the other side of the world.
9. It is more sociable as there's more space to walk around and meet people.
10. It is less stressful and there are fewer health risks (such as deep-vein thrombosis).

Some trains are now equipped with car-carrying carriages. In the UK, the Eurotunnel Shuttle (formerly known as Le Shuttle) travels from Folkestone to Calais. Its prices are comparable with the cost of a ferry, but with a crossing time of just 35 minutes it's a faster option if you wish to take your car. When you arrive in continental Europe some countries have similar carriages for cross-country travel – the best example of this that we've seen are the ICE trains in Germany. With a top speed of 300 kilometres (186 miles) per hour, there's perhaps no safer or more relaxing way of crossing the country.

FACTS ABOUT EUROSTAR

- Carbon emissions when taking the Eurostar from London to Paris are 10 times lower than flying from Gatwick to Charles de Gaulle airport.

- With the 'Tread Lightly' initiative, introduced in November 2007, all Eurostar passenger emissions are 'offset' and so each journey is effectively carbon neutral. This means that part of the ticket money is invested in schemes that reduce carbon emissions elsewhere – for example, planting trees that will absorb carbon or buying solar panels for villages in the developing world to reduce the use of fossil fuels.

- There is 845mm (33in) of leg room (compared to 736mm/29in on a budget airline) and if you're travelling Business Premier class the leg room increases to 945mm (37in).

- When booking Eurostar you have a choice of a single seat, two seats next to each other or a table for four. There are also special seats set aside for wheelchair users and a companion may travel at a discounted rate.

- You can often get hotel deals included in the price of your ticket if you book online.

- With a Eurostar ticket you can book in advance your connecting train to some European destinations for a cheaper price than you would pay for a standard ticket. A Eurostar ticket to Brussels enables you to travel to any other station in Belgium free of charge as long as it is on the same day of travel.

Going by coach

For a less expensive alternative to train travel, and an even more environmentally friendly option, consider travelling by bus or coach. The main non-charter coach company in Britain is National Express. We've both travelled extensively with them and have found that the coaches have improved enormously in the last 10 years. They've got a lot more comfortable, all coaches have a lavatory and air conditioning and some are equipped with wi-fi access and on-board television.

It's always worth looking at the National Express website, www.nationalexpress.com, for their current offers before you travel. The company offers tickets called 'Funfares'. These tickets work in a similar way to some of the budget airlines', gradually going up in cost depending on demand and availability. Some fares (to and from London from certain towns in the UK) can be as low as £1. They also have occasional offers of cheap fares to other destinations, often starting at around £10. At the time of writing, Bristol to Edinburgh could cost as little as £4 return if you book in advance and travel at certain times of the day. The downside of these tickets is that they're non-refundable and you have to go via London, which can add considerably to your journey time.

The disadvantage of travelling by coach is the fact that you're travelling by road so are subject to traffic congestion, although this has eased somewhat with the implementation of bus lanes on some busy stretches of motorway. Avoiding peak travel times such as rush hour and Friday afternoons can help to make the journey a much more peaceful affair.

Mega-bus also offers a service between many UK cities and we've found that their updated fleet of vehicles is also very comfortable and reliable.

Travelling by sea

There's definitely something quite romantic about a sea crossing – you feel as if you're following in the footsteps of countless explorers, artists and historical figures. Stress levels are much lower than with air travel, because you don't feel like you're on such a tight schedule somehow. The holiday starts once you're on board with facilities similar to those at a holiday resort. There are shops, restaurants, bars and a mini casino, and some ferries even have a cinema, nightclub and/or live entertainment. Although Dave describes the on-board entertainment on his Norwegian trip as cheesy at best, it is still one of his most treasured holiday memories.

There are no baggage allowance limits on ferries other than what you can actually physically carry or fit in your car. This means that you can carry bikes, camping equipment, sports equipment or a big musical instrument without having to pay more than its value to get it on board. Security checks are still in evidence, but these tend to be much less stringent or obtrusive than for flights. If you're on a tight budget you can save on accommodation by travelling overnight on a ferry; sometimes breakfast is even included on night crossings. Once at the other end you can link up with a railway network that will take you on to your required destination.

SEA SICKNESS

The downside of ferry travel can be seasickness for some people. With some preventive measures your suffering can be reduced.

● Try not to stay below deck for long periods.

● Don't read or do anything that means you are concentrating on one fixed point. Instead, gaze out at the horizon or approaching land but try not to focus too much on it.

● Drink plenty of fluids and eat or drink some ginger 30 minutes before boarding and then once an hour. A packet of ginger biscuits will suffice. Basil and peppermint can also be beneficial.

● Wear a pressure band (these are usually available in an on-board shop).

You might expect us never to mention the car as a sustainable form of transport, and frankly it isn't, but compared to air travel it's certainly the lesser of two evils from an environmental point of view. The beauty of using your own car means that you don't have to follow a strict itinerary and you can even tow a caravan, which brings costs down once you're at your destination. If you're travelling as a family or in a large group, car ferries can be a considerably less expensive option than flying plus car hire. Strange as it may seem, some ferry operators state that you have to have a vehicle and don't allow foot passengers on some routes, although you're allowed on if you're travelling with a bicycle.

There is a number of ferry ports all over the UK serving routes to Ireland (Eire), Northern Ireland, the Isle of Man, the Isle of Wight, the Channel Islands, Holland, Belgium, Norway, Denmark, France and Spain. (See Useful addresses & further reading, page 387.)

CO_2 EMISSIONS FOR TRAVEL

The graph below illustrates the varying amounts of carbon dioxide that are emitted per passenger (in kilograms) when travelling by coach, car, train or plane. The calculations are based on a one-way journey from London to Edinburgh, a distance of approximately 650 kilometres (400 miles). The flight emissions figure takes into account the 'radiative forcing index' (RFI) multiplier of 2, which scientists consider should be the minimum when calculating CO_2 emissions, because of the fact that carbon dioxide released at altitude creates a greater greenhouse effect that is considerably more damaging than the same amount of gas released at sea level. Some scientists believe the RFI should be multiplied by 3 or even 4.

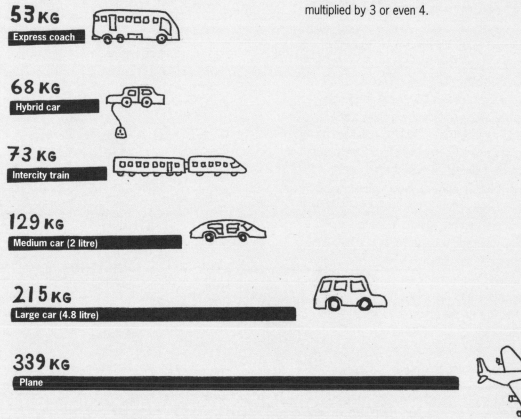

53 KG
Express coach

68 KG
Hybrid car

73 KG
Intercity train

129 KG
Medium car (2 litre)

215 KG
Large car (4.8 litre)

339 KG
Plane

TRAVELLING OVERLAND FROM BRISTOL TO MARRAKECH

We've taken several short breaks in Europe over the past few years, including Amsterdam (12 hours by coach) and Berlin (9 hours by train, stopping off at Brussels and Cologne). But one of our most exciting overland trips was travelling to Marrakech. We've both made the journey, taking different routes, and although it's a long way we really enjoyed our experiences. Travelling to Marrakech by land feels so different from travelling by air. The sense of adventure and connection with the past simply isn't there when you board a plane. Watching the people and culture slowly change through France, Spain and finally into Africa gives you a rich sense of history and accomplishment not achieved by sitting on a plane eating peanuts for 3 hours.

This is an account of how Dave made the journey. It's a suggestion of just one route you could take to Marrakech, or might consider taking part of if you don't want to go the whole way. This route took 8 days and allowed for a day's sightseeing in both Paris and Barcelona as well as some time spent in Andorra and Chefchaouen, a lovely Moroccan mountain town. Three of the nights were spent on sleeper trains to save time and money, but you could travel by day if preferred.

An alternative, quicker route would be to travel from London to Paris, take the sleeper to Madrid then the high-speed train to Algerciras, where you could spend the night, then travel on to Tangier in the morning. You could spend the rest of the day in Tangier and take the sleeper train on to Marrakech.

Day 1: Bristol–London–Paris

Bristol to London (coach: 2½ hours)

There are numerous ways of getting to London these days. Advance train and coach tickets for a fraction of the cost of full fares and budget bus services mean that there is very little reason to travel by plane to the nation's capital. The coach from Bristol takes you right into central London at Earl's Court or Victoria.

Walk from Victoria Coach Station to the underground (about 10 minutes) and travel directly to the Eurostar at St Pancras (King's Cross underground). Alternatively, jump on the 73 bus. Give yourself plenty of time for this leg of the journey, as transport around London can be very slow.

London to Paris (Eurostar: 2¾ hours)

Travelling straight from the heart of London to central Paris (Gare du Nord) in under 3 hours is really possible only by train. A flight from Gatwick to Charles de Gaulle Airport takes only 1 hour but when you consider checking in, security at both ends and travelling to and from the airports to your desired destination the time as well as the cost soon rises rapidly.

Overnight stay in Paris

Day 2: Day in Paris

Paris to L'Hospitalet, South of France (overnight sleeper train: 9½ hours)

After a day exploring Paris we boarded a sleeper train to the South of France. It's well worth travelling long distances overnight by sleeper train, as you travel while you sleep, saving time and the cost of accommodation.

Night spent on sleeper train

Day 3: South of France–Andorra–Barcelona

L'Hospitalet to Andorra (bus: 1½ hours)

Once you arrive at L'Hospitalet, in the South of France, you need to take a short bus journey across a spectacular mountain pass to get to Andorra la Vella. Andorra is right in the middle of the Pyrenees and is a principality, a tax haven and a ski resort set in some of the most stunning scenery in Europe. There are plenty of walks around the main town, Andorra la Vella, and the surrounding area. We spent only a matter of hours in Andorra and if we were to do this journey again we'd certainly spend longer there, as it's stunning.

Andorra to Barcelona (bus: 4 hours)

Snaking through the Pyrenees, the bus from Andorra to Barcelona took us through some of the most scenic parts of northern Spain. Watching the mountains slowly give way to foothills under the late afternoon sun meant this leg of the journey flew by.

Overnight stay in Barcelona

Day 4: Day in Barcelona

Barcelona to Cadiz (overnight sleeper train: 12½ hours)

You have a day to explore the lovely Catalan city of Barcelona before taking another night train, leaving late in the evening and arriving at a good time in Cadiz the following morning. The beds were comfortable and the staff friendly, and there was a small café bar on board.

Night spent on sleeper train

Day 5: Cadiz–Algeciras–Ceuta

Cadiz is a very traditional Spanish town and lays claim to being the oldest continuously inhabited town in Europe. It's a little off the beaten track for the British tourist, and as the last stop on the most south-westerly tip of the Spanish railway system it's well worth the train journey.

Cadiz to Algeciras (bus: 4 hours)

Algeciras is half a day's bus ride away from Cadiz and acts as the main gateway to Morocco. There are ships sailing constantly day and night and tickets are available both in advance and at the dockside.

Algeciras to Ceuta (boat: 35 minutes)

Heading to the African continent for the first time, we had romantic images of standing on the deck with the wind in our hair as Europe drifted slowly away and Africa came into view. Unfortunately this was one of the most disappointing parts of the trip – the sun rapidly set before we left the harbour, it was raining so most of the windows were steamed up and we were told we couldn't go out on the deck of the ship. In hindsight, travelling straight to Tangier and missing out Cueta

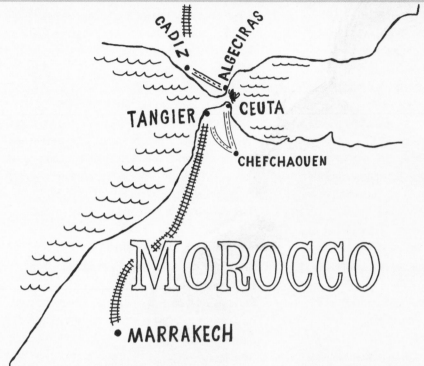

altogether would have been a better option. However, the Spanish colony of Cueta isn't without its charms – the beach is man-made but clean and at the right time of year the sea is warm and pleasant to swim in.

Night spent in Ceuta

Day 6: Cueta–Chefchaouen
Cueta to Chefchaouen (taxi: 2½ hours)
The land border crossing into Morocco resembles a town in the Wild West – hawkers, beggars, government officials and bogus government officials are everywhere. You'll need to take a taxi across the border – a 120-kilometre (75-mile) trip to Chefchaouen. It's a beautiful little town with blue-washed buildings nestled high in the Rif Mountains of north-west Morocco. After the long overland journey, this is the perfect town in which to put your feet up for a few days if you have the time.

Night spent in Chefchaouen

Day 7: Chefchaouen–Tangier
Chefchaouen to Tangier (bus: 3 hours)
Chefchaouen has one main bus station just out of town but countless bus services running to most of the major cities including Tangier, where we boarded the sleeper train to Marrakech.

Tangier to Marrakech (sleeper train: 9 hours)
The difference in the cost of living meant that first-class sleeper trains were very affordable, especially considering the distance we were about to travel. They're very comfortable and when we travelled there was a guard stationed in the carriage for extra security. It's advisable to book well in advance, especially in peak season.

Night spent on sleeper train

Day 8: Arrival in Marrakech
There's a real sense of the exotic when you're sitting in one of Marrakech's many rooftop cafés, sipping on mint tea overlooking the main square with its snake charmers, monkey trainers, acrobats and all manner of hawkers selling wonderful fruits, spices and potions. Knowing you got there in the same way travellers did over a hundred years ago makes it hard to not sip that tea with a big fat smile on your face.

Marrakech has been receiving tourists for a long time, and it's very good at it. There's no shortage of places to stay for every budget and there's plenty to do. Just walking around the city is an experience in itself, and if you've never experienced Islamic culture first-hand, Marrakech is the perfect introduction.

Memories of the overland journey to Marrakech.

Cycling is the healthiest, most inexpensive form of travel.

CYCLING HOLIDAYS

Cycling is by far the most environmentally friendly way to travel; it's also a great way to stay fit, get fresh air and feel at one with the surrounding countryside. We've cycled over much of England, Scotland and Wales and most of the time it's a thoroughly enjoyable experience, provided you're properly equipped and sufficiently fit for the holiday you've planned.

We try to take a cycling holiday in Britain at least once a year. Climate change means it's considerably warmer than it used to be, we have spectacular scenery, delightful pubs and a vast number of places of historical interest to visit, scattered throughout the country. Most people don't have to go far to find areas of outstanding beauty. In the north of England there's the Lake District, the Peak District and the Yorkshire Dales. Scotland is so full of naturally stunning places we could write an entire chapter about them (one of our favourites is Loch Ness). In the south there's the New Forest, the Forest of Dean, Cornwall and Devon. The Midlands has Derbyshire and Ironbridge, and vast areas of rural Wales are breathtaking, especially Snowdonia.

Cycling practicalities

We've learned a lot about cycling over the years, often by making our own mistakes. Here are some tips to help you avoid the common pitfalls:

● Plan your trip carefully and don't be over-ambitious – 32 kilometres (20 miles) a day is a good, steady pace that most people will be able to cope with, although obviously this depends on your fitness levels.

● Buy an Ordnance Survey (OS) map that shows you the contours of the land and work out the flattest route. A distance of 1 kilometre (½ mile) uphill can take longer than 10 kilometres (6 miles) on level ground.

● Eat carbohydrate-rich foods, such as pasta and rice, for at least 3 days before any long journey and during the trip if you can.

● Get your bike checked before leaving to ensure it's roadworthy, particularly the brakes.

● Pack for all weathers.

● Travel as light as possible. Think what you desperately need and what you can buy or forage on the way. The more weight you carry, the harder it is to cycle.

● Take a pump, a puncture-repair kit and a spare inner tube. Learn how to carry out simple cycle repairs (see below and overleaf).

● Buy or borrow some bike lights and reflective clothing. Even if you don't plan on cycling in the dark, your journey could take longer than you think and you may want to keep going until you find a suitable place to bed down for the night. It's best to be prepared.

● Wear a helmet.

● Carry plenty of water to stop yourself from dehydrating. Try to have at least 2 litres (3½ pints) of water with you at all times. More will be needed if you're not going to be anywhere near civilization for a bit.

Simple cycle repairs If you cycle you'll one day get a puncture – it's inevitable. You can get them fixed at most cycle shops but this can sometimes cost far more than you would expect; besides, they're not open all the time and are not on every street corner. It's much cheaper and more convenient to know how to do the job yourself.

There's a great invention known as tyre sealant, which helps prevent the most frequent smaller punctures of around 3cm (1¼in). Many trial cyclists and courier riders rely on this product, as they don't always have time to fix a puncture properly. It's pumped inside the inner tube and coats it when the wheel revolves. For more serious punctures, see the instructions overleaf. If you get the puncture while out, move your bike to a safe, level spot off the road or cycle path before trying to fix it.

Removal of the wheel is made easier these days with the invention of quick-release wheels. There should be a lever that you pull up then turn to loosen your wheel. On some bikes, especially older ones, there's a nut keeping the wheel in place, so you'll need to use a spanner to take this off. The back wheel on any bike is the trickiest to take off and you'll need to move the derailleur (smaller cogs for the gears) back and move the brake pads to release the wheel.

MENDING A PUNCTURE

1.

Turn your bike upside down and remove the offending wheel, using a spanner if you don't have quick-release wheels.

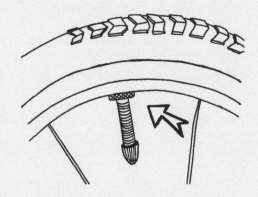

2.

Remove the tyre – you can undo the nut that keeps the valve in place with your fingers. In your puncture-repair kit there should be some levers with one flat end and one hooked end. Put the flat end between the tyre and wheel and hook the other end onto the spokes. Use another lever to do the same about two spokes up, then another two spokes up again and run this one around the rim of the tyre to take it off.

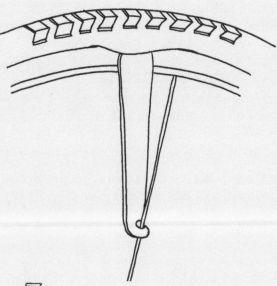

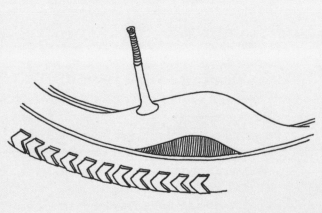

3.

Take out the inner tube and try to find the puncture. Pump up the inner tube until it looks fatter than usual, then hold it next to your lips. You should feel the air coming out. Mark this area with a bit of chalk or the crayon that comes with your repair kit. Once you've found the puncture, test for further damage by putting your finger over the hole and doing the same again until you're satisfied there aren't any more punctures. (Go to step 5.)

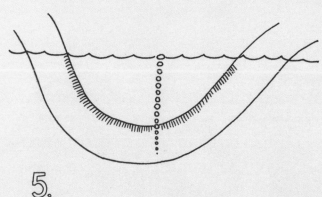

4.

If you can't find the puncture, immerse the inner tube in a bucket of water or run it through a puddle or nearby river. You should see bubbles coming from the hole. Dry off your inner tube and mark the location of the bubbles. If you still fail to find a puncture the chances are that the valve has gone and you'll have to replace the whole inner tube.

5.

Rub the area around your puncture with the small square of sandpaper from your repair kit. Pick a patch of corresponding size to the hole and apply the rubber solution around the puncture. Allow this to dry a little, then peel off the patch backing and press the patch into position.

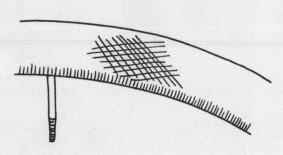

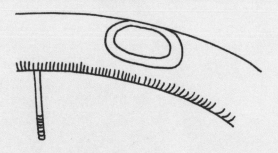

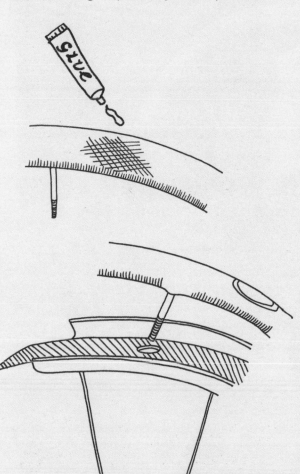

6.

Check the inside of your tyre for glass, thorns or anything else that might have caused the puncture. When you're satisfied that it's clear you can start to reaffix the inner tube. Push the valve into the hole in your wheel and work around the tyre, tucking the inner tube into place. Pumping up the tyre a little will make this easier. Use the tyre levers to help get the last bit in place if you need to. Run your fingers around the tyre to make sure it's in place, then attach it back on your bike and pump it up.

It's important for cyclists to be able to carry out simple repairs such as fixing a puncture.

Theft of bicycles
Sadly we've both had bikes stolen over the years; bike theft has doubled since the early 1990s, so unless you secure your bike it's likely to suffer the same fate. There are a few steps you can take to lower the likelihood of bike theft.

- Bring your bike indoors, when possible, and if it's stored in a garage or shed make sure that it's locked and that the bike is secured to something solid.

- Buy a decent bike lock or even two. D-locks can be broken with car jacks and bolt locks with wire cutters, so doubling up can provide additional security.

- Attach your bike to an immovable object such as a fence or lamp post. One of Andy's bikes got stolen when he nipped into the pub for a pint, leaving the bike outside locked to itself.

- Always wrap the lock around the wheel and the frame of the bike.

- If you have quick-release wheels, take the front one off and lock it to the back wheel.

- If you have a quick-release saddle, take it with you when you lock your bike.

- Lock your bike in full view of people or CCTV cameras. Thieves are less likely to steal in front of an audience.

- Write your postcode on your bike with a UV marker pen, make a note of the frame number and take a photo of your bike to help recovery if it's stolen.

- Try not to lock an expensive bike in the same place all the time as it could be stolen to order.

- Get decent cycle insurance (see below).

Cycle insurance
It's vital that you report a stolen bicycle straight away. Some household insurance policies also cover theft of cycles outside the home. However, you'll need to check your policy. Most claims will not be honoured if you don't secure your cycle.

Household insurance will not cover you if you're in an accident, and with roads getting busier it would be churlish for the frequent cyclist not to consider a stand-alone policy just to cover liability. Although the risk of being sued as a cyclist is pretty low, it might be a wise precaution. Cycle insurance means that you're protected against any claims and your insurance company may even provide someone to help you out with court proceedings.

To avoid the likelihood of being sued, cyclists should observe the Highway Code at all times and try to use cycle paths whenever possible. Cyclists can be deemed to be at fault if they ride too fast, undercut traffic, or have drop handle bars and are in the crouch position, because they're considered not to be looking at the road.

Making a bike from scrap parts
If you're mechanically minded and have the space to store bike parts you could make up your own bike from various components collected from skips or the dump. Andy once found an almost complete working bike in a skip – all it needed was a new brake cable costing £2.50 and he was able to travel the 64-kilometre (40-mile) distance from Oxford to Northampton on it. Although this was a lucky find, a series of smaller discoveries could have you cycling around for next to nothing.

Andy is slowly trying to kit out his friends with working bikes and so his garden is starting to look a bit like a scrapyard, with countless wheels, frames and miscellaneous bike parts collected over the space of a year. These parts have all either come from skips or have been obviously discarded. He has made up one bike and is currently one wheel short of another.

Look around for spare parts of bikes. If you see a bike in a skip, remember to ask the skip hirer before you take anything – some people have been known to report taking their rubbish as theft. Also, it's well worth asking in cycle-hire and cycle shops for spare parts. They may be happy to help out. Avoid collecting parts that you suspect could be stolen. Contact the police if you're unsure – you wouldn't want to be arrested for theft or handling stolen goods. Get a good cycle maintenance book and make sure that every part of the bike is in full working order before you use it.

Camping is a wonderful way of experiencing the outdoors.

CAMPING HOLIDAYS

Camping has always been second nature to us – we used to go camping with our parents when we were growing up, we were in the Scouts, and as adults we've camped all around Britain and continental Europe. We've even camped in February and awoken to find snow on the ground outside – with the right equipment, this can be a great deal more enjoyable than it sounds.

There's something very romantic about sleeping 'outdoors' and feeling close to nature. One of Andy's most magical trips was to Transylvania, where he camped with friends in the depths of the countryside. Since there was no light pollution from any nearby town, it was the first time that he saw the whole of the Milky Way – an awe-inspiring experience. Another major benefit of camping is that it's so much less expensive than staying in a hotel or even a hostel, and it can make the difference between staying somewhere for a weekend or staying for a week.

Wild camping and campsites

In England and Wales it's illegal just to put your tent up anywhere without permission from the landowner, and almost every square inch of our fair isles are owned by someone. However, this is not to say wild camping isn't tolerated in some very remote areas – for example, if you're more than half a day's walk away from an official campsite or other accommodation. The main thing is not to make a nuisance of yourself – camp as discreetly as possible, in small groups and for one night only. Don't light fires, take all your rubbish with you, don't let your dog run around with livestock, bury human waste at least 30m (100ft) from water, and if there's a nearby house ask them if they mind you camping. In Scotland you have a right to camp wild in many places such as hills, mountains, moorland, woods and forests – again, it's vital that you camp responsibly and respect the environment. Generally, there are plenty of campsites around in the UK, so the need for wild camping shouldn't really be an issue unless you're planning a long-distance trek.

It's worth doing some research into campsites, as they vary enormously. The most basic will have a toilet block and showers, and bigger sites may have a shop, clothes-washing facilities and electrical points as well as entertainment areas such as a restaurant, bar and swimming pool. Many campsites now offer ready-pitched tents, which will really help to keep the baggage weight down if you're on a walking or cycling holiday. Travelling in a group can be tricky, and unless you're all from one family some sites won't allow groups of more than four non-related people. Some campsites won't allow fires, others allow fires made only from wood that they sell you. Campsites are often slightly out of town – this is no trouble if you're cycling or driving, but we've both been caught out in the past, finding that there's no public transport to a site with limited facilities. Do your research beforehand and try to find a site that will suit your needs.

In Europe camping laws differ from country to country. For example, in Norway and Sweden anyone is allowed to camp anywhere that's out of sight of a house. In Romania many people in busy tourist areas will offer you their garden to pitch a tent (at a price), but do beware of wild camping in Romania as there are bears and wild boar living in some of the remoter areas. However, the general rule for most countries is that you're expected to pay to camp on a campsite. There are plenty of excellent campsites across Europe – France in particular is full of them.

Entertainment

If you're used to package holidays, or even holidays in popular tourist destinations, you may wonder what there is to do while camping. We celebrated our 30th birthdays at a campsite and it was certainly one of the best weekends we've ever had. Many of our friends came along, including musicians, a stand-up comedian and a poet, and they entertained us for the evening. But it isn't necessary to have a whole host of performers – just sitting around a campfire telling ghost stories, singing or playing games can provide hours of fun.

During the daytime, foraging for mushrooms and other wild foods (see pages 204–29) can be a great activity, especially when you come back to the site and cook your findings over an open fire.

If none of the entertainment suggested appeals, don't despair. On bigger campsites there are often bars and amusement arcades and obviously if you're close to a town or city you can still head off out for the evening. It's also worth noting that just being on the campsite can be entertainment itself. In tourist areas there are frequently people camping from all over the world and for some reason individuals tend to be much more receptive to new people when camping, so chatting and playing cards can take up much of your time.

Camping paraphernalia

Unlike a package holiday, camping requires a few essentials. The first consideration is the tent. You can buy a tent for very little these days, but it's worth investing in a good-quality one, because if treated well it will last you a lifetime.

You should always check that you have all the tent paraphernalia before you set off – it's not a good feeling to be in the middle of nowhere and find that you're missing some poles. Andy once did this and had to 'wear' his tent like a big sleeping bag, and despite it being a hot Cornish summer he still froze in the middle of the night. You'll also need tent pegs and a wooden or rubber mallet to knock them in. It's a good idea to put your tent up beforehand in your back garden, just to check that all of the bits are there and you know how to do it.

Another essential is a sleeping bag. For general camping, it's best to get an all-purpose one. Ask at your local camping suppliers for advice. Some people opt for a duvet and will also have an airbed. This is a real luxury, but if you're driving and have the boot space, why not be comfortable?

Other recommended items include:

⬤ Rucksack – If you're on a cycling holiday or trekking from campsite to campsite you'll need a large rucksack for carrying camping equipment. Even if you've driven to the campsite, a small backpack is always useful for day trips.

⬤ A camping gas stove – If you're camping away from civilization or in a site or spot that outlaws open fires, this is essential. There are basically two different types available – a single burner or a double burner with a grill. Hikers and cyclists can easily make do with one burner.

⬤ Matches/lighter – Essential for making a camp fire and for lighting camping gas stoves.

⬤ Torch – Not all campsites are well lit and guide ropes are a real hazard in the dark.

⬤ Change of clothes – The countryside is often muddy (bring Wellington boots), and if you camp somewhere like the West Country or Wales there is a strong possibility of rain at some point during your stay.

⬤ First-aid kit – You should always take a first-aid kit as a precaution in case of injury.

⬤ Insect repellent – This is essential if camping in parts of Scotland in summer.

⬤ Solar shower – This is available from some of the bigger camping shops. It's basically a bag with a hose attached that warms up in the sun and you can have a hot shower underneath. You could be the most popular camper in Glastonbury if you invest in one of these.

⬤ A push lawn mower – OK, not really essential, but we know a couple of brothers who always take one to the Reading Festival to ensure they have a nice 'front garden' to their tent.

Sweetcorn is ideal food when camping, as it's easy to cook on a small barbecue and you don't need plates or cutlery.

REEN ELECTRICITY·SOLAR
OWER·WIND TURBINES·WA
R POWER·BIOMASS FUELS

RENEWABLE ENERGY

Over the last century we've become increasingly energy-hungry and our appetite has been satisfied by a plentiful supply of fossil fuels such as gas, coal and oil. However, we now know that the supply isn't going to be available forever. Many petrochemical analysts believe that within the next ten years or so we'll reach peak oil production, after which point supplies will start decreasing until they disappear entirely. It's vital that we do everything we can to come up with a sustainable alternative for the future.

Prices of all fossil fuels are set to increase, and with a reliance on these old technologies the cost of living can only rise. In addition, the majority of scientists believe that there is a direct correlation between rising carbon emissions, caused by the burning of fossil fuels, and the current rise in temperatures. The only way to prevent complete and irreversible climate change is to replace the use of fossil fuels with a sustainable form of energy.

Renewable energy is energy that doesn't come from fossil fuels and is instead naturally replenished and therefore sustainable. It could be produced by wind, water, sun, biomass or even geo-thermic means (that is, generated by harnessing heat from under the earth's surface), all of which are naturally abundant. As well as being entirely sustainable, these sources have the added advantage of not polluting the environment.

GREEN ELECTRICITY

There has been a growing shift towards renewable energy over recent years, as we've become more aware of the damage caused by atmospheric carbon produced by fossil-fuel power stations. At the time of writing, only 3–4 per cent of our energy in the UK comes from renewable sources, but this figure is certainly set to rise in the near future. The government has planned to have 10 per cent of all our energy produced from renewable sources by 2010.

At present there are limited sources of 'green energy', but as demand for sustainable energy rises and becomes a necessity the investment put into it will inevitably increase. In Scotland the majority of the green energy comes from hydropower (see page 318), while in the rest of the UK wind farms are more prevalent (see page 316), followed by hydropower, then solar power (see page 315). Using a green-energy supplier doesn't automatically mean all your energy will come from renewable sources but a percentage of your total energy will. In the UK there are quite a few companies supplying electricity solely from renewable sources. The website www.greenelectricity.org lists all the companies providing sustainable energy and a quick postcode search on the site will show all available suppliers in your area.

Many of the major electricity suppliers are now offering 'green tariffs', which refers to a promise by the electricity company to buy a proportion of energy from a renewable source. However, it's worth noting that under government legislation (known as the 'Renewables Obligation') all electricity companies in the UK are required to purchase a proportion of their energy from a green supplier, and some companies are simply selling off their green quota at a premium to the customer for profit rather than actively investing in renewable energy and development. It's well worth asking what company policy is before signing up with an energy supplier.

Once you change to a green supplier there's a temptation to use more energy, but this defeats the object – with limited renewable energy available, a collective reduction in energy consumption would mean there would be a lot more to go around.

One of the ways the government's planning to reach the renewable energy targets they've set for the country is to encourage businesses to invest in renewable-energy generation in the community – for example, in schools and colleges. As a shareholder, you could put pressure on businesses to invest in such schemes (see Buying shares, page 352).

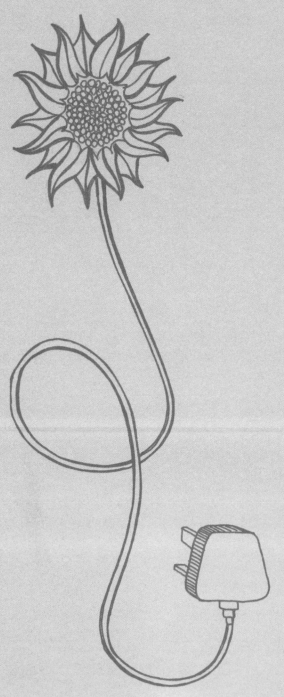

A solar-powered telephone at the Centre for Alternative Energy, Wales.

A solar array, consisting of photovoltaic cells that convert sunlight into electricity.

SOLAR POWER

Solar panels are often seen as the *crème de la crème* of eco living and a full solar array, glistening on the roof in the sunlight, makes a big, bold statement about the house's occupant. Solar panels can produce electricity with no sound or air pollution from a practically limitless source of energy – the sun. Unlike coal or gas power stations they don't produce any carbon dioxide, and there is no controversy over their safety as there is regarding nuclear power. Solar power is a particularly effective energy source in hot, arid areas of the world.

Solar power works by converting sunlight into electricity by means of photo-voltaic (PV) cells. Each cell contains silicon crystals that produce an electrical charge when exposed to sunlight. This electrical charge is then carried to the next cell and the next and so on along a module. A number of modules are grouped together into a panel and the panels are grouped together on a solar array, which is then mounted on the roof. The array works more efficiently if there's a slight gap under it to allow air beneath to cool it down – paradoxically, the hotter the array becomes, the less efficient it is. In each solar array the energy generated is a direct current (DC) and this needs to be converted to an alternating current (AC) to be of any use in powering electrical goods and lighting within a house. An AC/DC inverter can be used for this, or the power can be stored in batteries.

It's very important when positioning an array that there is no obstruction – for example, from trees or tall buildings: it must have direct contact with the sun. Wherever possible, the array should face south to get the optimum amount of energy. However, east- and west-facing orientations will receive a certain amount of energy at different times of the day. The ideal angle to position the solar array to obtain the maximum amount of direct sunlight hitting it throughout the day depends on where you live. All the towns across the M4 corridor – London, Bristol and Cardiff, which all lie on the same line of latitude – benefit from the solar array being set at 35 degrees. For towns north or south of the M4, the angle will be more or less than 35 degrees respectively. The slant of the roof will also determine the positioning of the array. Anywhere between 20 and 50 degrees will yield sufficient solar energy.

Despite their green credentials, large solar panels don't suit everyone because it takes so long to see a return on the considerable investment (anything between 10 and 80 years). This calls into question their effectiveness when compared with other green technologies, such as water and wind power, solar-water heaters and biomass or wood-burners. However, the cost of PV cells is steadily falling as interest in them increases and the technology is also improving all the time.

Other factors that can help bring down the costs of a PV array and should be taken into account are as follows:

- Government grants are often available to help with the overall costs.

- Old and damaged roofs can be replaced with solar panels/tiles offsetting some of the overall cost.

- Electricity can be sold back to the electricity company if you're attached to the local grid.

- Second-hand solar panels are becoming increasingly available as people invest in newer models.

- If you live in a remote area, it's often far cheaper to install solar energy than attach to the grid.

- As it's not attached to any centralized power source, solar energy is portable and can be used on boats, caravans, vans, trucks and any other mobile living space.

- Not being part of a centralized power source decreases the chance of power cuts in these times of diminishing fuel reserves, increasingly unpredictable weather, flash floods and perhaps even terrorist attacks.

In the future you may be able to rent a solar array. At the time of writing we found rental schemes only in the United States, but this may change in the near future as the government aims to produce more of its energy from renewable sources. Leicester City Council used to rent out solar water heaters, although this was stopped because of lack of funding. It's possible that in the future similar schemes or private businesses may eventually rent out solar arrays, making them an extremely affordable source of renewable energy.

WIND TURBINES

The rising cost of energy and the threat to the environment from increased carbon dioxide emissions has brought with it a resurgence of interest in wind power. We have an abundance of wind in Britain, ready to be converted into power, especially in the more exposed coastal regions and in hilly and mountainous areas.

Wind turbines are not quite as new as you might think. Old photos, newsreels and films from the United States in the 1920s and 1930s often show wind turbines outside remote farms. The Great Plains cover vast distances and often these farms were so remote and far from any power station, or even power cabling, that the only alternative was to generate their own electricity in the form of wind power. The turbines were invaluable for remote farmers and sometimes doubled up to pump water from underground sources for their crops and cattle. Unfortunately, it was seen as progress when the US government started the Rural Electrification Administration, centralizing power and introducing cables the length and breadth of the country to link isolated farms to the national grid. However, it's testament to the longevity of wind-power generators that some of these turbines installed over 70 years ago are still fully serviceable and are bought and sold across rural areas of the United States today.

The popularity of wind turbines is steadily increasing and they are now available in some of Britain's major hardware stores. We've seen second-hand turbines appear on internet auction sites, such as eBay, and some people have been known to make turbines from scrap and salvaged parts. Making your own or buying one second hand does mean a considerable saving in the initial outlay, but even a brand-new turbine should more than pay for itself during its lifetime if you're in a sufficiently windy area.

Turbines that are situated in rural areas have a lot more output than their urban counterparts. In some cases, an open-countryside turbine will produce 4 times more electricity than an urban one. In towns and cities, buildings tend to block the flow of wind and the amount of energy available is severely reduced. Ideally, wind turbines should be situated in exposed sites, such as offshore or on hilltops. For the urban wind-catcher, you'll need to mount your turbine on the roof or on a pole, preferably over 10m (30ft) tall. Chimney-mounted turbines are not a good idea, because the constant movement will cause structural damage to the chimney and they're not particularly effective as the chimney provides wind-resistance.

Before installing a wind turbine you have to seek planning permission from the local authority. You can measure local wind direction and speed using a wind vane and anemometer respectively. Data obtained from these devices can be backed up with data from a local meteorological office and you can work out if a turbine is for you. As a rule of thumb, the Department of Energy in the United States suggests wind speeds should be a local average of at least 14 kilometres (9 miles) an hour to make a large turbine worthwhile. For the entire home, the average energy use is around 500–700 watts for a 24-hour period, so a 1kW turbine with 3m (10ft) diameter blades and a 6m (20ft) tower would be more than enough to cover the entire household's needs. However, it's difficult to power your home by wind power alone. This is because wind speeds are highly variable – on still days you won't have any power – also, you may find you'll need more than average power at certain peak times. For these reasons, many choose to sell power back to the grid, effectively building up a credit of power when the turbine is running at full capacity and when energy consumption is low.

If your local wind-speed average is low, or if your budget won't stretch to a large-scale turbine, smaller turbines for small electrical needs, such as charging batteries, driving motors and pumping water, might be more suitable. Many boats and caravans have these small, low-watt turbines and there's no reason why homeowners couldn't utilize this source of energy too.

There are mixed feelings concerning wind turbines. Although they're undoubtedly a clean and efficient source of power, many people who live near them are offended by the noise and their appearance. One self-sustaining community in Nottinghamshire was repeatedly refused planning permission because the local residents thought the sound of the turning blades would cause distress. Also, some ornithologists believe that the vibrations of the turbines can affect the patterns of migratory birds and that the blades themselves can be harmful. However, many argue that they would soon get used to the turbines and would adapt their flight patterns accordingly.

Wind turbines are becoming an increasingly popular
source of power in Britain.

WATER POWER

In days gone by, water wheels were a chief source of mechanical power in Britain. Most water wheels fell slowly into a state of disrepair in derelict industrial buildings as the need for mechanical energy dwindled, but today we're reassessing the value of water power – rather than being used to drive a mill, fast-flowing water can be employed to turn a generator and produce electricity for our homes.

Water power can be one of the most efficient types of energy production: over 90 per cent of the energy available in water can be converted into electricity, while more traditional power stations utilize only 30 to 50 per cent of the energy available. Hydroelectricity is also a non-polluting and useful 'green' energy source. The supply depends on water currents, which themselves depend on gravity, so the supply is limitless.

Hydroelectricity works by utilizing the kinetic energy in water dropping from a height – the higher the starting point of the water, the faster it will fall and the more energy it will generate. Britain's geography means that it lacks the height differences needed to produce large quantities of electricity, and for this reason hydropower accounts for only about 2 per cent of the nation's power generation. Worldwide the figure is quite different – hydropower produces almost a fifth of the world's electricity. Emerging economies such as China and Brazil are among the biggest producers of hydroelectricity. China is home to the world's largest hydroelectric dam – the Three Gorges dam – and it has more major building schemes for hydroelectric dams in progress than any other country in the world.

Despite hydroelectricity being a totally renewable energy source, there have been environmental concerns regarding the construction of hydroelectric dams. Dams throughout the world have been blamed for a catalogue of social and environmental problems, including social upheaval, flooding, threats to freshwater fish and damage to farmland. Loss of habitat through construction of the Three Gorges dam has pushed both the Chinese paddlefish and the Siberian crane to the brink of extinction.

Although it is without question that some of the bigger plants do cause environmental problems, vastly scaling down their size and increasing their number could be the answer to these problems. Small-scale hydropower systems, or 'micro-hydroplants' as they're sometimes known, frequently consist of single turbines producing around 100kW of energy or less. They cause little or no disruption to the surrounding environment and are perhaps the greenest of all energy sources. A few fortunate individuals have running water at a sufficient height to produce electricity, and the cost of installing a water wheel can be recovered over time.

The future of small hydropower plants lies more in small communities than with the individual. In the Welsh village of Talybont on Usk, villagers raised £90,000 in funding to set up a community hydroelectric scheme. The scheme will provide energy for 500 homes and bring in £17,000 a year, paying for itself in just over 5 years. Many other small towns and villages have similar access to running water and, with the help of government grants or private investment, they could set up schemes like this.

A micro-hydroelectric power plant can make use of running water, even in the smallest rivers.

BIOMASS FUEL

Biomass is an umbrella term for any organic matter that can be used as a fuel. The organic matter can be plant-, vegetable- or occasionally animal-based. Biomass fuel is often called bio-energy or bio-fuel. The most common of all biomass fuels is wood, but other sources include straw, coppiced willow and animal manure. Bio-diesel also comes under the general umbrella term of biomass, as it's a fuel that originates from an organic source. A big benefit of bio-fuels is that unlike fossil fuels they don't increase the amount of carbon dioxide present in the atmosphere.

Wood-burning in the home

People from earliest times have burnt wood and other organic material for cooking and heating their homes, but in more recent times gas and electric boilers and cookers have largely replaced the burning of wood in the West. However, many people are now rediscovering wood as a fuel source and are investing in modern wood-burning stoves and boilers. The savings can be considerable and with the prices of fossil fuels on the increase, biomass will continue to be a cost-effective as well as greener way of heating the home.

There's a wide range of biomass burners available – some use logs and others burn pellets made from condensed wood shavings and discarded wood. There are stand-alone wood-burning stoves available that burn wood from behind a layer of glass, with air vents allowing movement of air. These reach very high temperatures with very little wood and are far warmer than a conventional open fire. Some are fitted with a back boiler and can provide hot water or be linked to the central heating. There are even models that are self-feeding, so there's no need constantly to refill the stove. These models come equipped with a hopper that you fill with wood or (more usually) pellets and they're fitted with a time-release to top up the wood-burner before it runs out of fuel.

The main drawback of biomass in the home is storing the fuel ready to burn, so it's important to take this into consideration if space is limited.

Bio-diesel

One of the most talked-about of all biomass fuels, bio-diesel can be used as a direct alternative to diesel in the running of all kinds of motorized engines. Its popularity is set to increase, in part because the British government has removed duty on certain biomass fuels, provided the consumer doesn't exceed the 2500-litre (555-gallon) annual threshold.

There are two main sources of bio-diesel. One type derives from recycled cooking oil used in the food industry, the catering trade and institutions such as schools and hospitals. This method has two benefits – not only does the oil, typically chip fat, present a good alternative to fossil fuels, but it also provides a home for used cooking oil that would otherwise be discarded down the drain and pollute the water system or be sent to a landfill site. One well-known high-street fast-food chain has decided to fuel its delivery trucks with the oil they use to cook their fries in.

FOSSIL FUELS & THE CARBON CYCLE

Fossil fuels represent carbon that has been trapped by plant and animal sources. Take coal, for example – millions of years ago, trees took in carbon dioxide from the atmosphere through the process of photosynthesis. Over time, the trees died and slowly became buried in ever-increasing layers of topsoil, decaying matter, plant material, dust and general debris. The weight of this compacted the trees more and more as time passed, until coal was formed. Burning these ancient trees as coal releases into the atmosphere carbon dioxide that existed millions of years ago, thus creating an imbalance in the carbon cycle and increasing atmospheric CO_2 and with it raising temperatures. By contrast, plant-based bio-fuels do not disrupt the natural cycle. Although plants do release carbon dioxide when they die or are burned as fuel, they take in carbon dioxide as they grow and so balance the amount of carbon in the atmosphere.

Pelllets made from compressed wood chips
can be burnt in a biomass heating system.

We can but hope that many other large corporations will choose to follow suit. Most environmental organizations and charities support this use of recycled oil. However, the problem is there's simply not enough recyclable oil to power all the vehicles willing and able to use this source of energy.

The second source of bio-diesel is oil-rich crops grown especially for the purpose of producing fuel: for example, sunflowers, corn (maize), rape and palms. This source is more controversial, because although it doesn't contribute to raised carbon levels in the atmosphere, it could present different environmental as well as humanitarian problems. The concerns are that growing bio-fuel crops might take away land that should be used for growing food or, in some cases, could lead to destruction of the rainforest. This could present a future humanitarian crisis if developing nations were persuaded to grow energy crops for the West rather than food for their own people. There are already signs of this happening in Mexico, where there is a shortage of maize within the country because Mexican farmers are now growing it for the United States to use as bio-diesel.

These are still contested viewpoints and many environmental organizations are divided on the issue of whether bio-diesel is a good or a bad thing. It's still an emerging technology and many of the problems will no doubt be ironed out in time. Some do consider the humanitarian issues surrounding bio-diesel a moot point in view of the present conflicts around the world caused by our dependency on oil.

Running your car engine on bio-diesel

A friend of ours frequently drives his car to the local supermarket, buys the biggest bottles of vegetable oil he can find and fills his car up with the oil. He started doing this long before bio-fuels came to the public's attention. His engine had been modified to use straight cooking oil, but most engines can use a vegetable oil/diesel mix or specially made bio-diesel.

Trends are slowly moving towards more bio-fuels as governments across the world are investing in these forms of fuel. Currently all vehicles can run on a 5 per cent blend of bio-fuel, although be warned that some car dealers and manufacturers advise that you shouldn't use any form of bio-diesel and may void the warranty if they detect it in your engine. Flexible-fuel vehicles, which are becoming more common, are able to use blends of up to 85 per cent bio-fuel. In Germany the move to bio-diesel has been happening for over a decade, with every car manufactured by Volkswagen since 1995 capable of running on bio-

diesel; in warm months the cars can run on 100 per cent bio-fuel, but in colder months weaker blends need to be used. The Germans have also set up over 1500 bio-diesel filling stations and the average distance between them is just 30 kilometres (19 miles). Bio-diesel outlets are increasing in number in the UK too. The website www.biodieselfillingstations.co.uk is a great source to find your local bio-diesel supplier. It is possible to make your own bio-diesel at home, but it can be a complex procedure.

Bio-ethanol

Bio-ethanol is another plant-based fuel that can be used in a motorized engine, but it is a petrol instead of a diesel substitute. Ethanol is an alcohol and is usually made from fermenting plant material with a high starch content. Typically, it is produced from sugar cane, but maize, wheat, trees and grasses can also be used.

Bio-ethanol is often mixed with ordinary petrol and most petrol engines can deal with a 10 per cent bio-ethanol and 90 per cent petrol mix without any modifications or risk to their warranty. At present this 10 per cent ethanol mix is about all we can hope for in Britain, because we lack the steady supply of bio-ethanol available in other parts of the world. A certain amount of land could be given over to growing sugar beet for the production of bio-ethanol, but this again poses the problem of where to grow our food. Advances in manufacturing this fuel from waste products have to be made if this is going to become a viable fuel in the UK.

Bio-ethanol works best in countries with an abundance of crops ready to turn into fuel. One such country that takes advantage of this is Brazil, which has had a long history of growing sugar cane. During the 1970s, when much of the world ground to a halt during the oil crisis and prices soared, Brazil invested in creating a fuel source from its surplus of sugar. The government launched an ambitious 'pro-alcohol' programme to get the nation's cars running on bio-ethanol. Today, most cars in Brazil are equipped to run on petrol or bio-fuel (these are known as 'flexi-fuel' vehicles) and there is a network of bio-ethanol pumps and filling stations up and down the country. Many other countries are now looking to Brazil's methods as a way of solving the impending energy crisis in the longer term. In tropical countries, growing sugar cane is a very good option, because it needs little water to grow. In fact, it grows better in Brazil's arid south than in the north, which is where the rainforest is situated, so there should be no need to cut down vast areas of rainforest if the requirement for Brazilian bio-ethanol increases.

THE WORKING DAY

We've worked in several offices and have always been astonished by how much electricity is wasted, even in Environmental Services departments. At night, many employees leave on their computers, printers, photocopiers, fans, lights and more. In many cases paper isn't recycled and kettles are invariably over-filled. Unsurprisingly, we've taken it upon ourselves to be the eco police and have always gone around switching off all manner of electrical appliances before heading off home at the end of the working day.

There are lots of things you can do to cut down on waste in the office and to help reduce carbon emissions – this chapter will explore the obvious and not so obvious ways you can do this. Most companies have someone in charge of the building: this might be a caretaker, building operator or company director. Ask your line manager who is responsible for your office and he or she will be your first point of contact to talk to about making changes for the better. Consider setting up an environmental group in your department – ask around and see if there's any support among your colleagues and then contact your manager with any proposals that you might have as a group – it's much easier to get results when there are a few of you. Be sure to mention how much the company will save in the process. Most managers will be happy to instigate ideas that will save the company money.

GETTING TO WORK

Next time you're about to hop in your car and drive to work, think of the other options. Walking and cycling are the greenest ways to commute; they also keep you fit and can be very pleasurable. Most of our towns and cities grew up around the time of the industrial revolution, when goods were transported along canals, so there are many canal-side walks and cycle rides across the country – it may just take a bit of research. Public transport is the next best way to get to work. If you must drive, consider lift-sharing, which will reduce carbon emissions and the amount of traffic clogging up our roads as well as fuel consumption and costs.

Cycling

Cycling is the greenest transport available – a carbon-free alternative to get you to work. Another benefit is that gentle exercise before work makes you more productive and alert, as studies have shown. Some offices actively support cyclists, offering money towards a new bike or a bike doctor, who comes in and helps out with minor repairs. Ask your employer about this and if you don't have such a scheme at your workplace suggest that they implement one. (For more details on cycling, including minor repairs, see pages 300–5.)

We were living in Nottingham during the fuel protests and blockades of 2000 and we witnessed cycle sales going up by 400 per cent. There was a sharp increase in cyclists during this time, but as soon as the petrol came back so did the cars. This was a real shame, but it does go to show that there are lots of people who can cycle, and have the equipment, but choose not to. We find that the thing with cycling is the more you do it, the easier it gets – you grow fitter with each passing day and more used to the traffic. Some people who haven't cycled for years find they lack the courage to ride on main roads. This is where the national cycle network can come to the rescue – there are cycle paths across the country; according to the cycling charity Sustrans, 75 per cent of us are within 3 kilometres (2 miles) of a route and the National Cycle Network (NCN) covers over 16,200 kilometres (10,000 miles). Cycling will save you money too. Consider a 16-kilometre (10-mile) round trip (which is within most people's capability) – this could be the 8-kilometre (5-mile) commute from your home to work and back every day, and by cycling you could save around £500 a year on petrol costs alone.

Public transport

If your workplace is too far to get to by bike it really is worth considering taking public transport. We won't pretend that rides on public transport are the most enjoyable of life experiences, or that buses and trains are never late and always clean, but ditching the car in favour of a bus, train or tram has a number of advantages, not least that you can read or catch up on work as you travel. You may also enjoy the experience of travelling with others – you get to see the same people day after day and the contact with familiar faces can get the morning off to a good start.

If your local transport network is inadequate, it's worth campaigning to improve things. In Bristol there has been a local train line for more than a century, but over the years it has slowly gone downhill – the timetable was cut to less than one train an hour and there were proposals to tarmac over the line to make a bus route. However, a local pressure group called Friends of Severn Beach Railway (FOSBR) has successfully campaigned for an increase in the number of trains. So don't lose heart: check the internet and local notice boards for similar campaigns, or set one up yourself – you might be successful too.

Car pool and lift share

Next time you see a traffic jam, count the number of cars with one person in them, often heading towards the same city centre or business district. If you're one of these people, send a group e-mail to your department or office complex offering a lift for a part share of the petrol costs, or suggesting you share the driving on alternate days. You might even be able to have an extra pint down at your local on the day the other person drives without fear of being over the limit the next day. If you don't get any takers, it's worth contacting car-share scheme websites, which introduce drivers undertaking the same journeys (see page 387).

Working from home

We're very fortunate in having a morning commute to work that simply involves walking downstairs – this is of course one of the most environmentally friendly commutes of all. With advancements in technology over the last 10 years, working from home has become an increasingly viable option for both the employer and the employee, and many companies now offer working-from-home schemes, where you spend one day or more out of the office. Technology such as VOIP (Voice Over Internet Protocol) gives you free web cam and telephone calls, so it's possible to stay in contact with the office whenever you need to. Also, broadband allows large files to be sent down the line at the click of a mouse. Some companies give out mobile phones to people working at home, which means you don't get called on your home phone.

Companies benefit from employees working from home, at least some of the time. It saves on desk space and helps to reduce the overall costs of running the office. And people frequently work more efficiently from home – there may be fewer interruptions and they're often more conscientious about the amount of work they do, thus increasing productivity. The benefits are also evident for the employee. Eliminating the daily commute allows you greater flexibility and better work/life balance, and if you have a young family it gives you the chance to be around more. It's also often better for health reasons – at home you're more likely to eat the right foods and take a proper lunch break rather than snack on what's available, and it tends to be a healthier working environment because there are fewer computers, printers, photocopiers and other electrical equipment emitting pollutants into the air (see pages 326–8).

The biggest winner of working at home is the environment – if you work at home for just one day a week you could reduce your carbon emissions by 20 per cent, and you would achieve the same saving on your commuting bill. If you're working from home, even for one day a week, set aside a dedicated space in your house to work. You'll be more productive sitting at a proper table set up for work than slouching in an armchair with a laptop. If you work a lot at home you'll probably need a home office, where you and your work will not be disturbed. This might be a spare room in the main part of the house or a basement or attic, or you might choose to convert a shed or outbuilding into a workspace. Take plenty of breaks, and if you find it difficult to motivate yourself go off and do something else for 10 minutes and class it as one of your breaks. Try to get out at some point during the day, preferably to take some form of exercise, and don't be tempted to switch the TV on. If you have friends or family who might pop in during the day make sure they know you're working and it's not a time for socializing. This can be hard, but working from home is not just a day off.

This alarm clock is powered purely by a reservoir of water; no electricity is needed.

GREEN ALARM CLOCKS

Unless you're woken up at the crack of dawn by a cockerel or are one of those people who can get up without the aid of a loud noise, you'll need an alarm clock. There are two alternatives to an electrical radio alarm, which once purchased will cost you nothing to run. The most familiar option is an old-fashioned wind-up clock, but a more novel idea is a water-powered alarm clock (see above). You just have to fill up the clock with water to power it into action, so there's absolutely no need for batteries or any other power source. A big advantage is that it's considerably quieter than a ticking, clockwork alarm, so it won't keep you awake at night as traditional wind-up clocks have a tendency to do. Water-powered alarm clocks are available online at www.ecotopia.co.uk.

ENVIRONMENTALLY FRIENDLY OFFICES

Next time you're at work, take a look around and think about the general office practices and the items you use. Offices are frequently very wasteful, and the chances are that electrical items such as computers, photocopiers and fax machines are left on unnecessarily, consuming large amounts of energy and exuding carbon and other pollutants into the atmosphere. Even non-electrical items such as paper, plastic pens and other commonplace stationery equipment take their toll on the environment. However, there are plenty of things you can do to make your office a healthier and more eco-friendly place to work, once you're aware of the issues, and you can save yourself or your company a lot of money in the process.

Natural and artificial light

Natural light is an important factor in creating a healthy and comfortable working environment, as well as saving energy, so try to maximize natural light as much as possible. It is less intense than artificial light, so is less tiring on your eyes, and is evenly distributed so doesn't cast as many shadows. Many people feel that a desk placed next to a window improves their productivity. However, you may need to use blinds to regulate the natural light, as the sun's glare can make it hard to see the computer screen and may cause eye-strain; Venetian blinds are good as they let air in but keep bright sunlight out. Other ways to enhance natural light are to place mirrors around the office, ensure that windows are clean and paint the walls light colours.

Many offices keep lights on unnecessarily during the day. When it's bright outside, try working with the lights out instead of switching them on automatically. Stairwells are often lit, despite being used infrequently if a lift is available. Where this is the case, look into fitting motion sensors. This might seem like an expensive move, especially for larger buildings, but it will pay for itself in time with the amount of energy saved.

Another thing you can do is to exchange all traditional, incandescent light bulbs for energy-saving bulbs. Old light bulbs are extremely inefficient, converting only 5 per cent of the energy they receive into light, while energy-saving bulbs last 12 times longer and use 80 per cent less electricity. Many countries, including the UK, are planning to phase out incandescent light bulbs by 2012 (Australia by 2009), and the initiative is expected to save 5 million tonnes of carbon a year.

If the above suggestions are beyond your control, remember there are two very simple things you can do – if you're alone in a big office, consider using a single lamp rather than having all the lights blazing away and switch off all lights and other items of electrical equipment when not in use.

Air quality
and sick-building syndrome

You might be surprised to hear that your workplace can be more polluted than the air outside. Pollutants such as low-level ozone, benzene, carbon monoxide, xylene and formaldehyde can build up in offices with poor ventilation and they can be spread through the air conditioning. If people are exposed to these compounds for long periods they can suffer symptoms of what is sometimes known as 'sick-building syndrome'.

Ozone at ground level (tropospheric ozone) is a pollutant and is given off by modern office equipment such as computers, printers, faxes and photocopiers. In a study by Loughborough University, almost half of the people who were subjected to small doses of low-level ozone reported significant reduction in lung functioning. To reduce the amount of low-level ozone in the office, switch off all electrical equipment when not in use, and in a large, open-plan office consider printer-sharing, to cut down on the number of printers that are being used at any one time.

Carbon monoxide exposure is deadly at high levels and companies should frequently check their boilers and avoid using fossil-fuel-powered, stand-alone heaters. Benzene, which is a solvent found in petrol, paint, some inks, plastics and dyes, has serious health consequences because it depresses the immune system, resulting in a higher chance of becoming ill; it has also been linked with cancers such as leukaemia. Exposure to high levels of xylene – used in paints, varnishes, adhesives, inks, dyes, plastics, synthetic fibres and in some art supplies and pens such as blender pens – can cause headaches, lack of muscle co-ordination, dizziness, confusion and loss of balance. If exposed to high levels of formaldehyde, which can be released by furniture made of chipboard or other pressed wood, synthetic carpets, curtains and some adhesives, you can become nauseous, have watery eyes and it can even trigger asthma symptoms.

Energy-efficient light bulbs last 12 times
longer than traditional bulbs.

Simply growing the right sort of plants in your office can neutralize many of these potentially lethal chemicals, giving you a cleaner and healthier office environment. The plants absorb the pollutants from the air through tiny openings in their leaves. This fact interested NASA, which conducted a 2-year study into 19 different types of indoor plants. It's a good idea to have a variety of plants in the office, because each plant removes different pollutants.

Spider plant (*Chlorophytum comosum*) removes carbon monoxide from the air (around 96 per cent), as well as xylene and formaldehyde. It needs natural light but not direct sunlight, so place it away from a window. Water once a week without soaking the soil. Each plant will reproduce by forming smaller plantlets from the stems. You can either leave these on the plant or, to produce new plants, place the plantlets in a pot of soil, leave them until they've established, then cut them from the main stem.

Boston fern (*Nephrolepis exaltata* 'Bostoniensis') removes formaldehyde from the atmosphere. It grows in medium to bright light, so place it near a south-facing window. Water regularly and do not allow the pot to dry out.

Areca palm (*Chrysalidocarpus lutescens*) absorbs the pollutant xylene. It grows best in sunlight and in humid conditions and needs filtered sunlight.

Mother-in-law's tongue (*Sansevieria trifasciata* var. *laurentii*) removes formaldehyde, carbon monoxide and benzene from the atmosphere. Mother-in-law's tongue is noted as an unkillable plant and it will grow in most conditions. Let the soil dry out between watering, as over-watering will rot the roots, and do not expose it to freezing or near-freezing temperatures.

Chinese evergreen (*Aglaonema modestum*) helps to reduce formaldehyde, benzene and carbon monoxide levels in the air. It grows best by a north-facing window, in indirect sunlight. Keep the soil moist but not soggy and don't expose it to temperatures below 10°C (50°F).

Ventilation and air conditioning

As global warming increases, so will the use of air-conditioning and ventilation units. The extra amount of energy needed will add to the heating up of our planet, thus compounding the problem of keeping cool. If you want to maintain a comfortable temperature without having to switch anything on there are other possibilities.

Although it's easy to turn round and switch on a fan, it's more beneficial to get some fresh air, which doesn't use any energy, so open a window before thinking about using a fan. In summer, ensure that the last one who leaves the building draws all the blinds shut. This can keep the office cooler, as the morning sun won't heat it up. Position photocopiers and other electrical items in a separate area from the main office, as they can generate heat, and for the same reason turn off all overhead lighting whenever possible. You could also consider installing a radiant barrier in the roof. A radiant barrier is made from a highly reflective material, such as aluminium, fixed to cardboard or plywood. To put it simply, this will reflect heat back out of a building during the summer months and will help reduce the need for air conditioning.

Another thing you can do is get an evaporation cooler – they don't emit any exhaust and use less energy than a conventional air-conditioning unit. Evaporation coolers work on a simple scientific principle: water is naturally cooler than air, so when water evaporates into the air it cools it. This is why temperatures are slightly lower when you're near a river or lake. It's not new technology: the ancient Egyptians developed an air-conditioning system whereby they placed 'wind catchers', which consisted of linen soaked in water, on house roofs; when the north wind blew, the moisture would evaporate and cool the air before it entered the interior.

Computers

When in operation, a laptop uses less energy than a desktop computer – between 15 and 45 watts, rather than 65 to 250 watts for a desktop model. These figures depend on what you have running: e-mailing and word processing use less energy than playing a CD or using a processor-intensive application such as Photoshop. The downside of a laptop is that it's more difficult and costly to upgrade, which could mean that you'll be more likely to replace it before you replace a desktop computer. You can easily upgrade the latter by adding more RAM, which can be bought for a fraction of the price of a new machine, as can more disk space. There will come a point when the cost of upgrading will be greater than the cost of a new computer. It is at this stage that you should look into disposing of your computer safely (see page 330).

Energy-saving hints Ideally, whenever you leave your computer you should shut it down, or at least put it into sleep/hibernation mode and turn off the monitor. There is controversy surrounding how best to deal with your computer at the end of the working day. Some consider

Many plants, including the Boston fern, spider plant and Areca palm, help to reduce levels of toxins in the air.

that putting your computer 'to sleep' keeps it running more efficiently, as the computer is not getting hot then cold again repeatedly, which means it will last longer. However, with computers being upgraded or replaced at an alarming pace, this benefit is negligible. You also need to consider that the heat generated when running a computer could mean more air conditioning has to be used when computers are left on, resulting in even more power consumption. We would highly recommend turning your computer off completely, as no power will be used.

If you think you won't remember to shut down or put your computer to sleep when it's not in use, the power-saving options are for you. All PCs and Macs allow you to set the times when you'd like your computer automatically to turn off the monitor and/or hard disk and the time taken before the standby and sleep/hibernate modes activate.

Battery life is always an issue with laptops. However, there are a few ways to keep your laptop on for longer while away from a power source.

- Don't use the CD/DVD drive – copy programs, games and music onto the hard drive instead.

- Turn off all of the scheduled tasks and Bluetooth capabilities.

- Turn off or turn down the volume.

- Turn down the screen brightness.

- Use the touchpad instead of an external mouse.

To reduce dramatically the amount of power needed for your computing, consider the Linutop, which is a 9-volt, 6-watt computer. It can run at such a low rate because it has no moving parts and uses a Xubuntu (Linux) operating system, which is a completely open source, meaning all upgrades and the actual system are free. Many public places such as libraries and cafés are using it because it's a cheaper way to connect to the internet. The disadvantages of this computer are that it can be a bit of a challenge to find software to run on it, it's slower than most computers and it doesn't have a CD-rom drive.

Greener components
Older monitors use cathode ray tube (CRT) technology, the same technology that is in an old TV set. CRT works by beaming an electron beam back and forth across the rear of the screen. It typically uses about 80 watts of electricity for a 17-in monitor. By comparison, the newer LCD (liquid crystal display) monitors use 35 watts of electricity.

Bamboo monitors make an interesting alternative to the usual plastic sort – the casing and adjustable stand are both made from hard bamboo. This is a tough, durable, panda-friendly material (these animals eat soft bamboo) and is completely renewable, as it can be harvested every year and grows back quickly. Bamboo monitors are for sale online at www.ecotopia.co.uk. The same company also makes bamboo keyboards and mice.

Disposing of computers
In 2005 over 2 million computers ended up in landfill in the UK. Fortunately, that has now changed thanks to the Waste Electrical and Electronic Equipment (WEEE) directive, which states that all electronic equipment has to be treated differently from other waste. By law, every producer, importer or 'rebrander' of electronic equipment has to work out how much electronic equipment they produce in a year and are held responsible for the collection and the disposal of all such equipment bought after 13 August 2005. Any equipment bought before this date is the responsibility of the end user, who will have to track down their nearest collection scheme.

There are approved recycling schemes across the country. To find a company in your area have a look at www.wasteonline.org.uk. If you prefer, there are charities that will recycle your equipment, meaning any money made from your electronic equipment will help a good cause. It's always worth wiping your hard drive before giving away your computer, because it can contain personal information that might fall into the wrong hands.

MOBILE PHONE ENERGY-SAVING TIPS

- When plugged in a charger still uses electricity; ensure that company mobiles are unplugged when not in use.
- If you drive to work, charge your phone in the car on the way.
- Invest in a solar or wind-up phone charger.
- Think before you upgrade – do you really need the latest phone? The average lifespan of a mobile is just 6–9 months. If you do have to upgrade, freecycle your old phone or give it to a charity.

RSI HAND REST

If you notice tightness, stiffness or pain in your hands, wrists, elbows or shoulders when at your computer, this might be the warning signs of repetitive strain/stress injury (RSI). This is quite serious and can leave people unable even to perform everyday tasks such as dressing. Prevention is easier than cure, which is why it's important to lessen the possibility of damage (see page 276). A hand rest will support your wrist and hand and spares the nerves from continuous pressure. There are several hand rests on the market, but it's just as good and less expensive to make your own out of old clothes.

1. Cut two lengths of strong fabric, 40 x 80cm (16 x 32in) – a tatty old pair of trousers or a shirt will be perfectly adequate.

2. Sew the two long edges of the fabric together and one of the shorter edges.

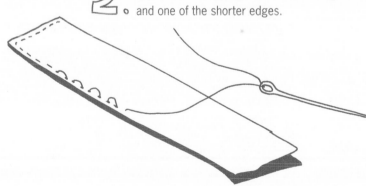

3. Tightly pack the 'sachet' with oatmeal or birdseed and sew up the remaining edge.

Stationery

Open your desk drawer and take a look inside – the chances are it's full of plastic items, all manufactured from new materials from around the globe. Most companies use disposable pens because they're inexpensive, but they have a short shelf life and are not biodegradable. Most of us don't think of pens as being waste, but 10 billion plastic pens go into landfill worldwide every year; if they were put end to end they could stretch over 4 times around our planet – think of this next time you throw one out.

Several companies are trying to make changes to the stationery world: for example, the company Remarkable (www.remarkable.co.uk), set up in 1996, produces a vast range of items including rulers, pencil cases, mouse mats and notepads, all from recycled materials from the UK. It uses car tyres and parts, coffee cups, computer parts and even old pens. You can also obtain biodegradable pens and gel pens made from sustainable wood that are refillable, available online from the Green Stationery Company (www.greenstat.co.uk).

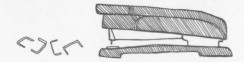

Paper

With the introduction of computers in the workplace, the notion of the paperless office was born. However, it seems to have stayed as just a notion and instead we're creating more paper than ever before, with far too many hard copies being printed off and stored in filing cabinets.

Simple ways to reduce paper usage:

- Think before you print – bookmark web pages you need and read e-mails on the screen.

- Print on both sides of the paper.

- If conducting a presentation, e-mail the handouts instead of printing them off.

- Reuse paper that has printed material on one side for short-lived documents such as agendas.

- Use the page-reduction option on a photocopier – two pages can easily be read on one sheet.

- Edit on screen instead of printing draft copies.

- Put instructions on the printer of how to load headed paper to stop upside-down misprints.

Recycled paper or FSC? According to the Woodland Trust, £800 million a year could be saved by not importing new paper. While there is much demand for recycled paper, there is currently not enough being produced to meet consumer needs. Forestry Stewardship Council (FSC) paper, which this book is printed on, fills the gap – 35 per cent of the paper comes from recycled sources and 65 per cent from managed woodlands. The FSC ensures that 100 million hectares (247,000,000 acres) of the world's forests are managed for efficient profit, without damaging the eco-system, and sets the standard for responsible forestry worldwide.

Meetings and travel

Meetings can be an inevitable part of office life but for environmental reasons as well as financial ones, consider if a face-to-face meeting is absolutely necessary. Think of the travel costs to send one person to take notes when a Dictaphone or Mp3 recorder could do the job for the price of the battery power. Also, ask yourself whether the meeting could be held over an instant messenger service? Most offices are set up with messenger services that can incorporate web cams but they're frequently not used. If your company doesn't have a messenger service there are many free options out there, including Skype, Microsoft Instant Messenger, Yahoo Messenger and AOL. There is also multi-client software available that will connect Yahoo users with AOL and Microsoft users, for example. Two of these are Pidgin and Trillian, which are both free to download.

Lunch and coffee breaks

Being in a rush in the morning can often mean you slip up from an environmental point of view. If you eat ethically at home, try to keep it up during the working day. If you have organic Fairtrade coffee for breakfast, make some extra and take it to work with you in a flask rather than buying coffee on the run, possibly from an unethical chain. Similarly, make your own lunch rather than popping out to buy plastic-wrapped sandwiches from the supermarket. The British Sandwich Association states that approximately 2.7 billion sandwiches are bought a year in the UK, which indicates we seem to have lost the ability to make our own, but you can so easily do so at a fraction of the cost – think before you buy a product that has been manufactured and packaged in a factory, then transported miles and miles by road. If you bake your own bread and grow your own fillings the cost of a healthy sandwich in financial and environmental terms will be negligible.

An ingenious example of recycled materials: a wastepaper basket made from an old, discarded car tyre.

'ORGANIC'
CUCUMBERS
29ᵖ EACH
or

THE SELF-SUFFICIENTISH CONSUMER

It seems a bit of an oxymoron to have 'The self-sufficientish consumer' as a chapter in this book, but as the 'ish' suggests this book isn't about total self-sufficiency. To live out of the system completely you'd have to grow your own wheat for bread and pasta, become a freegan (see page 338) and, if you live in Britain, never eat rice or bananas or drink tea or coffee. You wouldn't have a bank account, phone, water or electricity. To live like this would be extremely difficult in the modern age, but there are ways of being more environmentally friendly, by becoming more selective when shopping and abstaining from certain products and services.

Each time you buy something you pay into a chain, starting with growing, mining or drilling of the required raw materials through to the manufacturing and distribution of the goods and their packaging, and of course ending up at the shops you buy from. The idea of ethical or conscientious shopping is growing as consumers are becoming increasingly aware of the origins of the goods on their high street. Thinking about what you buy and where you spend your money can really make all the difference to a great number of people's lives.

MAKING CHOICES

Most of us are so far removed from the manufacturing or farming process we rarely stop to think about how the decisions we make as consumers will affect someone else down the line. Simple choices like starting the day with a Fairtrade tea or coffee rather than one bought from a large multinational corporation can make a huge difference to tea or coffee growers in developing countries. Similarly, buying something second hand or fixing a broken item rather than replacing it can have a positive knock-on effect for the environment, reducing potential carbon emissions and landfill. Considering how we spend our money is arguably the single most important thing we can do to aid our environment but sadly it is often the most neglected.

We often ask ourselves the following five questions before buying anything:

1. Do I really need this?
We often get need and want confused – for example, no-one really needs a giant plasma TV but a lot of people might really want one. It takes a large amount of energy to make a TV, ship it over to Britain and package it for sale. When this television is bought merely to replace an existing one in perfect working order, can we honestly say that we're buying out of necessity?

During a lifetime the average consumer will throw out 3 tonnes of electrical waste, not to mention waste from other sources. The website www.wasteonline.org.uk estimates that the amount of waste produced in the UK from all sources (including electrical goods) is a staggering 434 million tonnes a year. To put it another way, that's enough to fill the Albert Hall every 2 hours. We do have a choice as consumers and perhaps the most 'green' choice we can make is just not to buy in the first place.

2. Can I get it second hand or even free?
There's a well-known saying, 'One man's scrap is another man's gold.' If you look around in places that deal in second-hand goods (car-boot, table-top or jumble sales, charity shops or online auction sites) you'll see this for yourself. Buying second-hand items is not only less expensive for the consumer, but it can also often mean you're supporting a worthy cause, such as a local charity; just as important, it will save items otherwise destined for a landfill site, so will be helping the environment. Taking this one step further, if you're very lucky, you could get perfectly good items for free. Throughout this book we've mentioned Freecycle, the international community of people giving away unwanted items (www.freecycle.org). The majority of towns and cities have their own Freecycle group – it's the online equivalent of leaving your sofa outside the house. Once you've joined your local group you can post 'Offered' messages for items you no longer have any need for or post 'Wanted' ads asking for things you might need. The ultimate aim of the site is to stop unwanted items ending up in a landfill site.

Whatever you're throwing away, there's nearly always someone to take it off your hands. We've seen baby clothes and toys, long-distance train tickets, computers, bikes, TVs and even cars advertised. Dave once picked up a pumpkin someone was offering, as they'd grown more than they knew what to do with.

There are also other websites similar to freecycle.org – an online community that is building strength is www.dontdumpthat.com, and more are cropping up all the time. Also, in most parts of Britain, local newspapers and magazines often offer free advertising to people giving away or selling items for very little. In the south west, the classified newspaper *Trade It* offers plenty of items for no cost as long as the consumer is prepared to collect. Other classified papers, including *Loot*, provide the same service.

Remember, friends and relations are also a good source of unwanted items – always ask around before buying anything new.

3. Is it locally produced?
Unless you've had your head in the sand for the last 10 years or more, you'll know that British farming is having a very hard time, to put it mildly. Buying locally produced food is a very simple way of redressing this problem. Money generated from sales of locally bought food can be reinvested in the local economy. A recent survey by the New Economics Foundation states: 'Every £10 spent with a local food initiative is worth £25 for the local area, compared with just £14 when the same amount is spent in a supermarket.' The benefits are also passed on to the consumer, because the food is often fresher for not having been stored in a warehouse for days on end or on board a container ship.

Try to support small, local shops and buy organic produce whenever possible.

4. Is it organic? If you're not growing your own, organic food does cost a little more than intensively farmed fruit and vegetables. However, this is the only downside and if you're buying direct from a farm via a veg-box scheme or farmers' market the increased cost is usually negligible. Some of the positives in buying organic are:

- It's more nutritious – Organic fruit and vegetables are higher in nutrients, including vitamin C, iron and magnesium. Organic milk is higher in Omega-3 fatty acids and vitamins A and E.

- It's kinder to wildlife – Increased numbers of insects on organic farms lead to increased numbers of other wildlife higher up the food chain such as birds and small mammals.

- It's non-toxic – Non-organically grown fruit and vegetables can contain large quantities of pesticide residues. Some of these are fine in small doses but over time can build up in the body and have been linked with an increase in certain cancers.

- It's better for the land – Pesticides and artificial fertilizers can contaminate the soil and water supplies.

- The animal-welfare standards are higher – Organically farmed animals need to meet high welfare standards to achieve Soil Association accreditation.

It's worth looking out for some kind of certification mark when buying organic food. The main certification body for organic food in the UK is the Soil Association, but others include Organic Farmers and Growers Ltd, Scottish Organic Producers Association, Organic Food Federation, Bio-Dynamic Agricultural Association, Irish Organic Farmers and Growers Association, Organic Trust Limited, CMi Certification and Quality Welsh Food Certification Ltd.

5. Is it Fairtrade? The British charity Oxfam was one of the first organizations to champion the cause of ethical consumerism with its fair-trade campaigns, in which it highlighted the plight of coffee growers in developing countries. Combined with pressure from other organizations and individuals, this led in 1997 to the birth of the Fairtrade label – a certification body that inspects and certifies producer organizations in more than 50 countries, mainly in Africa, Asia and Latin America.

The aim of Fairtrade is to give farmers in the developing world a fair price for their goods, more reflective of the amount of labour put into growing their crops, and safer and healthier working conditions. It also encourages better environmental practices and strives to create a situation of sustainable development within communities. Many growers involved with Fairtrade now benefit from a variety of health schemes, school-building projects and improved sanitation.

At the time of writing, over 2000 Fairtrade items are available in Britain, including chocolate, tea, coffee, fruit and fruit juices, sugar, wine and beer, nuts and snacks, preserves and spreads and non-food-related products such as flowers, organic cotton items and even footballs. For further details visit www.fairtrade.org.uk or Oxfam's website (www.oxfam.org.uk).

WHAT IS A FREEGAN?

Freegans began emerging in the 1990s as a reaction to our modern-day consumerist society. In its true sense, a freegan is someone who disagrees with the inherent cruelty and unethical practices of a capitalist society, so chooses to boycott it altogether.

A lot of freegan principles are similar to those of the self-sufficientish community – they believe that food can be grown, found through foraging or bartered.

Freegans take foraging a step further than most: as well as foraging in the wild they look for food in bins (supermarkets provide rich pickings) and dumpsters. There's more than enough food for them – according to a BBC report, in the UK 17 million tonnes of surplus food is dumped by the food industry on landfills each year, of which 4 million tonnes is perfectly safe to eat.

Always take reusable bags when you go shopping rather than acquiring a new plastic bag each time.

BUYING FOOD & DRINK

Over the past 30 years or so numerous small, independent shops have closed down all over the country because they couldn't compete with the supermarkets in terms of price or diversity. It's easy to see the attraction of supermarkets, where consumers are seemingly able to buy everything under one roof. However, once you've driven there, found a parking space, battled with long queues and traipsed up and down the numerous aisles, you should ask yourself if they're really as convenient as they may at first appear. On the surface, the supermarket may seem to offer more choice, but at what cost?

In large urban housing estates and in rural areas the decline of the local high-street shops has hit residents particularly hard. Many supermarkets are in out-of-town locations and people without their own transport can find it a struggle to do their weekly shop. This has created what sociologists have called 'food deserts' – large areas where the locals are unable to buy the basics of a healthy diet including fresh fruit and vegetables – and it tends to be the most vulnerable members of society, namely the elderly and those on low incomes, who are most affected. Residents of areas designated as food deserts have begun to join forces to alleviate the problem of access to food. We've seen this happen close to home as our grandmother has recently joined a scheme with the local church, which provides her with fruit and vegetable bags for just £1 each.

Independent shops & suppliers

In many towns and cities, there is increasing demand for specialist shops, particularly in areas with ethnic communities – Asian, Greek, Polish and Jewish food stores are becoming more of a common sight on the high street. In the Gloucester Road area of Bristol, where Dave lives, there are many small, specialized shops selling above and beyond what a supermarket could ever offer. Loose dried fruit, nuts, seeds, rice and pasta at a fraction of supermarket prices are available at the local 'Scoopaway'. There are freshly made speciality breads (with no artificial additives), cakes and buns from the bakery, and the local butcher sells a huge choice of meat, cheeses and preserves – it even has a barbecue out at the front on Saturdays.

Farmers' markets have also become very popular and many towns around Britain now hold these weekly or fortnightly. At a farmers' market you can buy fresh fruit, vegetables, dairy products, honey and preserves direct from the farmers or their employees. Producers have to grow the food or source the ingredients within 40 or 48 kilometres (25 or 30 miles) from the market site,

depending on the market ruling, and produce may well have been harvested on the day you buy it.

The biggest shift in our shopping habits over the last decade has been the rise of online shopping, which has been a real boon to small producers and specialist producers alike. Many veg-box schemes have online ordering forms and chocolate-makers, bee-keepers and jam- and chutney-producers can now sell to a much wider market, improving customer choice and selling a higher standard of produce.

It's vital to support these independent shops and suppliers, because if we don't the large out-of-town supermarket, with its uniform selection of foods across the country and fruit and vegetables often air-freighted half way round the world, will be our only choice.

Fairtrade food & drink

For centuries, Westerners living in temperate regions have relied on countries in hotter climes to supply products we're unable to grow ourselves, such as tea, coffee, chocolate and tobacco. It therefore seems strange that none of the countries (with the exception of the United States) producing these foods has grown rich on our weakness for luxury goods. This is down to the simple law of economics – the cost of any product is always considerably higher in its processed form than in its raw state. Keeping the processing of these raw materials in a developed rather than developing country means the grower gets far less than the manufacturers and distributors of the goods.

Traditionally, societies in developing countries were based on subsistence farming, which meant farmers produced enough food for themselves and their families, possibly with a bit extra to sell or barter within their local communities. However, large Western corporations encouraged the farmers to grow cash crops for export, such as coffee and sugar, with the promise of a 'better

Just a few of the many Fairtrade products available to the consumer.

life', so these farmers who once grew organic fruit and vegetables for their families were soon growing goods for international trade. However, this change wasn't necessarily all for the good. The farmers are frequently paid a tiny wage, working conditions are often unreasonable and they sometimes use potentially harmful pesticides and herbicides to avoid the risk of losing their sole source of income.

The Fairtrade label was established to ensure that farm workers, their families and their communities in the developing world get a better deal. In this book, we've concentrated on the main five Fairtrade products – coffee, bananas, chocolate, tea and sugar – because these arguably provide some of the greatest benefits for poverty-stricken growers in the developing world. However, there are numerous other Fairtrade products to choose from.

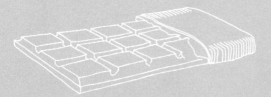

Chocolate Chocolate is one luxury many of us would find it very difficult to do without. Our appetite for it is so considerable that in the UK we eat about 200 million kg (440 million lb) of boxed chocolate, confectionery bars and chocolate bars per year, spending on average around £40 per person. With a cacao tree producing only 1kg (2lb) of cocoa every year, the amount of space, time and energy needed to satisfy our sweet tooth is staggering.

Chocolate has one of the strangest of all supply chains. The large confectionery companies such as Cadbury Schweppes, Nestlé and Mars buy the bulk of their raw cocoa beans from a series of smallholders in developing countries. The beans are then processed into cocoa butter, usually in a developed country, gaining in value before being made into chocolate, then the finished product is distributed by these confectionery giants at considerable prices. It's the economic equivalent of the blue whale relying on plankton to keep itself alive. An Oxfam report stated that over 90 per cent of our cocoa beans comes from the developing world. However, export sales of cocoa beans account for only $2 billion a year, while chocolate sales worldwide amount to over $60 billion.

This disparity is slowly being redressed through the emergence of Fairtrade chocolate. In Ghana, the Kuapa Kokoo (or cocoa co-operative) has over 30,000 members joining forces. Selling under the Fairtrade label means they receive a guaranteed minimum price in a constantly fluctuating market, securing jobs and increasing the standard of living. The Kuapa Kokoo also produces its own cocoa butter, adding further value to the product and keeping profits within the country.

The range of Fairtrade chocolate available is ever increasing and brands include the Divine, Dubble and Green and Black's (although now owned by Cadbury they still keep the Fairtrade label), and some of the major supermarkets are now selling their own Fairtrade range.

It's often only a matter of a few pence extra to buy Fairtrade chocolate and eating it without any guilt can make it taste all the sweeter.

Sugar Sugar is hard to avoid, cropping up in all the obvious places such as cakes, biscuits and confectionery, but also in canned goods such as baked beans and in many ready meals and processed foods. We get our sugar from two main plant sources – sugar cane, which is grown in the tropics, and sugar beet, which is grown in Europe including Britain. Despite the lower standards of living in developing countries (Ethiopian sugar farmers can receive as little as a dollar a day), subsidized European beet can often price out the cane-sugar crop from the world market, impacting considerably on the economies of cane-producing countries.

Our sugar habit can also be detrimental to the environment. The growing of beet sugar can have a corrosive effect on the soil, and as a refined product sugar cane doesn't have to undergo such stringent tests for pesticides as other food crops.

Fairtrade and organic sugar is becoming available, as consumers have begun to realize its humanitarian and environmental cost. It's still not that widely available and many of the major supermarkets at the time of writing don't stock organic or Fairtrade sugar. The Co-op seems to be leading the way, selling Fairtrade sugar sourced from Malawi, and many independent retailers, such as healthfood shops, stock a selection of Fairtrade sugars.

Tea Many of us start the day with a cup of tea and it's offered in all sorts of social situations. Although it's seen as a very British drink, tea is, of course, not a British-grown product, and we rely on India, Indonesia, China, Sri Lanka and Kenya for the majority of our imports.

The problem for tea-producing countries is fluctuating prices. For example, when the Indonesian economy collapsed in 1997 Indonesian tea prices plummeted, which in turn forced down the price of tea elsewhere; many growers around the world lost their only source of income as a result. Tea has continued to lose value on the global market and as recently as 2006 workers in Darjeeling were reported to be committing suicide because they were unable to feed their families.

Fairtrade tea ensures that the prices of tea are fixed, regardless of the fluctuations in the market. A stabilized price can prevent this human suffering and give money back to the tea-growing communities.

Coffee

As with tea, the market for coffee has also suffered because of globalization. Taking into account inflation, international prices for coffee are just 25 per cent of what they were in 1965 and since 1997 coffee prices have fallen by as much as 70 per cent. While this may appear to be good news for Western consumers, it's thought to have cost developing nations $8 billion in lost export sales. With coffee accounting for 60 to 80 per cent of export sales for Ethiopia and Burundi, for instance, it isn't hard to see how this reliance on a small number of exports can affect a nation's economy.

One reason for fluctuating prices is the fact that increasing numbers of countries are beginning to produce coffee, driving down prices elsewhere. For example, in an attempt to restructure its economy, Vietnam began growing coffee beans instead of the traditional crop of rice, which is much more suited to its climate. Excessive use of pesticides and fertilizers made the growing of coffee possible in the country, producing a product inferior to other nations' coffee but a lot cheaper.

It is again by offering a fixed price through the Fairtrade scheme that farmers can most benefit. The US equivalent of the Fairtrade label, TransFair USA, helped Latin American coffee growers receive twice the depressed market prices for their coffee. However, with supply outstripping demand, the Fairtrade coffee market faces an uphill struggle, and in Europe sales are reaching a plateau. It is only through continuing demand that the Fairtrade label can make a difference. The solutions are simple. First, when Fairtrade coffee is not available in a café, local shop or workplace, ask for it. If the demand is there, they will probably supply it. The second solution is always to have it at home and try to convince others to do the same.

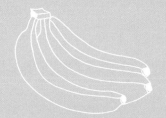

Bananas

The banana is the most sprayed of all food crops. This is largely a result of the growing method – bananas (particularly the Cavendish variety) are often grown as a monocrop, which reduces soil fertility and makes the fruit more prone to disease, forcing growers to use more fertilizers and herbicides. These chemicals run off into the water supply, affecting humans, animals and plants; in addition, large areas of land are frequently deforested to make way for banana growing, causing a decline in biodiversity.

The subsequent excessive use of pesticides has raised health concerns for banana growers and it has been reported that many banana workers suffer from skin complaints and lowered fertility.

A recent price war led to many of the leading supermarkets cutting prices of non-Fairtrade bananas. However, rather than take up this shortfall themselves they put the cost onto the banana growers, offering them less for their product. This has led to a greater disparity in prices between organic and Fairtrade bananas and those that are intensively farmed.

Organic and Fairtrade bananas do, therefore, come at a premium, but consumers have demanded them in ever-increasing numbers, despite the extra cost. Most notably, in December 2006 Sainsbury's announced they would sell only Fairtrade bananas, which doubled the number of Fairtrade bananas available in Britain.

REDISTRIBUTION OF FOOD

Many charities are aware of the huge amount of waste involved in the food industry and aim to redistribute it to their local community. One such charity is Fareshare (www.fareshare.org.uk), a national charity that redistributes food donated by wholesalers and retailers to day-care centres and hostels for the homeless. The food never has to touch a bin or skip, and rather than ending up in a landfill it can benefit vulnerable members of society. The charity ensures all the food is properly handled and prepared to strict food hygiene guidelines.

Buying milk

If given the choice, most of us like the idea of buying milk from our local farmer, or even milking our own cow or goat. However, the reality is that most milk is taken off the shelf and put into a trolley in a supermarket. Most of us don't know which country our milk comes from, let alone which county or farm.

In the past few years, supermarkets have been pushing down the price of milk in real terms and dairy farmers are experiencing real hardship. Between 2000 and 2004 an average of four dairy farmers a week were going out of business in Britain. Many farmers have to increase the size of their herds, which decreases welfare standards, in order to compete in a very difficult market.

To ensure that we're buying our milk to help dairy farmers rather than make matters worse there are a few things we can all do:

- Use a milkman – Milkmen do still exist, despite their decline. Milk rounds, especially ones based on a co-operative, will pay the farmers more for their milk. (To find a milkman, see page 387.)

- Buy local – Look in your local organic healthfood shop or supermarket for milk from a local dairy. Corner shops in Bristol sell local milk – perhaps ask at yours to see if they offer the same.

- Buy organic – Although organic dairy farmers don't get paid much more for their milk, the higher standards of feeding mean the cows are healthier and we get milk with more Omega-3, vitamin E and beta carotene. There are a few companies that sell milk produced in a sustainable way, such as Rachel's Organic (which donates some money to the Woodland Trust), Duchy Originals, White and Wild, and Farm Organics. Although these do cost slightly more, you'll be helping to keep milk at an overall lower price. If we lose all of our dairy farms, think of the price milk could rise to. Even substituting one carton of milk a week for an organic farm carton will help overall.

Alternatives to cow's milk Some people are allergic to cow's milk, so need to find alternatives. A few years ago there were reports in the media about a new, healthy, low-fat milk that was going to sweep our nation, namely horse's milk. It didn't take off, probably because of people's squeamishness. However, two alternatives to cow's milk are readily available – goat's milk and soya milk – and hemp milk is available in larger healthfood shops.

Goats take up less grazing space than cows and also create less methane (a greenhouse gas), which means that goat's milk is a more environmentally friendly alternative to cow's milk. It can also be a healthier option as it contains 13 per cent more calcium and less lactose: 4.1 per cent versus 4.7 per cent in cow's milk, making it ideal for those who are lactose-intolerant.

On first appearances, soya milk may seem to be the most eco-friendly alternative. However, with further research the humble soya bean does not come up smelling of roses. The new-found lust for soya has meant that vast areas of the Amazon delta are being deforested to make way for this crop. Soya is also being contaminated with genetically modified (GMO) soya; although it must clearly be labelled as a GM food in this country, the only way to be pretty certain it's not contaminated is to buy organic.

Another less common alternative is hemp milk, which is available in larger specialist stores, or you can make your own using the seeds, which you can find in the majority of healthfood shops. It's extremely nutritious and because it's high in Omega-3 and Omega-6 oils it's a viable alternative to oily fish. Hemp milk can be an acquired taste and even in tea and coffee you may prefer to add a teaspoon or two of honey to sweeten it. It's ideally suited to milkshakes and smoothies.

We've included a recipe for making hemp milk here (see overleaf), but it does take a while to make it. However, a company called Yaoh has developed a machine to take the hard work out of making your own. It claims that any nuts or seeds can be used to make milk, including hazelnuts, cashew nuts or sunflower seeds. You simply put the seeds or nuts into the machine with some water and it makes milk within a couple of minutes. It is available from www.yaoh.co.uk.

Getting your milk delivered rather than buying it in a supermarket ensures the dairy farmers get a better deal.

Hemp milk

In this recipe the seeds need to soak for quite a long time. The soaking time can be reduced to 24 hours, but the taste is superior and creamier if you take your time.

1. Place 150g (5oz) hemp seeds in a deep bowl and cover with enough cold water to come about 5cm (2in) or so above the seeds. Leave for 12 hours or until most of the seeds sink.

2. Rinse the seeds. Return them to the bowl with fresh water. Leave for 5 days, changing the water twice a day. Keep out of direct sunlight.

3. After about 5 days the hemp seeds should have sprouted small tails, about 1cm (½in) long. Don't worry if a few haven't. Provided the husks have opened you should be fine. Drain off the water and pound the sprouted seeds using a pestle and mortar or liquidize them in a blender. You'll probably need to add a little water to make this process easier.

4. Add 1 litre (1¾ pints) water and strain the liquid into a large bowl using a piece of muslin or an old tee-shirt.

5. Decant the milk into a plastic bottle and keep it in the fridge. Use the milk within about 3–5 days and shake well each time before using.

Use a pestle and mortar to pound the sprouted hemp seeds.

CLOTHES

During the past decade the ever-competitive clothing market has forced the price of clothes to an all-time low. Suits can now be picked up for a fraction of what they used to cost and even traditionally expensive items, such as wedding dresses, have had budget lines introduced.

There are several reasons for this, but a large part of it is that the majority of our clothes are made in developing countries in order to keep costs down. While this cost-cutting may initially seem good news for the consumer, there are a few serious drawbacks: the merchandise is shipped or flown half way across the world using valuable fossil fuels and there have been numerous reports about unethical work practices, such as employing child labour, in the garment industry. Intensive cotton farming is also having a serious impact on the environment and the health of the labourers who work in the business. As consumers, we can make a real difference. Buying second-hand clothes, rather than always buying the latest 'disposable' fashions, and choosing garments that have been made using sustainable farming methods, such as organic cotton and alternative fibres such as hemp (see pages 350–1), can both help.

Buying second hand

There are numerous benefits to buying clothes second hand – as well as cutting costs and in many cases giving money to a worthwhile cause, by not purchasing a newly made garment you're also taking an item out of the manufacturing chain and all that it entails.

Charity shops Many people feel there's a stigma attached to buying from charity shops, especially for children. However, the simple fact is that no-one has to know you spent a fraction of the price on perfectly good second-hand clothes, including your son or daughter. For adults the stigma hardly raises its head at all, as these days the clothes available in many charity shops rival those in any high-street outlet. Charity shops appeal to the bargain hunter and both of us have found good-quality designer clothes for almost nothing.

Charity shops have moved with the times. For example, Oxfam not only has an eBay store but it also caters for the designer market with Oxfam Originals. These shops are in

prime locations, such as London's Covent Garden and major cities such Manchester, Nottingham, Leeds, York and Preston. Oxfam Originals are slightly more costly than the standard Oxfam shop, but they're staffed by people who have a flair for fashion and they sell only vintage, retro and designer goods.

Vintage and designer seconds Good-quality vintage clothing looks attractive no matter what decade it's worn in. From 1950s dresses to 1960s mini and Mod suits, some styles will always appeal because they're classics. Vintage clothes can give your wardrobe that little bit of individuality somewhat lacking in modern, mass-produced garments.

Vintage clothes for both men and women have undergone a bit of a revival because of the internet.

Charity shops often sell good-quality, nearly-new items.

Online vintage shops, such as www.marthascloset.co.uk, www.candysays.co.uk and other companies selling their wares on eBay have added to this phenomenon. Many people still prefer to shop the more traditional way and thankfully vintage clothing shops exist all over the country.

Repairing and revamping

Rather than throw old clothes out, consider whether you could repair or revamp them. Adapting old garments is by far the most economical way to create new ones. For example, an old pair of jeans can easily be turned into shorts, or the more ambitious could turn them into a denim skirt by cutting the seams and restitching the two legs together. Dyeing is of course another way to revitalize old clothes (see right and opposite) – Dave once revamped a white suit jacket from a charity shop by tie-dyeing it, which had interesting results.

Not everyone can learn to fix a computer or TV, but anyone can learn how to repair holes or tears in clothes with just a few stitches. Here we've included instructions for how to darn a sock – rather than buying a new pair, you could just learn to mend the ones you already have.

How to darn a sock

This technique is best for small holes on thinner-weave cotton and man-made socks, such as sports socks and pop socks. It may not be the most professional way to mend a pair of socks but it does work and it's a method most of us can use without too much effort.

1. Turn the sock inside out and put an old non-energy-efficient light bulb into the sock. This should help the sock keep its shape and provide a guide for the needle.

2. Thread the needle and tie a knot at the end of the thread. Pass the needle into the sock just to one side of the hole. Make three or four stitches to the side of the hole, so the thread is secure, then take a stitch across the hole.

3. Continue stitching across the hole, ensuring the stitch is as tight as you can get it – the trick is literally to 'pull' the hole closed with the thread.

4. To finish, stitch again to the side of the hole, on the other side this time. Then stitch under the last stitch and make another knot with the thread. Do this at least a couple of times to make sure the thread is secure.

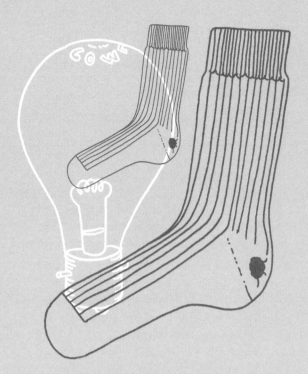

Home dyeing Before the invention of chemical dyes, plants were grown and used for dyeing yarn and cloth. This is still by far the most environmentally friendly way to dye textiles. If home dyeing, you may choose to grow dye plants yourself or gather them from the wild. Always harvest wild plants responsibly, ask the landowner's permission if you wish to dig up any roots and don't over-pick rare plants.

This chart shows you just some of the colours available from plant sources. However, results aren't always uniform and it's worth experimenting on small pieces of fabric before dyeing whole items. In some cases it's the leaves that are used, in others the flowers, roots or fruits.

Red	Beetroot, plums, dandelion roots, rosehips, rue
Yellow	Burdock root, St John's wort, onion skins, marigolds, chamomile flowers, sunflower petals, gorse
Green	Nettles, grass, spinach, self-heal, sorrel leaves and roots, rosemary
Purple	Plums, blackberries, elderberries, cherry roots
Blue	Blackberries, elderberries, woad
Black	Walnuts, iris roots
Brown	Hazelnuts, oak bark, acorns, hop leaves and flowers
Orange	Turmeric

HOW TO DYE CLOTHES

You can use a range of plants for home dyeing. Clothes that are dyed with natural dyes should not be machine washed as the colours can run. Before dyeing, treat the fabric with a mordant solution to fix the colour.

1. Soak the garment for at least 2 hours in a mordant solution. For fruit dyes, use a salt mordant (1 part salt to 16 parts cold water); for other plant dyes, use a vinegar mordant (1 part white vinegar to 4 parts cold water). Rinse the garment well before dyeing.

2. Finely chop the plant material, place it in a large pan with enough boiling water to cover the item you eventually want to dye, turn the heat down and simmer for an hour or so. The more water you use, the weaker the concentration. As a rule of thumb, use 500g (1lb) plant material per 20 litres (4–5 gallons) water, but bear in mind this will vary depending on the existing colour of the garment and the strength of the dye in the plant material.

3. Take the dye mixture off the heat and strain it into a large basin or washing up bowl.

4. Soak your garment in the dye. The depth of colour will depend on how long you leave it to soak. For deep, dark colours soak overnight and for lighter shades soak for a couple of hours. Wring out the garment and leave it to dry.

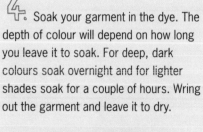

What's wrong with cotton?

The growing and production of cotton is one of, if not *the* most environmentally damaging of all agricultural practices. It has been calculated that around 25 per cent of the world's agrochemicals are used on cotton crops. These pesticides have had an extremely detrimental effect on the environment and are damaging the health of workers involved in cotton production.

Cotton is a very sensitive crop and the practice of growing it as a monocrop exacerbates the problem of pests and diseases. In the past, these were controlled by crop rotation – by planting only small numbers of plants together and taking the pests' lifecycle into account – but today they're controlled by vast quantities of chemicals.

The problems are perhaps most marked in the countries surrounding the Aral Sea in central Asia. Since the 1950s and 1960s, farmers in the region have diverted the rivers feeding the sea to irrigate their crops, especially cotton, which is a particularly thirsty crop. This has meant the Aral Sea has now just 3 cubic kilometres a year of fresh water running into it, in contrast to the 50 cubic kilometres in 1950. To add to the problem, the water that

WHAT IS HEMP ?

Hemp is a common name for *Cannabis sativa* and it is closely related to the drug cannabis or marijuana. However, industrial hemp is a different variety, grown for its fibres used in the manufacture of various items, including clothing, rather than for its narcotic properties.

Hemp has become an important sustainable crop in British agriculture. At one point it was forbidden to grow hemp, but a ruling in 1993 allowed farmers in Britain once again to cultivate the crop, as research showed that industrial hemp contains very little or no tetrahydrocannabinol (THC) – the narcotic compound found in other related varieties, particularly Indian hemp – and it would be impossible to get high from this variety.

So how is hemp environmentally friendly?

● Hemp needs few or no agrochemicals to grow and far less water than cotton – producing cloth that is 55 per cent hemp and 45 per cent cotton uses nearly 380 litres (84 gallons) less water than 100 per cent cotton cloth in its production.

● Hemp is very suited to the British climate and needs just over 3 months before it's ready to harvest. It's useful in the control of weeds in a crop-rotation scheme and its deep roots have been said actually to increase soil fertility.

● Clothing made from hemp grown in Britain has a relatively small carbon footprint, as it's not flown or shipped half way round the world, unlike cotton.

● It's a very versatile crop and can be used as a healthfood, to make bio-fuel and biodegradable plastics and in the manufacture of paper. It's been estimated that in its production hemp paper uses around a quarter of the land needed to grow trees.

does remain has become polluted, largely from agrochemicals (but also from weapons-testing in the area). The loss of habitat for many species is immeasurable. Oases on the edge of the sea have vanished and with increasing salt levels the number of fish and other aquatic life able to survive in the salty water has plummeted.

The impact on human health from cotton production is just as much a cause for concern. Poisoning is accumulative, building up with exposure to pesticides over time. Workers are often poorly educated and fail to read warnings on pesticides, so often wear no protective clothing and will even work in bare feet.

In 2005 a study was published in the *International Journal of Occupational and Environmental Health*. It studied a group of Indian cotton farm workers over a 5-month period and found 82 per cent of the group suffered from some symptoms of poisoning (symptoms were mild in 39 per cent, moderate in 37 per cent and severe in 6 per cent of the group). With over 10 million cotton farm workers in India alone, the health problems connected to the growing of cotton are immense. The World Health Organization (WHO) reported that around the world over 20,000 people a year die from exposure to the agrochemicals used in cotton production. This is reason alone to seek out organic cotton and alternatives.

Organic and Fairtrade cotton Organic cotton production uses traditional growing methods and various biological controls (where predators are introduced to deal with pests), negating the need for noxious chemicals and resulting in environmentally friendly, sustainable cotton. Many of the methods employed are no different from those used by an organic gardener.

- A crop-rotation system is used to increase soil fertility.

- Alfalfa is planted between the cotton plants, because many pests harmful to cotton prefer alfalfa and will eat that instead. The alfalfa plants and any harmful insects are destroyed at the end of each season.

- Organic pesticides, such as chilli, soap and plant extracts, are used on the crop instead of chemicals.

- Hedgerows are managed to encourage beneficial insects that prey on cotton pests; the insects are then released around the cotton plants.

- Birds that prey on harmful insects are bred for the purpose and released.

- Organic cotton is handpicked, allowing workers to choose only the best-quality cotton. This provides a higher-quality product and also takes away the need to separate low-quality cotton later in the manufacturing process.

Like many other products, cotton is subject to fluctuations in the world market. As organic cotton is often a Fairtrade product, workers on organic farms benefit not only from a lack of exposure to poisonous chemicals, but they are also guaranteed a fixed price for their product. With a secured income they can raise their standard of living, and further premiums allow money to be put into community projects such as schools and healthcare schemes. For environmental and humanitarian reasons, we should strive to buy organic, Fairtrade cotton.

Hemp: an alternative to cotton

Fashion designers, manufacturers and retailers are beginning to cotton on (pardon the pun) to the environmentally destructive nature of the cotton industry and, to a lesser extent, of man-made fibres. Leading the crusade is the non-intensively farmed hemp industry (see box, opposite). Hemp clothing has come a long way since its scratchy beginnings and has shaken off its hippy stigma in recent years to make its mark beside more traditional materials in the fashion world.

Despite there being only one main processor of hemp fibre in the UK, its prices have remained competitive. The Hemp Store (www.thehempstore.co.uk) is very affordable and sells lots of tee-shirts with an organic cotton/hemp mix, women's tops and a range of basketball shoes and trainers. The rather urban THTC (The Hemp Trading Company) has hoodies and tee-shirts available at competitive prices that also carry the Fairtrade mark. Even bigger retailers seem to be getting in on the act: Marks and Spencer now stocks a hemp/cotton bag and plans to stock more hemp products in the future.

Hemp can be sexy as well, with the emergence of the fashion label Enamore selling lingerie and women's clothing made from hemp mixed with other natural fibres. Enamore was set up by young designer Jenny Ambrose in an effort to support ethical and sustainable practices in the clothing industry. Her designs are a clear sign of how far hemp clothing has come and what is possible in the future from this entirely sustainable crop.

ETHICAL BANKING

When we pay interest to a bank, or have money sitting in our accounts, banks will loan this money on to other individuals or organizations. While some banks consider carefully whom they're lending the money to, others give loans to businesses that are less than ethical for profit – for example, to companies that deal in the arms trade, employ child labour or are involved in deforestation.

We don't wish to name and shame the banks and building societies with the worst records: just try typing 'ethics' and your bank name into Google and ask yourself how comfortable you are about the way your money is being used to fund such businesses. Fortunately, there are several ethical banks and building societies around, so perhaps it's time to start looking for a financial institution with an ethical policy.

Ethical current accounts

Some banks have established an active ethical investment policy and won't lend to companies they consider unethical. The Co-operative Bank (along with the internet bank Smile, part of the Co-operative Bank) is the pioneer of ethical investing, having led the way in 1992. There are now others, such as Triodos, the Ecology Building Society and the Charity Bank. They all invest only in companies that adhere to the highest ethical credentials and finance projects with social and environmental benefits.

Building societies such as Nationwide, Coventry, and Norwich and Peterborough have all made their money by offering individuals mortgages rather than lending to big business, so you can be safe in the knowledge that your cash isn't being invested in an unethical corporation.

Even if you never change banks, do at least ask your bank for paperless banking – a monthly reminder that you have to shred is an inconvenience and is wasteful. You can still keep track of your money online and by doing so you can be more aware of any fraudulent activity on your account.

Getting a mortgage

There's a huge choice of mortgages on offer. Mutual building societies and banks will lend money to fund only personal mortgages and they have no shareholders, so profits can be used to give customers a better deal. This means that your interest will go only to other mortgage holders or savers, funding people and houses rather than big business. Some banks are starting to offer so-called 'green mortgages', planting trees or otherwise offsetting your emissions. Before you jump at one of these deals, consider where the bank invests and look at the interest rate that it offers. You might find a lower rate of interest at a more ethical bank or building society and still, if you wish, give some money to an environmental organization.

Buying shares

To invest wisely and ethically, the first step is to do your homework or to find yourself a financial adviser with expertise in the ethical sector. The Ethical Investors Group (see page 386) or the Ethical Investment Research Service (EIRIS) can help you find ethical financial advisors.

Before you meet with your adviser, decide what you want to invest in and what you wish to avoid. For example, you might choose to invest in environmental housing schemes or clean-water projects for the developing world and avoid companies that have links with the arms trade or the oil business. Most organizations won't be 100 per cent ethical, so decide where you want to draw the line.

When you're buying shares, the whole ethical argument can be turned upside down because of the power of shareholders. If you make a large investment in a company with questionable ethics, as a named shareholder you get voting rights and can post shareholder resolutions. A classic example of this was used against the construction company Balfour Beatty in 2001, when Friends of the Earth asked its supporters to buy £30,000 worth of shares. This enabled Friends of the Earth to submit a resolution forcing Balfour Beatty to withdraw from building a dam in Turkey, which would have displaced 78,000 people and could have increased tensions between Turkey, Syria and Iraq over access to water. However, this sort of investment and action can have a real influence only if enough shares are bought in one company to put pressure on it. If considering a smaller portfolio, we wouldn't recommend investing in companies with questionable ethics, as you might be a lone voice among thousands and may actually be helping to make the situation worse.

GREEN FUNERALS

Despite its inevitability, we don't like to talk about death, let alone make provisions for it. For those left behind, this can mean that decisions are often made in haste, with the environment taking a back seat. Nonetheless, the fastest-growing green business at the moment is green funerals.

The majority of people in Britain are cremated, which can have some unexpected effects on the environment. During the process of cremation, mercury from dental fillings is released into the air. It's thought that around 15 per cent of mercury in our atmosphere is released in this way – a figure that will rise if we carry on cremating the deceased. The mercury can end up polluting our waterways and ground water. Huge amounts of gas are also used during cremation – the equivalent of a third of one person's average annual carbon emissions can be given off in a matter of minutes.

Traditional burials are not without their problems either, because over half a million coffins every year are made from chipboard, many with plastic handles, which take considerably longer than the memory of the person to degrade. In addition, chipboard leaches formaldehyde, which can pollute the ground water.

Eco-burials

When planning a green funeral, almost every aspect can be tailored to your requirements and what is appropriate to the deceased.

It's legal to be buried in your own back garden, provided you own the land and there's nothing in the house deeds that forbids it. Planning permission is required only if two or more people are to be buried there. You'll need to fill in an authorization form from the Environment Agency and the grave must be situated more than 10m (30ft) away from standing water and at least 50m (170ft) away from drinking water. It will also need to be deep enough so that larger mammals such as badgers, foxes or pet dogs won't dig it up. Accurate records of the whereabouts of the grave will need to be kept with the deeds of the house and you must tell prospective buyers of the situation.

Official natural burial grounds usually involve a choice between a woodland site and a nature reserve (see page 386). Think about which most people would enjoy visiting. You'll need to purchase the plot, either before or after the person's death. Some grounds allow you to dig the grave by hand, but this takes a lot of time and energy.

If you want to have a traditional headstone, talk to the stonemason and ensure you use a sustainable and if possible local stone. Alternatively, trees, bushes or wildflowers are sometimes used instead. In many woodland burial sites, a variety of trees is on offer – the most popular is oak, but consider the bio-diversity of the site before making this choice. Also, think about whether you'd rather have a tree that's more appropriate to the person – perhaps an apple tree, so you can make cider from the plot and toast your loved one's life for years to come.

A range of green coffins is available, including ones made from cardboard, wicker, pine or bamboo. These will all biodegrade, so you won't be contaminating the soil. Cardboard will biodegrade the most quickly, followed by wicker. If you use a pine coffin, do ensure that it comes from a sustainable source. Bamboo is very sustainable, because once cut it will soon grow back, but there are environmental issues to consider (see page 16). Using a hessian or woollen shroud instead of a coffin is greener yet, because these materials use less energy in their manufacture and will biodegrade very quickly.

We went to a green funeral where the coffin was made of cardboard and we were all given pens to write messages to the deceased on the coffin itself. Although this seemed odd at first, it actually really helped to say our last goodbye – making us focus on what we wanted to say to our friend rather than what was inside. We then lowered the coffin into the ground in a field with trees, a lake and sheep nearby. Despite the roar of the M1 it was an attractive resting place. Instead of buying flowers, many of us threw in dandelions because his allotment was full of them and it seemed to be more appropriate.

THE SELF-SUFFICIENTISH PARENT

We've now reached an age when everyone around us seems to be having babies or raising children. Indeed, just in the time it took us to write this book our agent, commissioning editor and three of our friends have produced babies and our second nephew or niece is on its way. We ourselves have no first-hand experience of parenting, but we can pass on what we've learned about the environment, knowing that most parents want their children to inherit a healthy, thriving planet.

Although we realize being a parent is a lot of hard work, it doesn't have to be at the expense of the environment. Non-eco options can sometimes seem easier in the short term, but our 'disposable' culture creates a lot of unnecessary waste and burning of fossil fuels and this way of life simply isn't sustainable. We're sure that if you persevere with the self-sufficientish lifestyle, taking the future of the planet into consideration, you'll feel better about how you're raising your children and will also save money in the process.

It's a good idea to explain to young children how our lifestyles can have an impact on the environment – they often have a surprising understanding of such issues. The old adage 'Give me a child for the first seven years, and you may do what you like with him afterwards' stems from the fact that childhood is the most important time for forming ideas and opinions – if you teach your children early enough, and lead by example, they'll quite possibly take it on as a way of life when they're older.

WHICH NAPPIES?

One of the biggest dilemmas that parents of a newborn baby have to face is the question of nappies. Most people opt for disposable nappies, because they're more convenient. However, this is having very damaging effects on the environment – around three million nappies in the UK end up on landfill sites every day, each taking hundreds of years to biodegrade.

It's not just the effect on the environment that you have to worry about with disposable nappies, it's also the cost, not only for the parents themselves but for everyone who pays council tax. For example, Nottinghamshire council spends over £1 million a year to dispose of nappies. For every pound spent on disposable nappies it costs the taxpayer 10 pence to dispose of them. As a parent, you're likely to pay around £1000 for disposables for the 2 years that your baby will be in nappies, while buying reusable nappies could cost as little as £200 to £300 new.

Reusable nappies

There are countless reusable alternatives available nowadays that are much kinder to the environment than disposables. It's important to get the right sort of reusable, so try a few out before buying in bulk.

You can buy second-hand reusable nappies on auction sites such as eBay or parent forums. It's worth looking around to ensure you're getting a good product. If you regularly see the same brands on eBay, you'll know they're durable and have resale value. If you've finished having children, you could perhaps sell yours on for half the price you paid for them once your child has grown.

Shaped nappies Probably the best of the reusable nappies are 'shaped nappies', which are formed to fit your baby and are worn under a wrap, which is breathable and kind to your baby's skin. They come in a variety of different materials including hemp (see pages 350–1), bamboo, cotton, organic cotton and fleece, often made from recycled plastics. One of the major advantages of the fleece variety is the drying time: they spin virtually dry just in the washing machine and dry very quickly on the line, which means you'll need fewer of them. According to our friends with babies, they're very absorbent and stay softer and whiter longer than most other nappies. Recommended brands are Tots Bots (www.totsbots.com) and Mother-ease One Size (www.babykind.co.uk). The latter have a slightly bigger cut, so suit babies who have taller parents or older children who are still in nappies.

Stuffable nappies Pocket nappies, or stuffables, make a good back-up when you're out and about. You have a two-layered cover, with a waterproof and breathable outer layer and a fleece inner layer. The layers are stitched together in such a way that there's a pocket at the back that allows you to 'stuff' between the layers whatever you want to use as the absorbent part – perhaps a hemp flannel or micro-fibre cloth, both of which are highly absorbent. The fleece varieties are excellent for babies with sensitive skin. Both the inner and outer layer will need to be washed at each nappy change.

Terries and pre-folds Other more traditional reusable nappies include terries, which are the least expensive option but are fiddly as they have to be folded. The only thing that has changed about terries since the old days is the fastening – rather than a nappy pin, nappy nippers can be used instead (see box, overleaf). Pre-folds are cotton (but non-terry) nappies that are folded into shape and are held in place with a separate waterproof outer wrap. If you're using a nappy laundry service it's likely that they will give you pre-folds.

Laundering nappies As cloth nappies are normally used with a flushable inner liner they're generally safe to wash with your regular laundry at 30–40°C (86–104°F). If there's stomach bug going round the family, it's advisable to wash at 70°C (158°F). We suggest using a detergent without fragrance or enzymes, because residual detergents in the wash can cause skin irritation. Soap pods are an excellent alternative to normal detergents (see page 55).

For the busy parent, there are laundry services that collect your dirty nappies and deliver clean ones. The drawback of a nappy-laundering service is the cost, which can be about the same as buying disposables, although your local council might offer a council-tax rebate for using the service. Other disadvantages are that you have to store the dirty nappies for a week, which can be smelly (some essential oil added to the bucket will help), and they tend to be pre-folds, which are not the best reusable

REUSABLE BABY WIPES

Rather than spending a fortune on disposable wipes, you could make your own reusable wipes that can simply be put in the wash after use. Make up a batch every couple of days to keep them fresh, storing them in a recycled ice-cream tub or other container, and in summer months keep them in the fridge.

1.
Buy 1m (3ft) of fleece from your local fabric shop or market stall. Wash the fleece, then cut it into 10cm (4in) squares.

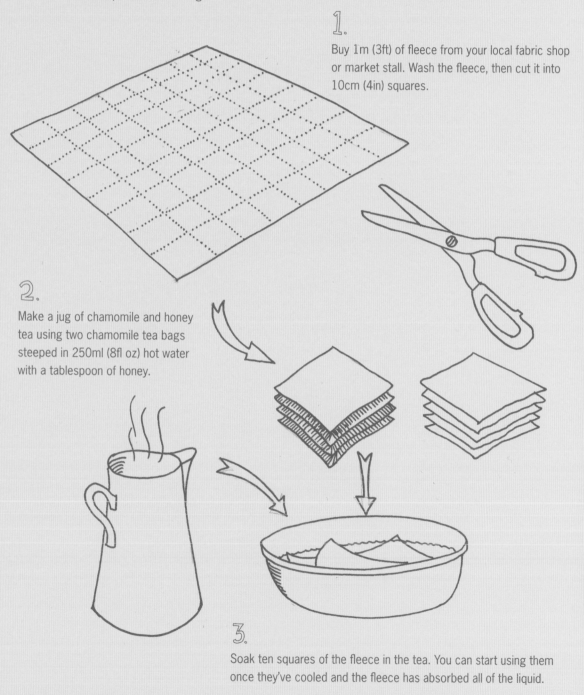

2.
Make a jug of chamomile and honey tea using two chamomile tea bags steeped in 250ml (8fl oz) hot water with a tablespoon of honey.

3.
Soak ten squares of the fleece in the tea. You can start using them once they've cooled and the fleece has absorbed all of the liquid.

nappies around. However, the green credentials of laundry services are not to be sniffed at – as they wash in bulk they use less water and detergent than you would if washing at home and some companies use bio-diesel vans to pick up the nappies.

To find a nappy laundry service in your area check the yellow pages or visit www.changeanappy.co.uk.

Eco-disposable nappies

We hate to be the bearers of bad news here – but biodegradable disposable nappies are not as eco-friendly as they may at first appear. The trouble with biodegradable products that end up in a landfill site is the fact that the landfill lacks the light and bacterial activity needed to help it degrade. The Garbage Project, a study conducted by a group from the University of Arizona, found newspapers from 1952 that were still readable in such a site. Yes, the nappies should biodegrade eventually, but the likelihood of your child having their own children by the time their nappies degrade is also pretty high.

To be sure that your nappies will biodegrade you should compost them yourself rather than send them to landfill. The compost from nappies should not be used for at least a year, preferably 2 years, and it should be used on trees and bushes rather than on the vegetable plot. Ideally, you should use a wormery (see pages 57–8), because the process of vermi-composting results in a 99.9 per cent reduction of the harmful pathogens (such as E. coli and salmonella) from human waste. Another advantage is that worms also help to neutralize odours.

When looking for nappies that are biodegradable ensure they're free of gel, perfume, latex, dyes and chemicals.

Using no nappies at all

One of our oldest friends – a journalist specializing in eco-issues called Adharanand Finn – started to use 'elimination communication' (also known as 'natural infant hygiene') instead of nappies when his second-born was just 8 weeks old. This involves looking out for signs that your baby needs to go and responding by placing them over a lavatory or potty, or whatever is convenient – perhaps under a tree in the garden or over a jam jar if that's all that's available. It's quite a common practice in parts of Asia and Africa, and he claims that it works.

If you do consider this method it's perhaps wise still to use a nappy at night and in the first few weeks. Also, make sure you tell friends and family before they visit or you visit them – it can take a while to be able to interpret the signs and the odd mess is unavoidable.

A WORD ON FABRICS + FASTENINGS

When choosing nappies, be aware of the qualities of the different fabrics used. Although bamboo is a renewable resource and has excellent natural antibacterial properties, bamboo fabric can take a long time to dry naturally. The longer a nappy takes to dry, the longer it is out of action and so the more nappies you'll need to buy. It could take half a day for bamboo nappies to dry during the winter if you don't want to use a tumble dryer. Also, bamboo is more than likely to be sourced from China, so there is the consideration of air miles to think about, as well as other possible environmental factors (see Furniture, page 16). Hemp can take a long time to dry too (you should opt for organic hemp). Fleece is probably the best as it's easy to wash and dries quickly. It's also made from recycled materials such as plastic bottles. Most renewable nappies use a biodegradable inner liner that you simply flush down the toilet.

Popper and Velcro fastenings are much easier to use than the traditional nappy pin. However, the wide Velcro band on some nappies can be uncomfortable for some babies as it's quite firm across the tummy and it's not advisable for newborns. Plastic poppers are a better bet, but ensure they're plastic and not metal, as your baby could be sensitive to nickel.

Nappy nippers are useful for nappies that don't come with in-built fastenings – they are rubber and in the shape of a 'Y', with plastic teeth that grip the fabric but not the skin. The advantage of these is that the nappies that they're used with are often less expensive; also, as the grips can be adjusted they can be tailored to your child's shape. The disadvantage is that they can be a bit awkward and take a while to get used to.

GETTING AROUND

All too often, busy parents get in their cars without considering other options, but walking and cycling with children is so much more beneficial for the family as well as the environment. Andy's godchildren have an eco-conscious mother who's always carried her young around in a sling, transported them by bike or walked with them. As a result, the children get a lot of fresh air and exercise and they've grown up to be very aware of traffic and other hazards – far more so than if they were just strapped into a car seat and driven everywhere. They're also very familiar with the area in which they live, which makes them more independent: the oldest child has become excellent at navigating his way around his home town of Bath.

Carrying babies and toddlers

For thousands of years many traditional cultures have used slings to carry around their babies. You can perhaps picture a Navaho tribesperson with their young strapped to their body. In a 2004 study by Dr Richard Ferber, the leading expert on children's sleep, it was shown that babies who are carried cry less, get sick less often, sleep more and even grow faster than babies who are transported in a pushchair. It's thought that this is because the contact with the parent reduces the baby's stress hormones.

A sling can be a lot more convenient than a pushchair – it keeps your hands free, you don't have to push around a big, bulky bit of equipment and it's much easier when travelling on public transport. The downside to slings is that you're carrying around the weight of the baby, and although most slings nowadays are suitable for carrying 16kg (2½ stone), you might not be. You also have to be very careful when bending over as your baby can slip out, so carefully cradle your baby. If buying second hand or if you inherit a sling, check the stitching thoroughly to ensure that it isn't worn.

There are several types of baby carriers. Make sure you buy one that's comfortable for you for long periods of time (the baby's weight should be distributed evenly between your hips, shoulders and back). Also ensure that the baby's legs are spread out at hip level, because this is essential for the development of their hips, pelvis and spine.

Ring sling This type of sling is made of a piece of fabric and adjustable rings. The fabric acts as a strap that goes over your shoulder and there's a resulting pouch where you put the baby. There's a huge range of ring slings available, made from a variety of fabrics including organic cotton and hemp, and some have additional padding for comfort.

Pouch sling One of the easiest slings to use, the pouch sling is worn over one shoulder, and the pouch is formed by the sash, which doubles over on itself. This is where you put the baby. The carrying positions can be changed for comfort for yourself and the baby.

Wraparound carrier This is the most secure and supportive baby sling carrier and it can also offer more comfort as the weight of the baby or toddler is distributed on the torso and hips. It takes a little more time to master but you can carry a baby on your front or back. The wraparound carrier consists of a length of fabric that is wrapped around the baby and parent and tied. The fabric can vary from a more stretchable type with Lycra in it to a woven fabric that has slightly less give.

Baby backpacks There are many kinds of baby carriers that are suitable for carrying your baby or toddler on your back. They're more appropriate for slightly older babies and toddlers, from 4 months up to 5 years depending on the size of the child.

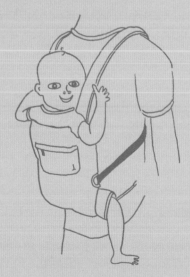

Cycling with children

Cycling is the greenest form of transport and a great way to keep fit. Instead of getting in the car for the school run, try cycling instead. Also, consider taking days out on your bike as a family – you can all enjoy it, regardless of the age or cycling competency of your children. When cycling with children it's more important than ever that you follow the rules of the road. Here are a few tips for you to remember:

● Always wear a helmet and reflective clothing and make sure that your child's helmet fits properly.

● Regularly check your bike's brakes, gears and lights, ensuring that they're all in full working order.

● Keep to cycle paths whenever possible. Always cycle in front of your child but don't go too far ahead.

● Take plenty of fluids on longer journeys.

● Smaller legs can get tired quickly, so don't plan to travel further than your children can manage.

● Teach your children basic road safety and how to fix a puncture from an early age (see pages 302–3).

There are several options available to the cyclist who wishes to transport a baby or child who is not old or proficient enough to cycle:

Child's seat This can be attached to the front or the rear of the cycle and the child is then strapped into a safety harness. There is a wide range of seats available, able to carry children from around 6 months to 5 years. Surprisingly, there are no specific safety standards governing child seats as a legal requirement in Britain. We would strongly recommend that you look for a seat with a CE or TUV mark on it, which means it has passed the EU safety standards test or has been assessed by a German safety organization respectively.

Bike trailer A bike trailer can carry one or two children. Some can carry up to around 45kg (7 stone), so there might even be room for shopping or luggage. If you have a baby of over 6 months old they, too, can be carried in a trailer, although you'll need to buy additional safety accessories. A bike trailer attaches to the back of your bike frame and most come with a rain cover. We'd suggest that you try to keep to cycle paths until you're accustomed to using a trailer. Also, be aware that on noisy roads you might not be able to hear your child, so pull over every now and then to check on their wellbeing.

Trailer bike A trailer bike is an attachment that basically turns your bike into a tandem. The crossbar attaches to the back of your bike, making your bike look like it doesn't have a front wheel. The child can either pedal with you or put their feet up and freewheel, letting you do the work. It's a good idea for learners, because the child can get used to the road and learn bike-handling skills.

Tow bar This is an ideal solution for children who have just learnt to cycle or are on stabilizers. It attaches to the adult bike and turns the child's bike into a trailer bike, so they can be pulled along or freewheel.

FIELD TRIPS + ECO SCHOOLS

There are numerous ways parents, schools and environmental organizations can help and encourage children to understand more about the environment. Perhaps the most hands-on way is to go on a field trip. The Field Studies Council (www.field-studies-council.org) provides enjoyable opportunities for people of all ages to discover and appreciate the natural environment. This educational charity runs a number of courses for families as well as exciting residential courses for schoolchildren of all ages.

Individual schools can take part in the international Eco-school programme. Set up by the Foundation for Environmental Education (FEE), the purpose of the programme is to help children look at how their school might impact on the environment and take responsibility for the future of our planet. Schools that participate in the scheme link the Eco programme with the curriculum in subjects such as science, citizenship and geography. The idea is to get the whole community involved, including local businesses, which may sponsor the school and provide funding. There are three levels of assessment for schools taking part, starting with Bronze, then Silver and, for schools making the most of the programme, the highest accolade of Green Flag status.

HEALTHY EATING

Food is especially important for developing bodies, and a self-sufficientish child should be a healthy child. We believe that children should start to be taught about where food comes from as early as possible. Getting them involved with growing fruit and vegetables at home or on an allotment, or visiting a city farm, are enjoyable ways to teach them about food and will help to get children interested in healthy eating from quite a young age.

Feeding babies

The advice 'breast is best' is often used when talking about feeding newborns. It is the most natural way for a baby to be fed and will help their developing immune system and natural bonding. In addition, the self-sufficientish mum doesn't have to worry about food miles, pesticides or animal welfare if she's breast-feeding. However, don't go beating yourself up if you don't take to breast-feeding – it's not for everyone and there are organic alternatives such as Babynat and Holle milk formulas.

When your baby is about 4–6 months, you need to start introducing solids alongside formula or breast milk. Many parents are keen to give their children a healthy start in life and so are choosing to feed them organic baby food, even if they don't eat organically themselves. You can feed your children puréed food you've grown yourself – carrots, pumpkins and indeed the majority of vegetables and fruit can be puréed and fed to babies. In parts of Africa, mothers feed their children avocados as a weaning food, because they're high in vitamins, minerals and essential fats and are easily 'mushed' and therefore very digestible. Nutritionists recommend that you also provide non-wheat-based cereals, such as white rice. It's important to note that a baby's digestive system can't cope with high-fibre cereals such as brown rice and that large amounts of fibre can reduce their intake of certain minerals. Vitamin C is good for babies, as it helps iron to be absorbed into the body. For this reason, many parents choose to feed their babies orange juice. This is especially important for vegetarian babies, who rely on getting their vitamins from fruit and vegetables alone.

The amount of food is sometimes hard to judge at this stage and can be fiddly to prepare on a meal-by-meal basis. A friend of ours makes up a large batch of puréed food and freezes it in an ice-cube tray. She starts by feeding her babies one or two defrosted cubes of food and as they get older the number of cubes increases.

Around this time your baby may also want to start chewing on some rusks, particularly when teething. To make your own, simply bake some bread or buy a loaf of unsliced bread. Cut off the crusts, cut into 12 x 12cm (5 x 5in) squares and bake in the oven on a baking tray at 150°C (300°F, Gas mark 2) until they've dried out.

When your baby reaches about 9 months you can start including pulped versions of your own meals. Introduce new foods at 4-day intervals. This is usually enough time for any allergies or intolerances to emerge. Never add salt or sugar to your toddler's food.

Healthy lunches

Growing up we used to always go to school with a packed lunch our mother had made for us. In those days there wasn't anything like the choice of lunchbox food available now but in retrospect this was probably a good thing, as modern lunchbox snacks can often be very high in fat and salt. Try to avoid buying these processed snacks, as they're not healthy, can be expensive and involve wasteful plastic packaging. Instead, make sandwiches out of wholemeal bread (preferably homemade) and try adding some seasonal fruit to your children's packed lunches, particularly 'fun', easy-to-eat fruits such as bananas, grapes and strawberries. If it's a real struggle to get them to eat fresh fruit, try adding dried fruit such as apple rings. You might also like to pop in a nutritious treat once in a while such as a homemade flapjack or piece of carrot cake.

Bread is the mainstay of the packed lunch. The easiest way to bake your own bread is with a bread machine. It takes about 5–10 minutes to fill it up and after that the machine does all the work for you. It's more economical to use a machine than a conventional oven to bake your bread as it heats up just enough to bake a loaf rather than heating up the whole oven.

Wholemeal bread

Wholemeal bread is much healthier than white bread, containing more iron and B vitamins. This recipe was posted on the Self-sufficientish Forum by Stonehead, who is a truly self-sufficient crofter living in Scotland.

Makes 4 x 500g (1lb) loaves
1kg (2lb) wholemeal bread flour
375g (12oz) strong white bread flour
125g (4oz) rye flour
900ml (1½ pints) plus 2 tbsp warm water
   (about 20°C/68°F)
15g (½oz) fast-acting bread yeast
30g (1oz) salt
30g (1oz) sugar

1. Combine the flours in a mixing bowl, then remove half of the blended flour to another large mixing bowl.
2. Add the 900ml (1½ pints) warm water to the flour in the second mixing bowl and mix to a batter.
3. Whisk the yeast together with the 2 tablespoons warm water in a cup or small bowl, then mix well into the batter. Cover the bowl and leave to stand for 15–20 minutes.
4. Add the rest of the flour plus the salt and sugar to the batter and mix into a dough. When it's thoroughly mixed, knead well for 10 minutes.
5. Run hot water into four 500kg (1lb) loaf tins to warm them up, then dry and grease the tins.
6. Divide the dough into four balls. Push the balls into the tins, then flatten them. Ensure there are no folds, holes or cracks in the dough.
7. Leave the loaves in a warm (but not hot) place or closed cupboard, such as an airing cupboard, for at least an hour or until they have doubled in size.
8. Preheat the oven to 230°C (450°F, Gas mark 8). Put a small, ovenproof container of water in the bottom of the oven (this helps to crisp up the crust).
9. When the oven is the correct temperature, put in the loaves and bake for 45 minutes. Half way through the cooking time, swap the loaves around so that the ones on the top shelf change places with those lower down.
10. Turn out the loaves onto wire racks and leave to cool.

Bread-machine apple bread

We were sent this recipe by one of our Self-sufficientish Forum members, Zoe from Swindon. She makes it in her bread machine and states that it tastes quite mild, so is perfect for children's sandwiches, as an alternative to traditional wholemeal bread.

Makes 1 loaf
150ml (5fl oz) apple juice
150ml (5fl oz) natural yogurt
1 tbsp sunflower oil
1 tbsp medlar syrup (or honey/maple syrup)
200g (7oz) white bread flour
175g (6oz) wholemeal bread flour
30g (1oz) barley flakes
1½ tsp dried yeast
1 tsp salt

Use the basic/normal setting on your bread-maker and put the ingredients in the order in which they're listed above.

BREAD-MAKING TIPS

* For a shiny brown crust, brush the loaves with single cream or full-cream milk before placing them in the oven. Glaze with whisked egg to get a dark brown crust or with melted butter to get a really crunchy crust.

* Don't leave the loaves to rise where the temperature is above 20°C (68°F), as it will make the loaves coarse and crumbly.

* Make sure the yeast is thoroughly worked through the dough or the loaves will be uneven.

* Let the dough rise properly – if it's not 'proven' you'll get a soggy loaf.

* If you're not intending to keep the bread for more than 48 hours, you can reduce the amount of salt.

Simple rice salad

You could eat this warm and put the remainder in packed lunches the next day, as it tastes good cold too.

Serves 6–8
425g (14oz) long-grain brown rice
½ tsp ground turmeric
1 vegetable stock cube
2 x 425g (14oz) tins kidney beans, drained
   and rinsed
1 tbsp chopped fresh coriander

1. Cook the rice as per the packet instructions but with the addition of turmeric and the stock cube (most brown rice should be boiled for around 20 minutes but this can be longer depending on the variety).
2. About 2 minutes before the end of the cooking time add the kidney beans.
3. Remove from the heat and add the fresh coriander.

Yogurt dip

A firm favourite, this dip is both quick and easy to prepare and a healthy alternative to many commercial dips. Children could take it in their packed lunches with carrot sticks or celery for dipping; it's also ideal for parties.

½ large pot of natural yogurt
¼ cucumber
Few sprigs of fresh mint, finely chopped,
   or 1 tsp dried mint
Few sprigs of fresh tarragon, finely chopped
Black pepper

Spoon the yogurt into a dipping bowl. Finely chop the cucumber into tiny pieces. Mix in the herbs and add some twists of black pepper.

Zingy salsa dip

This is an alternative to the yogurt dip for those children (or adults) who like slightly more fiery flavours. You could also use it in a tortilla wrap, perhaps with chargrilled chicken.

2 tbsp olive oil
1 chilli, deseeded and halved (optional)
1 red onion, chopped
2 cloves of garlic, crushed
425g (14oz) tin tomatoes, chopped
Generous pinch of ground coriander or small
   bunch of fresh coriander leaves
½ tbsp balsamic vinegar

1. Place the oil in a pan over a moderate heat and add the chilli (if using). Fry for about 1 minute.
2. Add the onion and cook for about 5 minutes until it has softened, adding the garlic for the last minute.
3. Add the chopped tomatoes and cook for a couple more minutes.
4. Stir in the coriander and vinegar. Leave to cool.

Spicy seeds

These are delicious and nutritious to nibble on at any time of day. Serve them in a bowl as you would peanuts. They're a good, healthy alternative to crisps at children's parties, or your child could take a small bag of them to school as a break-time snack.

1 tsp each cumin seeds and fennel seeds
2 handfuls each sunflower seeds and
   pumpkin seeds
2 tsp light soy sauce

1. Place a large, non-stick pan over a moderate heat (don't add any oil – the idea is to dry roast all the ingredients).
2. When the pan is hot, after about 5 minutes, add the cumin and fennel seeds. Keep the seeds moving in the pan by shaking it every 30 seconds or using a wooden spatula.
3. When you smell the aromas of the spices, after about 1 minute, add the sunflower and pumpkin seeds.
4. Once the seeds start to brown, after about 1 or 2 minutes, sprinkle the soy sauce into the mix and continue to cook for around 1 minute, ensuring the seeds don't burn.

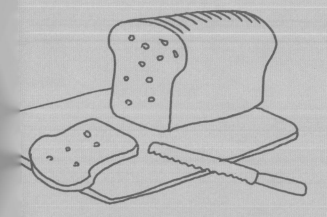

Fruity flapjacks

These are similar to the breakfast bars you can buy at extortionate prices. They do contain sugar but they also have plenty of goodness in them. This would be a fun recipe to do with your children – even if they're little they could safely join in with weighing the ingredients, greasing the baking tray or smoothing the mixture with a wooden spoon or spatula. The chocolate is optional – it's probably best avoided for everyday lunches but is a special treat for a children's party or gathering.

Makes 14 large flapjacks or 28 lunch-box sized snacks
250g (8oz) butter
75g (2½oz) soft brown sugar
60g (2oz) golden syrup
Pinch of ground cinnamon
½–1 tsp ground ginger
450g (15oz) rolled oats
2 tbsp dried apple rings, chopped, or other dried fruit
200g (7oz) chocolate (optional)

1. Gently heat the butter in a saucepan over a medium heat until melted.
2. Pour the sugar into the pan, stirring well, then add the golden syrup, cinnamon and ginger.
3. Turn up the heat. When the mixture starts to bubble remove the pan from the heat. Add the oats and dried fruit and mix well.
4. Grease a large shallow baking tin or tray. Pour in the flapjack mixture and smooth it with a spatula or wooden spoon. Give the saucepan and wooden spoon, when they've cooled, to your child – licking the spoon or scraping around the bowl is often the best bit.
5. Put the tin into the oven set to 180°C (350°F, Gas mark 4), and bake for about 20 minutes or until the mixture is golden brown.
6. Melt the chocolate, if using, in a microwave or in another pan on the hob.
7. Remove the tin from the oven and pour the melted chocolate over the top of the baked flapjack mixture. Cut the baked mixture (while it's still warm) into bar-sized squares, then leave to cool.

Carrot cake

The best way to make sure a cake has all natural ingredients is of course to make it yourself. Here is a delicious carrot cake recipe, kindly given to us by Naomi Walmsley. We've tried it and have to say that it's one of the tastiest carrot cakes we've ever tasted.

Serves 8
125g (4oz) self-raising flour
1 tsp baking powder
125g (4oz) soft brown sugar
125g (4oz) butter
2 eggs
2 carrots, grated
Grated zest and juice of 1 orange
30g (1oz) raisins
30g (1oz) walnuts, chopped
1 tsp ground cinnamon
60g (2oz) cream cheese (such as mascarpone)
3 tbsp icing sugar

1. Preheat the oven to 180°C (350°F, Gas mark 4) and grease and base-line an 18cm (7in) round cake tin.
2. Sift the flour and baking powder into a large mixing bowl.
3. Beat in the sugar, butter and eggs.
4. Stir in the grated carrot and orange zest.
5. Next mix in the raisins, walnuts and cinnamon. If you have children coming to visit who may have a nut allergy, add twice as many raisins and omit the walnuts.
6. Transfer the mixture into the prepared tin and bake in the oven for 30 minutes.
7. Turn the cake out of the tin, peel off the lining paper and allow to cool on a wire rack.
8. While the cake is cooling, make the icing. Put the cream cheese, icing sugar and orange juice into a mixing bowl and mix well. Whip until it becomes smooth. If it's too runny add more icing sugar; if it's too stiff add more orange juice. Smooth the icing over the top of the cake.

Children love helping you cook, particularly when it's something they like to eat, such as these chocolate-covered fruity flapjacks.

Soft toys made from calico and old scraps.

BUYING & MAKING TOYS

Children are perhaps the hardest to convince that environmental living can be fun and rewarding. It can be difficult explaining to a child that they can't have the latest toy that all their friends are playing with because it's made from non-sustainable materials under bad working conditions and has been shipped over from China. Depending on their age, try to explain your views to your child and offer interesting substitutes for them to play with. Also, seek out second-hand toys.

Second-hand toys

Many children lose interest in their toys very quickly, especially young children, so there's a large, varied market for second-hand toys. Websites such as eBay and Amazon are always a great starting point; it's also worth checking local charity shops, fêtes, jumble sales, table-top sales and car-boot sales. Sometimes you can find real bargains, often still boxed and unused by the previous owner. It not only saves money and space in a landfill site but often you're giving to a worthy cause at the same time. If you're buying a game, check all the pieces are there, and if it's an electrical item make sure it works before parting with your cash. You can always return items to a charity shop but you can't help feeling a little guilty about this, despite it being well within your rights.

Toy libraries

Toy libraries are an excellent way to save money on toys and thus greatly reduce the impact they make on the environment. They're also a way of meeting other parents in your area and provide help and advice along with organizing social activities. They work in a similar way to regular libraries. Just as you can read books in a library or take them home, the toy library offers a range of quality toys to play with on site or for you to borrow.

The first toy library was set up in 1967 and there are now over 1000 toy libraries across the country, catering for children of all ages and needs. They come under the larger umbrella of the National Association of Toy and Leisure Libraries (www.natll.org.uk) and are funded and run at a local level. They may charge a small membership fee. For details of your nearest toy library call 020 7255 4604 or e-mail membership@playmatters.co.uk.

Wooden toys

Wooden toys have come a long way since we were children. Although you can still buy the traditional, ever-popular wooden train sets and wooden trolleys with blocks for toddlers, much more complex and more educational wooden toys are also now available from a number of companies such as Treeblock (www.treeblocks.co.uk).

If made of wood from a Forestry Stewardship Council (FSC) or similar, managed woodland scheme they have a much lower carbon footprint than plastic toys, which are dependent on fossil fuels in their manufacture. Although initially more expensive than plastic toys they are much more durable, so can be passed to younger siblings, cousins and friends. Their durability also means there is a large second-hand market for wooden toys on internet auction sites, at car-boot sales, in charity shops and at jumble sales. Wooden toys are non-toxic, so can be suitable for very young children, who often put everything they come across into their mouth.

Making wooden toys For more practical parents, a rewarding alternative to buying wooden toys is to make them. A hand-made toy is likely to last for a very long time. It doesn't have to be too complex: a boat can be made by just attaching three pieces of wood together – a base, a cabin and a chimney. There are numerous books explaining how to make wooden toys – we found several in our local town library, in charity shops and in bookshops and toyshops. There are also relevant websites. Many of the toy-making books are quite old and may suggest varnishing or finishing toys with potentially toxic chemicals. With very young children who put toys in their mouth, this can be quite a concern for parents. Use paints that don't contain volatile organic compounds (VOCs), such as milk-based paints, and use natural wood finishes such as linseed; alternatively, just leave the toys unfinished.

As toys can be small, they're an ideal way of using scrap wood left over from other projects or found discarded. However, check the wood for woodworm and any other signs of deterioration before using it. Freshly cut wood should be dried before use as its shape can change, affecting the quality of the toy.

Toys from recycled materials

With an increasing demand for everything green and recycled, websites such as www.gogreen.cellande.co.uk and www.love-eco.co.uk now offer a range of toys made entirely from recycled materials. You could have a tepee, a rocket, a doll's house or a playhouse made from nothing more than recycled cardboard. At the end of play they can be folded flat and put down the back of the sofa or under a bed to take up less storage space.

Or course, rather than buying there's always the option to make toys from recycled materials. Old clothes can be cut up and sewn together to make soft toys, old washing-up or plastic soft-drink bottles can become rockets, shoeboxes can be turned into doll's houses and the cardboard tubes from inside toilet rolls can be transformed into kaleidoscopes and toy binoculars. Many readers will remember the children's TV programme *Blue Peter*, which championed the idea of making toys from recycled goods.

Toys from car tyres Tyres can be used in a number of imaginative ways for children's play. Here are just some ideas for using them:

🔹 Tyre sand pit – Suitable for young children, this is the most basic of all the car-tyre projects: you simply fill a used tyre with sand and it becomes a sandpit. The bigger the tyre, the better – tractor or lorry tyres are fantastic for this. When the child grows up and no longer wants a sandpit the tyre can be made into a small pond by simply digging a

ditch the depth of the tyre, then covering it with a butyl pond liner or similar non-permeable sheet (see Making a pond using a liner, page 92).

🔹 Tyre obstacle course – Old car tyres can make a great army-style obstacle course. Just peg the tyres down onto a lawn with one tyre next to another. Those lucky enough to have a large garden can include other obstacles such as slides, rope swings (see below) and a line drawn on the ground to run down (like a ground-level tightrope).

🔹 Tyre rope swing – When growing up we were fortunate in having a large tree in the garden with an overhanging branch, so we used an old car tyre and length of rope to make our own rope swing. The rope was doubled on itself to add to its strength and to tie it to the tyre. It's very important that the rope is not old and rotten and the branch is strong enough to take the weight of two children (at least) and the tyre. You should use solid wood such as oak, ash or beech; soft wood or dead or diseased branches should never be used. If you don't have a large, sturdy tree, you could construct your own frame for the tyre swing to hang from.

Cork toys Someone going by the name 'Rainy' on our web forum asked what crafts could be made from corks after inheriting 300 of them. The answer came from a member 'Vixnpips', an ex-childminder, and included the following ideas:

🔹 Paint the corks different colours – a colour per team or per child – and see how many corks each child can throw into a pot.

🔹 Paint a smiley face on some of the corks and float them in a washing-up bowl filled with water. Let the kids 'bob' for them; those with a smiley-faced cork get a small prize.

🔹 Make flower stamps with them by binding them together in a flower pattern.

🔹 Cut out 'clothing' from scrap pieces of cloth, draw faces on the corks and have a tribe of cork people.

🔹 Glue them together and make 'rafts', topped by a sail made of cocktail sticks and paper, and have a boat race.

🔹 Make animals by threading corks together and using cocktail sticks and pipe cleaners as legs, tails and necks.

🔹 Make jewellery by cutting up corks and threading the pieces together.

Old corks can be tied into bundles and used for making flower prints.

MAKING A BABY MOBILE

This inexpensive mobile will provide stimulus and should help to calm your baby, offering a distraction and something to focus on. It's very simple, made from a paper plate or cardboard circle, string and miscellaneous household items such as old CDs and DVDs, which are shiny and will capture the light and your baby's interest, and cardboard shapes, which will move in the breeze.

1.

Cut out cardboard shapes from an old cereal packet – these can be animals, smiley faces or whatever else you choose.

2.

Make a hole in the middle of a paper plate or cardboard circle with scissors or a skewer.

3.

Tie a knot in a length of string and thread it through the hole from underneath the plate. Depending on the size of your string and hole you may need to tie a few knots on top of each other to make a big knot.

4.

Draw two diagonal lines across the plate, crossing over the middle hole. Make four further holes in the plate, on the diagonal lines and about 1.5cm (½in) in from the edges of the plate.

5.

Tie a knot in four lengths of string (about 30cm/12in long but not so long the baby can grab them) and thread each length of string downwards through one of the four holes.

6.

Thread the dangling ends of string through the CDs or DVDs and the cardboard shapes.

7.

Attach the mobile above your baby's cot or nappy-changing area so that it's close enough to see but out of reach. Check regularly to ensure that all the bits of string are very secure to prevent the mobile from falling into the cot.

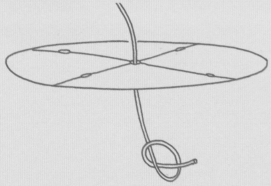

GAMES & ACTIVITIES

There can be plenty more to occupy a child's time than watching endless hours of children's television or playing the latest electronic game. This is where the parents' skills of distraction and imagination come into play. It's amazing how much can be spent on toys and games when kids (or even adults) can amuse themselves for hours with nothing more than a biro and a notepad or some scrap paper.

Paper games

Games like this are ideal for long car or train journeys, or simply just to while away the time, particularly on those wet bank holidays or summer holidays when you have to spend time indoors. Here are some of our favourites from when we were young, often played when travelling on long car journeys to Wales in the back of our parents' Vauxhall Viva. They cost nothing and are immensely enjoyable.

Four-in-a-row Four-in-a-row is essentially Connect Four on paper. A grid is drawn up in the same way as noughts and crosses, but usually 7 x 7 or larger rather than just 3 x 3. It's a game for two players – one player is 'crosses' and the other 'noughts', and the object of the game is to get four noughts or crosses in a row. This can be done horizontally, vertically or diagonally. The game can be played like Connect Four, as if gravity were pulling all the pieces to the bottom, so each nought or cross has to be played on the bottom row or on top of another nought or cross. Alternatively, you may prefer to play 'Hamilton rules', where the noughts or crosses can go anywhere.

Boxes This is a great strategy game and can be played with two to four players. Start by drawing a grid consisting of rows of five to ten dots across and the same down. Once the grid is drawn, each player takes it in turns to draw a line connecting one dot to the next. If any of the lines joins up on all four sides, making a box, the player writes his or her initial in the middle of the box and is allowed to draw another line. If this line makes another box they repeat the process until they can't make another box or there is no room left on the grid. At the end of the game the winner is the one with the most boxes.

Drawing misfits Also known as 'head, body and legs', drawing misfits can be as fun and silly as your imagination lets you be. Each person has a piece of paper and draws a head down to the neck. The paper is then folded to cover up the head, leaving just the two lines of the neck showing.

Then this is passed to the left and the next person draws the body, again folding it over but leaving two lines for the waist. The next person draws the legs to the knees from these lines and it's passed on to draw the shins and then the feet. Finally, a gap is left at the bottom to write the misfit's name. There's no winner or loser in this game – it's a joint effort and is just for fun.

Add-a-line stories This is a game we still play now and it's pretty self-explanatory. It's for two or more players. Each player takes it in turn to write a line and you eventually end up with a story. For example, you could start with the *Star Wars* opening: 'A long time ago, in a galaxy, far, far away' and the next player could come up with 'there lived a dragon by the name of Graham'. You can be kind and continue a theme someone else has started or try to throw the other player off course as much as you can. A slight variation of this game is add-a-word stories, which works on exactly the same principle but each person adds only a word at a time.

Active group games

Some games are much better played with two or more people and are slightly more energetic than sitting down with a pen and paper. Games like hide and seek have been played for centuries and it doesn't seem likely that it will be lost forever in favour of the Nintendo Wii. We used to play a couple of variations of hide and seek, namely stony 1, 2, 3 and sardines. Most people have their own names for these games and their own rules, but below is how we played them.

Sardines This is a great game to play with a group of people of all ages and is very environmentally friendly as the first thing you do is turn all the lights off! One person finds somewhere to hide while everyone else counts to a hundred. They then go and find the person who is 'it' and hides with them. Once everyone is in the same place the game is over.

Stony 1, 2, 3 This is best played outdoors with plenty of room to run about and lots of hiding places, ideally in large gardens, fields or parks. We used to play it around the streets where we lived, but that was when there were fewer cars on the road. Before everyone hides, a 'stony post' has to be agreed on – this can be a tree, a fence post, a lamppost or any immovable object. The person who is 'it' counts to a hundred while everyone else goes and hides. Each time he or she finds someone hiding they have to shout, 'Found you [name of person found],' and they both have to race to the stony post; the first person to touch it and shout, 'Stony 1, 2, 3' is safe and the one who didn't make it is now the new 'it'. There's no end to this game, so a set amount of time needs to be decided on before playing or you can play endlessly until you collapse through hunger and exhaustion.

Nature games

While working in the garden or on the allotment, or even on a walk, it can be very difficult to keep kids entertained. It's hard to blame them really – digging and weeding can be quite dull tasks, even for adults. Dave's neighbours on his allotment have to take it in turns to work or play with the kids. Both seem like hard work and sometimes it's difficult to tell who's got the easier deal of the two.

As adults who haven't really grown up, we've come up with some ideas that keep us amused when out and about and they're ideal for children and immature adults alike. Really young children may need supervision for some of the games, but for others you can just leave your child to play with their friends or brothers and sisters.

Bug bingo A game we actually invented when we were out foraging for food in our twenties is perfect for distracting kids when they're outdoors. We call it bug bingo and it's a game all about spotting bugs. A card is drawn up with the names of different types of bugs on it. As a bug is spotted, it's crossed off on the card until the card is full.

You can make a card for each person playing to make the game competitive or just have one card to encourage co-operation. We always play competitively, but then again little we do isn't competitive.

There's also a slightly more advanced variation of this game, which will expand your knowledge of wildlife. Rather than just marking the card with a cross, you can fill it out with different types of bug, so in the 'fly' box you could write 'horsefly', 'mosquito', 'blowfly', 'bluebottle', 'mayfly' and so on. If you don't have an extensive knowledge of bugs, you could take along a field guide and look up the

type of bugs found, or take a digital camera along and look them up on the internet or in books when you get home.

Tree bingo, plant bingo and bird bingo can all be played in the same way and all can of course be mixed together so that you have to name three each of birds, trees, plants and bugs all on one card.

The multi-coloured nature game An easier and quicker variation of bug bingo, which is ideal for younger children, is the multi-coloured nature game. It can be played when out on a walk but is perhaps best in a garden or on an allotment when everything is in full flower. You choose five to ten different colours for the children to find. For example, if looking for yellow you could choose the middle of a daisy, a chamomile flower, corn in a field, or a wasp, bee or butterfly. You'd repeat this until all the colours were found, one by one.

Pooh sticks For any Winnie-the-Pooh fan, this game needs no explanation. It was a game Pooh Bear played with Piglet and a game our family played whenever we came anywhere near a bridge with running water flowing underneath it. Each player takes a stick that is sufficiently different from those of the other players. You then face upstream, so the water is flowing towards you as you look out over the bridge. On the count of three, each player drops their stick from the bridge into the water. The winner is the owner of the first stick to emerge on the other side of the bridge.

If you're not near a bridge, you can play a slight variation of this game. The rules are much the same but each player drops or throws their stick into the river on the count of three and it's the first stick to reach a chosen mark, such as a large tree in the river.

Making and growing projects

If you think back to your schooldays we're sure that it's the hands-on projects that you remember most fondly. Things haven't changed much, and children today still enjoy making and growing things from scratch and learning in the process. For a parent, guardian or mentor, it can be very rewarding getting children involved in the self-sufficientish lifestyle from an early age.

Growing sunflowers When we were at primary school one of our fondest memories was the sunflower competition. It was set up across the whole school and each of us was given a seed – the aim was to grow the tallest sunflower you possibly could. Neither of us managed to grow a sunflower of any merit, but that wasn't the point – it got all the pupils interested in growing and caring for plants and we both still regularly grow sunflowers. So why not encourage your children to give it a go? Sunflowers attract bees, and if the plants are left standing over the winter the dried seeds can offer valuable food for the birds.

- Use the biggest variety of seeds such as 'Earth Walker' (a multi-headed variety that grows up to 3m/10ft), 'Panache' (a pollen-free variety, so good for hay-fever sufferers and grows up to 2m/6½ft) and 'American Giant' (which can grow to 3m/10ft).

- Start the seeds off in March indoors ready to plant out in April or May.

- Slugs love sunflowers, so do what you can to deter them (see pages 128–9).

- Sunflowers grow towards the sun, so try to avoid planting in a north-facing garden.

- Feed with an organic seaweed feed once a fortnight, when they have at least four leaves on them.

- Plant in well-drained soil.

- You may need to stake your sunflowers, especially in areas with strong winds and in the first month or so of growth.

- Save the seeds from the tallest sunflower for the following year – you might end up with a record breaker.

To give you an idea of the height of this sunflower, we're 1.75m (5ft 8in).

CRESS + MUSTARD HEADS

A staple of childhood has always been making cress heads. To spice them up a bit you can grow mustard seeds at the same time. It's a simple and quick way to teach children how plants can grow. When your cress or mustard has sprouted, add it to salads or cheese and salad sandwiches.

1. Eat a boiled egg with the top removed. Make sure all the egg is out of the shell and clean the inside of the shell.

2. Draw a face on the outside of the eggshell using a felt-tip pen.

3. Moisten a bit of paper tissue, cotton wool or kitchen towel and place it inside the egg.

4. Sprinkle some cress and mustard seed on top of the moistened tissue and place it by a window. Ensure the tissue paper or cotton wool stays moist.

5. Check the seeds regularly and watch them sprout. The cress should take about 2 weeks before it's ready to eat and the mustard about 2½ weeks. If you want them to be ready at the same time you could sow the mustard seed 3 days before the cress.

Making natural playdough This simple playdough recipe uses vegetable and herb juices to produce natural green, pink and orange colourings. The amount of vegetable juice you use depends on the intensity of colour you desire. If stored in a sealed container this playdough should last for at least 3 months.

250g (8oz) flour
125g (4oz) salt
2 tbsp cream of tartar
2 tbsp oil
250ml (8fl oz) water
Parsley
Beetroot
Carrots

1. Put the flour, salt, cream of tartar, oil and water into a large pan. Mix well and cook over a medium heat until the mixture becomes stiff and doughy.
2. Turn the dough onto greaseproof paper and allow it to cool.
3. Meanwhile, make the colourings. Put the parsley into a mortar and get your child to crush the leaves well using a pestle. For beet juice and carrot juice you'll need to blend the vegetables in a blender.
4. When the dough is cool, knead it until it becomes the consistency of playdough.
5. To add the colouring, divide the dough into three balls and add one type of vegetable juice to each ball.
6. Knead each ball of dough well to distribute the colours thoroughly before use.

Crushing parsley to make a green colouring for natural playdough.

PAPER MAKING

If you'd like your children to have a better understanding of recycling, what better way to start than to make your own recycled paper?

What you need
2 washing-up bowls, 1 of which must be
    big enough to fit the frame inside
Warm water
Scraps of used paper (including newspaper
    or tissue paper), about the size of half a
    credit card
A nylon frame (available from an art supply
    shop) or aluminium mesh and gaffer tape
Electric blender
J-cloths

1. Half fill the smaller washing-up bowl with warm water and submerge the used scraps of paper. Leave to soak overnight.

2. Meanwhile, if you haven't bought a frame, make your own by wrapping gaffer tape around the edges of a sheet of aluminium mesh so it resembles a framed picture.

3. When the paper has had a thorough soaking overnight, fill a blender to the 1-litre (1¾-pint) mark with warm water (roughly 60°C/140°F), add 2 tablespoons of the soaked paper and blend on a low or medium setting until the mixture looks like porridge.

4. Pour this 'porridge' mixture into the larger washing-up bowl and add about 250ml (8fl oz) more of warm water, mixing as you do so. Look out for clumps of paper and remove if necessary.

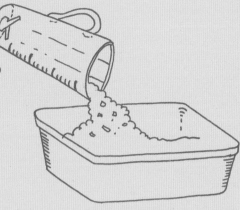

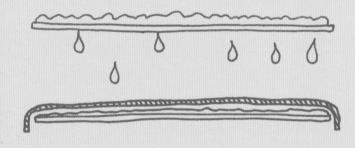

5. Slide the mesh frame into the pulp, then slowly lift up the frame, moving it back and forth while keeping it as flat as possible. The mesh should be coated in an even layer of pulp. Suspend the frame above the bowl to drip dry.

6. When the dripping stops, press down on the pulp a little to squeeze out as much moisture as you can, then place a J-cloth over the top.

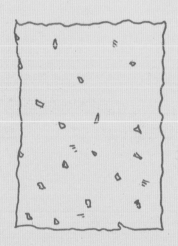

7. Flip the frame over and ease off the compressed pulp (or paper) so it ends up on the J-cloth. Get another J-cloth, cover the paper and leave it flat overnight in a warm place such as an airing cupboard. Repeat steps 3–7 until you have used up all the pulp.

Once the pulp has dried out completely the resulting paper is ready to use. You can experiment by adding colour to the pulp (see page 348 for details on natural dyes).

The traditional Halloween jack-o'-lantern.

PARTIES & FESTIVALS

From time to time adults and children alike need to blow off a little steam and enjoy themselves. Thankfully, most of us are given a holiday at Easter and Christmas and there are additional celebrations throughout the year. Just as in other areas of life, you can be self-sufficientish in your festivities and enjoy children's birthday parties, Halloween and Christmas without costing the earth or harming the environment.

Children's parties

Having a sister with a young son and numerous friends with children, we seem to be invited to more children's parties than adult ones nowadays. It's easy from the outside to be critical of the environmental side of these parties but neither of us is a stressed, busy parent. Nonetheless, there are several things you can do to make your child's party that little bit greener. There are quite a few companies that now supply green party products for children's parties.

Party bags Taking home a little reminder of the party they've just been to can be a real bonus for young partygoers. All too often the party bag is made of plastic, to be thrown away the moment the bag has been emptied. However, this needn't be the case. You can now buy environmentally friendly party bags, which are made from recycled or recyclable material and are sold empty for you to fill or pre-filled with environmentally friendly toys and gifts such as wooden toys, jewellery or notebooks made from recycled materials. (See www.ecopartybags.co.uk, www.happygreenearth.com and www.littlecherry.co.uk.)

An alternative to buying bags would be to use paper bags saved from grocery shopping and get the kids to decorate them themselves during the party itself. There could be a prize for the best decorated bag and you could fill them yourself with cakes, toys and treats.

Plates, cups and cutlery The biggest waste in catering for a children's party has to be all the plastic cutlery, plates and cups. Several companies now stock fully recyclable or biodegradable paper cups or biodegradable plastic cups, tumblers, cutlery and plates made from recycled material and bamboo along with organic hemp tablecloths and party bunting. You don't have to go to a specialist supplier for these, as many high-street shops sell paper plates, cups and napkins. Although they may not be made totally from recycled materials all can be composted after use.

Many choose not to buy in all these extras and instead rely on what they already have. If you regularly go camping, you will probably already have a supply of durable plastic cups, plates and cutlery, so there may be no need to buy any more. Loans from friends and family can always make up the difference. Otherwise, consider pooling together with other parents. A shared set between groups of friends can greatly reduce the environmental impact of buying many different items of party ware.

Balloons Foil balloons are made from non-biodegradable material, while traditional latex balloons are completely biodegradable and sustainable and, what's more, a lot less expensive. They're made from harvesting latex from living rubber trees, which doesn't harm the tree at all; it's a very similar process to tapping a birch for birch sap or a maple for maple syrup. The company Eco Party Bags (see left) claims that latex balloons take about the same length of time to biodegrade as oak leaves, around 6 months. Latex balloons are available just about everywhere.

Easter

An Easter-egg hunt can be a great way to amuse children and keep them active for an afternoon. It can be done using chocolate eggs or painted hard-boiled hen's eggs. Hide the eggs all over the garden or your allotment; you could offer a prize to the child who finds the most eggs.

The Fairtrade movement is entering the chocolate Easter-egg market and Green and Black's now has a wide range available. You could also try making your own chocolate eggs using moulds. We remember that our Mum's efforts when we were kids were a hit-and-miss affair, but they were always fun to make and tasted good even though they were sometimes less than perfectly formed. Chocolate egg moulds are available online and from specialist kitchen stores. Alternatively, use hard-boiled hen's eggs and paint the shells with poster paint. The designs can be as simple as rings of different colours or funny faces on the eggs.

SHRUNKEN HEADS

A great idea for spooky Halloween decorations is to make shrunken carved heads from apples. These have to be prepared a week or so in advance.

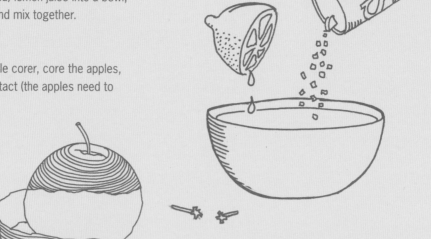

1. Pour 100ml (3½fl oz) lemon juice into a bowl, add 2 teaspoons salt and mix together.

2. If you have an apple corer, core the apples, otherwise leave them intact (the apples need to remain whole).

3. Peel the apples and put them into the lemon and salt solution, turning them if necessary so they're completely covered.

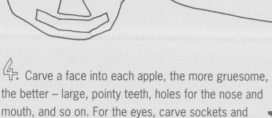

4. Carve a face into each apple, the more gruesome, the better – large, pointy teeth, holes for the nose and mouth, and so on. For the eyes, carve sockets and stick in raisins or cloves.

5. Using a pastry brush, coat the apples all over with the solution, ensuring it gets into all the little nooks you've carved. The salt and lemon will stop the apples from rotting; any bits that aren't coated will make them more prone to decay.

6. To dry the apples, pop them into an airing cupboard or place them on a rack hanging above a radiator. Alternatively, you could put them in the oven on a very low heat (the slow-cook option if you have it) for a few hours until they're completely dry (see Drying methods, pages 247–8).

These sinister shrunken heads make great table decorations for Halloween.

Summer and winter solstices

Many of our modern festivals stem from Britain's pagan past. The summer and winter solstices marked the longest and shortest days respectively. This would have been incredibly important for our farming and hunter-gatherer ancestors. In the northern hemisphere, the winter solstice falls just before Christmas on 21 or 22 December and the summer solstice on 21 or 22 June (it's the opposite in the southern hemisphere).

The solstices and the two equinoxes are all about the changing of the seasons and our link with the natural world. The summer solstice can be a great excuse for a family barbecue and is a good time to get out and enjoy the natural world with your family, when the days are at their longest. The winter solstice can be a time to sit round a fire, tell stories and toast marshmallows.

There are also organized festivals at Neolithic sites such as Stonehenge and Avebury at these times; many people take their children along for the experience.

Halloween

There's something about Halloween that can really fire a child's imagination – dressing up, ghost stories, trick-or-treating and Halloween parties all play a part in making this a fun evening for children. However, second to Christmas Halloween is becoming one of the most wasteful of all our festivals, with shops filling up with manufactured costumes and accessories weeks before the day. Many Halloween decorations can be made at home, often from recycled household items. For hundreds of ideas on Halloween crafts and decorations, including patterns and instructions, see www.allcrafts.net/halloween.

Jack-o'-lanterns The jack-o'-lantern is an ancient Irish tradition that goes back centuries. Before the time of pumpkins in the British Isles, people used to carve faces in large turnips, beetroots or potatoes, put a lit candle inside and leave them outside their doors to ward off malevolent spirits. This custom was taken to North America but they replaced the traditional vegetables with pumpkins, which were larger and easier to carve. By Victorian times we were doing the same in Britain.

Over a million pumpkins are now sold in Britain every year to make Halloween lanterns. Strangely, people often just throw away the insides rather than eating them, but both the seeds and the pulp can be very tasty and nutritious. The pulp is excellent turned into soup, roasted alongside other seasonal vegetables or made into a risotto (see Pumpkin and chestnut risotto, page 199).

Alternatively, make a sweet pumpkin pie – cook and purée the pulp, add sugar and spices and spoon the mixture into a pastry case. You could hand out slices to children trick-or-treating. The seeds can be toasted (see Spicy seeds, page 363) or saved and planted the following year.

Once Halloween is over, compost the pumpkin rather than sending it off to landfill.

Apple bobbing Apple bobbing is a simple game to set up. Just place a few eating apples in a bucket of water; without using their hands, kids have to try to pick up the apples with their teeth. For a drier alternative, suspend apples on strings and have them hanging down to the level of the children's mouths.

Christmas

Christmas need not be the consumer-driven festival it has become but is instead a much-needed celebration in the coldest and darkest months of the year. Whatever your religious beliefs, it is a welcome break from work and a chance to spend time with friends and family. Although Christmas can be a period when much is wasted, this need not necessarily be the case.

Christmas cards On average, between 740 million and 1 billion Christmas cards are sent every year, resulting in 250,000 to 340,000 trees being chopped down. Instead of sending cards you could send e-cards and donate the money you've saved to the billion-tree appeal, which aims to reforest large areas of the Scottish Highlands (www.treesforlife.org.uk). Alternatively, consider recycling last year's cards, cutting off the front and gluing it onto a new piece of card. Many of the major supermarkets have collection points for recycling Christmas cards and they can also be recycled with other cardboard waste.

Giving presents Presents need not cost the earth if you make them yourself and personal gifts are always well received. One idea that often goes down well is to make a memory album by assembling some important mementos in a scrapbook (you could make the album or buy one). This could focus on a special holiday or event that you and the recipient enjoyed together and could include photos, tickets and various other items of memorabilia. If you have a lot of digital photos, you could make a disk for all your relatives who have access to a computer. You could give it a personal touch by printing out covers for them too.

If you've got green fingers, take cuttings from your favourite herbs and pot them in painted pots. Another simple idea is to make personalized cooking oils. Buy some attractive glass bottles and fill them with olive oil and a few sprigs of rosemary or other decorative herbs and chillies. You could print off your own labels, saying something like 'Rosemary-infused olive oil bottled exclusively for...' You can do the same with homemade pickles and jams too.

Some people chose to bypass the commercialization of Christmas completely by buying gifts for those in developing countries. Oxfam seems to be the forerunner in this charitable gift-giving, offering the chance to buy a goat or cow or even an allotment. Check out its website www.oxfam.org.uk for further information.

Christmas trees Every year at Christmas our Dad would cut the top off a fir tree in our garden to act as a Christmas tree. If you don't have a large fir tree, you could grow your own for the following year. Norway spruce saplings grown in a pot are available from www.tree2mydoor.com.

If you prefer to buy a new full-sized tree each year, try to source your tree from the UK rather than from abroad, as this not only cuts down on CO_2 emissions from transportation but it also supports British farming. Many towns have Christmas-tree farms on their outskirts, so try to buy from these rather than supermarket or DIY chains, which rely heavily on foreign imports. Christmas trees spend their life soaking up carbon dioxide from the atmosphere and each tree is replaced by a new one, making it a fully sustainable crop.

When you've finished with your tree try to dispose of it responsibly. Check with your local authority, as it may pick them up after the Christmas period. Alternatively, take your tree to a local tip or shred it with a garden shredder and use it as a mulch in your garden.

Gingerbread men

Your children can help you make these and hang them on the tree. They don't have to be just gingerbread-men-shaped: cutters come in all shapes and sizes – reindeer, stars and snowmen are good for Christmas, and plain round ones are suitable at other times of the year.

Makes 15–20 biscuits
375g (12oz) plain white flour
1 tsp bicarbonate of soda
2 tsp ground ginger
125g (4oz) butter
175g (6oz) light soft brown sugar
4 tbsp golden or maple syrup
1 egg, beaten
Currants or raisins for decoration

1. Preheat the oven to 190°C (375°F, Gas mark 5) and lightly grease a baking sheet.
2. Sift the flour, bicarbonate of soda and ginger into a mixing bowl.
3. Rub in the butter until the mixture looks like fine breadcrumbs, then stir in the sugar.
4. Beat the syrup into the egg and add it to the mixture.
5. Mix to form a dough, then knead until smooth.
6. Divide the dough into two equal pieces and roll out each on a lightly floured surface until it is about 5mm (¼in) thick. Use cutters to cut out gingerbread shapes and put them on the prepared baking sheet.
7. Decorate with the currants or raisins to make eyes, mouths, buttons and any other additions.
8. Bake in the oven for 12–15 minutes or until golden. Cool the biscuits on the tray for a few minutes, then transfer to a wire cooling rack.

USEFUL ADDRESSES & FURTHER READING

GENERAL

Centre for Alternative Technology (CAT Centre)
Machynlleth
Powys SY20 9AZ
Tel: 01654 705950
www.cat.org.uk
An excellent resource for all aspects of environmental living, with a great online catalogue and fascinating visitor centre featuring interactive displays. Open every day (check website for opening times).

Department for Environment, Food & Rural Affairs (DEFRA)
Nobel House
17 Smith Square
London SW1P 3JR
Tel: 08459 335577
www.defra.gov.uk
UK government department that aims to tackle climate change and secure a healthy, productive natural environment.

Forum for the Future
Overseas House
19–23 Ironmonger Row
London EC1V 3QN
Tel: 020 7324 3630
www.forumforthefuture.org.uk
Charity that works with leading businesses and government to find successful ways of achieving sustainable development. Publishes Green Futures magazine.

Friends of the Earth
26–28 Underwood Street
London N1 7JQ
Tel: 020 7490 1555
www.foe.co.uk
Influential environmental campaigning organization with worldwide support.

Selfsufficientish.com
www.selfsufficientish.com
This website was set up by the two authors of this book. It is full of useful advice and includes a web forum populated by helpful people from around the world.

HOME

The Association for Environment Conscious Building (AECB)
PO Box 32
Llandysul SA44 5ZA
Tel: 08454 569773
www.aecb.net
Promotes environmentally responsible practices within building, providing information on products and materials that are safe, healthy and sustainable.

Composting Toilet World
http://compostingtoilet.org
Information about composting toilets and treating grey water.

Energy Saving Trust
www.energysavingtrust.org.uk
Tel: 0800 512012
Non-profit organization offering advice on saving energy in the home, including energy-saving grants and list of recommended retailers. Offices in England, Scotland, Wales and Northern Ireland.

Green Building Press
www.greenbuildingpress.co.uk
Online information to aid you in building a green home or finding environmentally friendly building products.

The Heat Project
Enact House
Tolvaddon Energy Park
Tolvaddon
Cornwall TR14 0HX
Tel: 0800 093 4050
www.heatproject.co.uk
Provides grant assistance for loft insulation and cavity wall insulation.

Low-impact Living Initiative (LILI)
Redfield Community
Winslow
Buckinghamshire MK18 3LZ
Tel: 01296 714184
www.lowimpact.org
A non-profit organization that provides information and courses on all aspects of low-impact living.

Natural Homes
www.naturalhomes.org
Website providing information on natural homes, including constructions made of straw, cob, wood and earth bags.

REUK
http://reuk.co.uk
Website covering all aspects of renewable energy, including wind power, solar power, solar water heating, rainwater harvesting, grey-water diverting and energy efficiency.

Solar Cooking Archive
http://solarcooking.org
Links to articles and practical advice on all aspects of solar cooking.

Solarwind
Gun Hill Poultry Farm
Swanbrook Lane
Horam
East Sussex TN21 0LA
Tel: 01435 812163
www.solarwind.org.uk
Suppliers of solar heaters, solar panels and wind turbines. Open Saturday 10am–1pm and by appointment at other times; phone before you plan to visit.

FURTHER READING

Anderson, Lorraine, and Palkovic, Rick *The Complete Guide to Solar Cuisine with 150 Easy Sun-cooked Recipes*, Marlow and Co., May 2006, ISBN 978-1569243008

Halacy, Dan and Beth *Cooking with the Sun: How to Build and Use Solar Cookers*, Morning Sun Press, May 1992, ISBN 978-0962906923

Hall, Keith (ed.) *The Green Building Bible*, Green Building Press, October 2006, ISBN 978-1898130031

Johnston, Jacklyn, and Newton, John *Building Green: Practical Guide to Using Plants On and Around Buildings*, Packard Publishing, August 1992, ISBN 978-1871045178

***Green Building* magazine** A quarterly journal about building your own home, published by Green Building Press.

OUTDOORS

Allotment websites
www.allotment.org.uk
Allotment website with online shop and web forum.

www.selfsufficientish.com/councilsaj.htm/
www.selfsufficientish.com/councils.htm
The best place to start looking for an allotment is a list of all the local councils.

www.allotmentforestry.com
A community project working with gardeners to increase the use of local woodland products in the garden and on the allotment.

www.allotments4all.co.uk
Website that helped out Self-sufficientish when we first started.

Garden Organic
Garden Organic Ryton
Coventry
Warwickshire CV8 3LG
Tel: 02476 303517
www.gardenorganic.org.uk
Formerly the Henry Doubleday Research Association (HDRA), this is the UK's leading organic charity and a great resource for organic vegetable gardeners.

National Pond Monitoring Network
www.pondnetwork.org.uk
Brings together organizations and individuals with an interest in recording or using data on ponds and pond species.

Royal Society for the Protection of Birds (RSPB)
The Lodge
Potton Road
Sandy
Bedfordshire SG19 2DL
Tel: 01767 680551
www.rspb.org.uk
UK charity set up to secure a healthy environment for birds and other wildlife.

The Royal Society of Wildlife Trusts (RSWT)
The Kiln
Waterside
Mather Road
Newark
Nottinghamshire NG24 1WT
Tel: 01636 677711
www.wildlifetrusts.org
The UK's largest voluntary organization dedicated to conserving the full range of habitats and species.

FURTHER READING

Clevely, Andi *The Allotment Book*, Collins, April 2006, ISBN 978-0007207596

Don, Monty *The Complete Gardener*, Dorling Kindersley, March 2003, ISBN 978-0751364415

Foley, Caroline *The Allotment Handbook*, New Holland, May 2004, ISBN 978-1843305835

Guerra, Michael *The Edible Container Garden: Fresh Food from Tiny Spaces*, Gaia Books, March 2005, ISBN 978-1856752206

Kruger, Anna (Henry Doubleday Research Association) *Encyclopedia of Organic Gardening*, Dorling Kindersley, 2001, ISBN 978-0751333817

Purnell, Bob *Crops in Pots: 50 Great Container Projects Using Vegetables, Fruit and Herbs*, Hamlyn, March 2007, ISBN 978-0600615514

Fergus the Forager
www.wildmanwildfood.co.uk
The famous TV forager's website featuring information about foraging mushrooms, plants and seaweeds (including the legalities) and recipes.

Wild-food courses
The following companies run foraging courses:
www.countrylovers.co.uk/wfs/index.htm
www.woodsmoke.uk.com/p/v/courses/wilderness+cookery
www.woodlandsurvivalcrafts.com/survival-courses/wilderness-cookery.php

Livestock-keeping websites/blogs
www.acountrylife.com
Informative web forum, ideal for newcomers to keeping livestock.

http://stonehead.wordpress.com
Smallholding blog offering great no-nonsense advice and the occasional pig for sale.

The British Beekeepers' Association
National Beekeeping Centre
National Agricultural Centre
Stoneleigh Park
Warwickshire CV8 2LG
Tel: 02476 696679
http://bbka.org.uk
Organization devoted to keeping bees,
offering nationwide courses and support
to new members.

National Institute of Medicinal
Herbalists (NIMH)
Elm House
54 Mary Arches Street
Exeter
Devon EX4 3BA
Tel: 01392 426022
www.nimh.org.uk
One of the UK's leading authorities on
herbal health matters. Find an NIMH-
registered herbalist in your area.

Plants for a Future
www.pfaf.org
Resource centre for rare and unusual
plants, particularly those that have edible,
medicinal or other uses.

FURTHER READING

Fern, Ken *Plants for a Future: Edible and*
Useful Plants for a Healthier World,
Permanent Publications, July 1997,
ISBN 978-1856230117

Graves, Will *Raising Poultry Successfully,*
Williamson Publishing, December 1985,
ISBN 978-0913589090

Harris, Carol *A Guide to Traditional Pig*
Keeping, Farming Books and Videos Ltd,
June 2005, ISBN 978-1904871101

Line, Dave *The Big Book of Brewing,*
G. W. Kent, June 1998,
ISBN 978-0961907297

Mabey, Richard *Food for Free,* Collins,
October 2001, ISBN 978-0002201599

McVicar, Jekka (RHS) *Jekka's Complete*
Herb Book, Kyle Cathie, September 2007,
ISBN 978-1856267410

Mercia, Leonard S. *Storey's Guide to*
Raising Poultry, Storey Books, December
2000, ISBN 978-1580172639

Waddington, Paul *The 21st-Century*
Smallholder: How to Go Back to the Land
Without Leaving Home, Eden Project
Books, April 2006, ISBN 978-1903919699

Waring, Adrian and Claire *Teach*
Yourself Beekeeping, Teach Yourself,
September 2006, ISBN 978-0071472708

Bushcraft Magazine A great read for
the wild-food and bushcraft enthusiast.
www.bushcraft-magazine.co.uk/index.html

LIFESTYLE

eBay
www.ebay.co.uk
Online marketplace where individuals and
small businesses can buy and sell a huge
diversity of goods and services.

Ecotricity
Axiom House
Station Road
Stroud
Gloucestershire GL5 3AP
Tel: 01453 756111
www.ecotricity.co.uk
The world's first green electricity company.

Ethical Investors
Montpellier House
47 Rodney Road
Cheltenham
Gloucestershire GL50 1HX
Tel: 01242 539848
www.ethicalinvestors.co.uk
Ethical investment specialists.

Fairtrade Foundation
Room 204
16 Baldwin's Gardens
London EC1N 7RJ
Tel: 020 7405 5942
www.fairtrade.org.uk
Organization that was founded by several
charities, including Oxfam, Traidcraft and
Christian Aid, to ensure workers in the
developing world get a better deal (it
licenses the Fairtrade label).

Good Energy
Monkton Reach
Monkton Hill
Chippenham
Wiltshire SN15 1EE
Tel: 0845 456 1640
www.good-energy.co.uk
This company supplies 100 per cent
renewable energy from natural sources
(wind, sun or running water).

Green Endings
141 Fortess Road
London NW5 2HR
Tel: 020 7424 0345
www.greenendings.co.uk
Arranges alternative and green funerals,
including woodland burials, in and around
London and the M25 region.

The Nappy Lady
15 The Stanley Centre
Kelvin Way
Crawley
West Sussex RH10 9SE
Tel: 0845 652 6532
www.thenappylady.co.uk
A useful resource for anyone who wants
to learn about reusable nappies. You can
even arrange a home visit by one of
the company's representatives.

Native Woodland
Tel: 08454 500165
www.nativewoodland.co.uk
Information about green funerals and
natural burial sites throughout the UK.

Oxfam
Oxfam House
John Smith Drive
Cowley
Oxford OX42 2JY
Tel: 08703 332700
www.oxfam.org.uk
A development, relief and campaigning
organization that works to overcome
poverty through shops, charitable gift-
giving and other fund-raising schemes.

Sustrans
National Cycle Network Centre
2 Cathedral Square
College Green
Bristol BS1 5DD
Tel: 0117 926 8893
www.sustrans.com
UK's leading sustainable transport charity –
if you've ever wondered who pays for most
of the new cycle paths, it does.

Tatty Bumpkin
Allens Farm
Plaxtol
Sevenoaks
Kent TN15 0QZ
Tel: 01732 812212
www.tattybumpkin.com
Organic and ethically sourced children's
clothing and toys (see page 366).

Traidcraft
Kingsway
Gateshead
Tyne & Wear NE11 0NE
Tel: 0191 491 0591
www.traidcraft.co.uk
Charity and trading company that fights
poverty through fair trade.

CAR-SHARE SCHEMES
Liftshare
Butterfly Hall
Attleborough
Norfolk NR17 1AB
Tel: 08700 780225
www.liftshare.org

National Car Share
PO Box 6311
Bournemouth
Dorset BH11 0AW
Tel: 08718 718880
www.nationalcarshare.co.uk

Shareacar
www.shareacar.com

TRAINS AND COACH TRAVEL
Eurostar
Tel: 08705 186186
www.eurostar.com

National Express
Tel: 08705 808080
www.nationalexpress.com

National Rail Enquiries
Tel: 08457 484950
www.nationalrail.co.uk

FERRY COMPANIES
Brittany Ferries
Tel: 08709 076103
www.brittany-ferries.co.uk

DFDS Seaways
Tel: 08715 229955
www.dfds.co.uk

Norfolk Line Ferries
Tel: 08708 701020
www.norfolkline-ferries.co.uk

P&O Ferries
Tel: 08716 646464
www.poferries.com

Stena Line
Tel: 08705 707070
www.stenaline.co.uk

FIND YOUR LOCAL SERVICE
Breast-feeding Network
www.breastfeedingnetwork.org.uk
Local breast-feeding support centres and
information about breast-feeding.

Charity Shop Finder
www.charityshops.org.uk/locator.php
Postcode search to find a charity shop
near you.

Freecycle Network
www.freecycle.org/groups/unitedkingdom
Freecycle is a website anyone can use to
find something they need or give away
something they don't to members of the
local community, keeping items out of
landfills and waste to a minimum.

Milkman Finder
www.findmeamilkman.net
Postcode search to help you find milkmen
in your area.

Organic Veg-box Finder
www.boxscheme.org
Website leading you to veg-box schemes
throughout the country.

FURTHER READING

Barker, Jill *Baby Green: Caring for Your*
Baby the Eco-friendly Way, Gaia Books,
September 2007, ISBN 978-1856751346

Boyle, Godfrey *Renewable Energy,*
Oxford University Press, March 2004,
ISBN 978-0199261789

Grace, Janey Lee *Imperfectly Natural*
Baby and Toddler, Orion, April 2007,
ISBN 978-0752885896

Harrison, Rob; Newholm, Terry; and
Shaw, Deirdre (eds.) *The Ethical*
Consumer, Sage Publications, March
2005, ISBN 978-1412903530

Jackson, Hildur *Ecovillage living:*
Restoring the Earth and Her People,
Green Books, August 2002,
ISBN 978-1903998168

Lynas, Mark *Carbon Counter,* Collins
(Gem series), January 2007,
ISBN 978-0787996222

D

damsons 220
dandelion coffee 277, 278, 283
dandelion cough syrup 275
dandelions 224–5
 roots 278, 283
 for treating warts 281
dandelion wine 266
dandruff 283
darning socks 348
demijohns 260
deodorants 65
depression 284–5
Derbyshire 301
designer clothes 347–8
developing countries
 buying gifts for at Christmas 383
 and the clothing industry 347
 and Fairtrade food 340–1
Devon 301
diarrhoea 278
digestive disorders 278
digging 76, 78–9
digital music 25–6
dill
 growing 158
  as companion plants 154
dioxins in sanitary products 69
dishwashers 52
disposable pens 332
doors, reducing heat loss from 33
double digging 78
double glazing 29–31
drainage systems 37
draught excluders 33
drawing misfits (paper game) 371
dry storage 246–9
 drying methods 247–8
  airing cupboards 247
  burying root vegetables 248
  ovens 247
  radiators 248
  string 247
dual-flush toilets 62
duck keeping 237
duvet cover, patchwork 22–3
DVDs 25, 26
dyeing clothes 348–50

E

earache 277
Easter eggs 379
echinacea 274
eco-balls 55
eco-burials 353
eco-disposable nappies 358
eco-friendly home 12–39
 furnishings and electricals 16–27

insulation and heating 13, 28–34
 outdoor areas 35–9
eco home 14–15
eco schools 360
eczema 286–7
Eden Project 76
eggs
 from chickens 232, 236
 from ducks 237
 Easter eggs 379
 in face masks 66
 and hair care 66
elderberries 220
 blackberry and elderberry jam 255
 elderberry wine 268
elderflowers
 cordial 228
 elderflower wine 266
 mallow and elderflower fritters 224
 wild 228
electrical equipment
 in offices
  and air quality 326
  computers 328–30
  switching off 323, 326
  and ventilation 238
 WEEE (Waste Electrical and Electronic
  Equipment) directive 330
 working from home 325
electricals see furnishings and electricals
electrical waste
 amount generated 336
 disposing of 27, 330
electric fencing, and pigs 238
electricity see green electricity
electric kettles 52
electric ovens 44
energy see renewable energy
energy, solar 315
energy-efficient fridges 48
energy-efficient lighting 25
energy-efficient windows 15, 29–31
energy-saving hints, computers 328–30
energy-saving light bulbs 326, 327
entertainment, and camping holidays 307–8
environmentally-friendly offices 323, 326–33
 air quality 326–8
 computers 328–31
 lunch and coffee breaks 332
 meetings and travel 332
 paper 332
 stationery 332
 ventilation and air conditioning 328
equinoxes 382
ethical banking 352
ethical shopping see consumers
European camping laws 307
European Energy Label and Ecolabel 43
Eurostar 292, 293, 296
Eurotunnel Shuttle 293
evaporation coolers 328
evening primrose oil, for dandruff 283
exercise
 and allotment work 97
 cycling to work 324
 and poor circulation 279

F

facial skincare 66
Fairtrade 338, 340–4
 bananas 343
 chocolate 342
 coffee 332, 336, 338, 343
 cotton 351
 sugar 342
 tea 342–3
fan-assisted ovens 44
Fareshare 343
farmers' markets 338, 340
fat hen/goosefoot 222–4
fennel
 Florence fennel 116, 134
  trout baked with fennel and herbs 194
 growing 106, 116, 134
 growing as a herb 158
fennel seeds, for digestive disorders 278
fermentation bins 260
ferns, in offices 328, 329
ferries 294–5, 387
 Algeciras to Ceuta 297–8
ferry ports 295
festivals 378–83
 Christmas 382–3
 Easter 379
 equinoxes 382
 Halloween 378, 380–1, 382
 summer solstice 382
 winter solstice 382
field blewits 210, 211, 212
field mushrooms 213
fig trees 139–41, 179
first-aid kits 308
fish
 and seasonal cooking 186
 trout baked with fennel and herbs 194
flapjacks, fruity 364, 365
flax-felt insulation 29
fleece nappies 358
flies, and kitchen waste 57
floods, and rainwater-collection systems 36
flooring, natural 18–20
Florence fennel
 growing 116, 134
 trout baked with fennel and herbs 194
flowers, wild 227–8, 229
fluorescent light bulbs 25
flu remedies 274–5
flying see air travel
food 184–287
 and allergies 277, 286
 brewing 258–69
 buying 340–8
  Fairtrade 338, 340–4
  independent shops and suppliers 340
  locally produced 336, 337, 344
  milk 344–5
  online shopping 340
  organic 334, 337, 338
  and supermarkets 340

ACKNOWLEDGEMENTS

This book is dedicated to the memory of Damian Michael Hendry (1974–2007)

Firstly, we wish to thank our Mum and Dad, who introduced us to growing our own and foraging and have given us their support in so many ways. Thanks also to Emma Wright for her support and encouragement and to the self-named 'ishers' for being there from the start, especially Nev Sweeney (Wombat), Shirlz, M3, Muddypause, Martin, The Fee Fairy, Boots, Red, Annpan, Tracey Smith, Ina (thanks for the bike too), Stoney, Hedgewizard, Hedgewitch, Shiney, Thomzo, The Chilli Monster, Wulf, Tigerhair, Gunners, Purple Dragon, Diver, Chickpea, Mrs Fibble, 2steps and Fluffy Muppet; also, to all the other members whose names haven't been mentioned. In addition, we're grateful to the people who helped us out when we first set up www.selfsufficientish.com, including Rowan Lawrence for a year's worth of free web space and advice, Kate Russell for mentioning us on BBC's Click and opening us up to a global audience and Laura Matless and Daryl Bullock for local exposure and giving us confidence.

Special thanks to Euan Thorneycroft, our agent, who helped us realize our dream of writing this book, our photographer Cris Barnett (and his assistants) for his amazing photographs and being a joy to work with, our editor Polly Boyd for her tireless work above and beyond what was expected of her, Will Webb for his excellent design and art work as well as his patience, Alice, Kate, Sarah, Hannah, Nicky and everyone else who helped us out at Hodder, and Katie Giovanni for cooking some of the recipes. The following kindly allowed us to photograph at their premises: Stella and Angelo at Stella's Greengrocers on Church Road, Bristol; CAT Centre, Machynlleth, Powys; Rocks East Woodland campsite, near Bath; the Wellspring Healthy Living Centre, Barton Hill, Bristol; and St Werburgh's City Farm, Bristol.

Both of us would like to thank the following for their enthusiasm, support and friendship throughout (in no particular order): Sharon Hamilton, our Nan, Amit Dutta, Bez (Steven Berry), Danny ('Two Hats') Cameron, Frag Ginbey, Sarah Jean Baptist, Spencer Rose, Ethan, Tony Fletton, Debbie, Sarah C., Rachel Jeffries, Amanda Butler, Alex Aldridge, Genine Blanning, Anthea Campbell, Herve Gulliman, Jim, Justin Porter, Liz Cooke, Paul Kerrison, Anthony Helm, Jay, Kaye and Ian, Maxine and Lorna O'Connor, Sam Riley, Chris and Brian Carter, Ben, Neil, Tom, Smit, our cousins, Paul Giles, Steph and Matt Small, John Randal, Sian Jones and Mark Watson. Also, to Noah Wood at the Little Lab café for the welcome diversions of backgammon.

Dave's personal thanks

I would like to thank all my friends and housemates who have put up with me and been supportive during the writing of the book, especially to Heather Elliot for keeping me sane and accompanying me on treks to find Bristol's best hot chocolate, Richard Jesshope for all the foraging outings over the summer, Simon Arthur for his help on the allotment and the rest of the Musty Men (Dicken and Tehs) for good food, boozy evenings and occasional home brewing. Very special thanks to Dom Read-Jones for providing me with musical projects in the form of *King Kong*, Vontergarten, Two Dead Dogs and of course the Funky Cheesey Wah Wahs, which pulled me out of the sometimes all-absorbing world of writing this book. Also thanks to: Helm, Rachel, Spencer, Ben and Chris of the Cheesey Wah Wah's; Dan Vernade for providing me with great company, food and a quiet place to write when things got too tough down in Bristol; my neighbours on the allotments in Oxford and Bristol; the women from the Children and Families Department at Bristol Council and staff at UWE, where I worked before getting the book deal; Octavia and Sarah for their games of online scrabble; Leila, Matt and Keira for Dorset and London getaways; Anja for her company on the long trip down to Morocco; Antony Armitage for his encyclopedic knowledge of mushrooms and bio-diesel; and last but not least all my friends in Oxford (including Canadian Matt, Tom, Holly, Dave, Will, Caroline, Duncan, Amy, Roz, Gary, Paul, Mick and Chris) and Bristol (Elizabeth, Ben, Ash, James, Alison, Phil, Jim, Sam, Rachel, Urah, Toby, Malcolm, Amy, Roderick, Amanda and Loz).

Andy's personal thanks

Although I've already thanked her I wish to give special thanks to my girlfriend Emma, who has put up with my stress and grumpiness over the years, often with good grace and humour. And in no particular order I'd also like to thank the following for being good friends: Harry Mann, Vashti Mayne, James Lloyd, Heather Bonsal, Stevo, George Fahina Dixon, Marleen, Daniel Wilkinson, Jass Trew, Dom Edwards, Arne Geshkie, Bob Cratchet, Mark Lewis, the staff at Hillview Lodge and Pat Solane.

I'm also grateful to John Rasbash and Hillary Browne for allowing me to slack a little at work when I first wrote the proposal, Michelle Easton for helping me with the Nature's Medicine chapter, Mel Fraiser for her nappy and wet-wipe advice, Adam Hart-Davis for his knowledge of straw-bale toilets, the folk at Plummer's Hill allotment for putting up with an influx of publishing folk and photographers on the allotment and Owen Mead for the late-night conversations.

We've both tried to remember everyone who's helped us throughout the years and with the writing of this book and our website – apologies to anyone we've neglected to mention.

First published in Great Britain in 2008 by Hodder & Stoughton

An Hachette Livre UK company

2

A CIP catalogue record for this title is available from the British Library

978 034 0 95101 9

Design by willwebb.co.uk
Illustrations © Will Webb
Project Editor Polly Boyd
Photographs © Cristian Barnett
Except the following photographs from:
Lucy Dickens 12. FLPA/Richard Becker 114, David Burton 149, Nigel Cattlin 113. GAP Photos/Mark Bolton 170, Tim Gainey 77 right, John Glover 145 top, Sharon Pearson 174, Friedrich Strauss 143, Maddie Thornhill 136. Garden Collection/Gary Rogers 173. John Glover 176, 221. Harpur Garden Library 141, 144. Andrew Lawson Photography 145 bottom centre, 154, Ivan Hicks 98. Marianne Majerus 139, 140, 147. NHPA/Ernie Janes 130. Nigel Rigden 14–15. Derek St Romaine 175.
Printed and bound by Butler Tanner and Dennis Ltd, Frome

Hodder & Stoughton policy is to use papers that are natural, renewable and recyclable products and made from wood grown in well managed forests. The logging and manufacturing processes are expected to conform to the environmental regulations of the country of origin.

Mixed Sources
Product group from well-managed
forests and other controlled sources
www.fsc.org   Cert no. SGS-COC-005091
© 1996 Forest Stewardship Council

Hodder & Stoughton Ltd
338 Euston Road
London NW1 3BH

www.hodder.co.uk